CASEBOOK SERIES ON EUROPEAN POLITICS AND SOCIETY NO. 3
Director, Stanley Hoffmann

The State in Capitalist Europe

CASEBOOK SERIES ON EUROPEAN POLITICS AND SOCIETY

The State in Capitalist Europe

A Casebook

Edited by
STEPHEN BORNSTEIN
DAVID HELD
JOEL KRIEGER
Center for European Studies, Harvard University

GEORGE ALLEN & UNWIN
Center for European Studies, Harvard University

George Allen & Unwin (Publishers) Ltd,
40 Museum Street, London WC1A 1LU, UK

George Allen & Unwin (Publishers) Ltd,
Park Lane, Hemel Hempstead, Herts HP2 4TE, UK

Allen & Unwin, Inc.,
9 Winchester Terrace, Winchester, Mass. 01890, USA

George Allen & Unwin Australia Pty Ltd,
8 Napier Street, North Sydney, NSW 2060, Australia

First published in 1984.

British Library Cataloguing in Publication Data

The State in capitalist Europe. – (Casebook series on European politics and society; no. 3)
1. Capitalism – History   2. Europe – Economic conditions – 1945-
I. Bornstein, Stephen   II. Held, David
III. Krieger, Joel   IV. Series
330.12'2'094   HC240.9.C3
ISBN 0-04-350058-7
ISBN 0-04-350059-5 Pbk

Library of Congress Cataloging in Publication Data

Main entry under title:
The State in capitalist Europe.
(Casebook series on European politics and society; no. 3)
"Center for European Studies, Harvard University."
Bibliography: p.
Includes index.
1. Europe – Economic policy – Addresses, esays, lectures. 2. Europe – Social policy – Addresses, essays, lectures. 3. Europe – Politics and government – 1945- – Addresses, essays, lectures. 4. Regional planning – Europe – Addresses, essays, lectures. 5. State, The – Addresses, essays, lectures. I. Bornstein, Stephen. II. Held, David. III. Krieger, Joel, 1951- IV. Harvard University. Center for European Studies. V. Series.
HC240.S673   1984   338.94   83-21358
ISBN 0-04-350058-7
ISBN 0-04-350059-5 (pbk.)

Set in 10 on 11 point Plantin by Fotographics (Bedford) Ltd
and printed in Great Britain by Butler & Tanner Ltd, Frome and London

Contents

Editors' Introduction and Acknowledgments

In recent years one of the most prominent debates among scholars interested in Western Europe and in Western capitalist societies more generally has involved the state—its nature, its functions, its relationship to the contending classes and organized interests, and the changes it has been undergoing in the period since World War II. Social and political theorists have produced a considerable literature on the 'theory of the state'. At the same time empirical social scientists in a variety of disciplines have generated numerous case studies of the operation of state agencies in specific areas of policy formation and implementation.

Despite these efforts, the available materials on the 'capitalist state' seem largely unsatisfying. The literature on the theory of the state remains difficult and mystifying, obscured by an arcane specialists' jargon. It has lacked, for the most part, not only concrete references to specific features of the contemporary state but also analysis, even in purely theoretical terms, of the state in earlier periods. As a result, the work on state theory has generally failed to cast much light on the changing landscape of European politics and, in the absence of an historical dimension, its claims for the distinctiveness of the contemporary state and for the magnitude of recent changes in state–society relations have seldom been convincing.

The available empirical studies do not, meanwhile, provide much help in filling these gaps. Much of the more empirical literature is too narrow to be relevant to the substantial macrosociological questions raised by theorists of the state. Even where it does reflect a theoretical and/or comparative concern, it has generally been formulated from perspectives such as organization theory or pluralist group theory which neglect crucial issues of class and the specificity of capitalist modes of political organization. Like the theoretical literature, moreover, much of the empirical material neglects historical matters and tells us nothing, therefore, about the important issue of whether or not the contemporary state in capitalist Europe differs significantly, and increasingly, from previous forms of the state.

This casebook was conceived as an attempt to remedy this situation by bridging the gap between theoretical reflections on the nature of the state and empirical studies of state activity in various sectors of capitalist society. We begin with an essay by two of the editors, David Held and Joel Krieger, assessing the competing claims within state theory, starting from Marx, Lenin and Weber and including democratic, corporatist and contemporary Marxist perspectives on class, state and bureaucracy. The essay offers, in closing, a set of propositions about state–society relations in capitalist Europe which raise many of the themes considered empirically in the remaining contributions to this volume. Each author brings serious theoretical concerns to bear on a discrete aspect of state activity, and each chapter reflects original research in the field. Chapter 2, by Peter Hall, presents a comparison of the actions of three major European states (France, Britain and West Germany) in the area of macroeconomic policy. He demonstrates that there are substantial and systematic differences among the patterns of policy in these countries, and he offers a model for explaining these differences that emphasizes factors not usually stressed in the literature on this subject.

In Chapter 3 one of the editors, Stephen Bornstein, reviews the evolution of relations between states and unions in a broad range of European countries. Arguing that these relations are as important as the more commonly studied relations between the state and capital he traces the emergence of a contemporary stalemate in state–union relations that reflects significant and often neglected features of the general crisis of the contemporary state.

Chapter 4, by Rosemary Taylor, considers the variety of different solutions to the dual crises of cost and efficiency in health care provision pursued in Britain, Italy and the USA, challenging the common contention that welfare policies in Western capitalist countries are tending to converge. Stressing the role of unions in shaping national approaches to the formulation and the implementation of strategies of prevention, Taylor shows how the evolution of health care systems reveals significant patterns in the general development of postwar state–society relations in Europe.

In Chapter 5, Dennis Smith demonstrates the connection between the structural transformation of the educational systems in France, Spain, Germany and Britain and broad problems of economic and political management faced by European states. Beginning from a perspective which includes revealing comparisons between Europe and the USA, and between Eastern and Western Europe, Smith traces back the current anguish in the educational sphere to roots in the nineteenth-century processes that spawned distinctive national educational systems.

In the final chapter James Lewis examines the evolution of regional policies in the postwar period, demonstrating that these policies provide a useful prism for examining general theoretical questions about the nature of the capitalist state. Describing a broad convergence in the regional policies of European states, Lewis argues persuasively that regional policy represents an important part of the relationship of the state apparatus to the contradictory demands of capitalist accumulation and political management responsibilities. He offers a trenchant analysis of the upsurge of nationalist and regionalist movements which views them as part of the decline of the social-democratic dream of managed capitalism and of the crisis of the state in capitalist Europe.

We wish to thank Stanley Hoffmann, director of this series, Abby Collins, Marilyn Arsem and the staff of the Center for European Studies for invaluable advice, encouragement and assistance at all stages of this project.

April 1981

1
Theories of the State: Some Competing Claims

DAVID HELD AND JOEL KRIEGER

In recent years there has been burgeoning interest in the state as an object of theoretical and empirical inquiry, triggered in part by practical concerns with the exercise of state power. The discussion has been particularly lively in the writings of contemporary Marxists, but questions concerning the relationship between state and society have long been on the agenda of social and political theory. These questions, however, have often been posed in radically different terms.

Responding to the rapid and disorienting processes of nineteenth-century industrial development in Europe, Marx, Lenin and Weber provided the crucial points of reference for subsequent debate on state–society relations, by focusing on class, bureaucracy and state power. Twentieth-century social and political science has, to a large degree, been preoccupied with an examination of the contributions of these classical thinkers. A variety of diverse and competing traditions has been spawned. A central, if not *the* central, tradition in Anglo-American political science has elaborated and defended a pluralist conception of society and posed a set of claims about the state which contrast strongly with Marxist traditions—rejecting all claims that state power has a class basis. Combating pluralists and democratic theorists in general contemporary Marxists have attempted to revise the interpretations of the state as a class state in light of the complex practices of Western postwar governments. While modifying Marx's original analysis, they have preserved some of the essential links he drew between political power and class power and adopted some of Weber's insights into the workings of state administration. A third school, which emerged forcefully in the 1970s, found the claims of neither democratic pluralist theory, nor Marxist theory, fully satisfactory. Theorists of 'corporatism' challenged the validity of these theories, focusing particularly on an explanation of state policies and institutional arrangements which sought to harmonize conflicting social interests.

Accordingly, in this chapter, we examine each of these approaches to the understanding of state–society relations: first, the contributions of Marx, Lenin and Weber; secondly, the analysis of contemporary democratic theorists which shifts the focus of attention from class, state and bureaucracy to the fragmentation of power within society; thirdly, the writings by theorists of corporatism which emphasize the importance of extragovernmental institutions; fourthly, the works of contemporary Marxists and their efforts to defend and reconstruct the Marxist project. Finally, we offer a set of propositions about state–society relations which synthesize what we consider to be the most salient contributions of state theory to date, and indicate a direction for future investigations.[1]

Class, Bureaucracy and State in the Writings of Marx, Lenin and Weber

Marx, Weber and Lenin never developed adequate theories of the relationship among class, bureaucracy and state. All three offered insights, however, which remain of lasting significance. Marx left a thoroughly ambiguous heritage, never fully reconciling his understanding of the state as an instrument of class domination with his acknowledgement that the state might also have significant political independence. Lenin forged a conception of capitalist state institutions which stressed their oppressive nature and the need for their demolition. In contrast to both Marx and Lenin, Weber resisted all suggestions that forms of state organization were directly caused by class relations (Wright, 1978). He stressed the internally homologous nature of private and public administration as well as their independent dynamics.

Marx

Marx's engagement with the theoretical problems

posed by state power developed from an early confrontation with Hegel, the central figure in German idealist philosophy and the crucial intellectual influence in his life. In the *Philosophy of Right* Hegel portrayed the Prussian state as cleft into three substantive divisions—the legislature, the executive and the Crown—which together express 'universal insight and will' (Hegel, 1967; see Perez-Diaz, 1978). For him, the most important institution of the state is the bureaucracy, an organization in which particular interests are mitigated by hierarchy, specialization, expertise and coordination on the one hand, and internal and external pressures for competence and impartiality on the other. According to Marx, in the *Critique of Hegel's Philosophy of Right*, Hegel failed to challenge the self-image of the state and, in particular, of the bureaucracy (Marx, 1970b, pp. 41–54).[2] Far from being the objectification of the general interest, the state, Marx argued, transforms 'universal aims into another form of private interest'. The state is not an independent structure above society, but deeply embedded in the total social process. Its dependence is revealed whenever civil society (the realm of business and family life) is beset by crises; for economic, professional and municipal organizations of all kinds create the material resources on which the state apparatus survives. The bureaucracy's interventions in the economy, moreover, have to be compatible with the objectives of manufacturers, otherwise civil society and the stability of the state are jeopardized. While the bureaucracy depends on those who produce resources, it is not in a simple relation of subordination to any interest within civil society. Bureaucrats have their own corporate identity and interest, and they seek not only to defend these, but also to strengthen them.

The bureaucracy is the 'state's consciousness'. Marx describes the bureaucracy, by which he means the corps of state officials, as 'a particular closed society within the state' (Marx, 1970b, p. 46). It extends its power or capacity through secrecy and mystery, 'preserved inwardly by means of the hierarchy and externally as a closed corporation' (Marx, 1970b, p. 47). The individual bureaucrat is initiated into the corporation through 'a bureaucratic confession of faith'—the examination system—and the politically dominant group's caprice (Marx, 1970b, pp. 48, 51). Subsequently the bureaucrat's career becomes everything, passive obedience to those in higher authority becomes a necessity and 'the state's interest becomes a particular private aim' (Marx, 1970b, p. 48). But the state's aims are not thereby achieved, nor is competence guaranteed. For as Marx wrote,

The bureaucracy asserts itself to be the final end of the state. Because bureaucracy makes its formal aims its content, it comes into conflict everywhere with the real aims. Hence it is obliged to present what is formal for the content and the content for what is formal. The aims of the state are transformed into aims of bureaus, or the aims of bureaus into the aims of the state. The bureaucracy is a circle from which no one can escape. Its hierarchy is a hierarchy of knowledge. The highest point entrusts the understanding of the particulars to the lower echelons, whereas these, on the other hand, credit the highest with an understanding in regard to the universal [the general interest]; and thus they deceive one another. (Marx, 1970b, pp. 46–7)

Marx's critique of Hegel involves several points, but one in particular is crucial: in the sphere of what Hegel referred to as 'the absolutely universal interest of the state proper' there is nothing but 'bureaucratic officialdom' (*Staatesbediententum*) and 'unresolved conflict' (Marx, 1970b, p. 54). Marx's emphasis on the structure and corporate nature of bureaucracies is significant because it foreshadows the arguments elaborated in what may be his most interesting work on the state, *The Eighteenth Brumaire of Louis Bonaparte*.

The Eighteenth Brumaire is an eloquent analysis of the rise to power in 1848–52 of Louis Napoleon Bonaparte and of the way power accumulated in the hands of the executive at the expense of civil society. The study highlights Marx's distance from any view of the state as 'an instrument of rationality' or 'ethical community', for he emphasized that the state apparatus is simultaneously a 'parasitic body' on civil society and an autonomous source of political action. Thus, in describing Bonaparte's regime, he wrote:

This executive power, with its enormous bureaucratic and military organization, with its ingenious state machinery, embracing wide strata, with a host of officials numbering half a million, besides an army of another half million, this appalling parasitic body . . . enmeshes the body of French society like a net and chokes all its pores. (Marx, 1963, p. 121)

Clearly, Marx's account of the state in *The Eighteenth Brumaire* represents a departure both from his early works and from polemical works like the *Communist Manifesto*. Far from a dependent or 'subservient' organization, the state is an immense set of institutions, with the capacity to shape civil society and even to curtail the power of the bourgeoisie (see Spencer, 1979; Maguire, 1978). Marx grants the state a 'primacy' in society. Political outcomes are disclosed as the result of complex coalitions interlocking with constitutional arrangements.

The analysis offered in *The Eighteenth Brumaire*, like that in the *Critique*, suggests that the agents of the state do not simply coordinate political life in the interests of the dominant class of civil society. The executive, under particular circumstances—for example, when there is a relative balance of social forces—has the capacity to promote change as well as to coordinate it. But Marx's focus, even when discussing this idea, is essentially on the state as a conservative force. He emphasizes the importance of the bureaucracy's information network as a mechanism for surveillance, and the way in which the state's political autonomy is interlocked with its capacity to undermine social movements threatening to the *status quo*. The repressive dimension of the state is complemented and checked by its capacity to sustain belief in the inviolability of existing arrangements. To the extent that private and public spheres are kept distinct, the state can, with a degree of legitimacy, claim to represent the community or the general interest, in contrast to the world of individual aims and responsibilities. But the opposition between general and particular interests—in fact, the very dualism between spheres of private and public interest—is, Marx argued, illusory.

First, this opposition becomes a basis on which bureaucrats justify their special position and privileges. Secondly, the state's claim to represent general interests is negated by the existence of classes. The state defends the 'community' as if fundamental differences of interest did not define civil society. In so doing, it not only masks the extent to which workers, among others, remain excluded from political power, but also articulates an ideological distortion (see Maguire, 1978, pp. 18–21). In treating everyone in the same way, according to principles which protect the freedom of individuals and defend their right to property, the state may act 'neutrally' while generating effects which are partial—sustaining the privileges of those with property. Moreover, the disjuncture between civil society and the state, the private and the public, the economic and the political, is ideological. The key source of contemporary power—private ownership of the means of production—is ostensibly depoliticized. The economy is regarded as non-political, such that the massive division between those that own and control the means of production, and

wage labor, is regarded as the outcome of private contracts, not a matter for the state. But by defending private property the state already has taken a side.

Marx attacked relentlessly the claim that the distribution of property lies outside the constitution of political power. This attack is, of course, a central aspect of Marx's heritage. In the *Communist Manifesto* and throughout many of his mature works Marx insists that the independence of the state from the dominant class is illusory, that the ownership of property largely determines political power: the notion that the state is a site of autonomous political action was progressively eclipsed. Class power became the major concern as is illustrated by the famous slogan of the *Communist Manifesto*: 'The executive of the modern state is but a committee for managing the common affairs of the whole bourgeoisie.' This formula does not imply that the state is dominated by the bourgeoisie as a whole: it may be independent of sections of the bourgeois class (Miliband, 1977).

The state, nevertheless, is characterized as essentially dependent upon society and upon those who dominate the economy: 'independence' is exercised only to the extent that conflicts must be settled between fractions of capital, and between 'domestic capitalism' and pressures generated by international capitalist markets. Marx's 'ideal picture' of bourgeois rule is thus a situation in which, as one commentator aptly put it,

the state can be seen by everyone as a pure instrumentality which serves the 'common good', by settling questions which have to be settled at a general social level, and by preserving the conditions for the market mechanism to reconcile individual and social benefit. (Maguire, 1978, pp. 19–20)

In operating this way the state maintains and serves the interests of the bourgeoisie in the name of the general interest.

While there is little doubt that Marx emphasized the political potency of class rule and, in particular, its repressive character, it is pertinent to recall his statement in the *Critique of the Gotha Program*:

'Present-day society' is capitalist society, which exists in all civilized countries, more or less free from medieval admixture, more or less modified by the special historical development of each country and more or less developed. On the other hand, the 'present-day state' changes within a country's frontiers. It is different in the Prusso-German empire from what it is in Switzerland, it is different in England from what it is in the United States. '*The present-day state*' is thus a fiction. (Marx, 1970*a*, p. 18, modified translation)

State forms, it is suggested, are not fixed from one modern bourgeois society to another. But the notion of 'state forms' is undeveloped and raises many questions, not the least of which is its consistency with the 'executive committee' formula of the *Communist Manifesto*.[3] Analysis of the development of state forms remained an unfulfilled project.

There are, then, at least two strands in Marx's account of the relation between classes and state institutions. The first (henceforth referred to as *position 1*) stresses that the state generally, and bureaucratic institutions in particular, emerge as a distinct sphere in society, may take a variety of forms and constitute a source of power which need not be linked to the interests, or be under the control of, dominant classes. By this account, the state retains a centrality in society: its institutional forms and operational dynamics cannot be inferred directly from the configuration of class forces. The second strand (*position 2*) is without doubt the dominant one in Marx's thought: the state and bureaucratic machinery are class instruments which emerged to coordinate a divided society in the interests of the ruling class.

On the basis of position 1 it is possible to conceive of the state as a potential arena of struggle which can become a key force for socialist change. The social-democratic traditions developed this notion: through the ballot-box the heights of state power could be scaled and used against the most privileged, while one by one the institutions of the state could be progressively turned against the interests of capital. In contradistinction, revolutionary socialist traditions developed from position 2. Following Marx's analysis, Lenin insisted that the eradication of capitalist relations of production must be accompanied by the destruction of the capitalist state apparatus: the state, as a class instrument, had to be destroyed (Lenin, 1971).

Position 1 has been emphasized above because it is generally downplayed, if mentioned at all, in the secondary literature on Marx.[4] Marx's work on the state remained incomplete. Position 1 left several important questions insufficiently addressed. What is the basis of state power? How do bureaucracies function? What precise interest do bureaucrats develop? Position 2 is even more problematic: it dogmatically postulates a particular capitalist-specific organizational form of state institutions and mistakenly

assumes a simple causal relation between the facts of class domination and the vicissitudes of political life. But Marx's combined writings do indicate how central he regarded the state to the integration and control of class-divided societies. Furthermore, his work, particularly on developed capitalist societies, suggests important limits to state intervention. If intervention undermines the process of capital accumulation, it simultaneously undermines the material basis of the state; hence, state policies must be consistent with capitalist relations of production. Accordingly, a dominant economic class can rule without directly governing, that is, it can exert determinate political influence without even having representatives in government. This idea retains a vital place in contemporary debates among Marxists, democratic theorists and theorists of corporatism.

Lenin

Lenin followed in the main the tenets of Marx's position 2. His views are stated succinctly in *State and Revolution*, where he listed his first task as the 'resuscitation of the real teachings of Marx on the state' (Lenin, 1971, p. 7). Lenin conceived of the state as a 'machine for the oppression of one class by another'. The modern representative state was 'the instrument for the exploitation of wage-labor by capital'. Thus, the distinguishing feature of the state, apart from its grouping of people on a territorial basis, is its dependence on force, exercised through specialized bodies such as the army, police and prison service. Taxes, state loans and special laws to protect officials are necessary for the survival of these institutions. Lenin affirms that the state is 'a special repressive force' (Lenin, 1971, p. 17).

The ruling classes maintain their grip on the state through alliances with government—alliances created both by government dependence on the stock exchange and by the corruption of officials. The vital business of the state takes place not in representative assemblies, but in the state bureaucracies, where alliances can be established out of public view. Further, even democratic rights such as freedom of association, freedom of the press or freedom of assembly are a major benefit to the dominant classes. They can claim these institutions are 'open' while controlling them 'through ownership of the media, control over meeting places, money, and other resources' (Lenin, 1971, pp. 72–3).

Although *State and Revolution* reiterates what we have called Marx's position 2, Lenin makes more than

Marx did of one central point: the crystallization of class power within the organs of state administration. For the Lenin of *State and Revolution*: 'So long as the state exists, there is no freedom. When freedom exists, there will be no state.' Strong central control would be necessary after the revolution, but a precondition of revolutionary success is the destruction of the 'old state machine': 'The bureaucracy and the standing army, direct products of class oppression, have to be smashed. The army would be replaced by armed workers and the bureaucrats by elected officials subject to recall' (Lenin, 1971, pp. 35–9). There would be 'immediate introduction of control and supervision by *all*, so that *all* may become "bureaucrats" for a time and that, therefore, nobody may be able to become a "bureaucrat"'. Officials and soldiers would be necessary but they would not become 'privileged persons divorced from the people and standing *above* the people'. Lenin never doubted that discipline was essential in political organizations, but he argued that this does not entail the creation of an elite of functionaries.[5] Following the lessons which Marx and Engels drew from the Paris Commune, Lenin maintained that the new socialist order must replace 'the government of persons' by 'the administration of things' (Lenin, 1971, p. 16).

The survival of the bureaucracy in the post-revolutionary period was frequently explained by Lenin in terms of the lingering influence of capitalism and the old regime. He continually affirmed a causal relation between forms of state organization and classes, even in his famous 'last testament' where problems concerning central administration and the bureaucratization of the party and the state were sources of great anxiety (see Lewin, 1975). This position had dire consequences: it led, in part, to the widespread belief among Bolsheviks that with the abolition of capitalist property relations (and the expansion of forces of production) problems of organization, control and coordination could be resolved.

There are many tensions in Lenin's treatment of the state and political organization. He thought that the work of the new socialist order could be conducted by workers organized in soviets, yet he defended the authority of the party in nearly all spheres. His argument that state bureaucracies need not entail fixed positions of power and privilege is suggestive, but it remains, especially in light of the massive problems of organization faced during and after the revolution, a very incomplete statement. Lenin failed to examine the degree to which state organizations are influenced by

diverse interests, political compromises and complex circumstances which do not merely reflect 'class antagonisms which must be reconciled from above'. To this extent his views on the state represent a regression from Marx's position 1.

Weber

Lenin's classic formulation that revolutionary transformation requires the institutions of the state to be smashed (and not merely appropriated) remains difficult to puzzle through. Centralized (bureaucratic) administration may be inescapable. Weber's consideration of this issue makes his work especially important. He dismisses the feasibility of 'direct administration'

> where the group grows beyond a certain size or where the administrative function becomes too difficult to be satisfactorily taken care of by anyone whom rotation, the lot, or election may happen to designate. The conditions of administration of mass structures are radically different from those obtaining in small associations resting upon neighborly or personal relationships...
>
> The growing complexity of the administrative tasks and the sheer expansion of their scope increasingly result in the technical superiority of those who have had training and experience, and will thus inevitably favor the continuity of at least some of the functionaries. Hence, there always exists the probability of the rise of a special, perennial structure for administrative purposes, which of necessity means for the exercise of rule. (Weber, 1978, vol. 2, pp. 951–2)

It is a dangerous confusion, Weber maintained, to conflate problems concerning the nature of administration with problems concerning the control of the state apparatus (see Albrow, 1970, pp. 37–49). He was in little doubt that the Bolsheviks had conflated these concerns.

Weber characterized the state as based on a monopoly of physical coercion which is legitimized, that is, sustained not by the power of an economically dominant class, but rather by a belief in the justifiability and/or legality of this monopoly. The legitimacy of the modern state is founded predominantly on 'legal authority', that is, commitment to a 'code of legal rules'. Foremost among the state's institutions is the bureaucracy—a vast network of organizations run by appointed officials. Although bureaucracies have been essential to states at many times and places in history, 'only the Occident', on Weber's account, 'knows the state in its modern scale, with a professional administration, specialized officialdom, and law based on the concept of citizenship'. This institution had 'beginnings in antiquity and the Orient', but these 'were never able to develop' (Weber, 1923, p. 232).

The modern state is not, Weber contended, an effect of capitalism; it preceded and helped promote capitalist development (Weber, 1978, vol. 2, pp. 1381 ff.). Capitalism, however, provided an enormous impetus to the expansion of rational administration, that is, the type of bureaucracy founded on legal authority. Weber extended the meaning of bureaucracy from officialdom or the civil service to a particular mode of organization. 'Today', he declared, 'capitalism and bureaucracy have found one another and belong intimately together' (Weber, 1978, vol. 2, p. 1465): private and public administration are becoming more and more bureaucratized—there is a growth of office hierarchy with supervision of lower offices; administration is based upon written documents (files); specialist training is presupposed and candidates are appointed according to qualification; formal responsibilities demand the full working capacities of officials; officials are 'separated from ownership of the means of administration' (Weber, 1978, vol. 1, pp. 220–1).

Under normal circumstances, bureaucracy is, according to Weber, 'completely indispensable'. The choice is only 'between bureaucracy and dilettantism in the field of administration' (Weber, 1978, vol. 1, p. 223). Weber explained the spread of bureaucracy in the following terms:

> The decisive reason for the advance of bureaucratic organization has always been its purely *technical* superiority over any other form of organization. The fully developed bureaucratic apparatus compares with other organizations exactly as does the machine with the non-mechanical modes of production. Precision, speed, unambiguity, knowledge of the files, continuity, discretion, unity, strict subordination, reduction of friction and of material and personal costs—these are raised to the optimum point in the strictly bureaucratic administration, and especially in its monocratic form. (Weber, 1978, vol. 2, p. 973).

As economic life becomes more complex and differentiated, bureaucratic administration becomes more essential.

While rule by officials (*Beamtenherrschaft*) is not inevitable, considerable power accrues to bureaucrats through their expertise, information and access to secrets. This power can become overwhelming. Politicians and political actors of all kinds can find themselves dependent on the bureaucracy. A central question—if not preoccupation—for Weber was, how can 'bureaucratic power' be checked? He was convinced that in the absence of checks public organization would fall prey to powerful private interests (among others, organized capitalists and major landholders) who would not have the nation-state as their prime concern; moreover, in times of national emergency, there would be ineffective leadership. Bureaucrats, unlike politicians, cannot take a passionate stand. They do not have the training—and bureaucracies are not structurally designed—for the consideration of political, alongside technical or economic, criteria. However, Weber's solution to the problem of unlimited bureaucratization was not one that depended merely on individual politicians' capacity for innovation. Writing about Germany he advocated a strong parliament which would create a competitive training ground for strong leadership and serve as a balance to public and private bureaucracy (see Mommsen, 1974). In so arguing Weber was taking 'national power and prestige' as his prime concern. As one commentator aptly noted, 'Weber's enthusiasm for the representative system owed more to his conviction that national greatness depended on finding able leaders than to any concern for democratic values' (Albrow, 1970, p. 48).

Weber's position on the relationship among social structure, bureaucracy and the state can be clarified further by examining his assessment of socialism. He believed that the abolition of private capitalism 'would simply mean that ... the *top management* of the nationalized or socialized enterprises would become bureaucratic' (Weber, 1978, vol. 2, p. 1402). Reliance upon those who control resources would be enhanced, for the abolition of the market would be the abolition of a key countervailing power to the state. The market generates change and social mobility: it is the very source of capitalist dynamism:

> State bureaucracy would rule alone if private capitalism were eliminated. The private and public bureaucracies, which now work next to, and potentially against, each other and hence check one another to a degree, would be merged into a single hierarchy. This would be similar to the situation in ancient Egypt, but it would occur in a much more

rational—and hence unbreakable—form. (Weber, 1978, vol. 2, p. 1402)

While Weber argued that 'progress' toward the bureaucratic state is given an enormous impetus by capitalist development, he believed that this very development itself, coupled with parliamentary government and the party system, provided the best obstacle to state power.

Weber's attempt to analyze the internal workings of public (and private) organizations and his observations about trends in bureaucratization constitute a major contribution to understanding the state and problems of centralized administration. His work provides a counterbalance to the Marxist and particularly Leninist emphasis on the class characteristics of the capitalist state, presupposing an intimate connection between state activities, forms of organization and class relations. The argument that private and public administrations are internally homologous—as opposed to causally determined by class power—is important and provocative; it is compatible with Marx's position 1, and reinforces the significance of the issues neglected by Marx's position 2.

At his most trenchant Weber posits a relationship between growing bureaucratization and capitalism, linked by the two-sided rationality of state agencies which mirrors the hierarchical rule-bound structure and the purposive logic that govern the operations of the capitalist firm. But one can search Weber's writings in vain for a satisfactory explanation of the precise character of that relation between the growing bureaucratic centralization of the state and modern capitalism. Weber does not specify the relationship between bureaucratization and capitalist development for two reasons.

First, in his historical account of patterns of bureaucratization in diverse societies he does not isolate the degree to which certain bureaucratic processes may be specific to, or influenced by, capitalist development *per se*. He seems to give equal weight to the 'impact of cultural, economic, and technological forces' on the growth of bureaucracy, even when these forces are wholly independent of capitalist development. The particular connection between bureaucratization and capitalism is left clouded within an admirably complex but insufficiently precise account of societal evolution. Secondly, in his analysis of Western society the specific connection between capitalism and bureaucracy is not structurally explicated. Rather, Weber suggests that bureaucratism in government and

in private capitalist administration have a common basis, are functionally interrelated and are homologous. This says quite a lot, but not enough to provide the basis for understanding patterns of state intervention. The assumption of functional, harmonious evolutionary codevelopment of private and public institutional forms obscures the issue of whether or not there is a real class basis to state power. It cannot take the place of a well worked-out theory of the complex development of state–society relations under modern capitalism.

In sum, we may say that neither the search for a form of state organization specific to capitalism nor excessive attention to the formal characteristics of bureaucracies is promising, if the intent is to understand the relation among classes, bureaucracy and the state. Although there can be little doubt, as Marx insisted, about the dependence of the state apparatus on the process of production and hence, in capitalist society, about the constraints on the initiatives of state agencies, there is certainly more to the theory of political and bureaucratic organization that Marx and Lenin suggested. Weber's account of bureaucracy and the state may be attacked on several grounds, but these must not be taken to imply any straightforward conception of the class character of the state and of forms of organization.

The state in capitalist society, then, facilitates the reproduction of class relations, the maintenance of private ownership of the means of production, and so on, but in so far as the state is a site of autonomous political and bureaucratic organization than Marx and Lenin suggested. Weber's account of bureaucracy and not empirically bounded. Discrete outcomes are uncertain. That being the case, what are the constraints on state activity? Why does the state in capitalist society tend to exercise power in a way which assures perpetuation of the key relations of domination and inequality? Although Marx never adequately answered such questions, it seems clear that he often assumed a commonality of interest between the dominant class and the governing/administering bodies which—against the backdrop of structurally determined class conflict in society—resolved the problem posed by the institutional separation between class and state. The resolution remains practical, expressed in explicit policies which are compatible with capitalist interests.

In Weber's formulation of the relationship between the state/bureaucracy and class power, there is no comparable assumption of shared interest between officialdom and bourgeoisie. State power, which is expressed through the myriad institutions of public administration, the parliament, the military, and so on, rests not on the economic power of a class, but on the belief that the institutions and commands of the state are legitimate. Accordingly, class and power are independent dimensions of social life, and are related only in a contingent manner.

Weber: Divided Against Himself

While we have emphasized the theoretical ground shared by Marx (position 1) and Weber, others have applied Weber's writings to a rather different end, relying on a reading of Weber's work which removes power from its structural context. In fact, Weber's writings have spawned an extensive literature which addresses the issues of bureaucracy and power, at the same time as it challenges fundamental Marxist axioms about class as the central structural determinant of state/bureaucratic action. In these writings the connection between state bureaucracy and (class) power is wholly recast. On the one hand, Weber's work helps orient the American tradition of empirical democratic theory which considers the institutional arrangements designed in principle to secure a high responsiveness by leaders to the mass of citizens, in particular, the competition of elites (political leaders) for electoral support and the influence exercised by organized interests between elections (see Pateman, 1970, pp. 8–14). On the other hand, public bureaucracies are treated by this school within a theory of organizations in which the general problems of rational administration are stressed at the cost of special attention to the consequences of a bureaucracy's structural position within the apparatus of the state.

Power is divorced from state power or class power and the notion of civil society divided by class antagonisms is replaced by an ill-defined conception of the social environment, which serves as a colorless background for state activities (see Giddens, 1979, pp. 88–9). The homologous and interdependent character of capitalist organization of private administration and bureaucratic organization of public administration is lost. Weber is divided against himself; a complex—if incomplete—interpretation of the growing rationalization of society is transformed and bifurcated into an internal account of the logic of bureaucratic institutions and an external account of voluntarist power, neither of which has any basic connection with class relations.

Empirical Democratic Theory: Power and the Fragmentation of Social Interests

Applying a Weberian notion of power—'the chance of a man or of a number of men to realize their own will in a communal action against the resistance of others who are participating in the action' (Weber, 1972, p. 180)—to a basic inquiry into the distribution of power in Western parliamentary democracies, a school of empirical democratic theory (widely referred to as 'pluralism') gained a commanding position within American university studies of politics, beginning in the 1950s. While its hold is probably not as secure now as then in academic circles and its understandings of power, class and the state are ones we ultimately reject, the application of American democratic theory to the issues we have raised is critically important. Although many have dismissed pluralism as a naïve, and/or narrowly ideological, celebration of American society, the tradition offers a clear framework for viewing political behavior—which is not always the case for Marxism and Weberianism—and one which rests upon the appeal of Madisonian democracy and the formidable logic of Utilitarianism.

The view of power in pluralist theory is, in Steven Lukes's apt terminology, 'one-dimensional' (Lukes, 1974, ch. 2). The dimension is voluntarist, and the consideration of institutional influences upon the expression of observable acts of power is neglected. As Dahl, perhaps the central figure in American pluralist theory, suggests, 'by "power" we mean to describe a . . . reasonable relationship, such as A's capacity for acting in such a manner as to control B's responses' (Dahl, 1956, p. 13). In other formulations Dahl refers to the power relation as involving 'a successful attempt by A to get a to do something he would not otherwise do' (Dahl, 1957; see Nagel, 1975, pp. 9–15). Whether one stresses capacity (the first definition) or actual behavioral outcomes in the exercise of power (the second definition), Dahl's notion of power, like Weber's, stresses the subjective elements of purpose and willing, and implies a comparable, narrowly conflictual basis. The issue is the overcoming of B's resistance—getting B to act against his or her preferences—and in that sense power hinges on the exercise of control over immediate events.

Dahl's research design for an empirical investigation of the distribution of power in American societies follows from this conceptual basis. Wanting to discover who had power over what in New Haven politics (hence the title of his famous study of 'pluralist democracy', *Who Governs?*) Dahl concentrates on discovering the capacity of actors involved in particular policy decisions to 'initiate alternatives that were finally adopted' or to veto alternatives initiated by others (Dahl, 1975). Which A could overcome the resistance of which B in securing discrete and observable political outcomes? Following a voluntarist understanding of power which focuses on the explicit results of the governmental decision-making process in New Haven Dahl concludes that the city is a pluralist democracy of multiple coalitions leading to the mayor. Power is disaggregated and non-cumulative; it is shared and bartered by numerous groups spread throughout society and representing diverse and competitive interests. There are inequalities of power, to be sure, as there is an unequal distribution of wealth, status, education, and so on, but nearly everyone can be 'more equal' than another with regard to some relevant resource. There are conflicts over the power to determine policy outcomes, as different interests press their sectional claims on the mayor, but the very process of interest bartering assumes a tendency toward equilibrium and assures a general direction of policy which is positive for the citizenry at large.

The Madisonian Assumptions

This last notion—that the process of diverse interests competing for power is a source of democratic equilibrium and generally favorable policy articulation—remains, alongside the voluntarist notion of power, a second critical assumption of American empirical democratic theory. It is a vintage argument, and one which provides 'a basic rationale for the American political system' (Dahl, 1956, p. 5). Beginning from the Hobbesian assumption that people's natural inclinations include the desire for power over others (a desire which can be realized because of unequal natural endowments), James Madison wrote in The Federalist, No. 10, that 'the latent causes of faction are ... sown in the nature of men' (Hamilton et al., 1945, p. 56). He argued accordingly that factions are a necessary part of political life unless snuffed out by repression, a process he likened to the elimination of air out of concern for the danger of fires. Madison's additional point, that 'the most common and durable source of factions has been the various and unequal distribution of property', has unfortunately been undervalued by contemporary democratic theorists who assert a relative equality of influence among diverse sources of faction/divisions of interest. Characteristically, Dahl argues that

religion, race, ethnic group and regional identities are as significant as class (what Madison terms the unequal division of property) in the division of society into distinctive 'subcultures' or interests (Dahl, 1971, pp. 106–7). Democratic theorists accept, however, that Madison's factions—creditors, debtors, mercantile interests, and so on—persevere in today's voluntary associations, interest groups, peak organizations of business and labor and, one step removed, in political parties. Mainly, Madison argued for a strong American state negatively, as a safeguard against tyranny and a means to 'break and control the violence of faction'. His contemporary adherents, however, radically (if unwittingly) alter Madison's argument. Despite substantial disagreement among themselves, contemporary democratic theorists claim that factions are more than the natural counterpart of free association—and they are not an obstacle to democratic government. Rather, Madison's factions in their modern expression as interest groups are viewed positively as the structural source of stability and the central expression of democracy.

This direction in democratic theory is perhaps most clear in the case of group theorists, who focus on the competing 'claims through or upon the institutions of government' by interest groups, and assert the importance of group interaction for securing equilibrium in American democracy (Truman, 1951, p. 505). According to David Truman,

Only the highly routinized governmental activities show any stability ... and these may as easily be subordinated to elements in the legislature as to the chief executive ... [O]rganized interest groups ... may play one segment of the structure against another as circumstances and strategic considerations permit. The total pattern of government over a period of time thus presents a protean complex of crisscrossing relationships that change in strength and direction with alterations in the power and standing of interests, organized and unorganized. (Truman, 1951, p. 508)

Power for group theorists like Truman is conceived along Weberian lines, while the configuration of power, expressed through factions, is strictly Madisonian. The state is not autonomous in either the Weberian sense, or that of Marx's position 1. Rather, the state reacts to the purposive exercise of power which is fragmented within society, non-hierarchically and competitively configured. Moreover, Truman is explicitly Madisonian in providing mechanisms for guaranteeing that out of the diversity of competing interests relatively coherent policy (and policy within 'the democratic mold') will nevertheless emerge. Beginning from Madison's assumption that the very diversity of interests in society will protect the republic from the 'tyranny of the factious majority' (by splintering potential factions that would threaten the rights of others), Truman suggests that 'overlapping membership' is an additional safeguard. Since, in Truman's language, all 'tolerably normal' persons have multiple memberships scattered among groups with diverse—and even incompatible—interests, each interest group remains too weak and internally divided in purpose to secure a share of power incommensurate with its (assumed to be small) numbers and (assumed to be narrow) interests. Policy emerges behind the backs of state officials as the result of a series of uncoordinated impacts upon government, directed from all sides by competing forces (Truman, 1951, pp. 503–16).

Dahl, writing later than Truman, criticizes Madison for theoretical sloppiness and notes the anachronistic character of his eighteenth-century views. Nevertheless, Dahl assimilates the central Madisonian concern with factional interests recast in its positive guise as the exemplary expression of—rather than a formidable threat to—democracy (Dahl, 1956). Indeed, Dahl argues that democracy may be defined as rule by multiple minority oppositions. For Dahl, a tyrannous majority is improbable, since elections, the central democratic procedure for selecting and 'controlling' leaders, express the preferences of various competitive groups, rather than the rule of a firm majority. Hence, supporters of democracy need suffer no fear of tyranny by an excessively strong interest. Rather, what Dahl calls polyarchy (a situation of open contest for electoral support among a large proportion of the adult population) ensures competition among interests (minorities)—and the existence of competitive interests is the safeguard of democracy. Thus, Dahl writes in *A Preface to Democratic Theory*:

The real world issue has not turned out to be whether a majority, much less 'the' majority, will act in a tyrannical way through democratic procedures to impose its will on a (or the) minority. Instead, the more relevant question is the extent to which various minorities in a society will frustrate the ambitions of one another with the passive acquiescence or indifference of a majority of adults or voters.

... [I]f there is anything to be said for the

processes that actually distinguish democracy (or polyarchy) from dictatorship ... [t]he distinction comes [very close] to being one between government by a minority and government by *minorities*. As compared with the political processes of a dictatorship, the characteristics of polyarchy greatly extend the number, size, and diversity of the minorities whose preferences will influence the outcome of governmental decisions. (Dahl, 1956, p. 133)

More sophisticated than Truman in his appreciation of the nuances of power and in his comparative understanding of institutional arrangements in Western parliamentary democracies, Dahl nevertheless reinforces the view that competition among organized interests structures the policy outcomes and secures the democratic character of the regime.[6] To this degree, at least, whatever their differences, nearly all contemporary democratic theorists preserve their Madisonian heritage and perpetuate an interpretation of democracy as a set of institutional arrangements which allow for the rule of multiple minorities through competition for the selection and influence of elites, subject to the periodic control exercised by voter approval (Pateman, 1970, p. 8).

Even 'participationists', the dissidents of democratic theory who criticize the assumptions that participation should be confined to the choice of decision-makers and that popular control be limited to the sanction of electoral rejection, tend to accept elite and interest group competition as the appropriate framework for the national political system. In this vein Carole Pateman insists, 'it is only if the individual has the opportunity directly to participate in decision making and choose representatives in the alternative areas [for example, the workplace] that, under modern conditions, he can hope to have real control over the course of his life'. She admits, however, that 'it is doubtful if the average citizen will ever be as interested in all the decisions made at the national levels as he would be in those made nearer home [i.e., in the alternative areas of his life]' (Pateman, 1970, p. 110). The limits of the critique are clear: participation in the workplace; polyarchy in governmental affairs. Once the Madisonian terms of reference are accepted, even some critics have difficulty avoiding the pluralist conclusions. However, these terms can be directly challenged.

In combination, a Weberian notion of power and a Madisonian view of the necessity of factions (transmuted into the positive basis of democracy), mark a dramatic turn in democratic theory and invite a series of substantial criticisms. Empirical democratic theory projects a narrow 'economistic' view of human rationality and potential, reduces democratic theory to a kind of economic theory and excuses inequality as the necessary side-effect of political stability.

Empirical democratic theory takes for granted a very particular and problematic Utilitarian notion of the individual as a satisfaction-maximizer, a 'consumer of utilities', and views the individual as only incidentally 'a doer, a creator, an enjoyer of his human attributes' (Macpherson, 1973, pp. 4–5). Democratic theory was not always like this. C. B. Macpherson rightly criticizes Dahl and others for their attack on the classical theory of democracy—represented, for example, by Aristotle—and the violence done by empirical theory to the more radical and libertarian traditions of democratic theory which struggled to survive in post-Benthamite Britain. 'The traditional theory of Mill, carried over into the 20th century by such writers as A. D. Lindsay and Ernest Barker', he argues, 'gave democracy a moral dimension; it saw democracy as developmental, as a matter of the improvement of mankind' (Macpherson, 1973, p. 5). Once democracy is reduced to elite competition and interest group pressure, however, democracy may be treated as an equilibrating mechanism. As Jon Elster observed, empirical theory has become 'an economic theory of democracy'. Economics concerns individuals maximizing their self-interests and politics concerns sets of individuals maximizing their common interests. Politics is reduced to 'the study of ways of transcending the Prisoner's Dilemma' (Elster, 1976, p. 249).

The implications for democratic theory and for what we consider democracy are very serious. Gone are the visions of greater equality and a guarantee of the best conditions for human moral and social evolution through a rich culture of civic participation, replaced by the Madisonian/pluralist ideal of elite competition for the seat of government. As a consequence of this theoretical shift, the concept of power itself loses its pre-Hobbesian meaning as uniquely human developmental capacities and becomes, merely, the power to control others, the narrowly purposive Weberian notion of power in society.

In an influential critique of the concept of power applied in pluralist theory, moreover, Peter Bachrach and Morton Baratz have drawn attention to an additional problem: that exercises of power may already have determined the observable instances of control by A over B which constitute power in pluralist

terms (Bachrach and Baratz, 1962, pp. 947–52). Bachrach and Baratz insist, adopting Schattschneider's notion of the *mobilization of bias*, that persons or groups may exercise power by 'creating or reinforcing barriers to the airing of policy conflicts'—in other words, through participating in the *non-decision-making* process (Schattschneider, 1960):

> Of course, power is exercised when A participates in the making of decisions that affect B. But power is also exercised when A devotes his energies to creating or reinforcing social and political values and institutional practices that limit the scope of the political process to public consideration of only those issues which are comparatively innocuous to A. To the extent that A succeeds in doing this, B is prevented, for all practical purposes, from bringing to the fore any issues that might in their resolution be seriously detrimental to A's set of preferences. (Bachrach and Baratz, 1962, p. 949)

While Bachrach and Baratz mark an important advance over 'one-dimensional' pluralist theory, their argument is hardly more satisfactory in the long run. The central problem with this 'two faces of power' approach (decision-making and non-decision-making) remains its partial adherence to the Weberian-cum-pluralist conception of power in society. As Lukes observes in his telling critique, 'the bias of the system is not sustained simply by a series of individually chosen acts, but also, most importantly, by the socially structured and culturally patterned behaviour of groups, and practices of institutions' (Lukes, 1974, p. 22). Accepting the view of power as the capacity of individuals to realize their wills against resistance, Bachrach and Baratz neglect consideration of 'collective forces and social arrangements'.

Lukes's objections to the approach of Bachrach and Baratz and, indeed, to the pluralists more generally, bring the critical issues into clear relief. Marx and Lenin consider power essentially to be a class matter: it is structurally determined, whether in society or the administration of the state. Pluralists reject a necessary connection between power and class and view power mainly in terms of discrete instances of control by one actor exercised over the conscious resistance of another. Between these extreme positions, Lukes argues for an understanding of power as the capability of A to affect B in a manner contrary to B's *real interests*—what people would want and prefer were they able to make the choice outside of the system which works against their interests and conditions their felt wants and needs.

Placing himself deliberately on radical—but not Marxist—grounds Lukes hopes to preserve both an understanding of power as conditioned but not *determined* by structures of domination, and voluntarily expressed by human agents. He is trying to reconcile the moment of active human subjectivity with that of structural/institutional constraint in accordance with Marx's famous assertion, set out in the *Eighteenth Brumaire*, that 'men make their own history but they do not make it just as they please' (Lukes, 1974; Lukes, 1977, pp. 3–29). Unlike Marx, Lukes continues to view interests in individual rather than class terms, at least partly adopting what one critic called the 'illustrative methodology' of pluralists, constructing arguments through 'a series of dynamic tableaux or mind experiments in which two individual actors, A and B, are manipulated through socially barren scenarios' (Bradshaw, 1976, p. 123; see Giddens, 1979, pp. 89–94). Thus, for Lukes, class is implicated as the source of power which separates (subjective) interest from real interest, but the relationship between class and power is not successfully drawn. Class society conditions interests, but power remains merely an attribute of agents—not a property of social relations collectivities and institutions.

Corporatist Theory

Beyond the debates about the concept of power, many have focused their attacks on empirical democratic theory in terms of the problems of policy formulation. These critics have viewed the policy process less as an issue about power and more as a concrete problem of institutional arrangements, both within and outside the traditional structures of the state bureaucracy. In the late 1970s none so forcefully attacked the assumptions of empirical democratic theory as the new generation of theorists of corporatism, many of whom nevertheless share some important conceptual ground with democratic—and particularly pluralist—theory.[7] How far have they come from an assumption that stability is the 'invisible hand' result of diverse pressures and from an understanding of state policy as the contingent outcome of diverse societal influences?

At first glance, corporatist theory and empirical democratic theory—for simplicity here reduced to pluralism—seem wholly incompatible. The corporatist

view of state–society relations began, as one of its most able practitioners, Leo Panitch, explains, from the 'common premise . . . that class harmony and organic unity were essential to society and could be secured if the various functional groups, and especially the organizations of capital and labour, were imbued with a conception of natural rights and obligations somewhat similar to that presumed to have unified the medieval estates' (Panitch, 1977, p. 61). This principle of organic unity is central to many versions of corporatist theory and incompatible with the tenets of pluralism. In corporatism, observed J. T. Winkler, '[s]ociety is seen as consisting of diverse elements unified into one body, forming one *corpus*, hence the word corporatism'. Whereas pluralism assumes a competition among divided interests with the struggle for factional advantage resulting in a political equilibrium which defines the policy options of a weak state, corporatism presupposes 'a shared interest in collective existence' and cooperation expressed through the strategic exercise of power by a strong central state (Winkler, 1976, p. 105).

Until recently, corporatism has referred exclusively to state corporatism—corporatism from above—and pointed to the Fascist states of Italy and Germany in the 1930s as 'exemplary' instances of modern European corporatism. In these cases corporatism was no more than a 'decorative façade, for an organic unity won through the consistent exercise of repression' (Harris, 1972, cited in Panitch, 1977). With growing academic support, however, a new conceptual variant of corporatism—corporatism from below or societal corporatism—has emerged as an explanation of contemporary European political realities which challenges the understandings of both Marxist and democratic theory.

In the central work of societal corporatism (or liberal corporatism) Philippe Schmitter defines corporatism as the specific political structure which typically accompanies the 'post liberal, advanced capitalist, organized democratic welfare state' (Schmitter, 1974, p. 105). As an ideal type, argues Schmitter in the definition which has become the standard reference point for subsequent debates, contemporary corporatism can be conceived as:

a system of interest representation in which the constituent units are organized into a limited number of singular, compulsory, hierarchically ordered and functionally differentiated categories, recognized or licensed (if not created) by the state and granted a deliberate representational monopoly within their respective categories in exchange for observing certain controls on their selection of leaders and articulation of demands and supports. (Schmitter, 1974, pp. 93–4)

With Schmitter and others, the relationship between corporatism and pluralism both as empirical accounts of the existing pattern of state–society relations, and as alternative conceptions, is explicitly drawn. The 'needs of capitalism to reproduce the conditions of its existence' and particularly varying requirements generated by the changing balance of class forces since World War I, have led to 'the decay of pluralism and its gradual displacement by societal corporatism' (Schmitter, 1974, pp. 107–8; see also Schmitter, 1977). There *was* pluralism, but there is no more; there are critical class forces which structure political relations, but the state was never the instrumental reserve of capitalist interests, and policy was never directly linked to the requirements of accumulation. The assumption of class struggle is, albeit with new institutional specifications, appropriated from Marxist theory and, at the same time, the lines are drawn sharply against pluralism as an account of contemporary politics. Any models in democratic theory, argues Schmitter, which suggest that diverse interests are pursued by 'an unspecified number of multiple, voluntary, competitive, non-hierarchically ordered and self-determined ... categories' (Schmitter, 1974, p. 93) are no longer valid.

By the corporatist account the directive capacities of the state have increased, and 'interest intermediation' has become systematized along stricter (less plural and less voluntary) lines of power: membership is compulsory in the few peak associations (trade union or business confederations) with clout; a single organization negotiates binding settlements which are recognized as legitimate by the state; and in return for this 'representational monopoly', the representatives of the corporate interests (for example, the Trades Union Congress in Britain or Confindustria in Italy) deliver support for agreed policies and discipline their members.

Some of the appeal of corporatist theory follows from its presentation (by Schmitter, for example) as a descriptively rich 'synthesis' of central conceptual premises of Marxist and pluralist theory. From pluralism, corporatists adopt the basic understanding that policy outcomes are determined by the competitive claims of interest associations—but the associations are now oligopolistically configured. Equally significant, corporatist thinkers adopt the pluralist assumptions that competition among disparate groups tends to result in state policy equilibrium, with no shifts toward labor or capital which would force a fundamental revision of the structural arrangements of capitalism. From Marxist theory, the liberal corporatists accept that beneath the intricacies of 'interest intermediation' lie basic class conflicts, and beneath the apparent indeterminacy of policy lie activities which are designed to reproduce class relations.

Remarkably, within this theoretical amalgam, the traditional corporatist premiss of organic unity is also preserved. In the liberal corporatist model an incomes policy, for example, jointly agreed between government and peak trade union associations—ideally, with tripartite negotiations securing the support of business as a full partner—becomes the modern cathedral, whose painstaking construction represents the solidity, organic unity and ostensible harmony of the society. Claims above class, the higher claims of stability and the pursuit of economic well-being, forge unity among societal factions which are manipulated by the state to disengage from class conflict and to achieve a compromise which freezes the balance of class power.

There is a conceptual ingenuity to the corporatist enterprise and a descriptive elegance which is noteworthy. More successfully than Marxist theory or modern democratic theory, corporatist theory exposes one of the most significant patterns of postwar state management, that is, the proliferation of tripartite agreements, the tendency for the conventions of collective bargaining to be writ large in the processes of governmental decision-making, particularly in areas of macroeconomic policy. Moreover, by highlighting these extraparliamentary negotiations about critical policies (wages, prices, investment and planning), corporatists seem to explain best the much-discussed weakening of formal representative structures, the undermining of the sovereignty of parliamentary bodies, the 'crisis of democracy' in the face of excessive economic pressures.

Nevertheless, serious weaknesses limit the utility of corporatist theory as a general framework for understanding the contemporary state. Descriptively, for a start, few things besides incomes policies reflect the attributes of the tripartite model and even agreements over incomes have often been insubstantial, voluntary, ineffective and transitory. Indeed, corporatist arrangements remain fragile, because they require the consistent presence of a relatively uncommon set of conditions which secure the integration of organized labor, including:

(1) an attitude within the labor movement which favors 'crisis management' over structural or redistributive measures of macroeconomic policy;

(2) the presence of state institutions for tripartite management initiatives;

(3) the institutionalization of trade union and party power within a coordinated working-class movement;

(4) sufficient centralization that decisions by confederations are binding upon individual industrial unions;

(5) adequate elite influence within unions to ensure rank-and-file compliance with agreed policies.

While broad corporatist arrangements have been generally successful in Austria and the Netherlands, these five conditions have been so difficult to realize elsewhere that even incomes policies—the minimal and most common corporatist arrangement—have failed to appear (or proved to be transitory). The failure in France has been due to the anticapitalist attitude of the largest and Communist-oriented union, the Confédération générale du travail (CGT) (absence of condition 1); in Germany, due to the low level of institutionalization for tripartite management at the federal level (absence of condition 2); and in Britain the failure is distinctly overdetermined, due (at a minimum) to the absence of factors 3, 4 and 5 (see Lehmbruch, 1979a).

Temporary, one-sided agreements to limit wages, while profits and prices are left to private and market determination, hardly rival the mediaeval cathedral as examples of organic social architecture. Not only is instability frequently associated with efforts at the construction of durable agreements, but the central premiss—that incomes policies involve freely contracting parties who represent functionally equivalent partners—seems illusory. More likely, corporatist structures temporarily obscure the asymmetries in the distribution of power (see Martin, 1975). Rather than demonstrating the end of class conflict, corporatist arrangements institutionally fix a balance of class power, endowing an unequal equilibrium—well within safe limits for the reproduction of capitalism—with quasi-legal justification. Class struggle continues, partly integrated within the institutional structures of the state. At the same time the presence of corporatist institutions which take away the responsibility for economic management from representative organs, challenges the pluralist interpretation of democracy as a set of institutional

arrangements subject to the control of periodic voter approval.

Developments in Contemporary Marxist Theory

In the last fifteen years there has been a massive revival of interest in the problems of state, power and bureaucracy among contemporary Marxist writers (see, for example, Gold et al., 1975; Frankel, 1979; Jessop, 1977). Ralph Miliband provided an important stimulus with his publication of The State in Capitalist Society (1969a). Noting the growing centrality of the state in Western societies he sought on the one hand to assess the relationship Marx posited between class and state, and on the other to evaluate the pluralist model of state–society relations which was then the reigning orthodoxy.

Against those who held that the state is a neutral arbiter among social interests, he argued (1) that in contemporary Western societies there is a dominant or ruling class which owns and controls the means of production; (2) that it has close links to powerful institutions, political parties, the military, universities, the media, and so on; and (3) that it has disproportionate representation at all levels of the state apparatus, especially in the 'command positions'. The social background of civil servants ('in many cases overwhelmingly ... from the world of business and property, or from the professional middle classes'), their own interests (a smooth career path), their ideological dispositions ('accepting beyond question the capitalist context in which they operate'), mean that the state bureaucracy 'is a crucially important and committed element in the maintenance and defense of the structure of power and privilege inherent in advanced capitalism' (Miliband, 1969a, pp. 128–9).

Nevertheless, Miliband contends, there is an important distinction between governing (making day-to-day decisions) and ruling (exercising ultimate control). Members of the dominant economic class do not generally comprise the government. However, the state remains an 'instrument for the domination of society' acting on behalf of ruling-class interests. The socioeconomic constraints on Western governments and state institutions—constraints imposed by the requirements of private accumulation—systematically limit their policy options. The system of private investment, private property, and so on, creates objective exigencies which must be met, if economic growth and stable development are to be sustained. If these arrangements are threatened, economic chaos quickly ensues and the legitimacy of governments is undermined. Hence, social-democratic or labor-oriented governments are constrained: confidence in their ability to manage is easily eroded.

According to Miliband, the commitments of state administrations to private enterprise and market rationality define their class character. Miliband insists, however—defending Marx's position 1—that in order to be politically effective, the state must be able to separate itself routinely from ruling-class factions. Government policy may even be directed against the short-run interests of the capitalist class. He is also quick to point out that under exceptional circumstances the state can achieve a high order of independence from class interests, for example, in national crises and war.

Nicos Poulantzas challenged Miliband's views in a debate which has received much attention (Poulantzas in Blackburn, 1972). In so doing, he sought to clarify what we have called Marx's position 1. He rejects the view that the state is 'an instrument for the domination of society' and what he considers Miliband's subjectivist approach—his attempt to explore the relation among classes, bureaucracy and the state through 'interpersonal relations' (what Miliband refers to as the social background of state officials and links between them and members of powerful institutions). As Poulantzas wrote: 'The direct participation of members of the capitalist class in the state apparatus and in government, even where it exists, is not the important side of the matter' (Blackburn, 1972, p. 245).

Although Poulantzas exaggerates the differences between his position and Miliband's, his starting-point is radically different. He does not ask: who influences important decisions and determines policy? What is the social background of those who occupy key administrative positions? The 'class affiliation' of those in the state apparatus is not, according to Poulantzas, crucial to its 'concrete functioning' (Poulantzas, 1973, pp. 331–40). Individuals are 'bearers' of the system. Accordingly, if the functions of the state and the interests of the dominant class coincide, it is because of structural necessity and not personal preference.

In order to grasp this structural necessity, it is crucial, Poulantzas argues, to understand that the state is the unifying element in capitalism. More specifically, the state must function to ensure (a) the 'political organization' of the dominant classes, which because of competitive pressures and differences of immediate interest are continually broken up into 'class

fractions'; (b) the 'political disorganization' of the working classes which, because of the concentration of production, among other things, can threaten the hegemony of the dominant classes; and (c) the political 'regrouping' by a complex 'ideological process' of classes from the non-dominant modes of production (for instance, peasants) who could act against the state (Poulantzas, 1973, pp. 287–8).

Since the dominant class is vulnerable to fragmentation, its long-run interest requires protection by the state. The state can sustain this function only if it is, in Poulantzas's well-known term, 'relatively autonomous' from the particular interests of diverse fractions. What is more, the state itself, Poulantzas stresses, is not a monolithic bloc; it is an arena of conflict riddled with contradictions (the 'condensation of class forces') (Poulantzas, 1975). The degree of autonomy actual states acquire depends on the relations among classes and class fractions and on the intensity of social struggles.

The state's autonomy is incomplete, Poulantzas stresses, because the bureaucracy does not in itself have political power. Bureaucratic power is 'the exercise of the state's functions', articulating political power actually belonging to classes. Insistent, at least in his early works, that power is 'the capacity to realize class interests', Poulantzas contends that state institutions are 'power centres'; but classes 'hold power'. Relative autonomy 'devolves' on the state 'in the power relations of the class struggle' (Poulantzas, 1973, pp. 335–6).

Thus, the modern state is both the 'centralising instance made necessary by the anarchic competition of civil society' and a force in the reproduction of the social division of labor. Its hierarchical-bureaucratic apparatus along with its electoral institutions simultaneously represent unity (the 'people-nation') and atomize and fragment the body politic (Poulantzas, 1980). The state does not simply record socioeconomic reality, it enters into its very construction by reinforcing its form and codifying its forces.

There is, however, a number of inconsistencies in Poulantzas's formulation of the relationship among classes, the bureaucracy and the state. These are especially acute in his early work, Political Power and Social Classes, where he at one and the same time grants a certain autonomy to the state and argues that all power is class power. Apart from such inconsistencies, he grossly underestimates the state's own capacity to influence critical social and political developments. Viewing the state essentially in terms of its protective role vis-à-vis the capitalist class

Poulantzas loses sight of an entire range of concrete undertakings—from military adventures to welfare expenditures—which cannot be explained in simple class terms. To this extent, Poulantzas's formulation collapses into Marx's position 2 (as reinforced by Lenin) which assumes that state organization directly expresses class power. Among the attendant problems is a peculiar de-emphasis of the capacity of the working classes to influence the course and the organization of state administration (Frankel, 1979). By stressing that the state responds to the functional requirements of capitalism Poulantzas may, as Anthony Giddens has argued, 'overestimate the "relative autonomy" of the state in capitalist liberal democracy'. As Giddens points out, 'if the state participates in the contradictions of capitalism', it is 'not merely a defender of the status quo . . . nor a mere functional vehicle of the "needs" of the capitalist mode of production' (Giddens, 1981).

Further, Poulantzas's emphasis on the state as the 'condensation of class forces' means that his account of the state is drawn without sufficient internal definition or institutional differentiation. How institutions operate and the manner in which the relationship among elites, government officials and parliamentarians evolves are neglected. Poulantzas's disregard for non-structural considerations—the behavior of actors which represents the central focus, for example, of democratic theory—leads him to ignore the concrete social practices through which structural relations are reproduced.[8]

Invigorating the debate in Marxist circles about state, bureaucracy and class Claus Offe has challenged—and attempted to recast—the terms of reference of both Miliband and Poulantzas (see Keane, 1978; Frankel, 1979). For Offe, the state is neither simply a 'capitalist state' as Poulantzas contends (a state determined by class power), nor 'a state in capitalist society' as Miliband argues (a state which preserves political power free from immediate class interests). Starting from a conception of contemporary capitalism which stresses its internal differentiation into four sectors (the competitive and oligopolistic private sectors, the residual labor sector and the state sector) Offe maintains that the most significant feature of the state is the way it is enmeshed in the contradictions of capitalism. Hence, the state is faced with contradictory tasks. On the one hand the state must sustain the process of accumulation and the private appropriation of resources, on the other hand it must preserve belief in itself as the impartial arbiter of class interests, thereby legitimating its power (see Offe, 1972; 1974).

The institutional separation of state and economy means that the state is dependent upon the flow of resources from the organization of profitable production, through taxation and finance from capital markets. Since in the main the resources from the accumulation process are 'beyond its power to *organize*', there is an 'institutional *self-interest* of the state' and an interest of those with state power to safeguard the vitality of the capitalist economy (see Offe and Ronge, 1975). With this argument, Offe differentiates himself from Miliband and Poulantzas. As Offe puts it, the institutional self-interest of the state 'does not result from alliance of a particular government with particular classes also interested in accumulation, nor does it result from any political power of the capitalist class which "puts pressure" on the incumbents of state power to pursue its class interest' (Offe and Ronge, 1975, p. 140). For its own sake, the state is interested in sustaining accumulation.

Political power is determined, then, in a dual way: by formal rules of democratic and representative government which fix the institutional form of access to power and by the material content of the accumulation process which sets the boundaries of successful policies. Given that governments require electoral victory and the financial wherewithal to implement policy, they are forced increasingly to intervene to manage economic crisis. The growing pressure for intervention is contradicted, however, by capitalists' concern for freedom of investment and their obstinate resistance to state efforts to control productive processes (seen, for example, in efforts by business to avoid 'excessive regulation').

The state, therefore, faces contradictory imperatives: it must maintain the accumulation process without either undermining *private* accumulation or the belief in the market as a fair distributor of scarce resources. Intervention into the economy is unavoidable and yet the exercise of political control over the economy risks challenging the traditional basis of the legitimacy of the whole social order—the belief that collective goals can be properly realized only by private individuals acting in competitive isolation and pursuing their sectoral aims with minimal state interference. The state, then, must intervene but conceal its purpose. Thus, Offe defines the capitalist state '(a) by its exclusion from accumulation, (b) by its necessary function for accumulation, (c) by its dependence upon accumulation, and (d) by its function to conceal and deny (a), (b) and (c)' (Offe in Lindberg, 1975a, p. 144).

He argues that if these analytical propositions are

valid, then 'it is hard to imagine that any state in capitalist society could succeed to perform the functions that are part of this definition simultaneously and successfully for any length of time' (Offe in Lindberg, 1975a, p. 144). To investigate this hypothesis, he focuses on the nature of state administration and, in particular, on its capacity for rational administration. The problems of administration are especially severe, Offe suggests, since many of the policies undertaken by contemporary governments do not simply complement market activities, but actually replace them. Accordingly, Offe argues in an interesting parallel to the corporatist view, that the state selectively favors those groups whose acquiescence and support are crucial to the untroubled continuity of the existing order: oligopoly capital and organized labor. The state helps to defray the costs of production for capital (by providing cheap energy for heavy users through the pricing policies of nationalized industries, for example) and provides a range of benefits for organized labor (for instance, by tacitly supporting high wage demands and enhanced wage differentials and relativities). In a recent article Offe contends, furthermore, that the representatives of these 'strategic groups' increasingly step in to resolve threats to political stability through a highly informal, extraparliamentary negotiation process (Offe, 1979, p. 9).

Starting from a critique of Weber's basic assumption that the main reason for the expansion of bureaucratic forms of organization in modern capitalist societies is their technical superiority, Offe attempts to demonstrate that no method of state administration can be 'adequate for solving the specific problem of the capitalist state'. This he characterizes as the 'establish[ment] of a balance between its *required functions*' which result from a certain state of the accumulation process on the one side, and its '*internal structure*' on the other side (Offe in Lindberg, 1975a, p. 140). Offe argues that the 'three "logics" of policy production' which are available to the capitalist state—based in turn on bureaucratic rules, purposive action and consensus formation—necessarily undermine its operation once the burgeoning demands from the economic sphere impel the state decisively into market-replacing activities (Offe in Lindberg, 1975a, p. 136). For Offe, each logic of policy production encounters a particular dynamic of failure: bureaucratic policy production cannot escape its dependence upon fixed hierarchical rules and therefore cannot respond flexibly to externally determined policy objectives; policy production governed by purposive action fails for lack of clearcut, uncontroversial and operational goals transmitted from the environment; the consensus mode of policy production fails because it generates conflict by inviting 'more demands and interests to articulate themselves than can be *satisfied*' by the capitalist state, bound as it is by considerations of accumulation (Offe in Lindberg, 1975a, p. 140). Modern states are hamstrung by a bureaucracy which operates by invariant rules and procedures and by too limited goals or with overly narrow and strict jurisdictional areas of responsibility which limit the flexibility and, in a word, the rationality of administrative responses to externally formulated demands.[9]

Offe's writings on the internal workings of bureaucracy within capitalist states are important: he has offered significant insights about the limitations of rule-bound administration in promoting aims which are beyond its jurisdictional competence. When, for example, national railways consider the elimination of an 'unprofitable' service, by what rules—and from what rational stance—can they evaluate the complex consequences of the decision for the pursuit of leisure activities, investment in local industry, employment, settlement patterns, tourism, and so on? Moreover, Offe's emphasis on the way capitalist states are pushed into providing a range of services which directly benefit the best-organized sectors of the working class, surmounts some of the limitations of Poulantzas's account of the state as functionally interlocked to the needs of capital. As Offe and Ronge argue provocatively, the state 'does not defend the interests of one class, but the *common* interests of all members of a *capitalist class society*' (Offe and Ronge, 1975, p. 139).

But Offe may skew his understanding of state power and administrative capacity in assuming that because of the logic of policy production state administration cannot successfully execute policies with political ramifications. This argument, which recalls Weber's specific analysis of the limitations of bureaucratic initiative and the necessity for parliamentary direction in Germany, underestimates the capacity of state administrators to be effective agents of *political* strategy. In an essay on the politics of French planning, Peter Hall argues that there is an implicit intelligence in a state seemingly divided against itself and torn by competing pressures:

A state faced with multiple tasks and well-defined conflicts of interest among the social classes it governs, or the groups within these, may find it necessary to maintain a degree of deliberate malintegration among its various policy-making arms so that each can mobilize consent among its particular constituencies by pursuing policies which, even if never fully implemented, appear to address the needs of these groups. In many cases the pursuit of incompatible policies renders all of them ineffective, but this strategy prevents any one group from claiming that the state has come down on the side of its opponents. (Hall, 1981a)

Offe's tendency to explain the success and failure of state policy by reference to functional imperatives (accumulation and legitimation) encourages him to ignore the strategic intelligence which government and state agencies often display.

Conclusions: Summary and Propositions

The traditions of state theory we have examined focus on different aspects of state–society relations and defend positions which seem radically at odds. For too long, these differences have been stressed with such vehemence that possibilities for fruitful synthesis have been neglected. We have already argued that what we called Marx's position 1 shares significant ground with Weber's account of bureaucracy, such that its elaboration and reconsideration—as attempted by Offe, for example—signals a powerful approach to questions of class, bureaucracy and the state. In addition, the undeniable importance of examining the exercise of power within the context of interest group intermediation, as emphasized in empirical democratic theory, recommends a significant area of inquiry which has been too frequently ignored by Marxists concerned with general structural arrangements. Indeed, the theorists of corporatism we have discussed have attempted to assimilate an understanding of interest group behavior within an appreciation of the boundaries restricting state–society relations under capitalism. Moreover, if these relations are understood with the subtlety expressed in the best works of contemporary Marxists, a powerful framework is available for the historical and comparative analysis of patterns of state activity in parliamentary capitalist societies.

We have already indicated our reservations about each of the traditions discussed and noted points of incompatibility. In summary, we offer a set of propositions about government and state administra-

tion; and hope that the chapters that follow in this volume will serve as a basis for their clarification.

(1) *State power:* Power is not merely the voluntarist expression of the capacity of an actor to influence the conduct of others, nor is it merely structured power following from institutional bias. Rather, power is the facility of agents to act within institutions and collectivities—to apply the resources of these institutions and collectivities to their own ends, even while institutional arrangements narrow the scope of their activities. Hence, state power expresses at once the intentions and purposes of government and state personnel (they could have acted differently) and the parameters set by the institutionalized context of state–society relations.

(2) *Administrative capacity:* The state's capacity to administer is constrained by dominant collectivities (for example, the willingness of corporations to invest limits the scope of intervention into the process of accumulation and appropriation of capital, while trade unions block attempts to erode hard-won social benefits). The capacity of regimes to govern is limited not only by the power of dominant groups, but by the requirements of parliamentary and electoral accept-ance. The power of regimes and the pattern of state policy are determined in three ways: by formal rules which set the mode of access to governmental power; by the institutional arrangements which determine the articulation and implementation of state policies; and by the capacity of the economy to provide sufficient resources for state policies. As Offe argues, the state is not controlled directly by the dominant class; the state defends democratic capitalist class institutions.

(3) *Policy formulation:* The criteria by which state agencies make decisions are distinct from the logic of market operations and the imperatives of profit maximization. The criteria for failure in the policy realm are not the same as in the economic realm, for example, bankruptcy. The state can make its policy alternatives visible to clients with conflicting interests, thereby creating a possible opportunity for compromise. State managers can consciously formulate objectives and alternatives which respond to different pressures and in accordance with a regime's strategy for electoral/parliamentary success.

(4) *The primacy of the state apparatus:* The state apparatus has sufficient primacy over social classes and collectivities that discrete political outcomes—

constitutional forms, coalitional arrangements, particular exercises of state coercion, and the like—are not foreordained. Political developments cannot be inferred directly from the configuration of class forces (although the latter surely will condition outcomes). As Marx acknowledges, considerable power may accrue to the executive, and as Weber stresses, state managers will be influenced in practice by particular interests, although they are independent from direct control by the capitalist class (or any other sectional interest). No groups are secure from (unfavorable) administrative intrusion.

(5) *Displacement strategies:* The capacity of a regime to maneuver is enhanced by its ability to displace the effects of economic problems onto vulnerable groups, for instance, the elderly, consumers, the sick, non-unionized, non-white, and so on, and onto vulnerable regions, while appeasing those able to mobilize claims most effectively. Thus, crucial fronts of social struggle can be repeatedly fragmented.

(6) *The limits of corporatist arrangements:* A displacement strategy can be successful only to the degree that crucial policies sustain the electoral/parliamentary viability of a regime and, at the same time, the arrangements for economic and social management. Hence, corporatist arrangements are simultaneously attractive to regimes and problematic. On the one hand tripartite arrangements may secure the support of the dominant trade union and business associations and their direct constituencies; on the other hand the favoritism toward these dominant groups expressed by corporatist arrangements—and the content of the tripartite bargains reached—may erode the electoral/parliamentary support of the more vulnerable groups, which is required for regime survival. Moreover, corporatist arrangements may also erode the mass acceptability of institutions which have traditionally channeled conflict, for example, party systems and conventions of collective bargaining. Thus, new arrangements may backfire, encouraging the formation of opposition movements to the *status quo* based on those excluded from key decision-making processes, for instance, shopfloor workers and shop stewards, those concerned with ecological issues and the women's movement activists (see Offe, 1979).

(7) *The limits of state intervention:* To the extent that all states in democratic capitalist class society defend their core institutions (notably property and a variety of democratic norms), state policies are limited to 'crisis management' (for example, incomes policies to fight inflation). While these policies might mitigate the worst effects of crises, thus preserving the social order, they cannot by design threaten these core institutions. Nevertheless, policies may erode the basic principles of capitalist market relations (for example, planning erodes the traditional private capitalist prerogatives in determining investment).

(8) *The ambiguity of the state:* The state may introduce a variety of policies which increase the social wage, extend public goods, enhance democratic rights and alter the balance between public and private sectors. As a result, social struggle is 'inscribed' into the organization, administration and policies of the state. The multiplicity of economic and electoral constraints on state action—and regime survival—means that the state is not an unambiguous agent of capitalist reproduction.

Notes: Chapter 1

We should like to thank Anthony Giddens and Albert Weale for extensive comments on earlier drafts of this chapter. Some of the issues raised in this introduction are pursued by David Held in 'Central perspectives on the modern state', in David Held *et al.* (eds.) *States and Societies* (Oxford: Martin Robertson, 1983).

1 Our discussion of competing claims within state theory and, indeed, the chapters which follow represent only an incomplete effort to illuminate the patterns of state–society relations in contemporary Western Europe. For example, theoretical debates—and empirical investigations—concerning the emergence of the international system of nation–states and the continuous influence of international political and political-economic forces upon the practices of state intervention will not be discussed here at length.
2 In the process of attempting to sustain this claim, Marx offered not only one of his most important statements on the state, but also his most elaborate analysis of the internal workings of state apparatuses and bureaucracy.
3 Marx did offer a series of remarks on different state forms, particularly those of the USA, France and Prussia, throughout his working life. These are always interesting, but they do not amount to a systematic statement.
4 Some important and highly informative exceptions to this are Maguire (1978), Perez-Diaz (1978) and Hunt (1974).
5 Lenin was far from consistent on these matters. For example, after the revolution he continued to emphasize the importance of technical experts, 'scientifically trained specialists of every kind', for the new state administration. Accounting and control were to be an essential part of the socialist order. A useful introduction to these issues can be found in Brown *et al.* (1979, pp. 72–87).
6 There is always danger in presenting as telescoped a view of

pluralism 'in general', as we have done here. We are particularly concerned not to imply an inappropriate equivalence between Dahl's and Truman's positions. For example, Dahl preserves a crucial distinction within his argument about polyarchies, which we do not wish to blur. He argues (a) that if competitive electoral systems are characterized by a multiplicity of minorities who feel intensely enough about diverse issues, then rights will be protected and severe inequalities avoided with a certainty beyond that guaranteed by mere legal or constitutional arrangements; and (b) that there is empirical evidence to suggest that at least certain polities—for example, the US in light of findings about New Haven—satisfies these conditions. These two claims are logically distinct in Dahl, which separates him in an important way from Truman. Moreover, Dahl's insistence that concepts in political theory be operational underlies his preference for a behaviorist/dispositional, as against a more structural, understanding of power. Indeed, it should be noted that Dahl's views have changed considerably over the years, and that he is not quite the champion of American democracy he was often assumed to be. For a useful overview of Dahl's work, see Von der Muhll (1977) and for an example of Dahl's more critical stance, see Dahl (1978). Of course, both Truman and Dahl tend to shift the terrain of the discussion from 'what is the state?' to 'what is democracy?'—a change in emphasis which we have accommodated in our discussion of empirical democratic theory. We are indebted for many of these clarifications to discussions with Albert Weale.

7   Corporatist theory includes various schools of interpretation and normative perspectives. For Winkler, corporatism is 'an economic system in which the state directs and controls predominantly privately-owned business' (1976, p. 3), while for Schmitter, it is a 'system of interest representation' or 'interest intermediation' (1974, p. 85; 1977, p. 9). For Panitch (1977), corporatism is an ideology and a structural tendency in advanced capitalism, viewed within a Marxist perspective. In this chapter we do not raise the normative issues explicitly, and emphasize Schmitter's interpretation of corporatism, since it is the most influential stance within American university circles.

8   In his last work Poulantzas took several steps to resolve these difficulties: State, Power, Socialism (1980) is his most successful work. However, we do not think that it fully surmounts the problems we have noted.

9   In a recent paper Offe states that 'only if economic policy makers loosen their institutional ties to their parties and parliaments can they hope to remain effective in responding to rapidly changing economic imperatives' (1979, p. 18). The suggestion seems to be that the corporatist mode of organization may present the state with a fourth form of policy formation.

2
Patterns of Economic Policy: An Organizational Approach

PETER A. HALL

The interruption in economic growth of the 1970s brought to the advanced industrial nations of Western Europe a renewed concern for the relationship between the economy and the polity.[1] This relationship had been obscured in the preceding two decades of almost unparalleled prosperity by two sorts of factors. In the first instance, impressive rates of economic growth acted as a solvent for the political tensions associated with underlying conflicts of interest over the distribution of the national product (cf. Lipset, 1964; Dahrendorf, 1964). Thus, it was often difficult to see the relationship between such conflicts and economic policies of the period. Secondly, economic growth was presented in many influential formulations as the result of a demographic or technological dynamic virtually independent of political machination (Carré *et al.*, 1972; Denison, 1969). Accordingly, the role of the state seemed to be negligible in the face of a self-equilibrating economic system.

The economic crisis of the recent period, however, has called both of these notions into question and raised again a twin set of issues which for many years have been obscured: namely, what are the political determinants of economic policy; and what is the role of the state in the capitalist economy? These are the questions which this chapter addresses. They are large issues which deserve much longer treatment than is possible here, and indeed there has been a resurgence of work on this subject. One of the objects of the chapter is to provide a preliminary review of this work, to place its disparate elements in some relation to one another and to indicate the contribution each has made to the resolution of these issues. But its purpose is also to go slightly beyond the existing literature to develop the outlines of a new approach, which argues that the distribution of power among social groups implicit in the specific organization of capital, labor and the state, has a determining influence on the economic policies adopted in the advanced industrial nations. Since this approach builds on existing theories, it may be useful

to begin with a review of the current literature before proceeding to brief case studies of Germany, France and Britain which are presented as a stimulus to further research. We find that the literature falls into two broad groups each of which encompasses several different approaches to a common set of problems.

Theories of the State

The first group consists of theories of the state often, although not exclusively, associated with neo-Marxist analyses. This body of literature represents the most ambitious attempt to describe the role of the state in the capitalist economy and has undergone an extensive development in recent years. In general, these theories are united by their concentration on a common aim, namely, the 'attempt to establish theoretical guarantees that the state in a capitalist society necessarily functions on behalf of capital' (Jessop, 1977, p. 352). This is an important issue, not least because it has been contested by those on the right who argue that the activities of the state in recent years constitute not an advantage, but a threat to the interests of capital (Bacon and Eltis, 1976).

Since these theories have been reviewed in detail elsewhere (Gold *et al.*, 1975; Jessop, 1977; see also Chapter 1 of this volume), only their main lines of argument will be noted here. Three such lines of argument have emerged each of which represents a step forward in the attempt to move beyond the classic observations that the state is 'a committee for managing the common affairs of the bourgeoisie' (Marx and Engels), the 'ideal collective capitalist' (Engels), or a 'machine for the oppression of one class by another' (Lenin). The first line of argumentation, often labeled 'instrumentalist theories' and associated with Domhoff (1967) and Miliband (1969*b*), maintains that the state can be relied upon to pursue policies which further the interests of capital, because the organization of politics in pluralist systems places capitalists in privileged positions both inside and outside the state from which they can exercise a decisive influence over policy-making. These theories emphasize such factors as the social interaction of political and business elites, the role of financial advantages in the electoral arena and the commercial bias of the media.

A second line of argument, which might be labeled 'functionalist', suggests that the influence which capitalists are able to exercise over policy via their role in the political arena is 'not the important side of the matter' (Poulantzas, 1969, p. 245). Rather, the functions which the state is compelled to perform by virtue of the exigencies of the capitalist system itself dictate that the policies of the state will conform to the interests of capital. Whereas instrumentalist theories emphasize the constraints imposed by the operation of a pluralist political system, functionalist theories emphasize the constraints entailed by the operation of a capitalist economic system, and in particular those associated with the requisites of accumulation or the reproduction of capital. Poulantzas (1972; 1975; 1978b) is the most distinguished defender of this position, but it has been adopted with varying emphasis by Altvater (1973) and Yaffe (1973), and in versions which stress the political requirements of capitalism by O'Connor (1973), Offe (1972; 1974) and Hirsch (1978).

Finally, a group of theorists who might be termed 'synthetics' explains the behavior of the managers of the state in terms of a direct link between pluralist politics and capitalist economics. They argue that under a capitalist mode of production the prosperity of all classes depends ultimately upon the profitability of the private sector and hence on the well-being and cooperation of individual capitalists. In order to remain in power under a liberal democratic electoral system, the state managers must secure such prosperity and cater to the interests of the private owners of the means of production. Transformation to a socialist system of production is ruled out by the politically intolerable period of economic hardship which the resistance of capital to any such attempt would impose. In other words, political survival within a capitalist democracy dictates the pursuit of prosperity via profit. Block (1977), Lindblom (1977) and Przeworski and Wallerstein (1980) are the most prominent exponents of this position.

There are some unresolved difficulties in these theories. In particular, neither instrumentalists nor functionalists have been able to present a convincing account of how the highly individualized interests of the actors who populate the state apparatus are aggregated in order to ensure that they act in the interests of a particular class. Instrumentalists tend to imply, rather implausibly, that social background confers a highly integrated class consciousness or to assume that even left-wing politicians will be responsive to the personalized inducements of the representatives of capital. Functionalists, on the other hand, tend to neglect the question of how individual interests are integrated into class interests and to imply that occupancy of positions in the state apparatus itself confers an understanding of, and concern for, the requisites of the capitalist economic system. Although the reproduction of a social or economic system is undoubtedly contingent on the performance of certain functions by the individuals within it, even functionalist theories must contain a plausible explanation for why individuals act in such a way as to perform those functions. And any such explanation must ultimately be couched in terms of the conscious-ness of individual subjects, even if in totality their actions constitute an objective function. It is on these grounds that synthetic theories may be seen as an advance on their predecessors. These theories are able to explain the performance of functions central to the reproduction of a class-based economic system in terms of the concrete interests of the managers of the state in retaining power. Accordingly this line of analysis is very persuasive.

But the very persuasiveness of these theories poses a problem. They suggest that the state in the capitalist societies of Western Europe can be expected to act so as to reproduce the economic system and to serve the interests of capital. But when we compare the experience of several European nations, such as Britain, France and Germany in the postwar period, we find there has been wide variation in the range of policies adopted by these states and in the efficacy of these policies for capitalist reproduction. The basic theories of the state are unable to explain this variation. Indeed, to the extent that some of the policies adopted in this period were counterproductive, the funda-mental thesis of these authors is called somewhat into question. In general, theories of the state have provided a powerful set of explanations for why the state tends to function on behalf of capital; but when confronted with the need to account for systematic variation among the policies of different nations, these theories explain too much.

Studies of Economic Policy

The second body of literature to which we might turn for an explanation of this variation in policy is the more detailed comparative studies of macroeconomic and industrial policy which have appeared in recent years. Here, too, there are three kinds of study, each of which takes a slightly different approach to the explanation of variation in the economic policies of the European nations. All have made a substantial contribution to our understanding of the European economies.

The first group consists of comparative studies by *economists* of the economic policies pursued by several European governments. Representative works in this group range from the pioneering studies of Kirschen (1964; 1975) and Hansen (1969) to the more recent investigations of Krause and Salant (1977), Lieberman (1977) and the OECD (1977). These works provide valuable accounts of the economic policies implemented in postwar Europe and, in some cases, useful insights into the differences between the policy-making procedures of various nations. But the capacity of these accounts to provide a systematic comparison of the political factors underlying the differences in economic policy across nations is limited by their tendency to treat policy primarily as a response to prevailing economic circumstances, and policy-making as a process that is determined by the resolution of a set of technical issues. There is very little room for the influence of political variables in such analyses (cf. Kirschen, 1964, p. 154; Keohane, 1978); yet unless economic policy-making is peculiarly immune to the sort of influences found in other policy areas (Heidenheimer *et al.*, 1975), political variables can be expected to exert a decisive impact on national patterns of policy.

As a result, the work of a second group of analysts represents a significant advance in this sphere. These are the *political economists*, such as Cowart (1978), Hibbs (1978; 1980), Tufte (1979) and Frey (1980), who have developed formal models to measure the impact of different political parties on macroeconomic policies and outcomes and to assess the impact of electoral competition on such policies. In most cases, their results suggest that we can expect the economic policies of a state to be affected by the approach of an election, by cross-national differences in the preferences of the electorate and by the entry into office of a different political party. These are important findings. But, leaving aside problems associated with model specification and parameter measurement here, the ability of these studies to explain economic policy-making is limited by their concentration on the electoral arena and by the assumption into which they are forced by this kind of

modeling that the state is a unitary and relatively rational actor. Such models inevitably neglect the non-electoral modes of interest intermediation which can be of substantial importance to policy-making (Schmitter and Lehmbruch, 1979), and are susceptible to the sorts of criticisms which Allison (1971) leveled at rational actor models in the foreign policy sphere.

Some of the problems of both these lines of analysis have been resolved by a third body of literature which might be described as *institutionalist*. An influential series of cross-national analyses organized by Shonfield (1969), MacLennan *et al.* (1968), Vernon (1974), Hayward and Watson (1975) and Warnecke and Suleiman (1975) has drawn attention to the institutional differences in economic policy-making among the European states in such a way as to reveal broadly different national patterns of decision-making. By moving beyond the description of discrete policies to identify distinctive national patterns of policy, these analysts have made an important contribution to our understanding of the variations in European economic policy. But, ultimately, their work has been limited by the difficulty they have had in locating the *sources* of these national differences. In several instances (cf. especially Hayward and Watson, 1975, ch. 1; Shonfield, 1969) these authors have resorted to a form of explanation which attributes differences in policy and policy-making to the culturally specific attitudes or aptitudes of national elites. But the national specificity of these attitudes remains nebulous and unproven and, to the extent that they exist, their origins remain unexplained (Hall, 1981*b*).

In general, if theories of the state seem to explain too much, these studies of economic policy ultimately seem to explain too little. We are confronted, on the one hand, with a set of theories which effectively link the operation of the state to broad structural determinants within the polity and the economy but at a level of generality which is unable to explain particular national patterns of policy. And on the other hand, we face explanations for particular policies which do not fully capture the structural factors which may lie behind cultural accounts of the national patterns of policy. Is there any way of bridging this gap?

An Alternative Approach

What is needed is an alternative view of the political determinants of economic policy that links those policies to the structural constraints implicit in the socioeconomic organization of each nation. Equipped with such a view, we could explain the broad differences in the patterns of economic policy among the European nations by reference to the distribution of power among the key social groups affected by such policy, since the socioeconomic organization of a nation both conditions and reflects this distribution of power. This section develops the broad lines along which such a view could be constructed, and subsequent sections assess its effectiveness for explaining the patterns of policy in Britain, France and Germany.

The construction of such a view begins with the observation that national economic policy is influenced most significantly, first, by what a government is *pressed* to do, and secondly, by what it *can* do in the economic sphere. To a large extent, in a liberal democracy the former defines what is desirable and the latter defines what is possible. This dualism reflects the fact that implementation is the obverse of the formulation of policy. Governments are frequently prevented from adopting a particular policy by the absence of any means to implement it.

To this observation should be added the hypothesis that both the pressures for a particular policy and the possibility of implementing it are most fundamentally affected by the organization of three basic facets of the socioeconomic structure of a nation, namely, the organization of labor, the organization of capital and the organization of the state itself. The first refers primarily to the organization of the working class in the labor market. The second refers principally to the organizational relationship between financial and industrial capital. And the third refers to the internal organization of the state apparatus as well as to the organization of the electoral arena.

Why is organization so important? Four reasons can be adduced. First, policy is generally formed in response to pressures from various groups according to the interests those groups have in the outcomes of policy-making. But the facility with which particular interests can be articulated and the force with which they can be pressed on policy-makers is dependent upon the organization of the structures within which they are expressed. Secondly, and of equal importance, the very interests of the actors themselves are critically affected by the organization of the economic and political structures within which they operate. Interests of the sort relevant to economic policy do not exist independently of the organization of particular markets. Thirdly, economic policy-making is invariably a collective endeavor. That is to say,

economic policy is the output not of individuals, but of organizations which aggregate the endeavor of many individuals in particular ways. Accordingly, the structure of these organizations has an immense impact on the nature of the policies produced. It is an 'organizational intelligence' rather than the intelligence of individuals which ultimately determines such factors as the capacity of the state for strategic thinking or the quality of policy. Finally, in order to implement economic policy, the state relies on access to organizational resources in both the public and private sectors. Variations in organization among these sectors put significant constraints on the ability of the state to secure acquiescence for its policies from both the electorate and producers groups.

It should be apparent that this approach draws some inspiration from a recent line of analysis in the literature which explains differing economic policies in terms of the broad coalitions of economic interests that converge around specific policy alternatives. Maier (1978) has examined the coalitions which lie behind inflation policy in these terms. Gourevitch uses a similar approach to explain tariff policy in the late nineteenth century (1977) and economic responses to the Great Depression (1980). And Esping-Andersen and Friedland (1981) suggest that changing economic coalitions underlie the contemporary economic crisis in Western Europe. The antecedents for this work are analyses which have stressed the impact of the evolving power of the working class on public policy (cf. Martin, 1975; Gough, 1975).

The approach adopted here accepts the contention of this body of literature that economic policies are often a response to the demands of groups with particular economic interests. In contrast to some of these analyses, however, it regards the process whereby those interests are defined, articulated and aggregated as especially problematic. Such an approach posits that the organization of both economic and political arenas plays a critical role in determining which interests will be most effectively articulated and what sort of response they will elicit from the state.[2] Organization does more than transmit the preferences of particular groups; it combines and ultimately alters them. Accordingly, economic policy may not faithfully reflect a struggle among competing economic interests precisely because organization refracts that struggle.[3] Thus, for instance, the notion that the state embodies the 'institutionalization of class conflict' or a 'condensation of class forces' (Poulantzas, 1978a) must be modified to take into account the fact that the state acts as a distorting mirror to reproduce a highly imperfect reflection of these conflicts and one which imprints its own image on their resolution. In the long run, of course, organization itself is shaped by the conflicts which underlie it. But this is rarely a rapid process, and in the meantime the institutions which organize intergroup relations act as a kind of social memory, imprinting the conflicts of the present with the institutional legacy of the past.

Let us turn from the general elaboration of this approach to the concrete experiences of Germany, France and Britain in the postwar period. The object is to see if an account of the organization of capital, labor and the state in each nation can contribute to the explanation of some of the most significant differences in the economic policies they have adopted over this period.

The Federal Republic of Germany

The most distinctive features of the German state with relevance for economic policy are the strict division of control over fiscal and monetary policy between the Ministry of Economics and the Deutsche Bundesbank, the central bank, and the entrenched power of the latter within the German system. The independence of the Bundesbank is guaranteed by the German constitution which has given it a mandate to protect the value of the currency and established it as 'a special part of the executive, entrusted as an autonomous body with responsibility for monetary and credit policy' (Wadbrook, 1972, p. 89). Since the majority of its Board of Directors is chosen by the central banks of the German Länder, and those chosen by the Federal Government are given minimum terms of eight years, the Bank is relatively insulated from pressure from the Ministry of Economics. Most authorities agree that the officers of the Bank are 'on a par with the highest federal authorities and not subject to instructions from the federal government' (Wadbrook, 1972, p. 89). As a consequence, while the operation of fiscal policy remains in the hands of the government, the instruments of monetary policy, which are also potent weapons for influencing the level of economic activity, are in hands that are subject to an entirely different set of influences than those normally associated with the parliamentary arena.

The organization of capital in Germany is also distinctive in important respects. Among our cases, the most salient feature of that organization is the relationship between the institutions of financial and industrial capital. In Germany this relationship is characterized by the concentration of financial capital itself and by arrangements which permit financial capital, represented primarily by the major banks, to exercise a high degree of detailed control over the operations of industrial capital at the economic level. Although there are over 3,000 quasi-banking institutions in Germany, the financial world is dominated by three large 'commercial' banks— Deutsche Bank, Dresdner Bank and Commerzbank—which work closely together to exert vast leverage over the rest of the banking sector and much of industry (Medley, 1981; Shonfield, 1969, ch. 11). A series of legal provisions and customary business practices combines to make this possible. German banks, unlike their American counterparts, are allowed to hold equity in other firms. Moreover, almost 85 percent of all shareholders in Germany generally deposit their shares with a bank which, in the absence of specific instructions to the contrary, enjoys the privilege of voting those shares as it likes. In addition, these banks are entitled to lend their voting rights to other banks and are accustomed to doing so. Since, under German law, the votes of 25 percent of the shares in a company are sufficient to block any measure coming before the shareholders, the banks are generally in a position to influence the major decisions of a firm. At the most recent count, the banks voted 70 percent of the shares of the 425 largest firms in Germany, accounting for three-quarters of the value of all the shares on the stock exchange. And 318 of the top 400 companies had on average two bankers on their supervisory boards (Medley, 1981, p. 48; and see **Document 1**).

Two consequences of particular importance follow from this. First, by virtue of these arrangements, the German banks have a direct and extensive interest in the long-term performance of the major firms within Germany industry. Secondly, the banks, and in particular the big three, are in a position to exercise immense influence over the activities of these firms. In keeping with this, the banks have developed considerable technical expertise in industrial matters and the capacity to provide detailed direction to the firms whose shares they hold. Similarly, the banks have become accustomed to collaborating with each other on their plans for particular industries (Shonfield, 1969, ch. 11). This stands in stark contrast to the situation in Britain or America where commercial banks are prohibited from taking shares in companies, where competition is more common than collusion in the banking sector, and where the debtor–creditor relationship is a more distant one, based less on the assessment of a firm's strategy and more on a mechanical consideration of the creditworthiness of its balance sheet.

The organization of labor in Germany is distinguished by the concentration of the labor-market organizations and the highly regularized nature of their collective bargaining arrangements. Following World War II, the German working class was reorganized into sixteen large unions, each covering entire industries with up to several million members in them. Almost all became affiliated to a central federation, the *Deutschegewerkschaftsbund* (DGB). In the view of most authorities these two organizational innovations —unions organized along industrial lines and a unitary union movement—set the basic framework for the coordination present in the industrial relations of postwar Germany (Markovits and Allen, 1980). On this framework has also been built a system for collective bargaining which is highly regulated by statute and quasi-judicial procedures. Its principal features include the use of legally sanctioned contracts running as long as two or three years during which strikes are prohibited, regulations which render wildcat strikes illegal and the employment of a Federal Labor Court as well as arbitration procedures to adjudicate many disputes (cf. Müller-Jentsch and Sperling, 1978). In most of these respects the organization of the German labor market differs substantially from that in Britain or France.

Is there any relationship between these features of the organization of political and economic activity in Germany and the distinctive patterns of German economic policy? To answer this, we must first identify the patterns in German policy which most broadly distinguish it from the policies of Britain and France and then locate the roots of the differences. For this purpose, it will be useful to break down economic policy into its three major components, macroeconomic policy, industrial policy and incomes policy, and examine each in turn.

To begin with the macroeconomic sphere, German policy for most of the postwar period has been distinguished by two unusual characteristics. The first has been the persistent maintenance of the Deutschmark at an undervalued level on the foreign exchange markets. The second has been the presence of bias in favor of deflationary macroeconomic policies consistent enough to constitute a repudiation of Keynesian anti-cyclical policy and severe enough to culminate in the artificial creation of the peculiarly German recession of 1966–7 (Kreile, 1978; Wadbrook, 1972).

The longstanding undervaluation of the mark was not dictated by economic circumstances. On the contrary, it was a controversial policy with distinctive costs and benefits for different segments of society and real risks for the German economy as a whole. In distributive terms the effect of the policy was to provide an immense subsidy to export sectors and a measure of protection to domestic capital financed by imposing higher costs on German workers and consumers in the form of higher-priced imports. Over a period of time the policy dramatically strengthened the export sector of the economy. As a percentage of GDP, exports rose from 8 percent in 1955 to 25 percent in 1980. By 1975 exports accounted for 47 percent of sales in investment goods, 36 percent in chemicals, 56 percent in machine tools and 52 percent in automobiles (Kreile, 1978, p. 201). This brought clear employment benefits, but it caused a series of balance of payments problems and rendered the economy especially vulnerable to imported inflation (Wadbrook, 1972, p. 251). Since the German populace is generally supposed to be hypersensitive to the risk of inflation (Krause and Salant, 1977, p. 591), the adoption of such a policy especially requires explanation.

As early as 1955 it became apparent to many observers that the mark was undervalued, and several prominent economic institutes, mindful of the inflationary consequences, began to urge that the mark be repegged (Kaufmann, 1969). In 1966 even Ludwig Erhardt, the Minister of Economics known as the 'father of the social market economy' and a man of considerable influence, began to urge revaluation. Throughout the late 1950s most of the senior economic officials in the unions and both major parties, the CDU and the SPD, also began to advocate *de facto* or *de jure* revaluation (Kaufmann, 1969, pp. 199–200). But nothing was done until 1961, and then a halfhearted revaluation of 5 percent continued to keep the mark below its natural parity. Two forces converged to ensure that this would be the case. The first was the power of the Bundesbank which, while unable to initiate a revaluation, could effectively veto one. The second was the singular relationship between financial and industrial capital in Germany, which meant that they could combine to oppose the move.

Since undervaluation shields the profit levels of both export and domestic sectors, industry tends to support it in most countries. But whereas financial capital in Britain supported an overvalued exchange rate, the

German banking community joined with industry against revaluation. In part this may be attributed to the natural aversion of central banks to exchange rate movements, but it is also apparent that the German banking community had an equity interest in the industrial sector and thus an immediate concern for its performance, which was more intense than that of the British banks. In Germany the two segments of capital interpreted their interests as congruent, and together they were a potent political force. Accordingly, the president of the German Federation of Industry (the BDI) announced that 'an open or concealed revaluation of the mark could result in a catastrophe for the entire economy (Kaufmann, 1969, p. 205) and the president of the Bundesbank, acting on behalf of the banking community, opposed revaluation, declaring that 'exchange rate parity is sacrosanct' (Kaufmann, 1969, p. 191). The president of the BDI and the influential leader of the Deutsche Bank both put pressure on the Chancellor, Konrad Adenauer, who vetoed the plans of his Minister of the Economy for revaluation (Kreile, 1978, p. 214).

Throughout the 1950s and 1960s this combination of Bundesbank influence and pressure from a coalition of industrial and financial capital effectively maintained the mark at an undervalued level. The revaluation to which Adenauer consented in 1961, in the face of overwhelming inflationary pressures, was barely half that which had been expected, and revaluation was secured again in December 1969 only after it had been made a central issue between the two major political parties in the preceding election. Only by means of an election were the interests of consumers and workers able to prevail over those of capital and the central bank. This situation prevailed for twenty-five years during which the pattern for postwar German economic policy was largely set. And it changed in 1973, with the floating of the mark, primarily because the Bundesbank itself switched sides, in the face of new economic circumstances, which meant that without a floating exchange rate it lost virtually all its power to control monetary policy (cf. Kreile, 1978, p. 216).

The second noteworthy feature of German macro-economic policy was that until 1967 it remained relatively contractionary. On the fiscal side the federal government tended to run a budgetary surplus, and a comparative study of the 1955–65 period chides the German authorities for failing to use fiscal policy as a countercyclical device (Hansen, 1969, pp. 233, 254). To a certain extent this can be explained by the anti-Keynesian doctrines of Germany's economic leaders, who believed that a 'social market economy'

would stabilize itself (Zinn, 1978). But the Bundesbank played an important role here as well. For most of this period it countered any laxity on the fiscal side with tight monetary policies. Its officials tended to regard recession as 'a necessary purge which restored labor discipline as well as confidence in the currency' (Kreile, 1978, p. 209), and their ability to counteract expansionary fiscal policies with monetary action may well have acted as an implicit constraint on the central government's behavior.

This *pas de deux* became explicit in 1965–6 when the Bundesbank played a central role in creating the first real recession Germany had experienced since the war. Angered by increases in public expenditure which preceded the 1965 election, and concerned that the accompanying expansion would lead to inflationary wage increases, Bank officials introduced a restrictive monetary policy in August 1964 and strengthened it during the following eighteen months. In the words of the president of the Bundesbank:

As late as May 1966 the Bundesbank felt obliged to raise the discount rate from 4 to 5 percent although private capital spending was already stagnating. It did so because government expenditure was still too high at that time . . . The bodies responsible for the public budgets did not see reason until the capital market, and later also the money market, failed them. (Klöten *et al.*, 1978, p. 31)

As a result GDP fell by 15 percent and unemployment rose from 140,000 to 600,000 in the space of a year (Lieberman, 1977, p. 207). Alone among the European nations, Germany experienced a recession at this time. Although German fiscal policy took on an anti-cyclical aspect with the enactment of the Stability and Growth Act of 1967, the Bundesbank continued to act as a restraint on expansionary policy in the following years, most notably in 1973–4 when it adopted a restrictive monetary stance in the wake of the oil price increases of that year (see **Document 1**).

In the sphere of industrial policy the German experience has been distinguished by relatively limited forms of state intervention, leaving the details of industrial reorganization up to the financial sector, and in particular to the three large banks. Thus, for instance, regional development aid in Germany is distributed via a system in which the banks 'play an active part in helping to choose the recipient' (Shonfield, 1969, p. 263). Applications for aid must first be approved by one of the banks. If granted by the

Ministry of Economics, aid is then administered in the form of a subsidized loan by the bank, which pockets a portion of the subsidy as a fee for service. Similarly, a number of schemes for sectoral rationalization, such as those for the steel industry in 1962–3 and again in 1971–4, were orchestrated almost entirely by the three big banks. In each case the government facilitated the reorganization when requested, but left the banks to play the directing role (Shonfield, 1969, p. 255; Medley, 1981, p. 53). Similar procedures were followed for the shipbuilding industry in the early 1970s, when the government provided a set of basic subsidies to German yards but left the nature of the reorganization itself up to the shipyards and their bankers (Medley, 1981, pp. 58 ff.; Peacock *et al.*, 1980, ch. 6). This contrasts strongly with the techniques used by both French and British governments for rationalization of the same sectors.

It should be clear that this overall approach has been possible only by virtue of the unusual relationship between finance and industrial capital in Germany. As a result of the organization of capital, the banks have had the interest, expertise and influence to make such an approach work. In Shonfield's words (1969, p. 261): 'The big banks have always seen it as their business to take an overall view of the long-term trend in any industry in which they were concerned, and then to press individual firms to conform to certain broad lines of development.' The banks were especially effective at this since they had the ability to plan for an entire sector and to impose cuts where necessary, a capacity which individual firms or even trade associations lacked, and since they were free from many of the political pressures to safeguard regional interests and employment that the government would have faced if it were seen as the instigator (see **Document 2**).

Finally, in the sphere of incomes policy, German policy-making is characterized by a pattern that might be described as one of 'tacit tripartism'. The distinguishing characteristics of this pattern are that on the one hand the unions generally exercise a substantial degree of restraint in wage negotiations, and on the other hand that they usually do so without the need for any explicitly or centrally negotiated bargain with the state to tie acquiescence to the delivery of other goods to them in return. Once again this pattern stands in contrast to both the French and British cases. Two sorts of explanations are often adduced for this. One stresses the unusual fear of inflation which was Weimar's legacy to the Bundesrepublik, and the other emphasizes the establishment of a procedure for 'concerted action' (*Konzertierte Aktion*) in the years following 1967. But neither of these are entirely convincing: the former because workers in many countries have reason to fear inflation, and the latter because the pattern of 'tacit tripartism' characterized German wage agreements long before the procedures for concerted action were established. Indeed, many knowledgeable observers, including the present Chancellor, have suggested that concerted action is a façade for something with deeper roots (Vogel, 1973, p. 186).

We should look for those roots in the organization of German labor, whose structure makes it rational on an individual level for German workers to accept wage restraint, while the equivalent organizational forms in Britain and France do not. To establish this, a brief analysis of the factors involved in consensual wage regulation is necessary.[4] In general, wage restraint can be seen as a public good—just as inflation is a public bad. It is a 'good' to the extent that, if achieved, it reduces subsequent price inflation and so raises real income, but it is 'public' in the sense that the benefits of restraint do not accrue only to those who exercise it, but to everybody (Olsen, 1971). However, wage restraint is an especially vicious public good because it must be exercised by almost everybody for *any* benefits to accrue; and if it is not, then those who exercise it not only fail to receive any benefit, but also suffer disproportionately greater losses of real income in the subsequent inflation.

In the face of this the most effective way to secure wage restraint is to turn it from a vicious public good into at least a semi-private good—that is, a good of the sort that those who pay for it can be assured of receiving its benefits. This is effectively what incomes policies do. By enforcing a measure of restraint on everyone, they provide assurance that a corresponding reduction of inflation will follow from an act of restraint. Depending on its form, the policy may also guarantee that others will not make disproportionate gains at the expense of those who exercise restraint. And it may offer certain key actors, such as union leaders, an additional set of goods in exchange for their acquiescence in restraint. These may range from organizational goods, which enhance the power of union organizations, to other sorts of public goods, such as fiscal or social policies of the sort that union leaders value (Pizzorno, 1978). These supplementary elements may be a significant component of particular bargains; but survey data indicate that the assurance that restraint will be universal is one of the most important factors in mobilizing support for restraint among rank-and-file workers.

In the terms of this analysis the organization of German labor is particularly conducive to the achievement of wage restraint in several respects. The centralized character of the German unions and the legal procedures available to enforce a particular wage bargain increase the likelihood that, once restraint is agreed upon, it will be widespread and thus have a payoff for rank-and-file actors. From their point of view, the risks associated with restraint are consequently lower, and the returns likely to be higher, than they would be under a system where the reduction of inflation was conditional on the acquiescence of many more unions competing within a less regularized set of bargaining procedures. Accordingly, restraint is proportionately more attractive to the rank-and-file. In addition, since the leadership of the German unions is relatively concentrated, to arrive at a norm agreement must be secured from a relatively small number of people and their subsequent compliance is relatively easily monitored. Similarly, the availability of alternative leaders is restricted, and any challenge to an agreement must go through the difficult process of finding alternative leadership before it can be expressed in an organized way. As the events of the 1969–71 period illustrate, this does not eliminate challenges, but it inhibits them (Müller-Jentsch and Sperling, 1978).

In such a context, once a reasonable wage norm has been identified, a series of organizational factors facilitates translation into policy with little need for an elaborate and intensely negotiated bargain at the center. Attention focuses on the identification of the norm rather than on political manipulation to secure consent for it. This has, in fact, been the German pattern. Here it is termed 'tacit tripartism', but it has also appropriately been called an 'incomes policy from below' (Kindleberger, 1965, p. 248). In the early 1960s, when inflation first became a problem, the Bundesbank took the lead in suggesting a norm; but when its conservative biases became suspect, a Council of Economic Experts was established in part to perform this function (cf. Roberts, 1979). It continues to do so. The operation of policy in this sphere has not been entirely unproblematic for the Germans, and from time to time other instruments, including the occasional induced recession and the unions' relationship with the SPD, have been used to bolster support for wage restraint. But overall, the distinctiveness of the German pattern of incomes policy, especially in contrast to the experiences of the British and the French, seems most attributable to factors associated with the organization of labor.

France

Turning to France and initially to the organization of capital there we find that relations between industrial and financial capital are such as to give the banking institutions associated with financial capital a detailed knowledge of the affairs of many firms in the industrial sector and considerable influence over their strategies. However, the organizational factors responsible for this state of affairs are slightly different than in Germany. Wheras real and proxy shareholding by the banks is of most importance in Germany the linchpin of relations between industry and the banks in France is the heavy dependence of industrial firms on long-term debt to meet their needs for finance. French industry has traditionally had one of the highest debt–equity ratios in Europe and one of the most underutilized stock exchanges. In 1977 for instance the debts of French industry were worth almost 140 percent of its assets, while the market value of equities listed on the French *Bourse* was barely 12 percent of GDP compared with Britain and the USA, where the corresponding figure was over 40 percent (Commission de l'industrie, 1980, p. 6). As a result of this, the French banks are in a position to exercise a proportionately greater influence over affairs of industry; and because most of the debt is medium to long term, these banks generally take an active interest in the production and marketing strategies of the firms they support (cf. Morin, 1974; Zysman, 1980, p. 266).

In contrast to Germany, however, the organization of French capital is further distinguished by the preponderant influence which the state wields in the banking sector. The history of state intervention in banking in France can be traced back to the reconstruction of the banking system under Napoleon III and to the efforts of the *Front Populaire* to take control of the Bank of France. But its immediate origins lie in the establishment after World War II of a series of state-controlled institutions for the collection of savings (Caisse des Dépôts, Banque Nationale de Paris, Société Générale and Crédit Lyonnais), and for the provision of funds to industry (Crédit National), agriculture (Crédit Agricole), housing (Crédit Foncier) and tourism (Crédit Hôtelier). Together these institutions collect and dispose of two-thirds of all the deposits in the French banking system (Morin, 1974, p. 175). In recent years they have been joined by an additional set of state institutions, such as the Fonds de développement économique et social (FDES), which provides as much as 2 billion francs (bF) a year to industry, the Institut de développement industriel

which administers another 1bF and the Banque
française du commerce extérieur which, along with
several other agencies, makes available up to 10bF a
year to facilitate exports (Ministère de l'industrie,
1979). By using these funds to enter into joint ventures
with the private banks of France and to rediscount
their bills, the state is able to exercise substantial
leverage over the activities of the private banking
sector as well. This leverage is further enhanced by the
system of quantitative controls used by the Bank of
France to govern bank lending. The result is that not
only does finance capital exercise a detailed purview
over the affairs of industry, but the state also exercises
substantial control over finance capital itself (Zysman,
1980; Caron, 1979; see also **Document 3**).

At the same time the state in postwar France also has
a distinctive organization. Three features are
particularly striking. First, in comparison with
Germany, the officials at the Ministry of Economics
and Finance, and in particular within its Trésor, are
able to exercise considerable influence over the actions
of the Bank of France through their joint participation
in the Conseil National du Crédit which supervises
national monetary policy (Adam, 1980). The central
bank of France is far less independent than its German
or even British counterparts. Secondly, the same
officials at the Trésor who are in charge of fiscal and
monetary policy are also closely involved in the
supervision of industrial policy (Adam, 1980). As a
consequence, the concerns of industry are likely to
receive greater consideration in the formulation of
macroeconomic policy than they would in Britain,
where responsibility for fiscal and industrial matters is
more clearly divided between departments. Thirdly, as
part of a deliberate strategy formulated by the ruling
elites immediately after the war and designed to turn
the state into an agency fostering socioeconomic
change, a set of institutions was embedded within the
French state for the purpose of inculcating its
personnel with the notion that they were to be the
grand strategists for the French economy and French
industry. Most prominent among these were the École
nationale d'administration (ENA) and the Commissariat général du plan. The former, which
became the principal source for recruitment into the
higher civil service, imbued its charges with a sense of
their own distinctiveness and a feeling of responsibility
for the performance of the French economy (cf.
Stevens, 1980; Suleiman, 1980). And the latter
attempted to fulfil that responsibility by generating
and coordinating the implementation of a general
strategy for the evolution of French industry (cf.

Gruson, 1968; Monnet, 1976). Together, these facets
of the French state gave its personnel a capacity to
influence the activities of industry and a willingness to
do so, which their counterparts in Britain and
Germany generally lacked.

The organization of labor in France also has several
features which are unique among our three cases. In
contrast to Britain or Germany, there is no single union
confederation in France. Instead, four unions of
substantial size, the Confédération générale du travail
(CGT), Confédération française démocratique du
travail (CFDT), Force ouvrière (FO) and
Confédération générale des cadres (CGC) find
themselves competing against one another, often to
organize the workforce in the same plant. Within these
organizations institutional linkages between the union
leadership and rank-and-file remain underdeveloped
in comparison with elsewhere (Schain, 1980).
Collective bargaining, itself, is largely unregulated by
law; indeed, until 1968 the unions had virtually no legal
status in the workplace at all (Ross, 1980). On a
national level the proportion of the workforce that is
organized in France is the smallest of any industrialized
nation, that is, about 20 percent compared with over 30
percent in Germany and 50 percent in Britain. These
factors combine to encourage factionalism within the
union movement and to put the working class as a
whole in a comparatively weak position within the
labor market. This weakness is compounded at the
political level by the attachment of most of the unions
to left-wing parties, which until recently had been out
of power for almost thirty years while a series of
right-wing coalitions with a declining base of working-
class votes had ruled (Birnbaum, 1978, p. 101).

What is the relationship between these organizational
factors and the patterns of French economic policy in
the postwar period? In the macroeconomic sphere it is
possible to discern a set of broad regularities in French
policy under the Fourth and Fifth Republics that
almost amount to a distinctive strategy of stimulating
investment above all else, usually through the
stimulation of demand. Fiscal policy played a role in
this strategy. With the exception of 1958 and 1965
when the government ran a slight surplus, demand was
stimulated almost continuously over 1954–70 by a
series of public sector deficits averaging 1–2 percent of
GDP (Hansen, 1969, p. 193; Salin and Lane, 1977, p.
550). Monetary policy, however, was the driving force
behind the French stimulus. Despite brief periods
when credit was tightened in 1963–5, 1968–70 and
1972–3, the money supply was allowed to grow rapidly

in France, reaching an average increase of almost 14 percent per annum in the 1960–8 period (OECD, 1974; Salin and Lane, 1977, p. 578). In general, the monetary aggregates were allowed to grow substantially faster in France than in either Germany or the UK. And lest one think that demand factors were primarily responsible for this rate, it should be noted that the French state played an important role in generating demand by using its control over the banking system to subsidize the interest rates at which vast quantities of funds were made available. As late as 1980 it is estimated that 44 percent of all business loans in France were at subsidized rates of interest (*The Economist*, 14 March 1981, p. 62). These, then, were the first two pillars on which postwar French policy was based: the rapid expansion of demand and the provision of large quantities of relatively cheap credit to industry.

The impact of this policy, of course, was highly inflationary. During 1950–75 the French cost of living rose by 6 percent more than the British and by 42 percent more than the German (IMF, 1977). From time to time the effect of this was to threaten the growth of French exports and to precipitate periodic balance of payments crises. At such points the government was faced with a choice between the pursuit of less inflationary policies, which would slow the rate of growth, and devaluation of the currency. The British faced a similar choice periodically as well; but whereas the British strenuously resisted devaluation during the era of fixed exchange rates over 1947–72, the French devalued frequently. They lowered the exchange rate of the franc five times in a twenty-five-year period: by almost 40 percent in 1948, by 22 percent in 1949, by 20 percent in 1957, by 17·5 percent in 1958 and by 11 percent in 1969 (cf. Lieberman, 1977). Devaluation was the third element of the triad on which their macroeconomic policy was based.

This is not to say that the French never adopted slightly deflationary policies. The periods of tightening in 1952, 1958, 1963–4 and 1974 have been noted. But each of these pauses was less severe than the one that preceded it, and each was mitigated in important respects (Carré *et al.*, 1972, p. 491). In the midst of the credit squeeze of 1963–4, for instance, the Conseil national du crédit sent a letter, drafted by the Planning Commissioner, to all the banks, declaring:

If the basic conditions for expansion are to be respected, our credit policy must be selective. In particular, as far as medium-term credit is concerned, there is a case for giving privileged treatment to the most dynamic firms serving foreign markets and to sectors especially hard-hit by foreign competition and for giving privileged treatment to the financing of projects for the reorganization of production. (Cited in MacLennan *et al.*, 1968, p. 165)

The letter was accompanied by instructions that these recommendations were to be implemented. Similarly, President de Gaulle, possibly under the influence of Jacques Rueff, opted for deflation rather than devaluation in the 1963–5 period, but he followed it with highly expansionary policies, and his successor reverted to devaluation very soon after taking office.

These are the policies of a state which subordinated macroeconomic management to the pursuit of industrial investment. When forced to choose between a variety of broader economic considerations which policy-makers in other nations often took very seriously, the French authorities opted consistently for industrial growth. Even Giscard d'Estaing, who had been one of France's more conservative economic managers, reflected this sense of priorities when he announced in 1969:

I consider that my mandate at the Ministry of Economy and Finance runs until 1976. My objective is, by that date, to bring France to an industrial level about equal to that of Germany and England. I would prefer to attain this objective without inflation. But if I have to choose, I would opt for industrial development and regard the fight against inflation as secondary. (Cited in Suleiman, 1978, p. 262)

This order of priorities and the consistency with which it has been pursued can be traced to the influence of several features of the organization of the state and capital in France. The emphasis on growth reflects, in part, the socializing effects of the ENA and the persistent pressure which officials of the Plan have been able to exert on the Ministry of Finance. These officials concede that their principal object was to convert not only French business, but also the economic managers of the state, to the view that all other considerations had to be subordinated to the need for growth (Monnet, 1976; Crozier, 1965). In this they were largely successful. The institutions of the Plan evolved in such a way as to generate and solidify close relationships between the managers of business and the state which had been lacking in prewar France (Shonfield, 1969). In fact by 1970 when some questions were raised about the desirability of rapid economic growth, the leaders of the Confédération nationale du patronat were able more or less to dictate the contents of the Sixth Plan. And the Planning Commissariat was widely recognized as an effective conduit reinforcing the voice of industrial capital within the state and articulating its demands for expansionary economic policy (Hayward, 1972).

The task of the planners was made much easier by the postwar reorganization of the Ministry of Finance which vested it with ultimate responsibility for industrial matters. In the interwar era the Ministry had been known as a bastion of fiscal conservatism heavily influenced by the banks (Cohen, 1977, pp. 37–8). Like the British Treasury, it resisted a series of attempts to use alternative departments of economic affairs to reorient economic policy. But under the influence of ENA graduates and planners in the postwar period and vested with new responsibilities for industry, the ministry became involved in, and committed to, economic rationalization and rapid growth. The success of French industry became the responsibility of the French Ministry of Finance in a way that it has never been the responsibility of the British Treasury.

Moreover, with the postwar reorganization of the financial sector, the Ministry of Finance gained control over a vast array of levers on the monetary as well as fiscal side of policy of a sort that was denied to the German Minister of Economics, who had to face a highly independent central bank. It became possible for the French Ministry to orient its growth strategy around an easy money policy punctuated by periodic devaluations, and to use selective exemptions to take the bite out of restrictive policies for critical industrial sectors. The reorganization of capital reinforced this by reducing the independence and influence of finance capital *vis-à-vis* the state at the same time as the Plan was enhancing the influence of industrial capital. It is not surprising that financial policy was subordinated to industrial policy in the subsequent period.

On the industrial side French policy in the postwar era has been distinguished from policies in Britain and Germany by the high degree of intervention which the state has been able and willing to exercise in the affairs of the private sector. Three characteristics of French policy particularly stand out. The first is the extensive role played by the state in the development of a strategy for individual industrial sectors. The second is

the degree of pressure the state has brought to bear on individual firms to comply with its strategy. And the third has been the willingness of the state to fund relatively profitable enterprises, often in growth sectors, rather than simply in the declining industries with high political visibility, which most states find they must support. The history of French industrial policy has been well documented (Shonfield, 1969; Vernon, 1974; Warnecke and Suleiman, 1975; Zysman, 1977; Stoffaes, 1978). In the period of reconstruction immediately following the war, the Planning Commissariat and Trésor collaborated to channel scarce funds to the six key sectors they had selected for rapid development and to draw up detailed plans for the division of production within these sectors. During the subsequent two decades of rapid expansion the state fastened on a strategy of creating 'national champions' who would carry France's banner against the multinationals, and to this end used a variety of devices to encourage mergers and to transfer resources to high-technology industries believed to be in growth sectors. The Airbus, Plan Calcul, Concorde and nuclear, as well as steel, programs were products of this attempt. In contrast to both the German and British governments, the French state assumed the task of rationalizing key industrial sectors time and time again. And it employed a multifarious range of techniques for accomplishing this (see **Document 3**).

Both the will and the capacity for doing this can be traced to several facets of the organization of French capital and the state which have already been outlined. Just as the socialization provided by ENA and the Plan dictated a macroeconomic policy fixated on economic growth, so it encouraged the managers of the state to undertake an activist industrial policy. They were designated the pilots of the 'strategic state'. The failure of French industry would be their failure. Of even greater importance, the reorganization of capital after the war provided them with the tools with which to exercise extensive influence over industry. Officials in the Trésor were given control over two-thirds of the funds within the French banking system and the manipulation of these funds became the fulcrum on which leverage was applied against all manner of French industries. For a period, all medium-term loans over 500,000 francs and all long-term loans over 2·5mF had to be approved by officials of the Plan and the Trésor (MacLennan *et al.*, 1968). The dependence of French firms on external finance and long-term debt increased this leverage. And the conjunction of inflationary macroeconomic policies and an extensive system of price controls bolstered the importance of the access to credit and exemption from controls that the state could provide. In short, the officials of the French state wielded a series of weapons that were absent from the public arsenals of Britain and Germany. Their major problem was deciding what to do with these. And for the most of the period French officials believed they knew what to do (Stoléru, 1969; Stoffaes, 1979). The Planning Commission, FDES and the other bodies associated with the allocation of credit provided Trésor officials with the industrial intelligence on which to proceed (see **Document 4**). These sorts of levers have sticky handles. Accordingly, long after the elites who had undertaken the reorganization of French capital and the state in the years following the war had been replaced by fresh, young technocrats, the organizational legacy which they left made it possible for the managers of the French state to play a role in industrial affairs which their counterparts in Britain and Germany never enjoyed.

In the sphere of incomes policy the French experience has again been unique: what distinguishes it from the German and British cases is the failure to develop any form of tripartism either tacit or explicit. Instead, the French state has relied primarily on price controls to stiffen the resolve of employers against workers' demands for higher wages and on periodic devaluation to neutralize the effect of sporadic wage increases on export prices. From time to time groups of officials, often within the Plan, supported by some union leaders, usually from the CFDT, have attempted to open tripartite negotiations involving the unions, employers and the state, aimed at achieving agreement on a national or sectoral policy on wages. But these attempts have never been fully successful. In each case the state agreed to such negotiations only when pressed by national crises of the sort generated by the steel strike of 1963 and the events following May 1968. On each occasion, while some of the parties favored a settlement, others acted to sabotage it. Thus, the Incomes Policy Conference of October 1963 was scuttled by the government's passage of anti-strike legislation in July 1963, its deflationary moves of September 1963 and by the refusal of the CGT and FO to trade wage restraint for contractual agreements covering social policy, minimum wages and public sector settlements. Similarly, although the government resorted to the tripartite Grenelle Agreements of 1968 to restore order after the events of May–June, it immediately undercut the wage gains these offered the workforce by devaluing the franc; and the *contrats de progrès* that were supposed to regularize public sector

bargaining in this period functioned for barely a year before union resistance intensified and the Chaban-Delmas government which had originated them was dismissed (Hayward and Watson, 1975). Indeed, for most of the postwar period the state's efforts have been directed at weakening the union movement rather than at attempting to strengthen and co-opt it by encouraging participation in national bargaining. Over a period of years union delegates were systematically excluded from the most sensitive negotiations at the Plan (Hayward, 1967). All attempts to secure legal recognition for unions at the workplace were frustrated until 1969, and industrial relations legislation was almost invariably contrived to strengthen alternative workers' committees rather than unions at the plant level (cf. Schain, 1980).

The strategy adopted by the state and the failure to develop any form of tripartism can be related to several characteristics of the organization of the labor market in France. In the first place, the weakness of the unions restricted their ability to secure extravagant wage increases or to disrupt the economy for a sustained period and, therefore, made it less necessary for the government to resort to tripartite bargaining to limit real wage gains. Secondly, the limited authority of union leaders over the actions of the rank-and-file made tripartite bargaining more difficult and less attractive. As one observer puts it, 'The employers and the state . . . can expect few benefits of social order from union organizations that have so little authority over their strike action' (Schain, 1980, p. 233). The presence of several competing union federations also hampered the achievement of a tripartite bargain. The temptation was high for some unions to score gains among rank-and-file militants by accusing those that bargained of selling out, and for union leaders the attractiveness of entering into a bargain was limited by the fear that their rivals might outflank them among the rank-and-file while they were immobilized by the agreement. Meanwhile, for the individual workers, these factors and the unregulated character of collective bargaining in France meant that there were few guarantees that any national bargain would be universally observed and, thus, there were high risks associated with the act of restraint. At the levels of the state, union leadership and union rank-and-file, therefore, organizational factors militated powerfully against the achievement of a tripartite incomes policy in France. Conversely, they meant that a strategy that employed rising unemployment and pressure on employers to depress wages was more likely to succeed, and such a strategy has generally been followed.

Britain

Turning to Britain we can see the impact of organizational factors on policy once again. In the organization of the British state two factors are especially significant. First, as in Germany, there is a strict separation between the organ responsible for fiscal policy, the Treasury, and that responsible for monetary policy, the Bank of England. And although its independence is not as constitutionally entrenched as that of the Deutsche Bundesbank, the Bank of England enjoys considerable autonomy and substantial influence over policy. This derives from its role as the principal manager of monetary policy, and as the representative within Whitehall for the financial markets. The Bank was nationalized after the war and its decisions formally subjected to Treasury approval. But according to most inside observers, 'This in no way legislated for a revolution in relations between the Bank and the Treasury' (Artis, 1965, p. 31; Select Committee, 1969–70). The Bank retained a virtual monopoly of expertise on both domestic and international monetary matters which made it difficult for any other political body to question its judgement on such issues, especially in the midst of a crisis. Moreover, the Governor of the Bank enjoys the unique rights of immediate access to the Prime Minister, which he exercises on a weekly basis, and of making his institution's views known to the public. Accordingly, when issues of confidence in sterling or the public debt arise, the Bank can both contribute to the definition of the conditions on which 'financial confidence' is deemed to rest, and interpret these conditions directly to the government of the day. In the face of this, as successive Prime Ministers have testified, formal limits on the Bank's authority dwindle into insignificance (Keegan and Pennant-Rae, 1979, p. 99).

Secondly, in contrast to both the German and French cases, where the central economic ministry has been charged with responsibility for industrial performance, the main responsibility of the British Treasury for most of the postwar period has been the control of public expenditure. Until 1962 the internal organization of the Treasury was geared almost exclusively to the performance of this function; and the National Economy Group, which was established at that time to oversee the impact of government operations on the real resources of the nation, was still oriented to the management of aggregate consumption and investment rather than to the sectoral organization or performance of British industry (cf. Shonfield,

1969, p. 104). Until 1975 the Treasury had virtually no capacity for assessing the detailed impact of its measures on industry. Indeed, for much of the postwar period the British government lacked a Cabinet-level Minister of Industry as well. The first steps to remedy this were taken in 1962 when the Board of Trade was given increased responsibilities for regional development. Not until the late 1960s when the Ministry of Technology began to assemble a staff of industrial experts, did the British government develop a capacity for the coordination of industrial policy. Moreover, the Treasury continued to exercise a kind of bureaucratic hegemony over economic policy-making within Whitehall throughout this period, despite the short-lived experiment with a Department of Economic Affairs (Shanks, 1977; Budd, 1978).

With respect to the organization of capital, the British situation is notable for the relatively strict division of interest and operations that persists between the managers of financial and industrial capital. It is often suggested that financial capital is more powerful than industrial capital in Britain and exercises control over the latter's operations (cf. Thompson, 1977, p. 196). But, in fact, the relative strength of financial capital is at the political level, that is, in relations with Whitehall, where its representatives enjoy superior access and wield more tangible sanctions in negotiations with the government than do industrialists. At an economic level the large clearing banks that account for most of British lending exercise none of the detailed control over the affairs of industry that is evident in Germany or France.

This situation is attributable to two sorts of factors. On the one hand, UK firms generally rely on internally generated funds for capital investment. During 1950–72 76 percent of gross capital formation in Britain was funded from earnings, compared to 62 percent in Germany and 49 percent in France. Furthermore, when forced to seek external sources of funds, UK firms have traditionally turned to equity rather than to debt. The average ratio of fixed interest capital to variable dividend capital of British firms in 1972 was only 0·55, compared with 0·74 in Germany and 0·92 in France (Thompson, 1977, p. 196; Lever and Edwards, 1980). As a result, industrial capital in Britain has been much less dependent on the banks for finance than its continental counterparts. Secondly, what capital *is* provided by the banks to British industry has been funneled primarily through short-term loans; in fact, a substantial portion of the funds available to even the largest corporations is still provided through regularized overdraft facilities. In

1972, for instance, 73 percent of borrowing by non-financial enterprises in the UK was short term, compared with 49 percent of the borrowing in France and 30 percent in Germany (Thompson, 1977, p. 263; *The Economist*, 9 October 1976). This is significant because when a bank grants short-term credit, it does not usually look closely at the details of a firm's performance or market strategy, as it might in connection with a long-term loan. Instead, it extends funds on more mechanical principles of credit-worthiness associated with balance-sheet figures such as the ratio of liquid assets to liabilities (cf. Thompson, 1977, p. 196). As a consequence, in comparison with the banks of Germany and France, the British banks appear to have more limited knowledge about the operations of British industry and less of a stake in the profitability of particular industrial sectors. British finance capital is thus more likely to define its interests in a way that is separate from those of industry (see **Document 6**).

The organization of labor in Britain is also somewhat different than in either France or Germany. In contrast to the French case, there is a central Trades Union Congress (TUC) in Britain to which most organized workers are affiliated and which has considerable moral authority among them; but it is a loose confederation with very limited bureaucratic resources and few sanctions to apply against its members. And in contrast to the German case, 112 separate unions are affiliated to the TUC, many of them still organized along craft lines. Within many of these affiliates a contest for control over union policy also continues among frequently autocratic leaders and an influential network of shop stewards (Clegg, 1979; Taylor, 1978). In broad social terms, however, this is a powerful union movement. At the economic level, over 50 percent of the laborforce is unionized, and in such key sectors as coal, railways and road transport over 95 percent of the workforce belongs to a trade union. In the face of severe inflation most of these unions have been able to bargain for and secure real wage gains for their members (cf. Sachs, 1979). Similarly, at the political level, the union movement has substantial influence within the Labour Party, which has been in office for at least eighteen of the last thirty-six years, and its ability to stymie the policies even of Conservative governments has been demonstrated on several occasions in recent years (Crouch, 1978; Dorfman, 1979).

How are these factors related to the patterns of British economic policy? In the eyes of most commentators the principal feature of British postwar macroeconomic policy has been the recurrence of a 'stop–go' cycle of reflation followed by sharp deflation (Hansen, 1969; Caves *et al.*, 1968; Brittan, 1971). Expansion in 1950 and early 1951 based on rearmament for the Korean War was followed in 1952 by sharp increases in bank rate, control on instalment buying ('hire purchase') and cuts in capital investment. The income tax cuts and investment allowances of 1953–4 led to renewed hire purchase controls, decreases in public investment and sales tax increases in 1955–6. The budgets of 1958 and 1959 employed direct and indirect tax cuts to initiate another expansion, but 1960 brought successive increases in bank rate, a more restrictive budget and hire purchase controls plus tax increases and reductions in public expenditure in 1961. In 1962–3 the chancellor embarked on another expansion, but this, too, came to a halt as the new Labour government imposed increasingly deflationary measures in the years 1964–70. In the 1970s a similar pattern was pursued as the deflationary policies of 1970–1 were followed by rapid expansion of public spending in 1972–4, deflation in 1975–7, expansion in 1978–80 and deflation in 1981. If these measures had been timed so as to moderate the effects of the business cycle on the British economy, we might attribute this 'stop–go' pattern to the application of Keynesian principles of economic management. But detailed analyses of the period suggest that these policies were timed in such a way as to reinforce rather than reduce the effect of cyclical fluctuations on investment and output (Caves *et al.*, 1968; Hansen, 1969, p. 443).

Accordingly, we have to turn elsewhere for an explanation—to factors which ultimately lead us back to the organization of the British polity. The expansionary policies pursued during the 'go' side of these cycles can be traced to the policy-makers' interest in stimulating economic growth. But this sort of stimulus invariably sucked imports into the economy which threw the balance of payments into deficit and precipitated an outflow of the foreign exchange reserves of the nation. Confronted with this situation, British policy-makers faced a choice between letting the exchange rate decline or deflating the economy so as to reduce expenditure on imports relative to exports. In similar situations the French devalued. But for almost thirty years after the war British policy-makers refused to devalue, except in 1948 and 1967 when they no longer had a choice. They consistently defended an exchange rate which by the end of the 1950s was seriously overvalued (Brittan, 1971, p. 299). And in tandem with this they maintained a policy of borrowing short-term funds to finance long-term capital outflows and a £3·5 billion overhang of overseas sterling balances, which exacerbated the effects of speculative pressure on the reserves (cf. Pollard, 1969, ch. 8). This meant that whenever the exchange rate came under pressure, British authorities moved to deflate the economy. It seems that in every one of these cases deflation was undertaken in response to an outflow of foreign reserves rather than as a result of domestic developments (Caves *et al.*, 1968, p. 78). The appearance of a 'stop–go' cycle in British policy was directly related to the defense of a high exchange rate and the maintenance of extensive international financial obligations (Blank, 1978).

The consequences for British industry were adverse in two respects. First, the increasingly frequent and severe deflations entailed by this policy discouraged capital investment which might have improved productivity and, thus, may have limited the nation's general economic growth. Secondly, the policy saddled industrialists with particularly high export prices while subsidizing the price of competing imports. British export prices rose by 14·5 percent more than the average price of world exports in the decade after 1953. Pollard (1969, p. 44) and others argue that this differential rather than the sectoral distribution of British manufacturing was the decisive element handicapping Britain's export industries. Moreover, deflation consistently depressed domestic investment in Britain, and the suggestion that it may have helped restrain prices is belied by the fact that prices rose as quickly in deflationary periods as at other times (Pollard, 1969, p. 483).

In short, for most of the postwar period, the British pursued a policy which appeared to be in the interests of finance capital and was detrimental to those of industry. Until the 1970s the representatives of the British financial community believed that the maintenance of a high exchange rate, of the overseas balances and of unfettered capital flows was essential to the profitability of British finance capital and to the survival of London as an international financial center. At each turning-point spokesmen for the City and for the Bank of England pressed the government to deflate rather than devalue (Brittan, 1971), and in each instance their views prevailed. To a large extent the position they took, and their success in defending it, must be attributed to the organization of British capital and of the state. The arms-length relationship between financial and industrial capital in Britain was certainly conducive to the different definitions of interests which emerged on the two sides when such issues arose. In this context the comments of a senior industrialist interviewed by Grant and Marsh (1977, p. 69) are revealing. He declared: 'There is a false assumption that all businessmen have common interests. Yet to me it is patently obvious that the interests of manufacturing business and the City are sometimes not coincident.' The contrast is with Germany, where the banks' direct stake in the profitability of industrial enterprise and their familiarity with its needs led the two sides to join in support of a low exchange rate.

At the same time the organization of the British state was such that the views of financial capital were more likely to be influential on macroeconomic policy questions than were the views of industrial capital. As we have seen, the Bank of England, which considers itself to be the guardian of the interests of the financial community, was vested with primary responsibility for exchange rate questions. In contrast with the French Trésor, the Treasury had little expertise in this area and was accustomed to relying on the Bank (Keegan and Pennant-Rae, 1979). In times of crisis the authority of experts is especially enhanced. The Bank used the crisis situations engendered by pressure on the reserves to press its demands for deflation on the government (Blackaby, 1979, p. 312). Similarly, even within the Treasury, there were few officials with specific responsibility for, or detailed knowledge of, the interests of manufacturing industry who might have successfully opposed deflation. On the contrary, the preoccupation of most Treasury officials with the control of public expenditure predisposed them to deflationary episodes during which public expenditure might be cut back. The organization of Whitehall was conducive to the formation of a consensus on the desirability of deflation over devaluation of the sort that Blank (1978) has found. The closed nature of the British bureaucracy, moreover, minimized the impact of outside advice from industry (Kipping, 1972, p. 90). Although politicians were ultimately responsible for these decisions, the power they wielded was, in many respects, illusory. It was difficult for even the most radical of them to contravene the received wisdom of many years and the advice of the most senior authorities in the field when it seemed that the country was in crisis and its financial viability was at stake (Brittan, 1971, p. 197).

In the sphere of industrial policy the British experience has displayed three distinctive characteristics. First, a coordinated policy aimed at the rationalization of key industrial sectors was not developed until late in the postwar period. Following the Labour government's failure to use the Industrial Organization and Development Act of 1947 to enforce a measure of planning on industry (Shonfield, 1969, pp. 98 ff.), the British government made only sporadic attempts to encourage rationalization in the private sector through the 1950s. The measures which were taken in ship-building, or in the textile industry via the Cotton Industry Act of 1959, were mainly extensions of programs begun in the 1930s (Grove, 1967; Blackaby, 1979, p. 403). Not until a growing concern about Britain's relatively slow rate of economic growth prompted the establishment of the National Economic Development Council (NEDC) in 1962 and the creation of a Secretary of State for Industry, Trade and Regional Development in 1963, did the British state attempt to mount an industrial policy aimed at the large-scale regeneration of British industry (Brittan, 1971, ch. 6).

Secondly, even after 1962, most of the government's activities in this area were oriented to the maintenance of employment in economically depressed areas rather than to the reorganization of industry (McCrone, 1969, p. 119). Regional considerations have continued to be the guiding principle behind British industrial policy. Even in the most recent period the vast majority of funds have gone to firms in declining sectors of the economy (Peacock *et al.*, 1980, p. 59). This contrasts with the activities of the French and the Germans who have focused most of their attention and a large portion of their funds on high growth sectors of industry.

Finally, the extent to which British policy has been seriously 'interventionist' is very limited. There was no attempt by the state to force industrial reorganization on critical sectors as in France. Even Britain's principal attempt at planning, associated with the NEDC in the 1960s, was a tripartite exercise based on mutual persuasion. As Hagen and White (1966, cited in Blank, 1978, p. 113) note, the British government approached producer groups 'not as a representative of the public interest seeking the recommendations of groups with special interests before it exercised its authority, but as one association approaching two other associations to ask them what they would be willing to do'. The Economic Development Committees and Sectoral Working Parties spawned by the NEDC operated on the same basis, and it is not surprising that they seem to have enhanced the influence of industry over government rather than vice versa.

This pattern of policy can be linked to several facets of the organization of British capital and the state. Most importantly, the British state lacked the instruments with which to enforce an active policy of sectoral reorganization even if it could have formulated one. Financial capital in Britain has been relatively independent of the state. The Bank of England attempts to influence the total quantities of credit extended in the economy and has occasionally suggested that the banks give priority to export industries in their lending, but the state lacks the detailed control over the flows of funds in the economy which the French state enjoys. Moreover, industry itself has been less dependent on debt, and thus on the banking sector, for finance in Britain than in France, although this may be changing (*Bank of England Quarterly Bulletin*, June 1979, p. 185). Thus, even if the state had nationalized the banks, its leverage over industry would still have been limited. The tax allowances on which the British have relied for most of the postwar period to stimulate investment cannot be focused on individual firms in such a way as to enforce a rationalization program. And the subsidies which several governments have made available to industry are not a substitute for more extensive control over an industry's sources of external finance.

At the same time the division of responsibility and allocation of expertise within the British state has not been conducive to the development of a strategy for industrial rejuvenation capable of being sustained in the face of conflicting economic demands. Power over the direction of economic policy and the allocation of public funds remained with the Treasury which, until 1975, had little responsibility for, or knowledge of, the needs of British industry. While the Department of Economic Affairs and NEDC were mandated to develop such a strategy, control over the priorities of economic policy never left the Treasury (cf. Budd, 1978; Brittan, 1971), and many of its decisions ultimately frustrated the planners (Leruez, 1975). Without an apparatus committed to sectoral planning and entrenched within Whitehall, the British state proved attentive to sectoral problems only in crisis situations. Initiative in this area remained at the political level where concerns naturally focused on the short-term alleviation of unemployment rather than on the long-term reallocation of investment toward growth sectors of industry.

In the field of incomes policy, the British pattern has displayed three distinctive characteristics. First, the government has made extensive efforts to secure an incomes policy at a number of junctures in the postwar period, and has implemented either voluntary or statutory wage norms in 1948, 1961–2, 1965–6,

1966–7, 1972–3 and 1975–8. Secondly, in each case, the imposition of a norm has been preceded by a serious attempt on the part of the government to reach agreement with the TUC and the Confederation of British Industry (CBI) on the need for a norm and on the outlines of a broader economic strategy. And finally, after one or two years under a wage norm, rank-and-file resistance to the policy has forced the union leadership to withdraw its support for such a policy and impelled the government to return to free collective bargaining. Thus, the British pattern has been one of alternation between incomes policy negotiated from above and free collective bargaining (Dorfman, 1979).

Once again, the roots of this pattern can be traced to the organization of the British labor market. On the one hand, the British government found it necessary to attempt to reach agreement on an incomes policy because of the power of the union movement. This power is reflected in the high proportion of the laborforce which is organized, especially in the key industrial sectors, and in the influence of the unions over the Conference of the Labour Party. At a political level this has meant that the unions have had the ability to turn the electorate, and in some cases a party's own supporters, against the government through widespread industrial disruption. A Labour government learned this lesson during the defeat of its industrial relations legislation in 1968; and a Conservative government had it confirmed when a confrontation with striking mineworkers contributed to its electoral defeat in February 1974 (Jenkins, 1970; Hurd, 1979). Of equal significance is the fact that, at an economic level, British workers have had an ability to maintain their real wages through periods of both inflation and state-induced recession (Turner and Wilkinson, 1972). Both of these factors have limited the usefulness of imposing deflation on the economy to deter the unions from seeking higher wages and have forced the government to look to negotiations over an incomes policy as an alternative.

If these negotiations have been made necessary in Britain by the power of the unions, however, they have also been made possible by the existence of a single union confederation. In both respects Britain stands in contrast to France, where the weakness of the union movement limits the need for negotiations, and the multiplicity of unions discourages any one of them from reaching an agreement with the state.

In part, these factors explain the attachment of British officials to 'tripartism', which Grant and Marsh (1977, p. 389) define as 'a belief that the peak organizations representing management and the trade unions are of special importance among all producers groups, that negotiations should take place with these peak organizations on the major issues of economic policy, and that agreement with these groups will provide a basis for the successful implementation of the government's economic policy'. It is also intrinsically difficult to secure adherence to a voluntary incomes policy in Britain without a substantial amount of bargaining. In contrast to Germany, where the acquiescence of a few major union leaders is sufficient to assure all concerned that restraint will be widespread and returns in the form of reduced inflation at least will be forthcoming, the TUC must persuade a large number of its affiliates to support a policy before any can be assured that it will stick. This requires a substantial effort at the mobilization of consent. Similarly, even if the CBI is involved primarily in order to lend weight to the government's demands for wage restraint, an institutional framework within which bargaining can take place on a regularized basis is essential if the British state is to realize a strategy of semi-voluntary restraint. In the absence of bargaining the generalized distribution of positive incentives to the unions has proved ineffective at securing restraint. An institutional framework of the sort the NEDC or TUC–Labour Party Liaison Committee provides, has made it possible for the state to demand a *quid pro quo* for each of the goods it distributes, to exact the maximum returns in exchange for those goods and to monitor any ensuing agreement. Once one turns from brandishing 'sticks' to offering 'carrots', bargaining produces more of a return than simple bribery (see **Document 7**).

While the TUC can strike a wage bargain with the government, however, there is an intrinsic limit to how long the bargain can be kept. Because the TUC is a loose confederation of affiliated unions with few sanctions short of expulsion to use against them, an enormous expenditure of organizational resources and institutional authority is required if it is to persuade its member unions—and they their members—to limit wage demands. After a period, those resources are exhausted, and a rank-and-file backlash begins to find alternative leadership with which to challenge prevailing personnel and policy. The existence of a large number of decentralized unions means that alternative leadership is more readily available in Britain than in Germany. Thus, any tripartite arrangement is bound to break down, and a period of free collective bargaining, often under more militant leadership, ensues before another tripartite bargain is attempted. Hence, the alternation between incomes policy and free-for-all which has characterized the British experience in the postwar period.

Conclusion

In conclusion, although only a preliminary analysis has been possible here, the economic policies of Germany, France and Britain seem to have followed distinctive patterns throughout most of the postwar period; and these, in turn, can be related to peculiar features of the organization of capital, labor and the state in each nation. A comprehensive analysis would have to deal with several facets of these nations' policies which are not covered here. In particular, within the context of these broad patterns, the individual policies of each nation have changed direction at several points since the war, and this internal dynamic should be accounted for as well. What seems striking, however, is not the occasional variation in a country's policies, but the persistence of broad patterns which differentiate the policies of one country from those of another. In a world of flux it is underlying continuities which most merit explanation; and the parallel persistence of both these patterns and specific organizational forms strongly suggests that the two are related.

To some extent, the effect of these organizational factors on political outcomes is independent of the power of individual groups. The very multiplicity of union confederations in France, for instance, works against the achievement of a tripartite incomes policy, and the separation between industrial and financial capital in Britain renders industrial rationalization more difficult. But in three other respects these organizational factors are clearly related to the distribution of power among social groups. First, the relative power of capital and labor at critical historical junctures when the organization of key institutions is in flux can have an important impact on the organizational relations which emerge during the period and are institutionalized. The political power of British capital in the critical years following the war, for example, played an important role in blocking the establishment of planning mechanisms there (Shonfield, 1969). Secondly, once a given pattern of socioeconomic organization is established, it instantiates a particular balance of power among key social groups and exercises a continuing influence over their ability to mobilize, to form coalitions and to wield power in the political arena. Finally, as in the case of German revaluation, the dimensions of socioeconomic

organization which specify the relations one group has to another can define the interests those groups will perceive themselves to have in a policy and, thus, structure their demands even before the groups mobilize to bring pressure to bear in a political forum. In this respect, these facets of socioeconomic organization can be thought of as intermediate factors in the determination of economic policy, lying somewhere between more transitory interest group pressures and the structural limits to policy-making in a capitalist state that structuralist or synthetic theories identify.

The relative autonomy of the state may also be affected by these sorts of organizational factors. More precisely, variations in socioeconomic organization may influence the proclivities of the state toward a particular course of action, its receptiveness to pressure from other social groups and its own capacity to put pressure on these groups. As a result of organizational variation, for instance, finance capital seems better able to influence the state in Germany than in France, and the ability of the state to strike a bargain with the union movement is greater in Germany and Britain than in France. Although a more complete examination of this issue would have to include a fuller discussion of how the political system in each nation operates, enough has been said to indicate that no state is ever entirely autonomous, since it faces a socioeconomic structure organized in such a way as to define its possibility for action. Yet neither is the state ever a purely passive respondent to social pressures, since its own organization endows it with peculiar capacities for, and inclinations toward, action.

A complete analysis of economic policy formation would also have to consider more fully the role of ideas or ideology in this process. Like many organizational analyses, this one begins from the premiss that one of the central factors underlying the preferences and behavior of particular groups is their perceptions of what actions are in their interest. It has been argued that variations in the organization of particular markets can alter these interests by linking the prosperity of some groups to that of others, by rendering some categories of action more or less difficult and by influencing the likelihood that certain collective outcomes will follow from the actions of individuals. The other tacit premiss here is that these facets of the configuration of interests are usually perceived by the participants. In general terms, over the period studied here, these assumptions seem to be borne out as the relevant groups articulate and pursue the options we would expect. But since the relationship between interest and action is always mediated by ideas, it is possible for ideology to exercise an impact of its own over the actions of these groups either by inclining them toward one interpretation of their interests over another, or by inducing them to forsake calculations of immediate interest for another goal. The term 'ideology' is used here to refer to any network of ideas used to interpret the parameters of social and economic activity by its participants. In this sense, ideology comprehends not only various political points of view, whether conservative, liberal or socialist, which specify what sorts of state activities are possible and desirable, but also economic theories of the sort associated with monetarism or Keynesianism, which specify what economic consequences will follow from the pursuit of particular policies. It should be evident that the preferences and actions of a group depend on its ideological, as well as its concrete social, position. This is especially likely to be true where issues of economic policy are concerned, since the relationship among economic aggregates is often opaque and open to interpretation. Thus, the mediating role of ideology places a natural limit on the extent to which organizational accounts of behavior can be sustained in this, as in other, spheres.

At the same time, however, the power of ideology is related to modes of organization. Ideas may not be created by organizations, but they are certainly disseminated by them. While the congruence between ideas and interests will not always explain why particular ideas are held, it can go a long way toward explaining the appeal of certain ideas to various social groups. Thus, the presence of ENA and the Plan within the French state played an important role in persuading state managers of the merits of industrial activism. Similarly, monetarist theories of the economy which dictated high exchange and interest rates gained a popularity in the City which they never enjoyed among British industrialists. In these instances key groups were not only gripped by particular ideologies, but also gripped these ideologies in turn to use as weapons against those with whom they disagreed. As was the case with technological developments during the Industrial Revolution, it is not the invention of ideas which has the most profound social consequences; it is their dissemination. And organizational factors, both inside the state and within the surrounding groups, contribute substantially to this process.

It is often suggested that the role of the state in capitalist society is to ensure the performance of two functions: that of *accumulation*, understood as the maintenance of conditions for the profitable accumulation of capital; and that of *legitimation*, understood as the maintenance of social harmony and of support for the regime (cf. O'Connor, 1973; Gough, 1979). In general terms, this may be true, but our understanding of how these functions are performed should be rendered more complex. Performance of the legitimation function, for instance, involves not only the expenditure of resources on transfer payments and other services designed to mitigate the political discontent arising from persistent economic inequalities. It also involves the use of ideological techniques designed to justify the prevailing economic conditions and to redirect popular apprehensions of responsibility for these conditions away from capital and the state toward labor organizations, foreign powers or seemingly immutable external events. Similarly, performance of the accumulation function involves not just the maintenance of adequate levels of investment through the organization of demand, the protection of profits and the limitation of wage gains, but also the periodic reorganization or rationalization of industry in such a way as to ensure the external competitiveness of firms and the effective use of resources.

Although all states may attempt to perform these functions, the patterns of postwar policy-making reviewed here suggest that they will employ different strategies for doing so and will experience varying degrees of success as a consequence of differences in their socioeconomic organization. A brief review of policy-making in the post-1974 period might be used to test this perception and to see if distinctive patterns were maintained in a period when all three nations faced especially acute accumulation problems.

The emergence of three sorts of problems rendered the 1970s a difficult period for economic policy-makers. A wave of working-class militancy, which began in the late 1960s, swept across Europe in the early 1970s, raising the share of national income going to wages relative to profits in each of the three countries studied here, prolonging an inflation which also had international sources, and reviving the spectre of continuing class conflict in societies which had become accustomed to the 'end of ideology' (Crouch and Pizzorno, 1978). Following this, slower rates of economic growth combined with increasingly interdependent world trade patterns to raise unemployment levels and intensify competition for world markets. Important sectors of European industry, including shipbuilding, steel, textiles and eventually even automobiles, began to suffer in the face of stiff competition from Japan, the USA and the newly industrializing countries (Cotta, 1978; Berthelot and Tardy, 1978). Finally, the massive oil price increases of 1974 and 1978 raised the relative costs of many goods and effected a real transfer of resources from OECD to OPEC nations. Rising rates of inflation and unemployment and falling rates of growth resulted in Britain, France and Germany. As a consequence, all of these states had to devise solutions to a common set of problems. The most important of these included how to shift resources away from wages to profits so as to restore investment to adequate levels and how to effect a reorganization of industry which would concentrate its resources in firms and sectors capable of meeting more intense foreign competition, while at the same time minimizing social conflict and the unpopularity of the regime.

In the context of the postwar era the experience of the 1970s posed a new challenge to these states and, as we might expect, in responding to it they had to diverge in some respects from their previous patterns of economic policy-making. In particular, since oil prices were denominated primarily in dollars and the oil price increases of 1974 had stretched the costs of French industry to their limits, further devaluation became too costly a strategy for the French state. Similarly, inflows of foreign currency forced the Germans to revalue the mark if they were to retain any control over their domestic money supply. But in most other respects, the old patterns which had characterized policy since the war could be discovered behind the attempts of each nation to cope with new economic circumstances.

British policy after 1974 was marked by the same stop–go pattern which had characterized the previous period. An attempt to deal with the oil crisis by reflation in 1974–5 was followed by enforced deflation in 1976–7, as sterling plummeted on the foreign exchange markets, and then by renewed reflation in 1978–9 and deflation in 1980–1. Similarly, in order to stem the inflation which rising primary goods prices and the union militancy of 1974–5 touched off, and to shift some of the costs of the oil price rise from capital to labor, the British government resorted to an incomes policy based on tripartite negotiation in 1975–8, as it had in the past. But by 1979 rank-and-file reaction had once again brought the policy to an end and a Conservative government to power. The Thatcher government was elected on a platform which promised to eliminate state intervention in industry and the aid to declining sectors which had characterized past policy (Joseph, 1974). This approach was part of an

ideological initiative advanced in the name of monetarist economics to dissociate the state from responsibility for inflation and for a declining industrial base (Gamble, 1979). But the government found it politically and economically impossible to abandon a series of failing industrial firms, and within two years of taking office, had returned to the policies of preceding governments, which meant providing substantial amounts of public funds to industries such as steel, shipbuilding, chemicals and automobiles, on the understanding that they would rationalize themselves. Faced with the same pressures as before and the same limited set of instruments, there was little else the state could do. Thus, in 1980–1 alone, over £3 billion of public aid went to industry in return for vague promises of rationalization (*The Economist*, 29 November 1980; 25 April 1981).

Like their British counterparts, the political leaders of the French state were also anxious to disassociate themselves from responsibility for the difficult economic conditions which followed the oil crisis of 1974. To this end, all quantitative projections for the economy were eliminated from the Plans, and the planning process itself was downgraded from an exercise designed to provide detailed guidelines for the development of the economy to a relatively limited statement of the government's spending priorities (Hall, 1982). Under Prime Minister Raymond Barre, the government embraced the concept of a 'free market economy' and announced that it would no longer provide aid to 'lame ducks' or attempt to direct the development of French industry. The Minister of the Economy revealed the state's new public posture when he declared:

> Industrial policy means nothing. What we need is an economic policy permanently oriented to free prices and financial flows. It is not up to the state to choose the way out to the future, it is up to the leaders of business. (Cited in Valance, 1978)

Behind this posture lay not only a desire on the part of French officials to disavow responsibility for the layoffs that would have to be made as industry was rationalized during a period of slower economic growth, but also a genuine feeling that, although the state had ample levers with which to influence industrial development, its officials no longer knew exactly what to do with them. In preceding decades the state had been able to use these instruments to speed up industrial investment, to create large firms and to ensure a French presence in critical industrial sectors; but they had never been able to ensure the competitiveness of the firms they supported, which now seemed to be the most important prerequisite for success on world markets (Stoffaes, 1978). Accordingly, even the most interventionist officials were inclined to make greater use of market pressures to winnow the weak from the strong in French industry (see **Document 4**).

However, while some institutions like the Plan could be altered fairly readily, it was not possible for the French state to extricate itself all at once from the socioeconomic relations within which it was embedded. National financial institutions continued to process a major proportion of the flows of funds through the economy. Officials at the Ministries of Finance and Industry, charged with the supervision of industrial development, were loathe to give up these responsibilities altogether. And pressure for state aid from firms facing massive layoffs proved too strong to resist. Therefore, despite the rhetoric of senior political officials, a number of agencies were mandated to distribute state aid to firms experiencing economic difficulty (cf. Berger, 1980). The state continued to channel substantial amounts of capital to high-technology sectors it identified as critical, including those of nuclear energy, telecommunications, aeronautics and automated machine tools (Cohen, 1980; Commissariat générale du plan, 1979). In fact, the total amount of aid which the state provided to industry in the 1975–80 period was substantially higher than it had been in the first half of that decade (Commission de l'Industrie, 1980; see **Document 5**).

The German response to economic developments after 1974 also followed patterns which for the most part had been established earlier. In the macroeconomic sphere, the tendency of the Social-Democratic government to relax fiscal policy in the wake of the 1974 oil crisis was tempered by the insistence of the Bundesbank on maintaining a relatively restrictive monetary policy (Anderson, 1980, p. 21). Once again, the independence of the Bundesbank made itself felt on the direction of economic policy. On the industrial side the amount of aid the state made available to the private sector was increased. As before, however, most of this aid took the form of grants for manpower retraining, research and development or regional development assistance, all of which involved little state intervention in the direction of rationalization itself. Responsibility for industrial reorganization remained with the firms themselves or with their

bankers. Thus, the steel industry managed to alter its basic product lines in favor of special steels and to shed 40,000 workers during 1974–9 without any substantial government aid, and the shipbuilders, who received some support, none the less devised their own rationalization scheme which eliminated half the workforce in the same period (Medley, 1981; Peacock et al., 1980, ch. 6). In the case of AEG-Telefunken, an electronics conglomerate employing 156,000 people, which ran into serious trouble in 1978, the banks directed a restructuring program that cost $307 million in 1979 virtually on their own. The government refused to provide aid to the firm, and a Bonn official took the opportunity to reiterate the view that 'the government isn't the repair shop of capitalism' (see **Document 2**). As if to emphasize who *was*, a government commission, appointed to reconsider the role of the banks in the German system, produced a report in 1979 which recommended very little change in the relationship between the banks and industry (Anderson, 1980, p. 15). The singularity of the German approach is also evident if the involvement of the British government in the affairs of British Leyland is compared to the response of the German state to the financial difficulties which Volkswagen suffered in the late 1970s, when the government refused to interfere with that firm's closure of plants, choosing instead to step up regional development aid to the areas most affected by its layoffs (Peacock et al., 1980, p. 65).

In short, changing economic circumstances inspired some rethinking of economic policy in all these states and several changes in the public presentation of policy. To a large extent, however, the basic patterns of policy continued to follow lines developed earlier in the postwar era which were rooted in the socio-economic organization of each society. In some respects, the response of these states to the new economic conditions were similar: all, for instance, increased the amount of aid available to industry. But the capacity of each state to effect a rationalization of its industrial sector or to depress wages in order to meet continuing accumulation problems seems to have differed according to the social and economic organization of each society. Thus, Germany has been able to depend on the banks to reorganize many sectors. The French state continues to control the financial instruments central to industrial reorganization, but has attempted to make greater use of market pressures in the absence of a clear notion of how to generate competitiveness. And the British state, without the instruments or inclination to direct a rationalization program, has been forced to allocate substantial sums to declining sectors in an *ad hoc* manner.

Many issues arising from this analysis remain to be explored. But it presents us with one way of understanding why states, which all exist within capitalist societies and are therefore subject to many similar constraints, nevertheless often pursue quite different policies in the face of similar economic circumstances. And it gives us a concrete basis for thinking that the differences in policy observed among capitalist states are more than contingent variations within states that are structurally similar in all relevant respects. There seem to be persistent differences in the patterns of policy adopted in these nations which can be traced back to fundamental differences in the organization of the socioeconomic relations which surround and encompass each state.

Notes: Chapter 2

1 An early version of this essay was presented to the British Study Group at the Center for European Studies, Harvard University in February 1981. The author is grateful to Jane Jenson, Peter Lange, Charles Maier, Andrew Martin, George Ross and the members of this group for their critical comments, as well as to Harvey Rishikof and Joel Krieger for the detailed criticisms which they made of the manuscript.

2 The formulation of this approach has been heavily influenced by two recent works which also pay particular attention to organizational factors, but which are otherwise very different. These are Samuel H. Beer's seminal reassessment of the operation of pluralism in Britain (1982), and the analysis of New Deal legislation in America prepared by Kenneth Finegold and Theda Skocpol (1980). Peter Gourevitch's thought-provoking essay (1980) finally forced me to grapple with these issues, and the work of Peter Katzenstein (1978) and John Zysman (1981) was very helpful in doing so. However, it is clear that many facets of this approach remain to be worked out, and none of these authors should be held responsible for the imperfections of this particular analysis.

3 The impact of different modes of organization on class struggle has been a central theme of the growing number of theorists writing about the appearance of 'corporatism' in the contemporary state (see Panitch, 1981). These theories share the concern of this chapter with the impact of variations in organization on the activities of the state, but the forms of organization which they consider most salient differ from those emphasized here, and they tend to be concerned with explaining the organizational forms themselves or very broad capacities of the state to legitimate itself rather than more specific patterns of policy (see Schmitter and Lehmbruch, 1979). The two approaches are not necessarily inimical to each other, however, and occasionally converge, as on the analysis of incomes policy.

4 On this point I have been influenced by a series of valuable discussions with Peter Lange, who is engaged in extensive research on consensual wage regulation.

Documents

1   Industry and the Banking System in Germany

Extract from Richard Medley, 'Monetary stability and industrial adaptation in Germany', staff study prepared for the US Congress, Joint Economic Committee, June 1981.

The German banking system has been a subject of interest to many other governments. The following excerpts are drawn from a report prepared by Richard Medley for the Joint Economic Committee of the US Congress. They highlight and illustrate the relative independence of the Bundesbank and describe the relationship between the private banks in Germany and the industrial sector.

The West German economy dealt successfully with a series of shocks through the first half of 1980 that left most Western European countries in some economic trouble. Central to Germany's continued health have been its monetary policy, administered by the independent central Bank, and the capacity for industrial adjustment of the German private sector. In both areas the overriding concern of all actors, public and private, has been the same: economic stability.

Economic stability does not mean simply low inflation rates, although they are an important element of any stabilization program. The range of concerns that run through economic planning are set forth in the 1967 *Act to Promote Economic Stability and Growth*, they are: stable prices, appropriate growth, high employment and balanced trade. There is general agreement that all of the policies are important, and that the successful implementation of any one of them requires stability in the other areas.

The remarkable consensus that spans all economic sectors from the private bankers to the trade unions is reinforced by the formal and informal arrangements that characterize the German system. At the center of this system stands the Deutsche Bundesbank. Since its creation in 1957, the Bank has carved out a reputation for intelligent planning and forceful implementation that keeps all other sectors of the economy reacting to its moves. That is exactly the way the Bundesbank wishes it to be . . .

In contrast to the government's crucial role, through the Bundesbank, in monetary policy, it plays an extremely limited one in industrial policy. While there is a bewildering array of tax incentives, and research subsidies, these provide only a small share of the money and resources used by the private sector to develop new products and production methods. Investment decisions are left largely to the companies themselves, in concert with the major private banks . . .

The Central Bank

The German Central Bank (Deutsche Bundesbank) was created in 1957 by merging the state (Länder) banks and the *Bank deutsche Länder*. Its primary goal is to assure the continued high performance of the Deutschmark. It is secondarily charged with assisting the federal government's economic policy, but in the case of conflict between the two goals, it must choose to assure the Mark's stability. This ordering of goals is evident in the DBB reply to questions from the UK House of Commons Treasury and Civil Service Committee in June 1980:

> The accepted interpretation of the relevant sections of the Bundesbank Act, which has never been disputed by the Government, is that in the event of a conflict with the objectives of the Government's general economic policy the Bundesbank has to give priority to its primary task, namely safeguarding monetary stability.

The few outbreaks of conflict between the central bank and the federal authorities illustrate that this is the true state of affairs and not merely public relations.

One of the most interesting tests of DBB autonomy came in March 1970. At this time, the stability of the Mark was threatened from many sides. First, there were foreign exchange pressures. The Mark had been upvalued by over 9% only six months before, in the wake of its emergence as the second major reserve currency in the world, after the dollar. Because of the small German economy, in relation to that of the United States (roughly one-eighth the size), the reserve currency status left the DBB faced with profound difficulties in its attempts to control the domestic money supply. Compounding this was the Bundesbank's pledge to support the dollar, if not within the old Bretton-Woods parity range, then at least within moderate parameters. Finally, the DBB had to note a surging inflation rate that officials believed to pose a danger of destabilizing the entire economy. The coincidence of all these circumstances was feared sufficient to spawn the widespread inflationary psychology the bank was determined to avoid.

Following the Federal Government's failure to invoke the strong inflationary program proposed by then-Economics Minister Schiller, the DBB raised the rates at which it loans to banks to their highest level since World War II. It took this action against the advise of labor, management, banks and the government itself. Coupled with this was a 30% increase in the reserves which banks had to hold on deposit with the Bundesbank against *non-resident* liabilities. This double-barreled action was intended both to slow credit expansion, and to decrease the huge foreign capital inflow resulting from speculation about new upvaluations of the Mark.

This did not end the DBB action to slow the economy. It continued to pressure the Federal government for strong fiscal measures to dampen inflationary pressures in the economy. Political pressure from business and labor to avoid such 'restraining policies' caused the newly elected SPD coalition to reject the Bank's pressure. Finally, after four months of behind-the-scenes lobbying with no results, the Bundesbank took a step it had never taken before. It announced considerations about raising the banks' reserve requirements by 10–20%. While the effects of such a squeeze would be severe, the DBB chose this announcement of intent as the most dramatic signal it could give, of its seriousness to follow whatever course necessary to smother the rising inflation rate. Only 4 years earlier the bank had generated a recession sufficient to oust the Chancellor when it was forced to use its rather broadstroke instruments in the face of fiscal impotence by the government. Since that time the 1967 Act to Promote Stability had been ratified, offering the government a broad range of counter-cyclical weapons that stood less chance of over-compensating for the liquidity glut than did the additional weapons at the disposal of the DBB. The Cabinet met shortly after this announcement to reconsider anti-inflationary measures it had shelved in March, but no action was taken.

After seeing that no governmental action was forthcoming, on July 1, the Bundesbank raised the reserve requirements by 15%, hitting the middle of its threatened range. It believed no more increases in its lending rate were possible, since higher rates would attract more speculative capital from abroad compounding the liquidity glut. The continued pressure of the Bank, and its clear determination to blunt the economic upsurge finally outweighed private sector pressures, and the Parliament ratified a government plan to increase personal and corporate taxes and suspend certain capital depreciation provisions. On the same day that this measure passed the upper house of Parliament the DBB reduced the rate at which it lent to banks to guard against more speculative capital inflows.

It is exactly the DBB's willingness to press its case against strong political opinion, along with the undeniable intelligence it has brought to its goal of monetary stability, that makes the bank a major force in determining the course of the German economy. The Bank is fully aware that public perception of its determination, and a thorough understanding of its instruments and goals are crucial to its task. It does not operate in a vacuum guided only by neo-Keynesian or monetarist theory, but recognizes the importance of presentation, persistence and consensus for the success of its policies . . .

Banking Institutions

There are over three thousand banks in Germany, but the three largest control about 10% of the banking business, by volume. This figure drastically understates the big three banks' role in German industrial policy. The three banks sit on the supervisory boards of seventy of the top 100 companies in Germany. They own stock in such German stalwarts as Daimler-Benz, AEG-Telefunken, and many others. Their influence over German industrial life is profound.

The Big Three—Deutsche Bank, Dresdner Bank and Commerzbank—are private commercial banks. They are the only ones considered to be 'national banks' in Federal reports. Other commercial banks are known as regional and local banks, whether or not they operate nationally and internationally. The domination of the big three is so complete in the commercial bank category that they and their formally independent subsidiaries in Berlin are listed separately in Bundesbank reports as the 'big banks' . . .

The relationship between banks and the private business sector in Germany is extremely close. It is based on many formal and informal contacts, and has generated a consensus in the private sector that banks have an important and legitimate part to play in corporate investment decisions. The banks have gained this leverage through four roles that have become a central part of private sector planning: (1) they supply the necessary funds for investment; (2) they offer export assistance; (3) they own and control a large number of shares in private corporations; and (4) the bank managers hold a large number of supervisory board seats. The first two roles are relatively noncontroversial and familiar to the American system, but both are altered somewhat by conditions peculiar to Germany.

Providing venture capital is different for banks in the Federal Republic because companies rely on loaned capital to a much greater extent than in the United States. This reliance is caused by the lower average return to capital and less-developed stock market in the Federal Republic. Therefore banks have more control over, and a greater interest in, the plans of a corporation than would otherwise be the case.

The advice on exports given by banks is magnified in importance by the greater export-dependence of West German corporations. Twenty-five percent of Germany's national production is ear-marked for export, and many of these products come from medium-sized firms. There is, therefore, a need for more sophistication in international transactions than most companies of that size can afford. The banks, particularly the large commercial and savings banks, offer help in this area, and companies rely on them to do so.

Both the financing and export dependence of many German companies bring them into a closer relationship with their banks than is traditionally the case in the United States. Banks and businesses defend these arrangements as both necessary and positive. However, critics of the banks' power point to the collusive aspects of these policies, and ask if such a small group of people should have as much influence on investment decisions throughout the country as is exercised by bank executives.

The investment and export roles of banks, combined with their direct participation in decision-making, lead to a relationship between banks and businesses that is called 'house banking'. Although larger companies often deal with many banks, most medium and small sized firms concentrate all their service requests with one or at most a few banks . . .

Ownership and control of corporation stock by German banks is one of the two major differences between American and German banking practices that is coming under increasing criticism within the Federal Republic. Bank ownership of companies is an integral part of the German economic scene. The basic claim made in favor of such participations is that banks can be of greater help, and are less likely to desert German corporations, because of them.

There are four levels of participation and control: (1) there is permanent participation, which is tantamount to ownership; (2) there is stock holding; (3) there is proxy holding, which means that a customer of the bank has put stocks on deposit with the bank, and that after clearing a set of procedures, the bank can vote the stock; (4) there is loaned stock whereby one bank can lend its voting rights in stock to another bank . . .

While each of these four tiers may account for a small proportion of the shares to be voted in German companies, when they are combined, the results are startling. In 74 of the nation's largest corporations, banks voted 63% of the shares at annual meetings. The Big Three voted 35%, accounting for three-fourths of the value of all issues on the stock exchange . . .

The second area of major controversy about the relationship between banks and businesses revolves around bank directors sitting on, and often chairing, business supervisory boards. Such participation gives banking executives a direct word in the conduct of business investments, as well as providing them with detailed information on the investment plans and financial status of firms on whose boards they sit.

The boards on which bank officials sit are known as Supervisory Boards. Governance of German companies is divided between a Supervisory Board and a Management Board. Supervisory Boards deal with questions of major investments, new production techniques, new product introduction and so forth. The Management Boards govern the day-to-day business of the company.

Of the top 400 companies in Germany, 318 have bankers on their supervisory boards. There are 570 bank executives on the boards of these 318 large companies: an average of 2 bankers on each board. The domination of the big three is displayed once more in this area. The banking industry controls 145 of the 1,480 seats on the 100 largest German companies. The big three took 65% of these seats and 15 seats as board chairmen.

2   A German Case Study: AEG-Telefunken

Extract from Bill Paul, 'AEG's troubles are a lot like Chrysler's, but the solution is likely to be different', *Wall Street Journal*, 26 November 1980, p. 16.

Since many of the schemes for the rationalization of industry in Germany are directed from within the private sector, they are difficult to document. However, the rescue operation for AEG-Telefunken, a huge electronics conglomerate, attracted international attention, and the following article by Bill Paul contrasts the way the Germans handled its reorganization with the rescue of the Chrysler Corporation in the USA.

Frankfurt—AEG-Telefunken, the West German electronics concern, has a lot in common with the Chrysler Corporation. Like Chrysler, AEG has been losing money hand over fist. In the first half of this year it posted a deficit equivalent to about $100 million. That was on top of $173 million loss in 1978. And AEG has a mountainous debt, about $3·8 billion.

AEG's critics charge that most of the company's problems stem from years of bad management. They compare Chrysler's sticking with big cars after Americans started moving to smaller cars with AEG's decision to continue concentrating on such high-priced consumer goods as TVs and stereos long after foreign competition started undercutting it. AEG does much better in such basic industries as power engineering, industrial systems and telecommunications.

But while AEG and Chrysler are trying to save themselves through a corporate reorganization, there is this important difference: Chrysler asked for federal assistance in the form of loan guarantees, but AEG has been told flatly by the West German government it won't get a bailout. 'The government isn't the repair shop of capitalism', says one influential Bonn politician. 'This is a test case of private enterprise', said a major German newspaper in an editorial supporting the government's decision to keep out.

Thus, it's up to AEG's management, creditor banks and unions to come up with a rescue plan, which is expected to be announced December 4. While none of the principals is willing to talk, an outline of the plan has emerged.

The banks, led by Dresdner Bank, AEG's biggest creditor, apparently will agree to restructure the company's debt, deferring most interest payments and agreeing to give the company more operating capital. But in return, the banks will effectively take complete charge of running the company, and management will be expected to sell off large chunks, starting with consumer-products divisions. Perhaps 20,000 employees, roughly a sixth of AEG's workforce, could lose their jobs, a prospect that union leaders say they'll fight. Sources close to the company also expect heads to roll in the executive suite.

What distinguishes the AEG case from Chrysler's is the position of the banks. In Germany banks are also major stockholders in companies. While this cozy relationship has come under increasing criticism in recent years, the banks essentially retain their strong influence over the affairs of most of Germany's biggest concerns.

By contrast, US banks are simply creditors. Thus, when a company such as Chrysler gets in trouble, a banker's first thought is to protect his institution's money, even if this means the company must go bankrupt and be sold off in chunks to satisfy bank loans.

Says a West German official: 'Our bankers realize their own reputation is at stake. If they even admit that the state should step in, they raise serious questions about why they should enjoy such sweeping power in corporate boardrooms.'

In the US it's the government, by virtue of the political pressure exerted by labor unions over the prospect of lost jobs, that feels an obligation to step in when a big company gets in serious financial difficulty. To be sure, the German government could also come under pressure from the unions. But with only a 3·2% unemployment rate in Germany, compared with a 5·7% rate in the US using a different method of measurement, the German government is in a better position to withstand the political pressure. 'The same number of jobs will be lost whether or not the government steps in', says an economic spokesman for Chancellor Helmut Schmidt.

3 The Control of Financial Policy in France

Extract from Stephen Cohen, James Galbraith and John Zysman, 'Credit policy and industrial policy in France', from a Staff Study prepared for the US Congress, Joint Economic Committee, June 1981.

The French state is equipped with a wide array of instruments for influencing individual industrial actors. The following excerpts from a report prepared by James Galbraith for the Joint Economic Committee of the US Congress provides a brief overview of these instruments and a more detailed discussion of the funds which have recently been employed by the French Treasury for the support of industry in France.

France has a set of institutions which grew out of the long postwar reconstruction effort, an understanding of which is prerequisite to an understanding of the current evolution of French economic policy. These institutions include the Planning Commission, various credit institutions and the Treasury itself. In the past ten years, however, their role has changed. Some have been restructured, and the influence of others, notably the Plan, has been dramatically reduced. Others have evolved in ways compatible with the new direction of French economic policy.

The Commissariat Général du Plan is the best known of the institutions of French reconstruction. The Plan was established immediately after the War, partly at the urging of the American administrators of the Marshall Plan, in order to establish coordinated five-year objectives for the reconstruction of France's devastated basic industries. Under the leadership of Jean Monnet, a simple but ambitious set of goals—for an average increase of 25 percent in basic industrial capacity—was established and substantially met in the First Five Year Plan.

Over the succeeding decades, the Plan grew both more sophisticated and less influential. A bent for econometric analysis reduced its audience, but did not permit it to keep pace with the growing complexity of the French economy or to adapt to its increasing openness to international markets. As of the mid-1970s, the Plan was essentially cut out of the day-to-day process of decision-making on French economic policy. It has survived, however, as a think-tank institution, and may be regaining influence as the focal point for thinking about the long-term structural adjustment of the French economy.

The instruments by which the objectives of the early Plans were put into effect were simple and direct. The State spent money, the State lent money, and the State owned and operated major enterprises in both the infrastructure and the final goods manufacturing sectors.

The direct budget funds of the State were channeled by the Treasury to industry and to subsidized housing—generally multi-family, moderate and low-income apartments—by the Economic and Social Development Fund (FDES). In addition, the State directly sponsored the expansion and/or modernization of the large nationalized industries, particularly the railroads (SNCF), the Parisian mass transit authority (RATP), and Electricité de France (EDF). In the competitive sector, a world-class automobile company (Renault) and a respectable aerospace industry were among those that grew up in the post-war years under state ownership or supervision (though not necessarily both).

In addition to direct subsidies, the post war French planners established or refurbished a series of specialized credit institutions to ensure the access of priority industries to credit at reasonable cost. The Crédit National was established to serve industrial needs, the Crédit Foncier to serve housing, and the Crédit Hôtelier to finance the modernization of the French hotel trade. All are parapublic joint stock companies which operate under the close supervision of the Treasury in the Ministry of Finance. In addition the largest private commercial banks were nationalized in 1946, and they cooperated with the state's objectives in reconstruction finance. The Banque Française du Commerce Extérieur (BFCE) took on part of the mission of financing the expansion of French exports. Thus, in the early years, the State either supplied, or directly controlled, a major fraction of available capital funds.

To moderate inflation, and also to prevent monopolistic pricing practices, a comprehensive system of price controls was kept in place and intermittently enforced from 1946 until 1976.

Interest rates were also controlled. Rates in the bond market were administered directly by the Treasury. The interest rate on bank credit was manipulated by the Bank of France, through its power to rediscount eligible commercial paper at fixed discount rate and thereby to control the marginal cost of funds to the banks. In general, interest rates were kept low and relatively stable from the 1940s until the late 1960s.

Its post-war economic institutions equipped the French State with the tools for a comprehensive strategy of promoting growth. The gamut of French industry (steel, shipping, aerospace, housing, telecommunications, computers, railroads and electricity) all benefited from state support and a state-created environment of steady increases in demand. There were also serious errors of economic judgement: The luxury liner *La France*, the Aerotrain, *Concorde* and La Villette (a mammoth and misplaced slaughterhouse in Central Paris) were among the showpieces of French industrial policy that were commercial or technical failures. But, in general, the policy was a success, which assured that resources were available for growth. France had the second highest average growth rate and the second highest standard of living among major European countries by 1970. French growth of real GNP averaged 5·6 percent from 1954 to 1970, compared with 5·7 percent for Germany and 2·8 percent for Britain . . .

The Treasury

The overseer of selective credit policy is the Treasury, the 'temple within the temple' of the Ministry of Finance.

The structure of the Treasury provides a bureaucratic road map of French financial and credit policy. There are three basic divisions: International, Money and Finance, and Investments and Participations. Roughly speaking, the Money and Finance division supervises the broad-gauge instruments of credit policy, including monetary targeting, the *encadrement*, stock and bond market policy, housing policy and the management of the public debt. The Investments and Participations division directs the narrow-gauge intervention of the Finance Ministry in the affairs of particular firms.

The activities of the Investments and Participations Division (IP division) of the Treasury mirrors the involvement of the French state as a whole in industry. Thus, they fall into two basic categories: management of crises in declining sectors, and the promotion of industrial exports and energy substitutes. The IP division in essence provides entrepreneurship for both activities, and a small but often critical portion of the funding. Crisis management, particularly in the steel industry, will be discussed a little later on. Industrial promotion—the schumpeterian aspect of the French state—is managed through a versatile and flexible maze of offices and committees whose effectiveness stems precisely from their rapid adaptability to specific problems. The maze can be broken into four components.

First, the IP Division supervises a range of institutions dedicated to private sector industrial finance. These include the specialized intermediaries in the Treasury's sphere: the CDC, the CN, the CNCA and the BFCE. There are also fifteen Regional Development Societies (SDRs), with a total capitalization of about 400 million francs, which

are devoted to financing small and medium enterprises. And there are a set of local institutions, known as *Instituts de Participation*, which exist to provide a regionally based source of capital to the private sector. Eventually there will also be fifteen such institutes.

Second, the IP division acts as the General Secretariat of three interministerial committees concerned with capital formation and economic development. These are the Special Industrial Adaptation Fund (FSAI), the Interministerial Committee for the Development and Support of Employment (CIDSE), and the Committee for the Orientation and Development of Strategic Industry (CODIS).

FSAI was created in 1978 to promote investment in depressed regions, particularly those hardest hit by the crises and employment attrition in the steel and shipbuilding industries. It has been responsible for 3·0 billion francs in government assistance to industry in such regions, half in direct capital grants and half in a special type of 'participation loans'. Under this arrangement, the government's assistance counts as an additional equity, and the payback is divided between an part that is fixed and a part that is dependent on the performance of the firm.

CIDSE was created in 1979 to help provide additional capitalization for successful firms, particularly exporters, and so to fill a perceived gap in the structure of state assistance to industry. The state will match private equity placements with participative loans on a one-for-one basis. Officials estimate that thirty to forty new loans are made each month, with the total over the first year or so of the program coming to 500 million francs. The participative loans go mainly to smaller enterprises, with an average loan size of about one million francs. Administration is handled by the Crédit National, Crédit Hôtelier, and the SDRs, with review of the completed dossiers entrusted by CIDSE to the IP division of the Treasury.

CODIS also dates from 1979. Like CIDSE, it is an interministerial committee concerned with succeeding or potentially successful smaller exporting firms. Its specific purpose is the promotion of six 'industries of the future', which have been identified (in the formation of the Eighth Plan, and elsewhere) as potential areas of significant export growth. CODIS operates without a budget. It serves as a coordinating, facilitating and red-tape-removing instrument, whose power stems from its affiliation with the Treasury. CODIS can mobilize all necessary administrative channels on behalf of the favored sectors, and it can spearhead the organization of financing for them as well.

Third, the IP division of the Treasury coordinates the investment activities of the behemoths of nationalized French industry in the non-competitive sector: Electricité de France, the national railways (SNCF), and the Paris regional transit network (RATP).

Fourth, and finally, the IP division oversees the foreign investment activities of French firms.

In the implementation of its policies, the IP division of the Treasury can count on close collaboration with the special intermediaries and on unimpeded access to several sources of finance. The latter include the FDES, which gets its funds from the checking accounts and national savings bank operated by the post office, and the CDC, which (as noted above) receives most of the moneys deposited in the savings banks. These moneys provide the Treasury with a bargaining chip in its relations to industry, and their use helps catalyze the cooperation of the commercial banking sector in large financial undertakings.

To summarize: The evolution of financial and credit policy under the Barre government goes far beyond the introduction of monetary targets and the institution of a monetarist anti-inflation program. There has been in addition, or perhaps instead, a substantial strengthening of selective mechanisms to affect the flow of credit on two levels. First, the encadrement and associated instruments have been perfected to assure state control over the aggregate quantity and composition of capital formation and over the broad sectoral outlines of bank lending. Second, an array of specific selective credit institutions, under Treasury control, have been developed to facilitate intervention in microeconomic planning and decision-making in a virtually comprehensive range of contexts.

4 Rhetoric and Reality in Recent French Industrial Policy

Extract from Paul Lewis, 'France aims for tomorrow's markets: the international economic survey', *New York Times*, 8 February 1981, p. 31.

The 1976–81 period was a difficult one for many European nations but it was especially important for France because in these years a government under Prime Minister Raymond Barre appeared to take the first steps toward dismantling the *étatiste* state apparatus built up in the preceding three decades. In the following article Paul Lewis examines M. Barre's record which suggests that there were underlying continuities behind the changes in emphasis of that period.

At a time when other Western industrial economies are stuck in the doldrums, France is staging an economic reorganization that it hopes will revitalize its industries by making them more competitive.

For the past four years, Prime Minister Raymond Barre has been coaxing French businessmen out from under the state's protective umbrella. He has scrapped France's centuries-old tradition of price controls, refused to rescue uncompetitive manufacturers by devaluing the franc, and is encouraging companies to trim their work forces to more efficient levels.

But he has not completely withdrawn the Government from participation in the economy. The Prime Minister is the first to say that those who describe him as a classic free market liberal have misunderstood completely.

By ending price controls and easing the Government ban on dismissing workers, Mr Barre has made French companies richer and sleeker. Corporate profits jumped a healthy 22·5 percent in 1978, 16 percent in 1979 and are expected to have repeated the increase in 1980. Last year, while US productivity declined, productivity in France grew by 6 percent.

While France could not escape the impact of two oil price explosions, it has gotten off more lightly than many other countries. Unemployment, at 1·5 million, or 6 percent of the work force, is on the high side by European standards. At the same time, with an economic growth-rate of 1·8 percent in 1980, France was close to the top of the European league, and this year's anticipated 1·2 percent growth contrasts favorably with the stagnation widely foreseen for West Germany, the traditional engine of growth.

Although getting inflation into single figures in 1980 was not accomplished, the French franc has become one of Europe's strongest currencies despite a 13 percent rate of price increase. And while France had an oil-swollen trade deficit of $12 billion last year, France's exports have climbed 30 percent since Mr Barre took office.

Mr Barre's policies have not made him popular; quite the opposite. But the French business community has come to trust and respect him. After four years in office, he is now the longest-serving French Prime Minister since General de Gaulle came to power, save for Georges Pompidou.

What has fascinated most foreign observers about the Barre program, however, is less its immediate impact on the economy's performance than the way the Government is trying to steer its newly liberated companies toward areas where it thinks growth will lie.

As France's traditional heavy industries, like steel, shipbuilding and bulk textiles, recede before their young third world rivals, the Government has selected six new 'strategic' growth areas in which it plans to invest $25 billion over the next five years. They are tele-communications, microelectronics, electronic office equipment, nuclear power, aerospace, biotechnology and undersea research.

Slowly, the Barre Government is maneuvering French companies into position for the coming world race to dominate these new, high-technology sectors: Companies are merged, new groups created, subsidies and state orders are dangled, advanced technology is bought from abroad, and foreign rivals are generally kept out.

Raymond Barre, far from being the 19th century free market liberal he is often depicted as, is indulging in the old game of trying to 'pick industrial winners'. Whether he will succeed is a matter of speculation, but economists and business leaders here point to two factors they feel will play a large part in determining the outcome.

First, many of the companies on which the Government is now lavishing attention are unsuccessful ones, like Saint-Gobain-Pont-à-Mousson, CII-Honeywell Bull and Hachette. The proven winners of French industry, such as

Michelin, Moulinex and Peugeot, traditionally make few calls on the Government's generosity.

Secondly, after four years with Mr Barre at the helm, the great mass of French companies still do not feel confident enough to plow back their newly increased profits into new investment. French industrial investment is lower today than in 1973 and below the Western average.

In a bid to end the trend, Prime Minister Barre placed $1·25 billion a year in new investment incentives over the next five years in this year's budget. Many analysts feel that the success of his economic revolution will depend on industry's reply.

5   The Eighth Plan and the Role of Planning in France

Extract from Jean Boissonnat, 'The planning syndrome', translated from *L'Expansion*, 17 October 1980, p. 5.

The most prominent feature of French economic policy-making in the postwar period has been their system of indicative economic planning. Like many facets of economic policy, however, the plan had an importance that was as symbolic as material. In the following article Jean Boissonnat documents the limitations of the most recent plan and examines the symbolic role which partially accounts for the planning system's longevity.

When one reads the proposal for the Eighth Plan (1981–5) which the Government has just presented to the Economic and Social Council, one wonders what justifies the existence of this text. Let us make no mistake: it is interesting, well written, full of useful information; all Frenchmen should read it, they will emerge more apprised of the realities. But it is not a Plan. Not only because it fixes no overall objective target—for neither rates of growth, nor rates of inflation, nor rates of unemployment, nor internal financial balance, nor external balance—but rather because the State itself does not enter into any commitment about how the particular objectives cited in the *programmes d'action prioritaire* are to be attained. Even these occupy only about 30 pages at the end of a document of 270. One reads there sentences as abrupt as the following: 'reduce by 20% between now and 1985 the annual consumption of alcohol per inhabitant'. How? That is a mystery.

The reality, which alone explains why hundreds of individuals—among them the best minds—have devoted thousands of hours of work to the preparation of this text, is that France has made the Plan into a syndrome. The latter belongs for ever more to our political mythology. In the same way that the pre-war Republic was known as secular, the post-war Republic has been 'planned'. The idea that this might no longer be the case is terrifying. The sweet drug of planning has become indispensable for all parties: on the left, one is a planner by principle: on the right, by

custom. The luminaries of the employers' association, of the unions and of the administration would suffer from a feeling of loss if the Plan did not exist. To sit on a commission of the Plan is to have one's power or expertise given official recognition by that one divinity which the French still venerate, after having forsaken all others: the State.

The Plan, then, performs several definite functions in French society, even if it is no longer anything but a speech in which one wraps a policy decided elsewhere. The Eighth Plan is 'Barrism'—itself only a short-term policy—explained to the French. The Plan, more than any other institution, symbolizes the osmosis, which is undeniable here, between the ruling class and the State. In so far as it can be conceptualized, it is the final bulwark of prediction beyond which it would be necessary to admit that the future is indecipherable. It provides a substitute, for better or worse, for a social consensus and grand design which are fading. The accomplishment of this task of substitution, after all, is enough to legitimate any institution.

6   Industry and the Banking System in Britain

Extract from Harold Lever and George Edwards, 'Why Germany beats Britain', *Sunday Times*, 2 November 1980, pp. 16–18.

The relatively slow rates of economic growth which Britain has experienced since World War II have inspired a great deal of concern in that country. The following is an excerpt from a series of articles in which Harold Lever and George Edwards argue that the causes for Britain's poor industrial performance can be traced back to the relationship between British industry and the banks. They provide a concise summary of the basic terms on which the banks lend to industry.

In the decade since 1966, Britain's annual improvement in manufacturing manpower productivity was 2·6 percent— by comparison with 8·6 in Japan, 5·6 in West Germany and France and 4·9 in Sweden. This represents billions of pounds of lost prosperity for Britain—the familiar litany of jobs, schools, houses and richer human choice in life.

Argument about the cause of all this has all the precision of the medieval debates about how many angels can dance on the head of a pin. Yes, the trade unions do restrict innovation. Yes, British management is weak. Yes, there may be some psychological change in the British national temperament.

Yes, if you like, believe any other bar-room theory, or last week's loftier but equally mystical and unhelpful observations of the Brookings Institution in Washington that the short-comings of Britain's economy 'lie deep in the social system' . . .

The hidden dynamic behind Britain's decline needs

setting out in figures—not particularly complex—but it can be easily characterized . . .

Many of Britain's economic ills can be traced in whole or part to the historic distortion in our credit system: the lowest rate of private sector investment in any OECD country, low output and productivity, a workforce with low wages and morale—and aggravated inflation. The average life of all plant and machinery in Britain is 35 years—almost double that of France, Germany and the USA.

This is not simply a hypothesis about what happens when credit is concentrated in certain ways. It is an observable reality.

It can be seen on the ground in Japan, Germany, France, and other countries. If investment credit is provided to industry, with little credit for consumption and government budgets, then economic growth will be high, housing will be of poor quality, the social infrastructure investments (roads, parks, sewage) will be unsatisfactory, and personal savings will be high. That is Japan.

If, at the other end of the scale, credit is provided to households and governments, while investment credit for industry is restricted, then there is a high level of public amenity and good housing—with a low-productivity industrial sector. That is Britain . . .

The difference between Britain and these other countries is that they have chosen during the 1950s and 1960s how savings are to be used for industrial, personal or government purposes and have tailored loans to that end. In Britain, the forces of history, errors of government and the conventions of the financial system have made the choice by default, providing consumption credit and inflation, and restricting investment credit and economic growth . . .

Observation of the successful post-war economies, Japan and West Germany, produces these conclusions:

(1) A much greater proportion of national product is re-invested. Britain's commercial and industrial companies' net investment is about 4 per cent of our gross domestic product in the economic engine of plant and machinery. Japan normally invests 12 per cent net (France and West Germany run at about twice the UK rate) . . .

(2) British industry has to try to raise most of its investment capital from its own profits. During the six years of 1974 to 1979, something like 70 per cent of the money for expansion came from within the industry itself. In Japan major finance comes from outside the company. The German entrepreneur is able to raise nearly three times as much money from the banks as the British.

(3) Britain's banks lend comparatively little to industry. Japan's banks provide five times more money than Britain's for private sector investment. In Japan, bank loans to business amounted to something like 15 per cent of the national product between 1974 and 1978. In West Germany, the comparable figure is 8 per cent. In Britain, it is as low as 3 per cent.

(4) Japan's industrialists have really long-term loans of 15 to 20 years. In Germany, the formal term averages seven years and in Britain the formal term averages two-and-a-half years (it is more in practice as we will discuss) . . .

(5) The league leaders in the world's productivity growth tables all have banking systems which make long-term loans to industry.

The Stock Exchange and bond market, though they make a contribution, have never provided more than a small fraction of the external funds industry requires.

There is an index to describe and document this hidden dynamic behind Britain's decline. It is the debt–equity ratio, which displays the extent to which our industry is forced to rely on raising its own money. For every hundred pounds a company borrows, the ratio says how much comes from outside the company (debt), and how much has been put up by the owners of the company (equity).

Japan's debt–equity ratio is 85, Britain's is 22 . . .

The banks' sense of security is high in our system, but it is bought at the expense of a sense of insecurity in the borrower which discourages risk-taking and expansion . . .

7 Tripartism and Producers Groups in Britain

Extract from David Marsh and Wyn Grant, 'Tripartism: reality or myth?', *Government and Opposition*, vol. 12, no. 2 (Summer 1977), pp. 195–211.

One of the concepts which has frequently been applied to British economic policy-making is that of 'tripartism'. Although David Marsh and Wyn Grant are skeptical about the applicability of that concept to British policy-making, they provide a clear elucidation of the concept in the following excerpt, as well as a discussion of its relation to 'corporatism' and an examination of the characteristics of British business and union organizations which have inspired attempts at tripartite bargaining yet have also ultimately undermined them.

Of course, as there have been many corporatist theories, so there have been many varieties of corporatist thought. Nevertheless, Schmitter's excellent review[1] of the history of corporatist thought makes it clear that corporatist theorists share an emphasis on unity, or more particularly class harmony, but differ substantially as to the role that they assign to the state in the corporatist system. Indeed Schmitter shows how the stress on harmony between classes in corporatist thought develops from its origins as a 19th century reaction against the individualism and competitiveness associated with capitalist development. The corporatist theorists believed that although labour and capital might have superficially conflicting interests they shared mutual rights and obligations. The organic unity of society is preserved if the organizations representing capital and labour are aware of these mutual rights and obligations. As Pahl and Winkler put it, 'Society is seen as consisting of diverse elements unified into one body, forming one *corpus*, hence the word corporatism. These elements are united because they are reciprocally interdependent, each performs tasks which the other requires'.[2]

There is no doubt that this notion of unity or class harmony is crucial in corporatist thought, but how is this class harmony to be obtained and preserved? On this point a sharp distinction can be found between different models of corporatism in terms of their account of the role of the state. Indeed Schmitter establishes a crucial distinction within corporatist thought between what he terms 'state corporatism' and 'societal corporatism'. He states, 'That most original and stimulating of corporate theorists, Mihail Manoilesco, provided the key distinction between two different subtypes. The one he called *corporatisme pur*, in which the legitimacy and functioning of the state were primarily or exclusively dependent on the activity of singular, non-competitive, hierarchically ordered representative "corporations". The second in contrast he called *corporatism e subordonné*, in which similarly structured "corporations" were created by and kept as auxiliary and dependent organs of the state which founded its legitimacy and effective functioning on other bases'.[3] In 'state corporatism' the state plays a directive role in the establishment of class harmony and the organizations representing the different economic interests within society are subordinate to and dependent organs on the state. In 'societal corporatism' the representative organizations are autonomous but cooperate with the state and each other because they recognize that they are mutually interdependent.

A similar distinction has been developed by Lehmbruch who distinguishes between 'liberal corporatism' and 'authoritarian corporatism'. Lehmbruch argues that the essential features of liberal corporatism are 'the large measure of constitutional autonomy of the groups involved; hence the voluntary character of institutionalized integration of conflicting groups' and 'a high degree of cooperation among these groups themselves in the shaping of public policy'[4] . . .

Indeed, tripartism might best be viewed as a sub-type of 'liberal corporatism'. In a 'liberal corporatist' state the emphasis would be on the relationships between government and a wide range of functional groups, or at least between government and all organizations that represent capital and labour. In contrast the notion of tripartism emphasizes the relationship between government and the peak organizations. Nevertheless 'liberal corporatism' and tripartism do appear to be closely related and by examining how far Britain has developed a tripartite system of economic and industrial policy making we hope to throw considerable light upon arguments about the development of 'liberal corporatism' in Britain.

We hope that we have established a link between corporatism and tripartism. However, as yet we have offered only a cursory explanation of the notion of tripartism. Before we can examine the empirical problems we have set ourselves it is essential that we give a more precise formulation of that term.

It seems to us that an ideal-typical tripartite system would have a number of distinct characteristics:

(1) Obviously it would involve three parties, here the government, the CBI and the TUC, interacting to evolve a commonly agreed industrial and economic policy within both formal and informal settings.

(2) The system would be underpinned by a basic consensus: whilst there would be disagreement between the parties, such disagreement would be limited in its character and therefore capable of resolution. In particular, the parties involved would be willing to set aside any fundamental disagreements about ultimate goals in order to arrive at agreed solutions to specific problems. Without such a consensus there would seem to be little chance of arriving at policies which would be acceptable to all parties.

(3) An effective tripartite system would not only involve elite accommodation. Such a system would involve the acceptance of decisions as authoritative by both leaders and members of the groups involved. The leaderships would have to be willing and able to persuade their memberships to comply with the agreed policies. Without acceptance of the policies evolved under such a system by the memberships of the groups, the chances of successfully implementing policy would be slight.

(4) The three parties would each have similar degrees of influence on the evolution of policy, otherwise the system would be tripartite in name but not in effect. If one or two parties became dominant, then not only would the term 'tripartism' be a misnomer, but also the disadvantaged party or parties would feel under no obligation to accept the agreed policies.

If these can be agreed as the main characteristics of a tripartite system, how far do we have a tripartite system in Britain? . . .

In particular, it is important to establish whether the groups involved are sufficiently representative, well organized and in control of their memberships to operate as component parts of a genuine tripartite system.

Both the CBI and the TUC are large interest groups with good access to the government. There are over 130 unions affiliated to the TUC and the latest available figures show that TUC membership is over 11 millions. The TUC estimate that about fifty per cent of the working population is unionized. These figures are impressive when compared with those for other major European countries. The CBI represents businesses who employ over 10 million people, one half of the total outside central and local government.

As Lord Watkinson has emphasized, the CBI 'primarily revolves at present around the pivot of the one hundred top manufacturing companies'. Indeed, approximately fifty per cent of the total income from the CBI comes from member companies in the top five hundred of *The Times* list of one thousand companies . . .

Overall both organizations have substantial memberships which is one of the reasons why each has good access to government. Government can view them as representing important interests within society. Each group is a member of a large number of advisory bodies and is regularly consulted by departments on all major issues which concern it. In addition these two groups are the only ones which enjoy continuing access at the Cabinet level. Strong memberships and good access might be taken to indicate that these groups are both representative and capable of becoming pillars of a tripartite state. However, both organizations have significant weaknesses.

Obviously, neither the CBI nor the TUC is fully representative of the interests which they purport to represent to government. The TUC has only about fifty per cent of the employed population in membership and no decision taken by the TUC General Council is binding on individual member unions. It is true that the TUC, through the operation of Rules 11, 12 and 13, can notionally exercise considerable influence over its membership in that it can demand to be informed in advance of any major impending wage claims and stoppages involving large number of workers, and can prevent further action until other means of settlement have been tried, but it can in reality do nothing to prevent determined dissident unions from proceeding with their intended courses of action. Dissident unions can be expelled by a vote of the whole congress, but the TUC is reluctant to use this sanction. Even if a union is expelled, the TUC will be unable to prevent it from taking strike action or from receiving unofficial support from other workers.

The TUC, then, cannot ensure that the leadership of individual unions acts upon General Council decisions. At the same time, the nature of British trade unions has changed considerably in the last two decades so that the individual union leadership cannot be sure that its member-ship will act upon *its* instructions. Indeed, as Fox stresses, 'Britain has the strongest semi-independent shop-floor union organisation in the world; a fact which obliges us to formulate propositions about corporate control with some care, in so far as they apply to the trade unions'. Of course, at any given time, the trade union movement may be more or less unified and the TUC may be more or less able to persuade its members that a particular policy line is advantageous. However, the TUC's financial resources are limited compared with its smaller European counterparts and the staff of Congress House is only around a hundred strong with thirty officials in the TUC's regional offices. The staff of the TUC is not really large enough to perform the range of tasks with which they are involved.

We have discussed the CBI's internal divisions in an earlier article and it would be repetitious to examine them in detail here. However, some new developments require emphasis. The organization's position in relation to the nationalized industries has been changed by the formation of a separate group from the chairmen of the state industries (the so-called 'Group of 21') and by the resignation from the CBI of the Post Office, the largest employer among the nationalized industries. Moreover, the CBI has encountered increased competition from three reinvigorated organizations, the Association of British Chambers of Commerce, the British Institute of Management and the Institute of Directors. There can be little doubt that these developments have weakened the CBI's position. It is also important to re-emphasize that the CBI is an organization which represents industrial capital; although City institutions are members, this is primarily for liaison purposes, and the CBI cannot claim to represent finance capital.

Notes to Documents, Chapter 2

1 Schmitter (1974).
2 Pahl and Winkler (1974), p. 7.
3 Schmitter (1974).
4 G. Lehmbruch, 'Consociational democracy, class conflict and the new corporatism', paper presented to IPSA Round Table on Political Integration, Jerusalem, 1974, pp. 1–2; see Lehmbruch (1979a).

3

States and Unions: From Postwar Settlement to Contemporary Stalemate

STEPHEN BORNSTEIN

The past decade has seen a proliferation of studies—largely within Marxist scholarly circles, but also among sociologists and political scientists of other orientations—concerning the nature, functions and development of the state in capitalist society.[1] The principal focus of the debate has, not surprisingly, concerned linkages between the state and the dominant class, the bourgeoisie. Sometimes at the level of abstract, theoretical reflection and less frequently at the level of concrete, empirical analysis, scholars have attempted to elucidate the ways in which the state is dependent, in its personnel, its policies and its modes of operation, on the capitalist class and the extent to which the state is a *capitalist* state.

In the discussion of the dependence, autonomy, or 'relative autonomy' of the state, one critical aspect of the class nature of the state has been seriously neglected—the relationship between the state and the other major class in capitalist society, the working class. How significant is the variety in state–working class relations in liberal-democratic capitalist societies? How significant are such variations for the character of class relations and the class content of state policy? As these questions illustrate, a comprehensive understanding of the capitalist state must include an analysis of the interactions between the state and the working class. Such an analysis is a vast undertaking. But even the narrower subject of the relationship between the state and one of the principal organizational expressions of the working class in capitalist societies, the trade union movement, has remained largely unexplained, despite its obvious importance.

More than other forms of working-class organization, such as political parties, unions involve the daily, universal experiences of working-class men and women. Even where they have been suppressed for years or denatured in form, unions tend to spring back into existence as soon as external circumstances permit—as the experiences of France less than a decade after the bloody repression of the Commune or of contemporary Poland demonstrate. The immediate sphere of action, industrial relations, constitutes, moreover, a central nexus of class conflict in democratic capitalist societies where the forms and niceties of parliamentarism have, for the most part, emptied political life of all but the verbal residues of class struggles (Anderson, 1976). Unions not only serve as vehicles for the expression of conflict by the working class in the narrow sense of the term (blue-collar workers), they also function as bridges between the traditional blue-collar working class and other strata of the dependent employed population, notably office workers, technical employees, teachers, and the like, who constitute a growing proportion of the working populations of Europe (Bain, 1970; Blackburn, 1967).

That the relations between such organizations and the state constitute an important field of interest, cannot be denied. The literature on this subject is, however, like that on the broader topic of state–working-class relations, disappointingly limited. Neither the traditional Marxist literature on unions, nor the traditional non-Marxist (Weberian, pluralist and elitist) treatments, are of very much use to students interested in state–union interaction. In the non-Marxist social sciences, a variety of subdisciplines has emerged to study unions and industrial relations—labor economics, industrial sociology, industrial relations research and labor history (see Shalev, 1980). Very little of the literature produced in these subdisciplines addresses the kinds of broad theoretical and comparative questions raised in the debates on the nature and functions of the state. Mainstream social scientists have examined in great detail and often with considerable sophistication such issues as the influence of unions on wage levels and labor market structures, the nature of collective bargaining systems and industrial relations practices, and the operation of unions as complex, bureaucratic organizations or as participatory political associations. Very few, however, have attempted to integrate these elements into a global consideration of the role of trade unions within the political economies of advanced industrial societies.

Marxists have done little better. While some scholars, particularly in Britain, have devoted considerable attention to unions and to industrial conflict, few Marxists involved in debates about the theory of the state have paid much attention to the relations between the state and unions. Many either ignore unions altogether, or follow Althusser and Poulantzas in labeling them cursorily as 'ideological apparatuses of the state' (in the case of 'reformist' unions) or as 'weapons of the class struggle' (in the rarer case of Communist-led unions) (Poulantzas, 1978a, pp. 224–38). Such an approach involves an oversimplification of the role of both radical and moderate unions. It ignores, as Leo Panitch has noted recently, the tensions involved in the actions of even the most anti-capitalist of union movements which invariably find themselves drawn into complex interaction with the institutions of the state. This approach also ignores the existence of considerable differences of orientation and action among so-called 'reformist' unions, with even the most moderate confronting organizational pressures to resist the state and oppose governmental policies.

The following pages present an introduction to the complex relationship between states and union movements in capitalist Europe. First, I shall discuss the effect of the state on institutions and practices of industrial relations and on the structures and strategic tasks of unions. How have the consequences of state intervention changed during the postwar period? How have these consequences varied from one capitalist state to another? Secondly, I shall consider the influence of the unions on the structures and processes of the state. Once again, I shall emphasize not only the general features of this impact, but also its variations over time and among capitalist societies. Throughout, I shall stress the epochal importance of the post-1974 economic crisis, and its effect on trends established in the previous periods. The Depression of the 1930s was the occasion, everywhere in the capitalist world, for major (and in the case of Germany and Austria devastating) changes in the relations between the state and organized labor. The current recession bears many similarities to the Depression. It is important to ask whether the parallel includes the relations between the state and the unions.

The Impact of the State on the Sphere of Industrial Relations

In the period prior to World War II the states of Western Europe did not, for the most part and with the exception of certain special interludes, play extensive direct roles in the sphere of industrial relations. In most of the major West European nations the state confined itself to regulating the basic framework of labor relations, legislating more or less extensively on certain aspects of work and remuneration (minimum pay, maximum hours, minimal health and safety standards), and sometimes providing labor courts for adjudication of violations of these codes as well as for mediating disputes. States differed in the extent to which they imposed legislative restrictions on the collective bargaining process, with the German state of both the Imperial and the Weimar periods standing at one pole of heavy legislative activity, and the British and Italian states occupying the other extreme, leaving many aspects of labor relations and working conditions untouched by legislation and uncontrolled by government inspection. Aside from fascist states, however, no state assumed much direct interaction with the union movement or much of an active role in structuring the labor market or orienting wage bargaining. The period of World War I constituted an exceptional interlude within this pattern. For a few years, in most of the countries involved in the fighting, industrial relations were briefly transformed, state, unions and capital becoming involved in networks of tripartite bodies for the organization of the war economy and the mobilization of domestic enthusiasm. Once the fighting was over, however, the state withdrew from most of its newly established positions in the industrial relations arena and left capital and labor to their traditional struggles (Maier, 1975).

By contrast, World War II was not followed by a comparable return to the prewar *status quo*. Rather, there occurred in most of the capitalist nations of Europe and North America, a set of important changes in the role played by the state in the economy and society. The new arrangements for the operation of Europe's capitalist economies involved two basic modifications in the role of the state. In the first place, governments assumed broad responsibility to use state power for macroeconomic management with the aim of preventing a recurrence of the Depression. In most of capitalist Europe neo-classical liberalism (according to which the market forces of supply and demand could, if left alone, adequately regulate economic life) was displaced as the conventional orthodoxy of government policy-makers by some version or other of Keynesian economics (according to which economic stability and acceptable levels of employment could be secured only if the state intervened regularly and systematically to supplement the forces of the market) (Skidelsky, 1979; Martin, 1979). Secondly, the state assumed responsibility for the provision of a broad range of social services to all citizens and not just for the poor and the disabled. Old-age pensions, unemployment insurance, medical care, child protection, family benefits and educational services—in all these areas and others the states of the major capitalist countries assumed, as had the Swedish state ten years before, a far greater obligation to assure that no citizen fell below a minimum standard of overall wellbeing. Thus, liberalism, the prevailing orthodoxy during the previous history of the capitalist state, gave way to Keynesianism in economics and to the 'welfare state' in social policy.

This general expansion of the role of the state in the economies of Western Europe did not leave the sphere of industrial relations unaffected, although we shall see that the growth of state intervention here was considerably more uneven than in other areas of social and economic life. The changes which occurred are easier to follow, moreover, if we divide the years since 1945 into three periods: (1) 1945–mid-1960s, the period during which the new political and social institutions and arrangements (the 'postwar settle-ments') came into being and flourished; (2) the period mid-1960s–73, during which economic difficulties and social unrest prompted efforts at rearranging some of the elements of the postwar settlements, including those pertaining to industrial relations; and (3) the period of severe economic crisis and political and social instability, 1974 to the present.

The Postwar Settlements and the Period of Postwar Boom

Throughout capitalist Europe the years immediately following the end of World War II saw efforts by political elites to use the power of the state to reorganize industrial relations in ways that might reduce or at least regularize industrial conflict and facilitate smooth economic growth. These efforts assumed different characters and attained very different degrees of success from country to country. Roughly speaking, the nations of Western Europe may be ranged into two groups: those such as Sweden, Austria and the Netherlands where political elites managed to transform industrial relations by means of institutional arrangements that have been called 'neo-corporatist', and those such as Britain, France and Italy where no such arrangements emerged and conflictual modes predominated. In addition, West

Germany constitutes an intermediate case which will be examined separately.

Neo-Corporatist Regimes

The most comprehensive institutionalization of industrial conflict occurred in a group of smaller states including Austria, the Netherlands and Sweden. Here, complex, centralized, hierarchically structured networks were constructed for the mediation of conflict between the national organizations of business, labor and agriculture, networks which scholars have recently dubbed 'neo-corporatist'— corporatist, to distinguish them from situations of unmediated class conflict, and neo, to differentiate them from earlier types of hierarchical group interaction found in mediaeval feudalism and in twentieth-century fascism (Schmitter, 1974; Pahl and Winkler, 1974; Panitch, 1981; Crouch, 1978; 1979; Jessop, 1979; Winkler, 1976; and Wilensky, 1976).

Although the precise contours of the institutions for class compromise established in the variour neo-corporatist political economies differed somewhat, their basic outlines were essentially similar. The unions were assigned important roles in a variety of official bodies involved in formulating and implementing state economic and social policy in return for their participation in a highly centralized system of wage determination alongside representatives of the state and of organized business. In the Netherlands top-level discussions of economic priorities and social policies were carried on in a Social and Economic Council and in an institution called the Foundation of Labor (Barbash, 1972, ch. 4; Akkermans and Grootings, 1978). Similar functions were performed in Austria by bipartite negotiations between the Chamber of Labor (an official, compulsory body linked to the unions) and the Chamber of Commerce, while, in Sweden, peak-level negotiations were carried on between the leaders both of the unions (LO, the blue-collar workers' organization, and TCO, the white-collar union, being the two most important) and of the Employers' Federation (SAF), and within a special body called the National Labor Market Board. In each case wage agreements were to be reached, first, at the national level on the basis of targets and criteria coordinated with long-term state policies, and then transmitted downwards through a series of inter-locking agreements at the level of industrial branches, regions, localities and individual plants.

The role of the state in these arrangements was sometimes a concealed rather than a direct one. Thus, in Sweden the state was ostensibly absent from the wage negotiations and from the other so-called 'cooperative agreements' between the unions and capital establishing national policy on such matters as safety at work, vocational training and industrial rationalization (Barbash, 1972, ch. 1). Indeed, the whole pattern of cooperative policy-making in Sweden was established by the Basic Agreement of 1938, in which the state was not involved (Korpi, 1978; van Otter, 1975). In reality, however, the state was no less involved in neo-corporatist arrangements in Sweden than in other similar countries: labor and capital negotiated the Basic Agreement after a period of intense industrial conflict when they were confronted with a threat of legislation by the recently established Social-Democratic regime. Indeed, all subsequent agreements depended on legislative enforcement and administrative coordination by the state. In particular the centralized coordination of wages was made possible by the state's acceptance of a major role in operating a vast network of manpower institutions whose establishment was demanded in the early 1950s as a precondition of its continued operation of the 'coordinated wage bargaining' which was crucial to the prevention of inflation (Barbash, 1972; ch. 2; A. Martin, 1979).

The effects of such neo-corporatist transformations on industrial relations and on the union movement were extensive. The pattern of industrial relations was transformed. The determination of wages and of the conditions of work was, to a great extent, removed from the hands of local bargainers and shifted upwards toward the central organizations of labor, capital and the state. When taken together with the growth of the welfare state and of the so-called 'social wage', this centralization of collective bargaining effectively transferred much of the struggle over income distribution between capital and labor into the arena of the state. As a result, as Douglas Hibbs has pointed out, one of the principal causes of strike activity by shopfloor and local union groups was eliminated and the rate of strikes thereby sharply reduced (Hibbs, 1978; see also Korpi, 1980b). Strike rates in Austria, Sweden and Holland have, as **Document 1** reveals, been extremely low throughout the period since 1950. Industrial relations in these countries became a highly centralized and regularized activity with periods of intense bargaining alternating with long spells of comparative quiet.

The impact on the union movements of these countries was also substantial. Their status as semi-official organizations, sanctioned by the state and sharing some of its functions and authority, combined with legislative protection of union rights, spurred rapid expansion of the already-large union movements. As **Document 2** suggests, during the first fifteen postwar years, the density of union membership in both Sweden and Austria increased markedly. The Dutch union movement remained stable in terms of the non-agricultural laborforce, but gained substantially in its coverage of the laborforce as a whole as workers shifted out of agriculture into industry. The unions also underwent important internal changes as power within them was transferred away from local and regional offices toward central headquarters, and within the latter from part-time and 'political' leaders toward paid experts and, in particular, toward specialists in economics. Finally, union officials at all levels and all types (both experts and 'political' leaders) tended to become enmeshed in the workings of state bureaucracies and semi-official consultative bodies and to become increasingly distant from union members and from traditional union activities (Zoll, 1978; R. Martin, 1978). This process had both advantages and disadvantages for the unions as organizations. On the one hand, it facilitated the management of incomes policies, since those responsible for negotiating wage bargains rarely had to come into contact with sources of potential rank-and-file opposition. On the debit side, however, this isolation allowed resentment to build up unheeded and, thus, produced the long-run risk of wildcat strikes against the authority of union leaderships.

Why was it that industrial relations in these countries assumed 'neo-corporatist' forms in the immediate postwar period (even earlier in Sweden) and what permitted the continuation of neo-corporatist patterns during the following two decades? The union movements in Austria, the Netherlands and Sweden shared a number of important traits. They were, to begin with, large movements organizing comparatively high proportions of the working population, as an examination of the table of comparative union densities in **Document 2** will reveal. The union movements in all three countries were, moreover, well-organized, well-staffed bureaucratic bodies possessing, by comparison with other national union organizations, considerable financial and human resources (Headey, 1970). In all three cases, furthermore, the union movements were appropriately structured for effective, coordinated action at the national level. First, the unions were all highly centralized with financial resources, personnel and decision-making authority concentrated in central leadership elites. Secondly, each union movement was composed either of one principal national peak organization (the Austrian ÖGB, for example), or of several such bodies with a long history of cooperation or peaceful competition unmarred by extreme conflicts of ideological orientation or political approach (in contrast to the extremely competitive and conflictual situation among union organizations in France and Italy, for example). In particular, none of the union movements contained a strong Communist component, so that they could all avoid the divisive impact of Cold War politics on union movements elsewhere.

In addition to these features of the unions, we should also note a number of traits of capital, of the state and of the national economies that appear relevant to the success of neo-corporatist mechanisms of class cooperation. In all three countries capital was highly organized into national peak organizations possessing many characteristics in common with the unions, notably, size, resources, centralization of authority and the absence of debilitating interorganizational rivalries. Moreover, the ideological orientation of business and its approach to labor is every bit as significant as its organizational features. Neo-corporatism does not appear possible without 'progressive' attitudes on the part of capital on such questions as the legitimacy of unions, the right of workers to strike, and the acceptability of state intervention in economic management and welfare provision. While these attitudes dominate organized business interests in Austria, Sweden and the Netherlands, they are notoriously absent in many other European countries.

The state, too, seems to share a number of traits in all countries that developed neo-corporatist structures at this time. In all cases the state was distinguished by a long tradition of welfare activities, even during the liberal era, as well as by the existence of efficient, centralized bureaucratic structures. In all three cases, again, the state enjoyed a special sort of linkage with organized labor. In Sweden, as in the other Scandinavian countries, this linkage was provided by the relationship between the social democratic party that dominated the state while maintaining a dense network of structural, financial, personal and ideological ties to the unions. In Austria and the Netherlands ties between the state and the unions were more complex and may best be categorized as 'consociational'. In these two countries, as in other small European societies which are split up into multiple linguistic-cultural-religious communities, political power—in both the governmental parliamentary arena and the state administrative machinery—was parceled out, according to compli-

cated consensually established proportions, among the various political parties. Each party was connected to its own linguistically culturally religiously based affiliates in various segments of civil society: business, youth, women, athletics and, most important from our perspective, labor (Lijphart, 1969; Lehmbruch, 1979a; McRae, 1974). These close connections between the state and the unions seem crucial in facilitating the regular and highly consensual communications between the state and union leaders required to make neo-corporatist bargaining work.

Finally, the national economies in our three cases shared several important traits. All three economies were strong and highly competitive, with traditions of high productivity and high wages. They were also economies that were highly dependent on exports, lacking populations large enough to permit the optimum scale of industrial production based on domestic markets alone. This export dependence of the industrial sector rendered their entire economies highly vulnerable to international competition and highly sensitive, therefore, to the impact of cost inflation on export prices.

Conflict-Based Regimes

If we turn now to those countries where these preconditions were absent and neo-corporatist mechanisms not possible, the efforts of political elites to reorganize industrial relations in the immediate postwar period were considerably less successful. In Britain, France and Italy the state was unable to bring strike rates down substantially from high prewar levels or to develop effective institutions for controlling wages. This is not to say that industrial relations in these countries were not affected by changes in the role of the state resulting from the postwar settlements. First, much as in the previous group of countries, the higher levels of employment sustained in the postwar period in Britain, France and Italy by the Keynesian intervention of the state contributed to a tightening of labor markets and a strengthening of the bargaining power of the unions. Secondly, the expansion of public services resulting from the growth of the welfare role of the state made the state into an employer of labor— primarily white collar, but blue collar as well—on an unprecedented scale. The same was true of the nationalizations, for example, of coal and steel in Britain or the Renault automobile firm in France, which brought large numbers of industrial workers into the employ of the state. This growth of public sector employment facilitated the growth of union memberships, since the state (particularly in the conditions of postwar socialist and communist participation in government) was far more ready to accept unionization of its employees than was private industry. In addition, the growth of the public sector and of public-sector unionism contributed to a shift in internal power configurations within national union movements just as much in France, Britain and Italy as in the neo-corporatist countries. Whereas in the prewar years the union movements had been dominated by the large, blue-collar private sector industrial unions, there now began a shift in influence in the direction of public employees' unions in general, and white-collar unions in particular (privately employed white-collar workers did not join unions as readily as government workers). Even within old industrial federations, such as the French and Italian metalworkers' organizations, locals representing workers in nationalized firms played an increasing role, and their distinctive orientations toward union strategy (deriving as they did from relations with a public rather than a private employer) began to affect the approach of their unions.

Thirdly, the states in all three countries acted to introduce legislation protecting union rights and improving the position of workers and union organizers within the workplace. This was partly no doubt because the state's new role as an employer gave it a highly visible, direct role in industrial relations, but also, more obviously, because of the new influence of left- and reform-oriented political parties in the governments of the immediate postwar period. Labour ruled as a majority government in Britain during 1945–51, while in France and Italy not only Socialists, but Communists as well, participated in the coalition governments that ruled during 1944–7.

In France, for example, the new constitution of the Fourth Republic enshrined the right of unionism and collective bargaining, and the same guarantee was provided in Italy. In Britain the Labour government made 'joint consultation' between unions and management compulsory in the public sector and repealed a 1927 law that had inhibited the organizing and political activities of the unions and of their national organization, the TUC (Clegg, 1978; Aaron and Wedderburn, 1972).

These changes aside, the patterns diverged sharply from those of the neo-corporatist regimes. Efforts to effect more substantial changes in the structure of the union movements, or in the institutions of collective bargaining, proved unsuccessful. In Italy an attempt was made with the encouragement of the state to reconstruct the union movement along unitary lines rather than on the prefascist basis of multiple religiously and politically constituted confederations. This attempt at institutional innovation proved a failure: conflicts between communists, socialists and Catholics within the unified CGIL (Confederazione Generale Italiana del Lavoro), exacerbated by the emergence of the Cold War and by American meddling, led to the resumption of the old pattern of three separate confederations by 1949 (Horowitz, 1963, chs. 5, 6; Lange and Vannicelli, 1982). The less ambitious effort at union unity in France—the Catholic CFTC (Confédération française des travailleurs chrétiens) refused to dissolve itself in 1944 and join communists and socialists in a united CGT (Confédération générale du travail)—had collapsed in similar circumstances even earlier. In Britain in the same period considerable pressure was exerted on the TUC (Trades Union Congress) by the Labour Party to modernize and rationalize its internal structures by replacing the welter of craft, local, regional and even plant-specific unions affiliated to it by an industry-by-industry approach along American (and now German) lines. This initiative came to naught, as it was rejected as desirable but impracticable by a special committee of the TUC (Clegg, 1978; Panitch, 1976).

So far as bargaining systems were concerned, reform efforts by the three states met with equally meager results. In Britain the traditional patterns of industrial relations were left pretty much alone. Neither the Labour government of 1945, nor the Conservatives who followed them during 1951–64, sought to alter the traditional patterns and structures of Britain's unusual industrial relations system—decentralized bargaining at the branch, regional and plant levels; competitive, highly fragmented union organizations; comparatively little legislative regulation of the labor market; and the absence of any legal status for collective agreements. While the unions' leaders were, as elsewhere, brought into increasing involvement in a variety of state bodies (sixty by 1947 compared to only twelve in 1939), bipartite and tripartite cooperation was confined to inconsequential matters of administration and implementation. In crucial areas of policy-making, the British state was unable to create lasting tripartite institutions with real executive power. Thus, the incomes policy attempted in 1948 by the Labour government was accepted only very reluctantly by union leaders, did not bring into being special institutional arrangements and was unable to last beyond 1950 when the opposition of rank-and-file union activists scuttled the entire venture (Panitch, 1976, ch. 1; Tarling and Wilkinson, 1977). In the early

1960s, again, government efforts to secure TUC participation in an incomes policy proved unsuccessful. In 1961 the Conservative government created the National Economic Development Council (NEDC), in which top union leaders were given generous representation alongside leaders of organized business. The government's objective, behind its widely publicized concern with economic growth and planning, was to involve the union leadership in a voluntary tripartite incomes policy, in order to curb Britain's comparatively very high inflation (Panitch, 1976, pp. 47–52; Corina, 1975). Unlike the 1948 incomes policy, however, union approval for this installment did not emerge, and the NEDC remained largely ineffectual. Thus, in the first two postwar decades British industrial relations remained decentralized and conflictual with fairly high rates of strikes and inflation, which the neo-corporatist arrangements of Sweden, Holland and Austria and the non-institutionalized controls of Germany rendered controllable.

In France and Italy, too, efforts by the state to restructure industrial relations met with very little success. Attempts in both countries to encourage collective bargaining by means of legislation giving collective agreements legal status and providing for the extension of the terms of such agreements from the firms in which they were signed to other similar firms, proved ineffective. The French Law on Collective Agreements of 1950 failed to stimulate the intended wave of orderly contractual bargaining, as did a similar Italian law of 1959 (Lorwin, 1954, pp. 215 ff.; Horowitz, 1963, pp. 312 ff.). Factory councils were set up in both countries partly in response to union demands for workers' control, and partly in an effort to pacify industrial relations by establishing networks of labor-management communication outside the existing union structures. These institutions, the *comités d'entreprise* in France, and the *commissione interne* in Italy, proved of little use both because capital generally refused to accord them much authority, and because of the increasing competition among union factions for influence within them (Lorwin, 1954, ch. 14; Regalia *et al.*, 1978). At the national level, similarly, attempts were made in both countries to involve the union leaderships in corporatist tripartite bodies. However, none of these bodies was given sufficient authority over matters of importance to interest union leaders, even the moderate Catholics and socialists among them, who were not politically predisposed against such participation. Thus, the 'economic parliaments' established in both countries (the Conseil économique

et social in France, and the Consiglio Nazionale dell'Economia e del Lavoro in Italy) never acquired much significance in the policy-making process. Similarly, the intentions of the various Resistance groups in France to give the unions important influence in the economic planning system were not realized. For a variety of reasons—from opposition to corporatism by radical CGT leaders, through collusion by bureaucrats and business leaders to exclude unionists from important discussions, and the lack of sufficient expertise and resources by the moderate unions—the delegates of the unions on the various commissions of the Plan played a minor and steadily declining role in the real process of the French planning system (Cohen, 1969; Nizard, 1975).

Finally, the failure of these tripartite bodies and the radical orientation of the largest union confederations of both countries combined to vitiate any efforts, during the first fifteen postwar years, at the creation of neo-corporatist concerted income policies. As in Britain, therefore, industrial relations in France and Italy remained conflictual and uninstitutionalized and no regular mechanisms for controlling wage levels were developed.

The Quasi-Corporatist Case

The West German case of state intervention in industrial relations in this initial postwar period must be considered separately. Here, the state succeeded in restructuring not only the industrial relations system, but the union movement itself. Yet the resulting system, while it did succeed in institutionalizing conflict and containing inflationary pressures at least as effectively as in the neo-corporatist regimes, did so without the emergence of a central wage-determination system or the widespread implication of union officials in state policy bodies. As such, the German system may perhaps be described as 'quasi-corporatist'. The Occupation forces that administered the Western parts of conquered Germany and the nascent West German state that gradually assumed power from them found a labor movement and an industrial relations system which had been smashed by the Nazi dictatorship, total war and military defeat (Markovits and Allen, 1980; Müller-Jentsch and Sperling, 1978). Drawing on features of both the American and the British patterns, they fashioned a new union movement and a restructured industrial relations system. The union movement was created as a single federal body, the DGB (Deutsche Gewerkschaftsbund), composed of a very small number (sixteen) of highly centralized industrial unions in place of the ideologically divided, factionalized and occupationally fragmented movement of the pre-Hitler years. The collective bargaining system created in the immediate postwar period was also carefully designed to reduce the possibility of conflict. Drawing on Germany's long heritage of detailed legislative regulation of industrial matters, the new German authorities fashioned a system of bargaining in which the right to strike was carefully confined and the unions were assigned a legally enshrined role as a 'force for order' (*Ordnungsfaktor*). Bargaining, concentrated at the industrial branch level, was heavily constrained by legal restrictions requiring long-term contracts, and no-strike provisions for their duration. Union wage-pressure was restricted not only by the difficulty of striking, but also by a number of other factors: the abundant labor supply resulting from the influx of population from the East; the weakness of the union movement and, in particular, of left-wing elements in the wake of Nazi repression and war; memories, shared across class lines, of the devastating inflation of the 1920s and its destructive political aftermath; and the considerable success of the new German economy. As a result, German state elites could avoid wage inflation without having to involve union leaders in any tripartite or bipartite bodies.

German state elites thus entertained a unique set of interactions with the union movement and the labor market. In terms of legislative regulation of the labor market, they intervened extensively to structure not only the pattern of collective bargaining, but also the very form of the unions themselves. Otherwise, however, the German state was much less involved in the operations of the labor market than most other West European states. Until 1967, they not only eschewed all forms of national economic or manpower planning, but also refused to assume the standard Keynesian set of responsibilities for maintaining full employment, preferring instead to combine moderate levels of welfare provision with free-market macro-economic policies—a combination baptized 'the social market economy'.

The involvement of German unions with the institutions of the state was, thus, comparatively limited. In so far as German unions and workers did become integrated into capitalist institutions it was at the level of the firm.

A number of institutions were established that involved unions and workers in the operations of capitalist firms. The Works Constitution Law of 1952 provided for the creation of works councils in all German enterprises and for the election of one-third of

the members of all firms' boards of directors by their employees (Kassalow, 1969, ch. 9; Clegg, 1979, ch. 7). In the coal and steel industries worker participation was even more extensive, with a system of 'co-determination' (*Mitbestimmung*) whereby half of the seats on the 'supervisory board' and one of three company directors were to be elected by the employees. True, the implications of these measures for control of industrial firms ought not to be exaggerated. Even in the coal and steel sectors the provision for a 'neutral' chairman of the supervisory boards, the allotment of part of the employee seats to white-collar workers and supervisory staff, and the existence of a separate and independent 'board of managers' served to minimize real worker influence on company policy, as did the exclusion of wage matters from the purview of the works councils. The same may be said of the insistence of the Christian Democratic political leaders, who formulated these reforms in response to union demands, that the works councillors and board members elected by the workers be entirely independent from the unions. Also there is considerable evidence that German elites saw these new bodies primarily as possible vehicles for undermining the influence of the unions and for creating alternative channels of communication with the workforce (Sturmthal, cited in Kassalow, 1969, pp. 181–2).

The Mid-1960s to Mid-1970s: Years of Unrest

By the beginning of the 1950s the patterns of industrial relations and policy-making described above had become well established and the decade that followed was one of generally untroubled continuity in the political economies of Western Europe. Those countries that had managed to institutionalize industrial conflict and set up barriers to inflation enjoyed the fruits of their organizational endeavors in terms of industrial peace and rapid growth. In other European nations the absence of such neo-corporatist or German-style quasi-corporatist arrangements was sometimes lamented but not sorely missed: the extraordinary expansion of world trade that followed the war produced growth rates so high by historical standards and conditions of international competition so relaxed that state managers and political leaders in such countries as Italy and France were easily able to tolerate the comparative inefficiency of their class systems, especially since the weakness and internal divisions of the unions, the availability of large pools of surplus labor from the countryside and the absence of any political challenge from the left allowed policy-makers to keep wages down.

By the mid-1960s, however, circumstances had begun to change; the long untroubled postwar boom was coming to an end, giving way to a period of more difficult accumulation and social relations (see Soskice, 1978). Inflation, which had not seriously troubled most European economies since the late 1940s, returned as a major problem as a result of the concurrence of a number of developments: the tightening of domestic labor markets resulting from the exhaustion of readily accessible supplies of surplus rural labor and from growing shortages of various sorts of skilled labor required for the ongoing processes of industrial modernization; the growth of union bargaining strength resulting from a decade of relatively full employment and improved conditions for unioniza-tion; and international inflationary pressures resulting from conditions in the US economy. At the same time the opening up of tariff barriers resulting from the progress of European economic unification and the intensification of international competition for export markets made it increasingly difficult for European economies to tolerate inflationary price increases. Simultaneously, and partly as a component of the same process, industrial militancy at the grassroots level began to emerge after a decade or more of quiescence. The result of these developments was that policy-makers and legislators in Western Europe began to reexamine their collective bargaining systems and wage-control mechanisms in an effort to find new strategies for keeping their economies and their societies running smoothly.

The next decade would witness a wave of state intervention in labor markets and industrial relations comparable to that following World War II. This process of attempted readjustment occurred both in the neo-corporatist group of countries, and in the others, although it was in the latter group that the process appeared most frenetic. In the countries with functioning neo-corporatist institutions political elites were generally successful in devising minor adjust-ments to the institutions of wage negotiations and plant-level industrial relations that enabled them to stabilize work relations and bring inflation under control. In the other group of countries, however, the state was required to go to considerably greater lengths in its efforts to restore economic and social order.

Austria, Sweden and Holland

Beginning with the neo-corporatist group of countries the smallest adjustments were required in Austria,

where the economy was comparatively unthreatened by recession or by inflationary pressures, and where after the strikes of 1951, industrial militancy had virtually disappeared. Thus, the highly effective corporatist postwar settlement with its centralized incomes policy continued to function unaltered, except for a few minor legislative concessions to the unions. In Sweden, on the other hand, more sweeping changes in the state's approach were needed to restore stability to the workplace and to the economy. Here, beginning in the mid-1960s, the Social Democratic leadership of the state undertook a reexamination of its labor market and industrial relations policies. This reappraisal was prompted by a combination of economic difficulties beginning in 1966 (inflation, recession, and a partial decline of the cohesion of the 'coordinated wage bargaining' system administered by the unions and crucial to the non-inflationary functioning of the Swedish economy) and political problems (challenges from left-wing elements within both the party and LO along with serious setbacks in the 1966 local elections engendering premonitions of defeat in upcoming national voting) (A. Martin, 1975; 1979; van Otter, 1975).

The response of state policy-makers came in two stages. First, beginning in 1967, they enacted a series of measures on what may be called 'industrial policy', giving the state an array of tools including a state investment bank for influencing the investment decisions of private industry, establishing new state bodies to subsidize research and development, and creating new mechanisms for regional and sectoral economic planning. Alongside a series of measures reinforcing the activities of the state in the training and relocation of manpower, these changes considerably increased the intervention of the state in the workings of the market economy in general and of the labor market in particular (A. Martin, 1979). Several years later, in the wake of the wave of wildcat strikes in 1969, the Social Democrats introduced a number of significant reforms under the rubric of 'industrial democracy', bringing about considerable changes in labor-management relations in the workplace. Most significant was the Joint Determination Act of 1976, which extended collective bargaining to a wide range of questions previously considered the exclusive domain of managerial prerogative (Logue, 1980). This reform played an important role in helping the unions reassert their authority within the workplace and thus facilitated their efforts to maintain the viability of the 'coordinated wage bargaining' system.

Of the various states in the neo-corporatist group,

the Dutch had the greatest difficulty maintaining its institutions for social collaboration and inflation control. As early as 1959 the operation of the Dutch centralized incomes policy began to show signs of trouble. The system of concerted wage rounds was increasingly difficult. By 1966 the system had completely broken down, wage restraint being secured only by direct intervention of the state. Thereafter, various state efforts to reconstruct the system, including the establishment in 1969 of a set of manpower policy boards, failed to restore the consensual character that wage bargaining had previously had (Barbash, 1972, ch. 4; Akkermans and Grootings, 1978).

In those countries whose postwar settlements had included corporatist mechanisms the state—with the exception of the Dutch case—succeeded in reorganizing industrial relations so as to preserve basic class harmony in the face of the new conditions of the 1960s. In countries which had not managed to institute such neo-corporatist arrangements in the earlier period, on the other hand, political elites responded to the challenges of inflation and militancy by attempting to create corporatist institutions *de novo* in the hope of duplicating the successes of their less troubled neighbors. These efforts were rarely very successful.

West Germany
The only case of a successful transition in the direction of neo-corporatism in this period was that of West Germany. The accession of the Social Democratic Party (SPD) to a share of political power for the first time in the postwar era, in 1966, brought with it a reworking of the postwar settlement along corporatist lines. The principal change was the establishment of the system of informal incomes policy called the *Konzertierte Aktion*. Although wage bargaining remained formally unrestricted as required by the Basic Law, the state now began to issue annual guidelines for wage increases (the so-called 'orientation data') which unions and management in practice accepted as authoritative. While Germany did experience a wave of strikes in 1969, the new arrangements managed to keep inflation well under control throughout this period (Lehmbruch, 1979; Markovits and Allen, 1980; Müller-Jentsch and Sperling, 1978; Clark, 1979).

Britain, France and Italy
Elsewhere, however, the efforts of the state to 'Swedenize' their social relations and collective bargaining proved fruitless. In Britain concern among

policy-makers and political elites about the defects of the nation's industrial relations and about the problem of inflation emerged earlier than elsewhere, as part of a process of national self-examination beginning in the mid-1950s and provoked by the increasingly obvious failure of the country's economy to keep pace not only with that of the USA, but also with the rapidly expanding and modernizing economies of its continental neighbors.

In the early 1960s a succession of attempts were made by both Labour and Conservative governments to use the power of the state to restructure this system of institutions and relations. The first Labour government of Harold Wilson attempted during its stormy tenure during 1964–70 to encourage the TUC to rationalize its internal structures, to impose authority on its own members to reduce the incidence of wildcat strikes and to bring about a centralization of collective bargaining. This effort occurred in two stages: an attempt at reform by persuasion in the form of a Royal Commission on Trade Unions and Employers' Associations, known after its chairman as the Donovan Commission (HMSO, 1968); and after the failure of this enterprise to generate any substantial movement in the desired direction, an attempt to impose change by means of legislation, in the form of a Bill entitled *In Place of Strife*. The Bill was no more successful than the Commission, as the unions used their influence within the Labour Party parliamentary group to block its passage. Nor were the Conservatives, who came to power in 1970, any more successful at introducing higher levels of rationality, centralization and state regulation into the collective bargaining process. Their Industrial Relations Act requiring all unions to register with a new state agency, and making them legally and financially responsible for the industrial actions of their members, was a complete failure: massively opposed by the unions, and ignored by many industrialists and judges, the act rapidly became a dead letter (Crouch, 1979*b*; Moran, 1977).

In addition to these ill-fated efforts at rationalizing the bargaining system, British governments also sought during the 1960s and early 1970s to institutionalize industrial relations by another path— the creation of corporatist institutions. Here, again, their efforts met with little success. In the 1960s first the Conservatives and then Labour tried to bring the unions into an economic planning operation modeled on French indicative planning and to induce them thereby to endorse a voluntary incomes policy. The planning venture bore very little fruit beyond the creation of a small bureaucratic institution called the

National Economic Development Office and a network of tripartite bodies called Economic Development Committees for various industries with a peak-level council, the NEDC, at the top (Leruez, 1975; T. Smith, 1975). The incomes policy established in 1965 under the auspices of the National Prices and Incomes Board was somewhat more successful for a brief period until it, like its predecessor in the late 1940s, collapsed under the weight of union hostility and grassroots wage militancy (Corina, 1975; Panitch, 1976, chs 3–5). Thus, when inflation accelerated in the early 1970s the Conservative government lacked a mechanism for a concerted, corporatist wage policy and found itself embroiled with the TUC over this issue as well as over the Industrial Relations Act. By the mid-1970s, when the oil crisis imparted a new intensity to the crisis of West European political economies, the British industrial system remained as unregulated as ever, and the British state continued to lack appropriate means for channeling industrial conflict or controlling wages.

Similarly, during the decade from the early 1960s through the early 1970s, the French and Italian states tried persistently to transform industrial relations in response to unprecedented levels of industrial unrest. There was, to be sure, nothing that corresponded in boldness and directness of approach to the Donovan Commission's ideas on the reorganization of the basic structures of the unions and of collective bargaining or to the Industrial Relations Act's straightforward attack on union rights. Still, in a variety of ways governments in both France and Italy sought during this period to stabilize industrial relations and to institutionalize conflict in the face of challenges from rank-and-file militancy that went beyond the high inflation and endemic strikes Britain was experiencing to produce, in Italy's 'hot autumn' of 1969, an unprecedented wave of radical mass strikes, and in France's May–June 'events' of 1968—the nearest thing to a full-blown revolution ever experienced in an advanced industrial society (Dubois *et al.*, 1978).

In both France and Italy the years preceding the strike waves were marked by state efforts to create neo-corporatist channels of communication and cooperation with labor and capital, efforts that in both cases were undermined by the anti-capitalist orientation of the principal unions, the reactionary attitudes of organized business and internal divisions within the ruling coalitions themselves. In France the Gaullist state, which consolidated itself rapidly after the coup of 1958, made a series of overtures toward the labor movement with the objective of luring moderate

union leaders, especially those of the Catholic CFTC, away from the radical orientation of the dominant CGT and into collaboration with state policy-makers and capital. These moves included: the introduction of a scheme for profit sharing in individual firms that had long been one of General de Gaulle's pet projects; a widely touted 'democratization' of the economic planning process to give union representatives of labor and of other organized interests greater say in the formulation of long-term economic policy; a reorganization of the Senate, the second chamber of the National Assembly, designed to convert it into a 'functional' parliament; and an attempt to organize a 'concerted' incomes policy beginning with a 'Conference on Incomes' held in late 1963 (Ross, 1980). None of these schemes proved capable of reducing the severe tensions that characterized France's highly politicized industrial relations system and the public sector wage squeeze. A general austerity program imposed by Finance Minister Giscard d'Estaing as a substitute for the failed incomes policy simply exacerbated tensions, created a united front between the CGT and the CFDT (the renamed and de-Christianized CFTC) and prepared the ground for the wave of unrest that began in 1967 and culminated in the May–June events of 1968.

The Italian state, meanwhile, was slightly more successful in its efforts but not successful enough to head off the strike waves of the late 1960s. The venture in economic planning that emerged from the inclusion of the Socialists in a new Center–Left governing coalition never got off the ground, nor did state efforts to encourage decentralized industry and firm-level wage bargaining. The state did manage to initiate bargaining with the unions in the public sector as a result of the creation of an organization of public sector corporate management (*Intersind*), which remained separate from the Confindustria, the major confederation of Italian business (Regalia *et al.*, 1978; Lange and Vannicelli, 1982; Hayward and Watson, 1975, ch. 10). From this modest success to Swedish-style corporatist incomes policy was, however, a long step that Italian unions and especially the left-wing CGIL refused to consider.

The responses of the Italian and French states to the vast waves of militancy of the late 1960s were essentially similar in intent but rather different in outcome. In both cases the state attempted to restore order in the labor market and in the political arena, to calm unrest by granting immediate concessions to workers and inducing capital to cooperate in this strategic retreat, and then to introduce reforms in collective bargaining and social policy that would grant some of the unions' long-term demands, while, at the same time, employing the newly strengthened organizations as bulwarks of order against the tide of rank-and-file militancy. The French state had less difficulty than the Italian in regaining its control of society, but, while its reform efforts in the years between 1968 and the onset of the oil crisis did augment considerably the state's direct involvement in the sphere of industrial relations, they did very little to establish a French version of neo-corporatist cooperation to replace the traditional conflictual relations in the labor market. Beginning in the midst of the strike wave the state initiated a series of tripartite talks leading to significant agreements between capital and labor and backed up by legislative commitments by the government; such were the 'Grenelle talks' that brought a resolution to the May strikes; the negotiations in December 1968 that established a new set of union rights in the workplace and later negotiations on such issues as continuing education, supplementary pensions, and health and safety at work (Ross, 1982; Dubois *et al.*, 1978; Crouch, 1978). The attempts of the new government of Prime Minister Jacques Chaban Delmas, however, to trade these concessions for union cooperation in wage restraint in the form of long-term no-strike contracts in the public sector (the so-called *contrats de progrès*) foundered on the opposition not only of the CGT, but also of the left-wing socialists who increasingly controlled the orientation of the country's second largest and rapidly growing union, the CFDT (Bornstein, 1978; W. R. Smith, 1981).

In Italy, meanwhile, the state was not as successful in reestablishing order in either the industrial or the political arena in part because of its own political and administrative weaknesses, and in part because of the surprising ability of the unions to capitalize on the militancy of rank-and-file workers by initiating a partially successful unification of the three confederations while rapidly expanding their coverage of the laborforce, increasing their workplace organization and enhancing their general influence within Italian society and politics (Regalia *et al.*, 1978). The series of important reforms undertaken by the state in the wake of the strikes of the late 1960s—a labor code (*Statuto del Lavoro*) granting the unions both legal recognition and significant elements of control over managerial activity within the capitalist firm as well as a radical law on worker education for example—must be seen less as maneuvers by the state to institutionalize industrial relations and incorporate the unions than as victories for the unions, reluctantly conceded by an increasingly unstable governmental coalition (Regalia *et al.*, 1978; Crouch, 1978). In the Italian as in the French case, the state entered the period of the post-1974 recession more deeply involved than before in attempting to manage the labor market but no less ensured of the cooperation of the unions or even of organized business in its endeavors.

The Crisis Period

Reviewing the developments of the period from the end of World War II through the early 1970s, what generalizations can we reach about the scope for state intervention in the sphere of industrial relations in capitalist societies? It appears that the state can exercise considerable influence on the sphere of industrial relations but that, so long as it is not willing to abandon the terrain of democratic legitimation (as did the fascist regimes of the interwar years), there are distinct limits to this influence. Collective bargaining institutions and processes at the level of industrial branches or individual plants appear to be open to considerable manipulation by the state. Political elites have been able to affect in important ways the relations between employers and workers not only by legislating advantages for one party or the other, but also by wielding the apparatus of the state—courts, police, inspectors, mediators and even the army—in ways that altered the stakes and the outcomes of industrial struggles. On the other hand, attempts by political elites to use the power of the state to alter not merely the environment of collective bargaining or some of its details, but rather fundamental features of a nation's industrial relations system have been much less successful. The basic organizational and ideological features of the unions themselves have proven largely immune to direct governmental manipulation as was revealed by the failure of the British government's efforts in the late 1960s to restructure the TUC and by the inability of the Gaullist regime a few years earlier to prevent the leftward drift of the Catholic union confederation, the CFTC. Similarly, states have demonstrated very little success in bringing into existence neo-corporatist arrangements of any durability and efficacy in countries without a long tradition of such interclass cooperation and a complex set of structural and cultural preconditions. The states in capitalist Europe seem more able, however, to secure less visible but none the less significant increases in moderation among union leaders by integrating them within state bodies and semi-official organs dealing with matters less controversial than incomes policy: for instance, in such areas as industrial training, recreation, or the administration of various welfare funds and institutions (Crouch, 1979).

The current economic crisis that began with the oil shock of 1973-4 with its unprecedented combination of hyperinflation, slow and often even negative growth, extremely high unemployment and international currency and trade instability has not drastically altered the nature of the state–union relationships just described. It has, however, significantly narrowed the margin of maneuver available to political leaders in their relations with organized labor and in their operations in the labor market.

Political elites in countries with functioning neo-corporatist arrangements found that both making deals with union leaders and getting those deals accepted by union rank-and-file were much more difficult than in previous years. In Germany relations between the SPD and the union movement and especially the largest and most radical union, the metalworkers' IG-Metall, deteriorated as both leaders and followers became disenchanted with slowly growing wages, rising unemployment, intensifying industrial rationalization and the increasingly cautious fiscal, social and labor-relations policies of the government. The winter of 1978-9 saw strikes of extraordinary magnitude in major sectors of German industry, including printing and metal (Markovits and Allen, 1980). While the unions were becoming more demanding in their approach to economic and social issues, the ruling coalition of Social Democrats and Free Democrats was losing interest in the kinds of reform project being advocated by the more advanced unions and by the left wing of the SPD. Tension between party and unions focused on two reform proposals: the unions' demands for an extension of the system of codetermination at the workplace to give workers half the seats on the boards of all large companies and the proposal by the metalworkers' federation for *Investitionslenkung*, the public planning—or at least supervision—of investment decisions (Markovits and Allen, 1982). In Sweden, too, the state became considerably less amenable to the economic and social proposals of LO. The coalition of bourgeois parties that replaced the Social Democrats in power in 1976 has done remarkably little to alter the basic structures of Sweden's unique industrial relations system. It has, however, proved implacably hostile to LO reform proposals and especially to those contained in the so-called Meidner Plan. Adopted as

LO's top priority in 1976, this document proposed a qualitative increase in union economic influence as the condition for continued LO participation in the centralized wage-bargaining system and in the wage restraint required for the regeneration of industrial investment. The profits generated by new investment would not simply flow into the hands of Sweden's capitalist elite but would also serve to feed a set of new 'wage-earner funds' to be owned collectively by the workers and administered by the unions. Every year a fraction of company profits would be transferred into these funds, thus giving the unions a growing voice in national investment policies and, over the course of a few decades, majority ownership of most large industrial firms (Martin, 1979). Not surprisingly, organized business and the bourgeois parties found this scheme utterly unpalatable and campaigned against it strenuously in the elections of the late 1970s. Opposition to the Meidner Plan was not, moreover, confined to the bourgeois parties. Repeated electoral defeats and the opposition of the white-collar federation, TCO, made Social Democratic politicians increasingly nervous about the scheme and induced them to press their union allies (ultimately successfully, as we shall see below) to tone down their proposals.

In those nations lacking neo-corporatist institutions efforts to bring such institutions into existence have been multiplied as governments, facing unprecedented levels of inflation, shrinking export markets and waves of factory closures have attempted to bring union leaders into the policy-making arena in order to secure workers' consent for an inevitably unpalatable mixture of policies. Taking France, Italy and Britain as illustrations, we find that governments have managed to hold real wages down rather effectively over the medium term but have not been able to construct the sorts of institutionalized collaboration of unions with capital and the state that could make such wage restraint a smooth, reliable affair or, even more important in today's hypercompetitive international market conditions, that could make possible cooperative schemes for the industrial reconversion and selective modernization that has been given the label of 'industrial policy'.

In both Italy and Britain the opening years of the crisis witnessed the beginning of neo-corporatist development, but in neither case was anything permanent achieved. In Italy the Commnist Party moved increasingly close, in 1975-9, to taking a full share of governmental power. Concomitantly, the CGIL, the country's largest union confederation and the dominant partner in the union movement's new cooperative umbrella structures, developed a new strategy for responding to the economic crisis, a strategy called the 'Eur line' and involving a union commitment to wage restraint and an acceptance of a wide variety of austerity measures in return for a series of social and industrial reforms. This project foundered not only on employers' resistance to the radical character of some of the union demands—notably the proposals for union control over investment decisions—but also and primarily on the inability of the Communist Party to make the necessary electoral breakthrough (Regini, 1980; Lange and Vannicelli, 1982).

In Britain the establishment of neo-corporatist arrangements went well beyond the preliminary stages reached in Italy. During the early 1970s, while the Labour Party was out of office and the unions were engaged in a bitter struggle with the Conservative government of Edward Heath over its Industrial Relations Act and over its statutory wage restrictions, the two wings of Britain's labor movement worked out a plan for economic and social policy-making under a future Labour government that contained very strong neo-corporatist features, as its name, 'the Social Contract', suggests. Wages would be restrained by the voluntary cooperation of the TUC's leaders (**Document 5**). In return, the government would deliver a package of reforms in the areas of industrial relations legislation, economic policy and social policy, while offering the unions a vastly increased role in the policy process through a number of mechanisms—privileged informal access to ministries under a friendly government, regular formal consultation through the recently created 'Liaison Committee' consisting of leading members of the TUC's General Council, the Labour Party's National Executive Committee and the Cabinet, and also through union representation on official bodies of all sorts and especially on those that were to be responsible for the revamped schemes for economic planning and industrial modernization (Taylor, 1978; Bornstein and Gourevitch, 1982; and Dorfman, 1979). The electoral victory of Labour in February 1974 allowed this project to be tried out. At first it worked quite well, and it even acquired an increased corporatist flavor when its highly informal wage-moderation component was converted into a formal incomes policy in the summer of 1975. Like all earlier British attempts at incomes policy, however, the Social Contract was unable to last beyond a few years. The increasingly conservative fiscal and social policies of the government in combination with the accumulation of worker resentment and the inability of unions to impose their will on their own shop stewards and members produced an explosion of wage militancy in the winter of 1978–9. The strikes, and the stubborn and maladroit manner in which the Labour Cabinet attempted to handle them, were instrumental in undermining the authority of the government and bringing its defeat in the election of May 1979.

The present Thatcher government has abandoned Labour's strategy of state–union cooperation for a policy of direct confrontation reminiscent of, but considerably more systematic than, the approach of the Heath government during 1970–2. Prime Minister Thatcher has undertaken to reduce substantially the influence of the unions within the British political economy. Her approach contains two basic strands, one macroeconomic and the other legislative. On the macroeconomic side, the government has deliberately sought to undermine the power of the unions by sapping their strength in the labor market. First among the states of Western Europe, the British state under Thatcher has explicitly abandoned the full-employment commitment that constituted one of the pillars of the Keynesian postwar settlement. With employment levels deliberately sacrificed to a rigorous pursuit of wage and price stability, rates of business failure and unemployment have skyrocketed. Seen from the perspective of the Thatcher government's 'monetarist' philosophy, rising unemployment acts as a disciplinary force upon workers and unions, confronting them with the choice between moderate wage behavior and joblessness in a context of severely reduced state spending on unemployment relief and welfare services of all kinds (Krieger and Amott, 1982).

The unions are to be cut down to size not only by the harsh winds of the unrestrained market economy, but also by a recasting of industrial relations legislation designed to reduce their freedom of action and their powers within the workplace. The Tory attack on the powers of the unions is embodied in two pieces of legislation—the Employment Act of 1980 and the Employment Act of 1982. Taken together, the two Acts mandate some major changes in the industrial relations system: (*a*) both union officials and unions as organizations are to be legally and financially responsible for damages suffered by employers and others as a result of industrial actions deemed to be illegal; (*b*) the scope of what is to be considered illegal is to be considerably broadened to include such traditional union activities as large-scale picketing, 'secondary' strikes (sympathy strikes or strikes against companies supplying the original company in the dispute) and politically motivated strikes such as strikes to protest government policies; (c) the institution of the 'closed shop', the exclusion of non-union workers from employment in a given unit of production, is to be challenged by requiring regular postal ballots needing massive (80–5 percent) majorities as well as by making unions responsible for financially compensating workers who lose their jobs because of the establishment of closed-shop agreements; and (d) the ability of owners to dismiss striking workers and union activists is to be considerably augmented. These legislative provisions involve not only the reversal of gains made by the unions during the Labour governments of 1974–9 and in particular as a result of the Trade Union and Labour Relations Act of 1974, but also, in a number of cases, the repeal of legal immunities enjoyed by the unions since 1906. As the experience of the Heath government with its Industrial Relations Act indicates, legislation can alter the balance of power in industrial relations only if it is successfully implemented. However, compared to its predecessor, the present Conservative government appears to enjoy a number of advantages—the legitimacy conferred by a large parliamentary majority; the weakness of the unions' mobilizing capacity in a period of unprecedented unemployment (as demonstrated in the decisive failure of almost every major strike undertaken by the unions in 1981–2); and the existence of a broad anti-union consensus among politicians and voters, a consensus reinforced by the emergence of a new party, the Social Democrats, whose program includes a critique of traditional patterns of union–state relations in Britain.

The French case provides an interesting contrast with the British experience during the crisis years. Whereas in Britain the economic downturn brought an unsuccessful venture into neo-corporatism followed by an attempt by a newly elected government to alter relations between the state and the unions in a strongly anti-union direction, in France precisely the opposite has occurred. The conservative government of Valéry Giscard d'Estaing responded to the crisis with a program of economic policies and industrial relations initiatives that resembled in some ways the schemes of the Thatcherites. In its approach to macroeconomics the Giscard regime, especially after the appointment of Raymond Barre as both Prime Minister and Finance Minister in September 1976, adopted a moderate version of the monetarist strategy. Price stability was given priority over employment, and fiscal and

monetary rigor was heavily emphasized, but public expenditures on welfare and relief were not so sharply cut back. With regard to the unions, Giscard and his ministers adopted a set of apparently contradictory policies. On the one hand, they declared their intention to 'loosen up' (décrisper) relations between the state and the unions and between the unions and capital, to upgrade (revaloriser) the status and working conditions of manual laborers, and to democratize the workplace. Some of these promises were made good, while others, such as the 'reform of the firm' promised by a special task force called the Sudreau Commission, never got beyond the public relations stage (Ross, 1980; Bornstein and Fine, 1977). On the other hand, the repressive and administrative apparatus of the state was often used under Giscard in decisively anti-union fashion: the police were used to break strikes and dislodge workers occupying bankrupt plants; organizers of the two radical unions, the CGT and the CFDT, were jailed on various pretexts or allowed to be fired by state labor inspectors and courts; and the representatives of small right-wing unions such as the Confédération française du travail were allotted seats on various official bodies in contravention of the Labor Code and established practice.

In the spring of 1981, however, a dramatic turn was taken with the election of Francois Mitterrand to the Presidency and of a Socialist government with a large parliamentary majority. These elections initiated a period of rapid political innovation in which the relationship between organized labor and the state as well as other important features of French industrial relations have begun to be substantially transformed. Even prior to the introduction of any new industrial relations legislation, the accession of the Left has brought with it several important changes. The access of union leaders to the state has increased dramatically: with a friendly government in power, the unions benefit from the kind of privileged contacts with administrative and political officials previously reserved for business interests. Similarly, even prior to any changes in the Labor Code, the administrative, judicial and police powers of the state have begun to be used very differently, thus allowing the unions to exercise rights and guarantees that were previously very difficult to enforce. Developments during the summer of 1982 in two of France's principal automobile firms, Citroën and Talbot, are indicative of the impact of this reorientation of the influence of the state. These two very large employers had previously managed, with the connivance of state inspectors and the police, to flout the intention of the laws and prevent all but phony company unions from operating freely in their plants. As a result of long and bitter strikes in which for the first time management could not rely on the courts and the police to support its efforts the unions have succeeded in establishing the right to organize inside several major Citroën and Talbot plants (*Le Monde*, 5 June, 30 June, 11–12 July 1982).

In addition to these non-legislative changes the government has also introduced a set of bills, collectively known as the 'Auroux Laws', which, if passed intact and applied effectively, will give the unions considerable new powers and alter substantially the character of industrial relations. The scope and effectiveness of collective bargaining, till now very underdeveloped in France, are to be improved by making annual negotiations on actual wages (rather than merely on minimum levels) and on real conditions of employment mandatory in all firms employing fifty or more workers and by the adoption of as yet unspecified measures to extend collective agreements to the more than three million workers presently not covered by any contractual arrangements. Unionization is, moreover, to be facilitated by extending to small firms, presently exempted from legislation, the rights of unions to be present within the workplace and of workers to join unions and to be represented by union representatives (*délégués syndicaux*), by worker representatives (*délégués du personnel*) and by works committees (*comités d'entreprise*). In addition, workers in all types of plant and office are to acquire a new 'right to self-expression', that is, to hold regular meetings of various sorts in the workplace and on company time and to invite outside speakers including political and union officials. The powers of the various workers' representatives and of the committees on which they sit are also to be considerably reinforced: the works committees are to acquire greatly increased access to company information and expanded rights to employ, at company expense, outside consultants to help them process it; the health and safety committees are to obtain expanded powers to secure information and to inspect working conditions; and all workers' representatives and union officials are to benefit from broader legal protection against unfair dismissal as well as greatly increased freedom of action within the workplace in terms both of the right to move freely inside the plant and of increased paid time off for the exercise of their functions. Moreover, the capacity of management to discipline not only union representatives but also ordinary employees will be sharply curtailed by restrictions on the content of company rulebooks (*règlements intérieurs*) and by changes in appeal procedures to state inspectors and courts (*Le Monde*, 5 June, 12 June, 13–14 June, 29 July 1982; *Nouvelles CFDT*, 30 April 1982). Finally, the workers in nationalized firms are, according to a separate piece of projected legislation, to be given a variety of new rights and powers ranging from the right of political self-expression through regular meetings in forums called shop councils (*conseils d'atelier*) to representation on company boards (*Le Monde*, 5 August 1982).

While these changes involve quite substantial alterations in French industrial relations, they do not appear likely to bring about the transformation of state–union relations in the direction of neo-corporatist institutions. None of the measures to facilitate unionization seems sufficient to overcome rapidly the very low level of union density and thus to enable the unions to play the kind of legitimate representative role required for effective centralized bargaining. Similarly, the ideological and political predispositions of many of the union organizations are not well suited to the development of institutionalized state–union cooperation. This is true not only of the politically moderate unions—the Confédération générale des cadres or the Confédération français des travailleurs chrétiens or Force ouvrière—but also of the two leftwing unions, since the Communist-led CGT is linked to the Mitterrand government by rather tenuous bonds and the CFDT, while very sympathetic to the aims of the government, is very sensitive to accusations of collusion with political parties and with the state and so decentralized as to have great difficulty administering an effective wage restraint program. The absence, thus far, of any pronounced trend in the direction of neo-corporatism in Socialist-governed France was dramatically illustrated in mid-June 1982. Facing rising inflation, deteriorating trade balances, currency reserves and exchange rates and growing state debts, the government—apparently without consulting union or business elites on the possibility of a negotiated austerity plan—abruptly devalued the franc, announced plans for large cuts in government spending and pushed through legislation for a four-month freeze on wages and prices. The critical response of most of the unions does not suggest that a concerted incomes policy will be negotiated for the period following the freeze (*Le Monde*, 15, 16, 17, 18, 24 June 1982).

The Impact of Unions on the State

The second part of this chapter will examine the other side of the state–union relationship by offering a relatively brief comparative study of the impact of the union movements of Western Europe on the policies and institutions of the state. As in the preceding pages, the analysis will use a historical approach, beginning with the period prior to World War II, then analyzing the postwar years in three distinct phases—the period of the postwar boom, the years of unrest beginning in the mid-1960s and the years of the contemporary crisis.

Before World War II, unions did not contribute prominently to the activities of the capitalist state. The influence of the union movements on the state was, in general, very limited in terms of direct access. In the first place, the leftwing political parties (socialist or communist) with which the unions were linked held office very rarely and briefly before 1945. Even where socialist parties did gain some control over parliamentary institutions—as in Austria, Sweden, Weimar Germany and Britain—weak majorities or early electoral defeats meant that they could barely begin to challenge the hegemony of the dominant classes over the institutions of the state. Even had socialist governments been stronger, the influence of the unions over state policy would have remained small during this period. The unions, even where they were most powerful, tended to grant priority of place to the political branch of the labor movement and, moreover, the narrow margins of maneuver available to leftwing governments during the crisis-ridden 1930s limited their responses to union pressure. The unions had even less access to state officials and policy-making bodies in states dominated by center or rightwing parties. Except for the brief period of wartime mobilization during World War I, the states of Europe tended to exclude union movements from extensive representation in administrative and consultative bodies (Maier, 1975).

Lacking direct modes of access to governments, the unions were confined to indirect influence on the state, through pressure-group techniques within the political arena combined with the use of labor-market action. The success of these strategies depended almost entirely on the capacity of the unions to mobilize the working population. This capacity depended, in turn, on a number of features of union organization—the number of officials, efficacy of propaganda activities, effectiveness of lines of communication between national leaderships and rank-and-file—as well as on the more readily measured issues of numerical strength.

Two different statistics are of interest as indicators of the potential power of a national union movement (see **Document 2** and **Document 3**). The first (**Document 2**), the proportion of the non-agricultural laborforce officially organized by unions, measures their success in recruiting industrial and office workers and gives us an idea of the credibility of their traditional claims to represent 'the working class'. According to this index, even the most successful European unions in the prewar period were not especially impressive. The second measure (**Document 3**), the proportion of unionized workers in the laborforce as a whole, reflects the extent of industrialization as much as it does the success of the unions, but it also gives a useful indicator of the overall weight of the union movement as an interest group within society as a whole. On this index even the strongest unions in Europe, such as the Swedish, with 36 percent of the laborforce as of 1939–40, only weakly foreshadowed the social force they would become (the Swedish union movement, in 1970, represented 75 percent of the national laborforce). Therefore, their ability to command the attention of governments and state officials, closely linked as these were to business elites and uninvolved as they were in management of the economy and in the direction of the labor market and social affairs, was limited except for brief periods of exceptional rank-and-file mobilization as in 1926 in Britain, and 1936 in France and Sweden.

Similarly, in terms of economic policy, the unions had very little success in pressing their demands on the state. Low wage shares of GNP (compared to profits and dividends) were typical of the interwar period as were high average levels of unemployment. Levels of wages and unemployment were, moreover, highly unstable in the cyclical swings of overall activity in these unregulated capitalist economies. Union pleas for state intervention to soften the human impact of the business cycle went largely unheeded, except for the relief that states provided to the unemployed and the disabled. At no time was the impotence of the unions more clearly demonstrated than during the Depression of the 1930s. With unemployment at unprecedented and brutal levels, unions throughout Europe called on governments to break with liberal economic orthodoxy and use public investment and expenditure to supplement the obviously defective market mechanism. Only in Sweden, however, did the state adopt such an expansive response to the Depression. Everywhere else—even under the Labour government in Britain in 1930–1—workers were forced to suffer severe unemployment and plummeting wages until the vast military expenditures associated with the runup to World War II gradually brought wage and employment levels back to more customary levels (Gourevitch, 1980).

It is important to recall, however, that the weakness of trade union influence on the state was not for lack of effort. For French and Italian unions, what may be called the 'political arena' as distinct from the 'market arena' figured very prominently in their strategic visions. This was the case for several reasons: (1) their own weakness in the market because of small numbers, divisions among the various confederations and the hostility of capitalists to unionization; (2) the comparatively prominent role played by the state in both countries within the activities of civil society; and (3) the radical ideological orientation of the major confederations in both countries. These were not 'associative' unions seeking gains exclusively for their own members but, rather, 'class' unions devoted to promoting the welfare of all the workers of their nation (see Pizzorno, 1978), and accordingly they inevitably looked to the state as the agent of change and to political action as the appropriate mechanism for gaining control of the state. Strikes in both France and Italy were frequently directed not against individual factoryowners or against a branch of industry, but, rather, against the state. Unions organized protest marches, demonstrations and work stoppages designed to put pressure on the government, to promote both specific policies and broad campaigns, such as the anti-fascist strikes in France in 1934 or the strikes against the conservative Daladier government in 1938. A large amount of the energy of many of these unions was, moreover, devoted to political action in a narrower electoral sense, that is, to efforts to help leftwing parties come to power (Lorwin, 1954; Horowitz, 1963).

Nor was such orientation toward the 'political arena' confined to the highly politicized, leftwing unions of the 'Latin' countries. Electoral political activism was a feature of all social-democratic unions, and political strikes were, though less common than in France and Italy, still not uncommon elsewhere. Thus in Germany, a general strike by the workers of Munich was primarily responsible for the defeat of the so-called Kapp Putsch of 1921, while in Britain strikes aimed at least partly at the state and its policies occurred in 1926, in the famous General Strike, and on several occasions during the 1930s as well. It was thus not lack of interest that made interwar unions weak at the level of the state but, rather, objective features of the balance of social forces.

The Postwar Settlements and the Unions

World War II and the new configurations of social and political forces that emerged in its aftermath set in motion a process of change which transformed the role of the unions in the activities of the state. In the first place, the unions in combatant Allied countries acquired a new status as legitimate and respected public organizations as a result of their contributions to the war effort or to the Resistance and of the discrediting of organized business and of reactionary anti-union forces in the areas of fascist rule or occupation. Secondly, the accession of socialist and communist parties to political office throughout Europe—either as new majority governments, or as parts of postwar coalitions—gave unions the possibility of new forms of direct access to political leaders and to appointed officials in state administration. Thirdly, this direct access of unions to government and to the state also took a form less directly dependent on their party connections. In most European states the war effort had inaugurated a variety of official and semi-official committees, councils and boards in which union appointees joined representatives of the state and of business in administering aspects of economic life. Whereas, in the case of World War I, most of these tripartite and bipartite bodies had been dismantled or phased out after the armistice, this time many were left in place and, sometimes, new ones were created as well, thus providing the unions with new channels of institutionalized access to state officials. Fourthly, the rapid expansion of the public sector of the economy by means of nationalizations and of the state services sector provided the union movements with a new opportunity for direct interaction with and influence over the state—negotiations between state officials and public sector unions representing their employers. Finally, the new economic and social functions assumed by the states of Western Europe as part of the postwar settlement made them potentially much more dependent on the unions than they had been before. In so far as the state now assumed much greater responsibility for managing economic affairs, the unions could be useful to it in a number of ways: by providing an element of predictability, or at least regularity, in the wage-setting process; by serving as a force for discipline, or at least for predictable behavior, in the workplace; by providing the possibility of controlling wage growth through voluntary wage restraint. Also, in the area of social policy, states were often eager to reduce their own administrative burden by enlisting union assistance in the administration of some of the less controversial programs such as pensions, health insurance, and the like.

The First Two Postwar Decades: Sweden, Austria and the Netherlands

Overall, then, the postwar settlements throughout Western Europe (as well as the settlement reached in Sweden in the mid-1930s) provided the unions with considerable opportunities to increase their role within the policy-making processes of the state and their influence over the outcomes of those processes. The success of union movements in taking advantage of these opportunities varied a great deal. It was in the Scandinavian countries and in the small 'consociational' polities such as Austria and the Netherlands the union movements had the greatest impact on state policies. In the first two postwar decades union pressure on the state was extremely successful in these countries. Legislation concerning the rights of unions and of workers was consistently the most advanced in Europe and the power of the state was rarely used overtly to curtail strikes or break unions, as it was in France and Italy, for example. In terms of economic policy, moreover, the unions did very well: the proportion of GNP going to wages as compared to profits was high in these countries by international standards and grew considerably over the first two postwar decades. Similarly, the unions succeeded in securing high rates of spending by the state on social welfare items such as pensions, health care and other components of the 'social wage'. As Table 3.1 indicates, Sweden, Norway, Denmark, Austria and the Netherlands all appear near the top of a ranking of countries according to what one observer has called 'welfare effort', that is, the proportion of national income allocated to non-military expenditures.

Table 3.1 *Percentage of GNI Devoted to Non-Military State Spending*

Denmark	49
Norway	45
Sweden	44
Austria	43
Netherlands	43
Finland	38
Belgium	37
France	37
UK	35
Germany	35
Italy	31
USA	21

Source: Stephens (1979), p. 118.

Another indicator of the comparative success of the union movements of these countries in orienting the economic and social policies of their states is the extent to which income taxation was structured to redistribute resources from the richer groups toward the poorer. This can be assessed by comparing a measure of the inequality of income distribution in a given society before and after taxes (using the 'Gini Index' of inequality—the higher the score, the more unequal the society). The comparison of the two Gini scores will give what might be called the society's 'redistributive tax effort'.

Table 3.2 *Income Distribution and 'Redistributive Tax Effort'*

	(a) Gini before tax	(b) Gini after direct tax	(c) Redistributive tax effort $(\frac{a-b}{a})$
Australia	0·313	0·312	0·003
Canada	0·382	0·344	0·099
France	0·416	0·414	0·005
Germany	0·396	0·383	0·033
Italy	n.a.	0·398	n.a.
Netherlands	0·385	0·354	0·081
Norway	0·354	0·307	0·133
Sweden	0·346	0·302	0·127
UK	0·344	0·302	0·122
USA	0·404	0·381	0·057
Mean	0·371	0·351	0·073

As an examination of column (c) in Table 3.2 reveals, Sweden, the Netherlands and Norway (also a country with successful neo-corporatist mechanisms and strong unions) score well above the mean in redistributive tax effort. It is also noteworthy that, in most of the countries that established neo-corporatism, the unions were successful in using the favorable postwar economic and political climate to set in motion a dynamic of steady union growth, whereas elsewhere initial postwar surges of membership often petered out within two decades. An examination of **Document 2** makes this pattern very clear. How can we account for the comparative success of the union movements in these countries in taking advantage of the opportunities provided by the new postwar environment?

It is clear that the unions in these countries secured comparatively large roles in the policy process. In these countries the 'corporatist' institutions for the tripartite discussion of social and economic policy, as noted above, were the most highly developed. It was also here that the level of informal contacts between union officials and state bureaucracies were most frequent.

The development of both formal and informal contacts owed much to party politics. Parties with which the unions in these countries maintain close connections—social democrats or Christian socialists—either monopolized, or significantly shared political power consistently during the period under consideration. With these parties holding political power, the unions could count on getting a better deal out of the state than could their counterparts in Italy, Germany or France, where conservative parties ruled consistently after the onset of the Cold War, or in Britain, where the Conservatives were in power during 1951–64.

The policy successes of the Scandinavian, Dutch and Austrian unions were not, however, simply the byproduct of the success of their political allies. In the first place, the unions were themselves largely responsible for these electoral successes, since they provided much of the funding and staff support for election campaigns and since their cooperation with the economic policy initiatives of their allies was an important ingredient in the longevity of these governments. Secondly, the unions were able to mobilize so much electoral support and to negotiate strong bargains with governments and bureaucracies, because of their extraordinary strength as labor market organizations. For these were the largest, most effectively structured union movements in the capitalist West. As **Documents 2** and **3** indicate, even the smallest of these movements, the Dutch, covered a proportion of the laborforce far above the average for Western Europe, while the Austrian, Swedish and Danish movements were unmatched in their densities.

Equally significant, these were not only large union movements, but ones in which power was, as we have already seen, concentrated in centralized national leadership elites who were able to make promises in negotiations with capital and the state without much fear that their own members or lower-level organizers would fail to comply (Headey, 1970). In nations where neo-corporatist arrangements were most significant national labor movements were dominated by one highly centralized body (for blue-collar workers at least, in Sweden, Denmark and Norway), or by a number of centralized bodies divided along linguistic or denominational lines with shared ideological orientations and closely allied strategic approaches. Central leaders could make decisions that were potentially unpopular without having to confront opposition from rank-and-file members. In all of these countries plant-level and local-level members had very little voice in approving wage settlements, in determining union policy or in selecting national leaders. This insulation of national union leaders from rank-and-file influence proved especially important in allowing union leaders in Austria and the Netherlands to endorse incomes policies through the 1950s and into the 1960s, although these policies consistently involved restraint in the use of union market strength in the effort to ensure that wage inflation did not reach levels that threatened profit margins and therefore rates of investment and employment. This ability to deliver wage restraint enabled union leaders to obtain from the state valuable concessions in terms of economic and social policies and industrial relations legislation.

Only the Swedes managed to secure these benefits without accepting a wage-restraint arrangement. They did so by developing a sophisticated scheme for the control of inflation without a formal incomes policy. Known as the 'Rehn Model', after the chief LO economist, Gösta Rehn, it involved a complicated set of policies which linked union bargaining strategy and government economic and social policy in such a way that the burden of preventing inflation while maintaining full employment was shifted on to capital (see Martin, 1975; 1979). That the Swedish unions were able to influence their country's economic and social policy so heavily and to secure considerable legislative and social tradeoffs without accepting an incomes policy was partly the result of the ingenuity of LO economists. Other factors cannot, however, be neglected; these include the rapid growth of the Swedish economy, the size and organizational structure of the unions and the growing hegemony of the Swedish Social Democrats over the state apparatus—a process they had begun much earlier than any comparable party in Europe—which makes the Swedish example remarkable, even when compared to the other neo-corporatist cases (Stephens, 1979).

The First Two Postwar Decades: France, Italy, Germany and Britain

Compared to their neo-corporatist counterparts, the union movements of France, Italy and Germany exercised much less influence over the policies of their respective states during the period from 1945 through the early to mid-1960s. Evidence of this lack of success abounds when we compare the patterns of economic and social development of these countries to those of Scandinavia, Austria and the Netherlands. The share of wages in GNP was so much lower in the former group of countries than in the latter that it is possible to claim that we are in the presence of two distinct patterns of postwar economic recovery and development—a high-wage, low-profit trajectory and a low-wage, high-profit path. Similarly, an examination of Tables 3.1 and 3.2 reveals that the state used its policies much less consistently and effectively to benefit unions and their members in the conflict-based systems than in the neo-corporatist systems. The 'welfare effort' of the state in Table 3.1 was consistently lower; income inequalities were, partly as a result, higher; and the use of fiscal policy as a tool for transferring income toward lower-income groups was much less in evidence. Finally, where the state in the neo-corporatist group of countries threw its weight on to the side of labor in much of its industrial relations legislation, in France, Italy and Germany, the power of the state was frequently used to impede unionization and to undermine strike activity. The actions of the French police and army in the strikes of 1953 and in the miners' strike of 1963 were blatant examples, while the rigorous legal restrictions surrounding strikes in Germany represented a more consistent and subtle form of intervention.

The relative policy weakness of the unions in France, Italy and Germany is not difficult to understand. It is clear that these unions were substantially weaker organizationally than those in the first group. Union density figures for France and Germany were quite low during this period (see **Document 2**), and the Italian figures, while high, are probably seriously inflated. In any case, all three unions were weak not only numerically, but organizationally, the German movement having to rebuild itself slowly in difficult political conditions after its destruction by the Nazis, and the Italian and French movements being severely weakened by internal divisions linked to the Cold War battles between Communists and non-Communists in the domestic and international political arenas (see Lange and Ross, 1982). Moreover, the weakness of the unions was exacerbated by economic conditions: in all three countries, the demand for labor was considerably lower throughout the first ten to fifteen postwar years than it was either in the first group of countries, or as we shall see in a moment, in Britain. Comparatively large surplus agricultural populations plus, in the German case, extensive immigration from the Eastern bloc, kept the labor market loose, kept wage levels lower than growth of output and productivity might otherwise have warranted and undermined the organizational and bargaining efforts of the unions. Similarly, the ability of the unions to bargain with the state was undermined by the absence, for most of this period, of sympathetic parties in government. Except for the brief interlude of three-party governments in France and Italy in 1945–7 when both communists and socialists shared power, the parties with union connections remained excluded from governments, thus making unlikely the development of corporatist bargaining networks or of informal channels of state–union communications. Nor have the radically anti-capitalist ideological orientation of the largest French and Italian union confederations, the CGT and the CGIL, proved conducive to such policy bargaining even with sympathetic governments (see Markovits and Allen, 1980; Müller-Jentsch and Sperling, 1978).

The British case must be treated separately. Here the unions made a number of major gains at the very beginning of the postwar period but then failed to maintain the sort of dynamic that developed in Scandinavia, Austria and the Netherlands. Real wage growth slowed substantially during the 1950s and early 1960s as inflation at comparatively high levels eroded the effects of union bargaining successes. Similarly, the British welfare state whose creation in 1945 constituted a spectacular triumph for the working class failed to keep pace, in terms of expenditure levels and overall redistributive effects, with the achievements of many of Britain's neighbors (see Table 3.1). Simultaneously, unlike the unions in our neo-corporatist sample, the British union movement failed to convert the dynamic of Keynesianism and of the welfare state into a pattern of organizational expansion. As **Document 3** reveals, the TUC grew very little within the period under consideration, gaining 2 percent of the non-agricultural laborforce in 1945–6–50 but then gradually shrinking to the earlier level by 1960.

The reason I wish to set Britain apart is that the TUC's comparative policy failures in the first two postwar decades cannot be attributed to the same factors that undermined the efforts of the unions in France, Italy and Germany. In terms of many organizational features, British unions resembled the unions of the neo-corporatist countries much more than they did those of the second group. As **Documents 2** and **3** reveal, in terms of organizational density, at the outset of the postwar period, the TUC was among the strongest union movements in Europe with 40 percent of the total laborforce and 45 percent of non-agricultural workers and employees enrolled in its affiliates. Nor did the British union movement have to face the kinds of internal ideological or denominational splits that played such an important role in France and Italy. The TUC was a single, unified national organization within which communists and moderate socialists coexisted comparatively easily (Kassalow, 1969, ch. 1; Crouch, 1978). Nor did the state of the labor market undermine union efforts as in France, Italy and Germany. Throughout the first two postwar decades unemployment rates in Britain were, with the Swedish, the lowest in the capitalist world. Unlike the cases of France, Italy and Germany, moreover, where the principal labor-oriented parties were effectively excluded from political power and even from the status of legitimate participants in the political arena, in Britain the Labour Party was in power for the first six years of the postwar period and remained, despite the long period of opposition that followed, a major and legitimate force in national politics.

How, then, can we explain the comparatively meager successes of the TUC in influencing the policies of the British state? Partly we can point to the slow economic growth achieved by the British economy as compared to that attained by its principal European competitors. Although the rate of 2·8 percent annual growth maintained by the British economy in the first two postwar decades was excellent by comparison with the interwar period, Britain's performance could hardly match the economic 'miracles' of 6·7 percent, 6·0 percent and 4·5 percent being recorded in Germany, Italy and France, or the steady and rapid growth of other European economies (Peaker, 1974, p. 11). Since, moreover, it was the British financial sector rather than the often outmoded and inefficient industrial sector that provided much of the country's output and income growth, the ability of the unions to secure a share of the proceeds was further restricted (Aldcroft and Fearon, 1969; Caves et al., 1968). Just as important, perhaps, as the poor performance of the country's industrial economy was the failure of the union's party ally, the Labour Party, to obtain hegemony within the party system or the state apparatus along Swedish lines. Labour managed to retain political power for only six years during which, moreover, it made very limited inroads into the personnel or the approaches of the principal bureaucratic agencies and especially of the crucial economic ministry, the Treasury (Miliband, 1972a; Rogow, 1955). While the Conservatives who came to power in 1951 and retained office until 1964 did not dismantle the basic elements of the newly created welfare state, their lack of real enthusiasm for the new institutions was an important factor in their relatively slow expansion in the 1950s. Similarly, the lack of personal and political links between the Conservative

elites and the leadership of the union movement goes a long way toward explaining the absence from British politics of the sorts of tripartism and associated tradeoffs that played such an important role in Sweden and the other countries of that group (for the importance of this alternation in office in a British/Swedish comparison, see Martin, 1975). That Labour lost control very soon after its sweeping 1945 victory was, at least in part, attributable, moreover, to the actions of the unions themselves as a comparison between Britain and Sweden suggests (Martin, 1975). Whereas the Swedish union movement succeeded in developing a scheme (the Rehn Model) for restraining inflation without undermining its own organizational unity, the TUC was unable to find any equivalent solution for an inflationary problem which, by 1948, had become quite troublesome. The TUC lacked not only the sophisticated economic expertise required to develop and implement something as complex as the Rehn Model, but also and more importantly the TUC lacked the kind of organizational structures and general strategic orientation that made the Swedish approach work. The 'solidaristic' wage strategy of the Rehn Model, made possible by the extreme centralization of Swedish bargaining structures, the concentration of authority within the union movement and the 'class' orientation of union ideology, was highly inappropriate to Britain with its fragmented bargaining, its extremely decentralized unions in which the authority of national leaders over their own officials and especially over factory-level shop stewards and work groups was often very limited, and its highly fragmented and competitive unions oriented, unlike their Swedish counterparts, not toward broad class objectives but, rather, toward the protection of the economic interests of their own members only (see Crouch, 1978; Clegg, 1978). Under these conditions not only was the Swedish scheme of inflation control inapplicable in Britain, but the incomes policy approach of the Austrians or the Dutch was also very difficult to match. As we have seen, the system of voluntary wage restraint accepted by the TUC's leadership at the request of the Labour government in 1948 broke down within two years as the national leaders of the TUC and of the individual unions proved unable to restrain the wage militancy of rank-and-file members. With inflation a major political issue as a result of the Korean War, and Labour unable to claim a unique ability based on its union links to control it, the Conservatives had little difficulty sweeping into office in the election of 1951.

For the period from 1945 through the mid-1960s,

then, the ability of the union movements of Western Europe to take advantage of the structural opportunities for influencing state policy provided by the postwar settlements depended not only on the performance of the national economy, the character of the state, the pattern of party domination in the political arena and the character of collective bargaining institutions, but also on several features of the unions themselves: their organizational strength, internal centralization, strategic orientation, party connections and, in the Swedish case at least, their economic expertise.

Years of Unrest and Union Gains

How enduring were these patterns? The period from the mid-1960s through the onset of the recession of the mid-1970s was, as we have seen, distinguished from the preceding two postwar decades of stable economic growth and comparatively peaceful industrial and class relations by the coincidence of a variety of forms of instability: economic instability in the form of alternations of recessions and booms; new inflationary pressures; and industrial unrest of unprecedented proportions (Soskice, 1978; Dubois, 1978). The states in capitalist Europe attempted, as we have seen, a variety of responses to these challenges, including, in most cases, both efforts to suppress inflation through wage-restraint arrangements, and attempts to reinstitutionalize and control industrial conflict either by using the unions' disciplinary agents, or by introducing institutional arrangements in the workplace to impose order directly.

The instabilities of this period, as well as the efforts of the state to deal with them, constituted a challenge for the union movements much like the institutional transformations of the postwar settlements some twenty years earlier. The establishment or renegotiation of incomes policies offered union leaders opportunities to increase their influence over state policies by exchanging wage restraint for increased input into economic and social policy and concrete benefits for their members (pensions, condition of work, and the like). Alternatively, unions could bargain for organizational benefits (legislation increasing union powers in the workplace or facilitating union recruitment activities). At the same time, participation in incomes policies also posed potential problems for union leadership, exposing them to criticism from below, a threat that was more serious in a period of rank-and-file militancy than it had been in the comparatively quiescent 1950s. Thus, for the unions corporatist bargaining was a two-edged

sword. The same could be said of the intensification of rank-and-file militancy. On the one hand, the rise of new forms of strike action and the emergence of politicized, independent-minded local activists threatened the established patterns of action and authority within the unions and undermined their organizational stability. On the other hand, the fact of new militancy gave union leaders a valuable bargaining chip when negotiating with capital and with the state. As in the previous period, national union movements differed in their ability to respond to this complex set of challenges.

In general, however, the increased vulnerability of state elites to rank-and-file wage militancy, on the one hand, and to an increasingly competitive and economically unstable international environment, on the other, induced them to open up the process of economic and social policy-making to negotiation with the unions. If they played their cards right, unions could achieve considerable material and policy gains for themselves and their members in return for relatively small concessions and sacrifices (Salvati and Brosio, 1979; Crouch 1978). Among the countries with longstanding corporatist institutions the success of union strategies depended on a combination of factors: the extent to which the national economy was troubled by inflationary pressures; the degree to which such inflationary pressures could be accommodated by raising market prices without endangering the balance of international payments; the extent and visibility of rank-and-file industrial militancy; the vulnerability of existing governmental coalitions and the extent of their electoral dependence on the unions. Thus, in Austria where the economy was comparatively unthreatened, industrial militancy essentially non-existent and the government (during 1966–70, at least) independent of union influences, the terms of exchange of the highly corporatist postwar settlement and incomes policy remained basically unaltered (Barbash, 1972, ch. 3; Lehmbruch, 1979a; 1979b). In the Netherlands where the economy was much more vulnerable to inflation and to international competition but where militancy was fairly low by international standards (though high compared to earlier Dutch experience) and consociational political arrangements stable, the unions succeeded, as we noted, in partially reshaping the mechanisms of wage control to their own benefit. The statutory control of wages was replaced by a system of negotiated wage restraint in which the unions were successful, in several stages during 1969–73, in trading off limitations in wage demands against concessions on welfare spending, housing policy, educational reforms, increases in the statutory minimum wage and tax reforms (Barbash, 1972, ch. 4; Akkermans and Grootings, 1978).

In Sweden, too, the unions made very far-reaching gains. The institutional reforms described in the previous section entailed important augmentations of union influence, both at plant level and over state policy. The industrial strategy measures gave the unions extensive representation on all the boards and panels established to oversee investment allocation and economic planning. Similarly, legislation on health and safety and on industrial democracy gave the unions' local officials access to information about managerial intentions and influence over managerial decisions unmatched in any other capitalist society (Logue, 1980; Martin, 1979).

Meanwhile, in those countries where the postwar settlement had not involved the establishment of corporatist institutions, political leaders were, as we have seen, attempting to create them as a means of responding to the challenges of economic and social disorder. In no case did a state succeed in creating a stable set of such institutions, but the policy bargaining that accompanied these efforts, and that persisted even after their failure, enabled the unions to begin a much larger public role in the state arena and to make some significant policy gains for themselves and their members.

Most impressive was the success of the Italian unions. They managed over less than a decade not only to win major legislative concessions from the state, but also to transform the entire character of union–state relations and to turn themselves from essentially powerless observers of the activities of the state and of capital into prominent participants in the highest levels of power politics. Taking advantage of the upsurge of grassroots activism in the labor market during and after the 'Hot Autumn' of 1969 the Italian unions expanded their memberships by an astonishing 20 percent during 1969–71, made themselves into powerful factors in the workplace by incorporating the militant shop stewards' movement (the *delegati*) into union structures and set into motion a partially successful process of unification among the three confederations. The result was a dynamic, popular-based, coherent national union movement able to win major gains not only from employers but also from the state. The indexing of wages (the so-called *scala mobile*) and of state subsidies and pensions to inflation was a significant victory with important implications for income distribution, the state's budgetary situation and union strategy in the subsequent period of economic crisis. Likewise the

new labor code, Statuto del Lavoro of 1972, gave the previously weak union representatives in the workplace significant powers over such traditional managerial prerogatives as the organization of work and the planning of investment (Lange and Vannicelli, 1982; Lange and Ross, 1982; Regalia *et al.*, 1978; Regini, 1980). Remarkably, the Italian unions secured these gains and made themselves into an indispensable interlocutor of the state on issues of economic and social policy without committing themselves to any formal corporatist institutional participation. True, the history of the Italian union movement in this period also involves important defeats: they did not succeed either in getting for the Communist Party a full share of political power (clearly the central objective of the largest confederation, the CGIL), nor were they able to secure many of their principal legislative demands (Lange and Vannicelli, 1982; Regini, 1980). Nevertheless, the Italian case illustrates very well the ability of a union movement to take advantage of the instabilities of this period in order to increase very markedly its capacity to influence the formation of state policy.

Less comprehensive yet still significant changes in the relation of unions to the state occurred in Germany and Britain. In Germany the accession of the Social Democrats to a share of political power in 1966 as part of a 'Grand Coalition' with the Christian Democrats brought, as we have seen, a reworking of the postwar settlement. The unions accepted the establishment of a non-coercive yet quite effective form of incomes policy (see Clark, 1979; Lehmbruch, 1979a), while the government assumed a commitment to full employment and granted the unions not only a newly enhanced status as participants in policy discussions, but also a number of their long-sought legislative objectives. Union influence has remained strong since 1969 when the Social Democrats became the dominant partners in a new two-party government with the Free Democrats, a governing coalition which has to date never lost power. Union legislative victories have included the establishment of a selective manpower policy in the Works Promotion Act of 1969; increases in the powers of works councils and in the unions' influence over them by means of the 1972 Works Constitution Act; and a commitment (as yet unfulfilled) to extend the 50–50 codetermination system from the coal and steel sectors to the economy as a whole (Markovits and Allen, 1980; Müller-Jentsch and Sperling, 1978). In Britain developments were much less consistent. As we have seen, over 1964–73 the unions' relations with the state, both under Labour and Tory administrations, were extremely conflictual. The unions were forced to accept several rounds of wage restraint and received very little in return, except largely ineffectual participation in the newly created economic planning bodies, amid efforts by both parties to curtail their legal rights and to reduce their bargaining autonomy. Under the terms of the 'Social Contract' of the Wilson–Callaghan government, Labour Party leaders promised the TUC that the unions would enjoy both an enhanced role in the policy process, and the enactment of a long list of legislative reforms corresponding to high union priorities.

Of all the countries under consideration, it was only in France that the developments of the mid-1960s to mid-1970s did not alter the role of the unions within the state to any substantial degree. Prior to May–June 1968, the attempts by the Gaullists to involve the unions in various corporatist schemes proved unsuccessful. After 1968, despite the extraordinary dimensions and intensity of the near-revolutionary strike wave and the persistence of a high level of militancy in the three or four subsequent years, the unions did not really manage to alter their status as outcasts within the Gaullist state. Still, the Gaullists did initiate some policy bargaining along lines broadly similar to that occurring elsewhere, although under much stricter state control. Thus, for example, the state followed up the tripartite Grenelle negotiations that had settled the May strikes with a series of tripartite and bipartite meetings culminating in legislation on such subjects as on-the-job training, unemployment benefits and supplementary pensions (Ross, 1980; Dubois *et al.*, 1978). Thus, even in the most conservative of the states under consideration, the unions did make certain legislative gains out of the militancy and economic instability of this period.

Conclusion

Whereas the unions of Western Europe were able to win important gains from their new or expanded role as policy bargainers in the late 1960s and early 1970s, the onset of the international economic crisis in 1974 has altered the balance of forces profoundly. The unions now find that the task of bargaining with politicians and bureaucrats over economic and social policy has become much more arduous. Also their new status as public actors now imposes many more costs and far fewer benefits than previously.

Politicians and state managers, even those most sympathetic toward workers and toward the goals of the unions, are now extremely exigent in their dealings with union leaders. With inflation rates often four or five times higher than before the oil crisis, the urgency of wage restraint for politicians became extreme. Governments have often sought not merely to slow the rate of wage growth, but to cut into real wages in order to transfer resources from wages to profits and thereby, in theory, into productive investment and economic growth. Similarly, unpredictable rank-and-file militancy has become a far more serious problem both because of its effect on wage levels, and because of its potential effect on output and productivity in a period of declining and often negative growth rates and intensified international competition. In their negotiations with the unions, then, politicians have become much more demanding. It is also true that politicians have become considerably less generous about the kinds of tradeoffs they can offer unions in return for wage restraint and industrial order. In earlier periods restraint in demands for market wages could be rewarded with increases in the 'social wage'. Today, such strategies are much less feasible because of the parlous condition of state budgets, constrained by falling growth rates and high levels of unemployment (O'Connor, 1973).

Nor can states readily resort to 'costless' benefits such as improved safety legislation, increased union rights in the workplace or even various schemes for 'industrial democracy' or 'economic democracy' (Salvati and Brosio, 1979).

Capitalists have become even more zealous of their managerial prerogatives now that declining profit margins and intensifying competition mandate new efforts at rationalization of production and intensification of work discipline. Thus, in Germany the SPD's proposed codetermination legislation has run up against concerted opposition from business groups and from the Free Democratic Party on whose support the government depends and has been watered down almost beyond recognition (Markovits and Allen, 1980; Logue, 1980). In Sweden, similarly, the far-reaching proposal by the LO to funnel profits into investment funds controlled by the unions—the Meidner Plan—has confronted similar obstacles, and has recently been substantially altered by a joint union–party commission. The new version (see **Document 4**) involves much less of a direct challenge to capitalist control of the economy: whereas the Meidner Plan sought to transfer equity from capitalists to unions, the new plan seeks to fund the wage-earner funds partly from an increase in the pension tax and partly from a levy not on all profits but only on surplus profits. Even were capitalists willing to accept such schemes as a way of pacifying the unions and securing wage restraint, it is not at all clear that union members or even many middle- and lower-level activists are concerned with such issues as industrial democracy or even health and safety legislation in a period of escalating unemployment and uncertain standards of living. In Britain, for example, lack of interest among rank-and-file members and organizers in many of the non-material components of the 'Social Contract' package was an important source of difficulty both for the Labour government and for the TUC's top leadership, who regarded economic planning and industrial democracy as important elements of the tradeoff arrangement (Bornstein and Gourevitch, 1982).

For the unions, the current crises of capitalist economies and of capitalist states pose serious strategic and organizational difficulties. On the one hand, unions fear that compliance with government demands for wage moderation—either through formal endorsement of incomes policies or through informal restraint—may provoke rank-and-file resentments that ultimately produce wildcat strikes directed as much against union leaders as against capital or the state. The experience of the TUC in the winter strike wave of 1978–9 is a case in point. On the other hand, failure to restrain wages may prove equally costly. Higher inflation may generate increased unemployment, which hurts both individual workers and the unions as organizations. Failure to restrain wages may undermine the political credibility of friendly governments and bring to power conservative regimes, eager to solve the crisis by breaking the strength of the unions and rolling back many of the basic elements of the postwar settlement. Thus, the British union movement accepted severe restraint at the hands of a Labour government in order to stave off, unsuccessfully as it turned out, the much less palatable approach advocated by Thatcher's Conservatives. The dilemma of the TUC in the years following 1974 was particularly poignant and in many ways representative of the plight of unions in the present crisis. After the second 1974 election victory of the Labour Party, and despite the rapid deterioration of the economy, the TUC enjoyed a period of grace lasting some eighteen months during which no wage restrictions were imposed, and the government delivered many of the reforms in industrial relations law and welfare provision promised in the 'Social Contract'. Once the level of inflation and the deterioration of the trade balance and of the pound sterling had become intolerable, the honeymoon came to an end. The TUC was compelled by its political allies to accept a stringent incomes policy without being accorded any significant policy tradeoffs from the long list of items remaining on the 'Social Contract' agenda. The TUC found itself the 'hostage' not only of its political alliances, but also of the public status it had won for itself in the previous period.

As long as the TUC's leaders helped the government enforce its incomes policy, they exposed themselves to rank-and-file resentment without being able to claim any abatement of the severe and rising unemployment as a tradeoff for stalled wages. When, however, the TUC lost control over local wage militancy, and when the resulting strike wave contributed to the defeat of the Callaghan government at the hands of Thatcher's Tories, it had to face not only severe recriminations from within Labour Party circles, but also the prospect of an assault by the new regime on working-class living standards, organizations and communities reminiscent of the interwar years (Krieger and Amott, 1982).

Most other European union movements have thus far escaped the worst aspects of the TUC's recent dilemma. Nowhere has the combination of inflation and unemployment been so devastating or the threat by the state to union influence and freedom of action so severe. Still, no union movement, regardless of its own market strength or of the relative health of its national economy or of the friendly disposition of the governing party or parties, has been able to escape completely from similar difficulties. Everywhere the growth of real wages has slowed considerably, even in Austria, Sweden, Germany and the Netherlands as capital and the state have put considerable pressure on union negotiators to moderate wage demands in the name of 'the national interest' or the good of the party. Everywhere, similarly, employment levels have come under pressure from declining international trade and shrinking economic growth rates, and governments have proved either unwilling to maintain full employment, as in West Germany, or unable to do so, as in Italy and Britain. Alternatively, they have demanded—and received—greatly increased union restraint, in terms of wages and legislative demands in return for keeping unemployment from rising as in Norway, Austria and Sweden (Salvati and Brosio, 1979).

While the unions everywhere have accepted (either explicitly or *de facto*) wage restraint, they have received fewer policy tradeoffs for their cooperation than in the past. Thus, a semblance of full employment has been preserved only in very few cases (Austria,

Sweden and Norway), while everywhere else unemployment rates have escalated. Moreover, the flow of legislative tradeoffs that unions became accustomed to receiving for wage restraint in the past has all but dried up. In Sweden and Germany proposals, dear to the unions, for increasing economic and industrial democracy—the Meidner Plan in Sweden and the new parity codetermination law in Germany—were shelved by the Social Democrats in favor of more cautious strategies.

As in Britain, then, though less dramatically to be sure, the unions have found themselves hostages to their newly attained public status and to their own political party allies. In Italy, for example, the unions—with the CGIL leading the way—first adopted and then dropped a program for economic austerity and administrative reform (as the CGIL's political ally, the Communist Party approached and then drew away from entry into a coalition government with the Christian Democrats) (Lange and Vannicelli, 1982).

The French case appears to be a partial exception to this general pattern. As we have seen, the 1981 elections were followed by substantial changes in the policies of the state in the sphere of industrial relations. These changes allowed the unions to make major gains during the first year of socialist rule in such areas as real wages, levels of welfare provision, hours of work (a fifth week of paid vacation was added and one hour was deducted from the work week) and the legal powers and rights of workers and union organizers as well as in the less quantifiable matter of general access to officials and policy-makers. The unions were generally pleased with the performance of the government during this period, although each of the major confederations judged the regime according to its own set of priorities and preferences. Only two negative items appeared on the unions' balance-sheets for this period. The first was the persistence of very high levels of unemployment. Despite government promises and policies, unemployment figures continued to climb, increasing by almost 15 percent during a year: that the performance of neighboring countries such as West Germany was much worse or that a continuation of Giscardian policies would certainly have produced much more distressing results was of limited comfort to union leaders. The second sore spot for the unions involved membership levels. Despite the election victory and a year of friendly government, neither of the two major confederations succeeded in recruiting significant numbers of new members. The wave of unionization that many observers thought might follow

a Left victory and allow the unions to break out of their congenital weakness did not occur (*Le Monde*, 25 May; 8 June 1982).

The summer of 1982 has, as we have seen, given the unions something else to worry about. The government's new austerity program has confronted them with the sort of dilemma faced in the 1975–9 period by their British counterparts. For the two leftwing unions, the CGT and the CFDT, the presence in power of a friendly government makes it impossible to reject out of hand proposals for wage restraint as would have been the case under a conservative government. For the CFDT's national leadership, matters are clear: the pressures of the international economic crisis will doom the socialist experiment unless the unions cooperate in restraining inflation and restoring the competitiveness of French industy. (*Le Monde*, 15 June 1982; *Syndicalisme*, 22 July 1982). For the CGT, the situation is more complex. The union's political ally, the Communist Party, is only a junior partner in the Mitterrand government and the union's economic analysis, unlike the CFDT's, does not regard austerity as an appropriate response to the economic crisis (*Le Monde*, 16, 17, 18 June 1982; *L'Humanité*, 17, 18 June 1982). Both confederations, however, face contradictory pressures: cooperation in the government's anti-inflationary program for more than a brief period is liable to produce dissatisfaction among the rank-and-file over stagnating wages; but, at the same time, refusal to cooperate exposes union leaders to the charge, both from their political allies and from their own militants and members, of sabotaging the efforts of France's first Left government in the postwar era.

The economic crisis has, thus, had paradoxical effects on the capacity of French unions to influence state policy and behavior. On the one hand, the inability of the Giscard governments to engineer economic recovery played a major part in bringing the Socialists to power and thus in placing the unions on the threshold of a significant breakthrough in their role within the French political economy. Yet, on the other hand, the persistence and, indeed, the aggravation of the crisis appear to be limiting considerably and increasingly the capacity of the unions to exploit this opportunity.

Thus far, this chapter has examined the two sides of the state–union relationship separately, looking first at the relationship from the perspective of the state and then from that of the unions. In this concluding section, I shall attempt to combine these approaches in order to seek an overview of the changing interrelations between states and union movements in postwar Western Europe.

From this synthetic point of view, we can discern two distinct modes of state–union relations emerging in the wake of World War II and persisting through the years of the economic boom. The first was the neo-corporatist mode in which large, centralized and comparatively moderate unions cooperated with the state and with organized business in a variety of mechanisms for the administration of industrial relations and the planning and execution of social and economic policy. In this mode, the state played a considerable role, at least indirectly, in ensuring social peace by enacting and enforcing legislative provisions protecting workers and guaranteeing union rights. In the second, or conflictual, mode comparatively small, ideologically divided and often quite radical unions refused, or proved unable, to participate in corporatist bargaining and administration. At the same time, the absence in these countries of a network of bargaining relations between labor and capital at the industry or plant level required the state to step in to regulate many aspects of industrial relations which elsewhere are subject to collective agreements.

These two models represent two different patterns of 'trade-offs' among the participants. In the neo-corporatist mode, state elites gave up the possibility of resorting to a variety of tactics for weakening the unions or for dealing directly with the workers over their heads while gaining in return the advantages of predictable labor behavior and stable industrial relations at the workplace. National union leaders, likewise, traded away much of their freedom of action in bargaining as well as the possibility of using radically anticapitalist appeals for mobilizing the working class, while receiving in return high wages, well-developed welfare programs and positions for themselves in administrative and policy-making bodies. Precisely the inverse set of exchanges characterized the conflictual model. State elites preserved their—and capital's—freedom of action *vis-à-vis* the unions but could not rely on the latter to discipline the workers and stabilize industrial relations. The unions, likewise, maintained their liberty to act freely in the labor market (within the constraints of legislative restrictions and police enforcement) and to mobilize workers on the basis of radical programs for societal change while sacrificing the advantages offered by corporatist institutions.

For the initial postwar period, most of the countries discussed in this chapter fell clearly into one of the two modes of state–union relations just described. West Germany displayed many of the features of the neo-corporatist mode except for neo-corporatist institutions themselves and has thus been treated separately in the opening sections. Britain was also a problem: its unions were larger and less ideologically oriented than those of France or Italy but their frequent strike behavior and their lack of incorporation into tripartite institutions put the British system of state–union relations closer to the conflictual mode than to the neo-corporatist.

For the first two postwar decades, then, we find two basic modes of state–union relations and two anomalous cases. This bimodal classification, based as it was not on accidental circumstances but on profound sociological and economic structures with deep historical routes, persisted substantially unchanged throughout the two subsequent stages into which I have divided the postwar period—the years of unrest from the mid-1960s through the early 1970s and the crisis years from the mid-1970s onward. During the first of these two periods, the impact of the 'new militancy' and the extent of the so-called 'industrial relations crisis' were felt very differently in the two groups of countries we have distinguished. Despite brief eruptions of strikes which astonished observers not so much by their dimensions as by the contrast they offered with the quiescence of the previous years, the countries of the neo-corporatist mode continued to have annual strike rates well at the bottom of the international rankings (**Document 1**). Similarly, wage inflation, the economic by-product of industrial militancy, remained decidedly lower in these countries than elsewhere, although in Holland the system of centralized bargaining did not prove resilient enough to sustain even such low levels of militancy and inflation.

It was the countries lacking entirely in neo-corporatist institutions and habits that experienced real industrial upheaval during these years. The 'new militancy' and the 'industrial relations crisis' were essentially French, Italian and British phenomena. The upheavals in these countries did produce an increased level of state intervention in the sphere of industrial relations and a certain number of important gains for the unions (this was especially true in the Italian case) but they did not result in any fundamental transformations in the basic structures of industrial relations or in state–union relations.

In the early crisis years, the broad pattern described above of two basic modes of state–union relations continued to exercise considerable influence over the course of economic and social developments. As Salvati and Brosio have noted, during the years 1974–9 the international recession appears to have had rather different impacts on Western political economies depending on whether or not they were managed through a system of neo-corporatist institutions. It was only in those countries with stable centralized bargaining networks that rates of inflation and levels of unemployment were kept close to those that had prevailed in the previous postwar decades. The importance of this difference for organized labor and for the tenor of social relations becomes clear when we note that in almost every OECD country the unions found themselves obliged to accept significant wage restraint whether explicitly or implicitly. It was, thus, only in countries such as Austria, Sweden and Germany that this moderate wage behavior was rewarded by the maintenance of reasonably full employment and by the preservation of stable prices and accordingly of working-class living standards (Sachs, 1979).

As the crisis has worn on, however, the distinction between the two types of system has begun to fade somewhat. In several of the neo-corporatist countries, state–union relations have begun to lose some of their cooperative flavor as the economic and political preconditions of centralized bargaining and policy-making have become increasingly elusive. At the same time, under the Mitterrand government, the highly conflictual French system of state–union relations is being significantly reformed, although neo-corporatist institutions have yet to be put into place. Indeed, in all the countries surveyed, although with less acuity in the neo-corporatist group, the problem of the interrelation between the state and organized labor under capitalism is being posed anew. The solutions provided by the various postwar settlements to the question of the compatibility of labor organization and social progress on the one hand and capitalist accumulation on the other no longer seem clearly viable. Should the economic instabilities and failures of recent years continue for much longer, the kinds of major effort at restructuring the role of the state in industrial relations now being undertaken in Britain may become the rule among capitalist societies rather than the exception.

Note: Chapter 3

During the preparation of this essay I benefited greatly from discussions with Electa Arenal, Keitha Sapsin Fine, Peter Hall, Joel Krieger, Andrei Markovits, Andrew Martin, George Ross and Maurizio Vannicelli.

Documents

1 Comparative International Strike Statistics, 1964–6

Extract from Richard Hyman, *Strikes*, 2nd rev. edn (Glasgow: Fontana/Collins, 1978), p. 32.

Different countries record strikes in rather different ways and, thus, statistics such as these are not strictly comparable. None the less, they are capable of conveying a general idea of conflictuality in the labor relations of different countries.

2 Union Membership as a Percentage of Total Laborforce

Extract from John D. Stephens, *The Transition from Capitalism to Socialism* (London: Macmillan, 1979), p. 115.

The figures from different countries are not, strictly speaking, comparable, because of different accounting and reporting methods. Still, they can provide rough comparisons of unionization rates across countries and from one period to another within the same country.

	No. of stoppages per 100,000 employees	Average no. of persons involved per stoppage	Average duration of each stoppage in working days	No. of working days lost per 1,000 employees
Australia	63·8	350	1·8	400
Belgium	7·0	680	9·2	200
Canada	15·8	430	14·0	970
Denmark	5·5	370	7·3	160
Finland	10·8	360	2·1	80
France	21·8	1,090	0·8	200
Federal Republic of Germany	n.a.	n.a.	3·6	10
Republic of Ireland	25·6	450	15·2	1,620
Italy	32·9	720	5·3	1,170
Japan	7·6	1,040	2·9	240
Netherlands	2·2	370	2·4	20
New Zealand	26·8	250	2·1	150
Norway	0·6	100	26·0	5
Sweden	0·5	570	15·4	40
UK	16·8	340	3·4	190
USA	13·2	470	14·2	870

	1905	1913–14	Postwar peak	1930	1935	1939–40	1950	1960	1970
Australia	10	25	30	38	33	35	50	45	44
Austria	3	3	39	25	—	—	40	46	51
Belgium	2	7	27	18	22	24	36	43	51
Canada	n.a.	6	12	8	6	8	19	24	27
Denmark	7	13	27	21	25	28	33	48	50
Finland	n.a.	2	11	1	2	3	17	19	45
France	4	5	8	7	7	17	22	11	15
Federal Republic of Germany	6	11	30	18	—	—	29	30	30
Italy	1	2	12	—	—	—	37	31	36
Netherlands	n.a.	11	25	20	22	22	31	33	34
New Zealand*	8	15	19	17	13	39	38	38	35
Norway	2	7	13	12	17	26	34	49	52
Sweden	5	6	11	20	24	36	51	60	75
Switzerland	n.a.	5	12	17	19	19	29	28	27
UK	11	22	43	23	23	31	40	41	44
USA	6	7	11	7	7	16	22	24	23
Mean	5·4	9·2	20·6	16·8	17·5	23·8	31·0	33·5	37·6

* Unions registered under New Zealand's Industrial Conciliation and Arbitration Act only. Excluded are many public servants, mine workers, chemical fertilizer workers and agricultural workers.

3 Union Membership as a Percentage of Non-Agricultural Wage and Salary Workers

Extract from John D. Stephens, *The Transition from Capitalism to Socialism* (London: Macmillan, 1979), p. 116.

	1930–1	1935	1939–40	1945–6	1950	1960	1970
Australia	57	49	53	63	63	61	53
Austria	41	—	—	51	70	72	72
Belgium	35	40	40	41	51	58	65
Canada	14	15	17	24	29	31	33
Denmark	42	41	46	59	54	69	66
Finland	4	7	11	46	32	33	62
France	18	21	43	85	47	17	20
Federal Republic of Germany	26	—	—	—	44	39	37
Italy	—	—	—	—	81	61	57
Netherlands	35	48	44	44	45	44	41
New Zealand*	36	21	67	60	60	54	45
Norway	21	33	42	51	54	62	67
Sweden	35	44	53	55	69	73	87
Switzerland	26	30	28	35	40	36	31
UK	31	29	34	45	47	45	49
USA	11	13	25	31	32	31	28
Mean	28·5	27·7	36·1	49·3	51·1	49·1	50·8

* Unions registered under New Zealand's Industrial Conciliation and Arbitration Act only. Excluded are many public servants, mine workers, chemical fertilizer workers and agricultural workers.

4 Employee Investment Funds in Sweden

Extract from *Arbetar Rorelsen och Lönetragar Fonderna (The Labor Movement and Employee Investment Funds)* a report by a joint working group of the Swedish Confederation of Labor (LO) and the Social Democratic Party (SAP). This report was adopted as official policy by both organizations at their congresses in 1981.

Summary of the Proposal

Organization

The Working Group proposes that an employees investment fund be established in each county. [Sweden is divided into twenty-four counties, or provinces, each of which is a unit of government primarily responsible for administering medical care.] Two alternative ways of choosing the funds' governing bodies and management are proposed for further discussion. According to the first, a council shall be elected in each county to govern the fund in that county. All employees shall have the right to vote in the elections for the council. According to the second, employee representatives shall be selected by the trade unions. These representatives shall comprise a clear majority on the council. The council shall also have representatives of the county councils and the local governments within the county. The method for choosing the employees'

representatives is to be decided by the employees through decisions in the trade unions.

Financing the Funds

The funds are to get their money in two ways: partly through an increase in National Supplementary Pension System (ATP) fees, and partly by giving the funds a share in company profits.

For this purpose an increase in the ATP fee of one percent is proposed. (The ATP fee is currently 12 percent. It is levied on all wages and proprietor income between 14,000 and 105,000 crowns.)

The funds are thus financed partly through ATP fees. The relationship between the funds and the ATP system is to operate in the other direction as well. The employee investment funds are to be required to deliver an annual return to the ATP system. The money can then be used to pay pensions. The employees thereby get their return from the funds in an indirect way.

The employee investment funds are also financed by sharing in company profits. The Working Group proposes 'surplus-profit sharing', which implies that the funds get a share of profits over a certain level. The level of return on equity capital not subject to profit sharing is to be determined on the basis of what is a necessary rate of return for risk-bearing capital. At the current inflation rate and interest level that rate of return may lie between 15 and 20 percent. It is proposed that a profit sharing levy be set at 20 percent of all profits exceeding that rate of return. The proceeds of the levy shall be paid in cash to the ATP system for transmission to the funds.

Profit sharing shall apply to all joint-stock companies, regardless of size, activity, or kind of ownership.

Investment Policy
The funds' money is to be channeled into industry as equity capital. The funds shall thus invest their money principally in shares.

Share ownership through the funds will give employees the possibility of playing a significant role in the financing of companies' development and in decisions about conditions within their own companies.

The funds are to be free to buy shares in all kinds of companies. They are thus not only concerned with [companies whose shares are listed on] the stock exchange but can introduce equity capital in any company whatsoever. Nor is their right to invest confined to any sectors of the economy or any regions.

The right which companies have hitherto had to issue shares with different voting rights is to be eliminated. In the future all newly issued shares shall have the same voting right as the average for all previously issued shares.

If a large company does not issue new shares despite economic evidence of the need for new equity capital, the local union can initiate negotiations on the question. If the negotiations do not result in agreement, the question is to be put to arbitration. The union's right of initiative shall apply to all listed companies and most joint stock companies with more than 500 employees, excluding opinion (newspapers, etc.), socially owned, or foreign owned companies and banks.

Voting Rights
Employees shall gain two kinds of influence through the fund system. Their influence is to be exerted partly through investment of the funds' money and partly through the exercise of ownership rights in companies. The proposal is for the exercise of ownership rights to be divided as follows:

50 percent of the voting rights of shares acquired by the funds shall be exercised by the funds and 50 percent by the employees of the companies whose shares are acquired. This division of voting rights continues until the employees and funds each have 20 percent of the voting rights in any given company. Additional voting rights resulting from additional share purchases shall be exercised by the funds purchasing the shares.

Origins and Motives

Capital Formation and Equality
A motion by the Metalworkers union at the 1971 LO Congress declared it urgent to work out a way to bring about increased resources for investment without having negative effects on the distribution of wealth. It called for a study of whether—and in what way—the trade union movement should engage in collective capital formation that would give employees influence over the development of industry.

For the trade union movement, it was a reasonable task to consider ways by which a greater share of the results of production could be brought to their own groups without threatening the investment necessary for the future. To enable employees to participate in the ownership of companies' capital seemed a natural solution which could also offer a necessary support for the democratization of working life.

From the mid-1970s, oil crises, structural crises and restrictive economic policies abroad and at home dominated development and debate. It was no longer possible merely to proceed on the basis of accomplished gains. The progressive, dynamic industrial society had to be restored anew if employment and welfare were to be maintained. That had to take place through a new industrial build-up and development, which require increased savings.

The National Pension (AP) funds [surplus accumulated in the ATP system] were the 1960s' source of increased savings. They made the high savings ratio in society possible by resolving the distributive policy dilemma that private savings at a corresponding level would have implied. It is entirely unlikely that it would have been possible to attain the 1960s savings ratio without extensive collective savings.

The AP funds were built up to provide a buffer for the pension system and to guarantee the savings needed for the strong industry which would assure future pensions. It was anticipated that the funds would grow more slowly as pension payments increased. But the decline has been faster than anticipated as a result of inflation and low economic growth. As the AP funds diminish as a source of new savings it is desirable to replace them by other collective savings.

It is not sufficient to increase the magnitude of savings and put them at industry's disposal. In a situation of strongly increasing uncertainty concerning future conditions, including the uncertainty that the complete lack of price stability implies, firms are generally unwilling to expand. A contributing factor is the high debt–equity ratio of firms, since it makes them vulnerable to instability.

Thus, industry needs not only capital, but capital in a form that is risk-bearing. This is needed to make firms more robust and able to withstand setbacks. It also enables them to a greater extent than today to take the risks always associated with new production whose sales and profits depend on an uncertain future.

The debt–equity ratio can be decreased either through increased profits that are plowed back or through the emission of new shares. Increased profits should be part of a program for industrial reconstruction, providing that distributive policy goals are satisfied. But the need to decrease debt–equity ratios is greater than can be met through increased profits. A large portion of the new risk capital that is needed must therefore be provided from outside the firms. This is especially important in a period when the industrial structure has to be transformed. The test that occurs when a firm has to convince new buyers of shares of its future prospects compels it to engage in more conscious judgments about the future than when the only firms that get money are those that have a profitable period behind them.

The proposal for employee investment funds that we now offer is a response to this new situation. Firms shall be able to increase their stability and robustness through the capital channeled to them by the funds. That must occur in the form of equity capital. At the same time, this implies that large Swedish firms can be democratized and the private concentration of power can be broken. Industry's resources can grow without the drastic distributive effects that would otherwise be very likely to thwart the whole program for a reconstruction of the economy.

To Abstain—for Whose Benefit and in Which Way?

It is correct that savings must increase. It is correct that we have to hold back consumption, that is, to abstain to some extent, if we are to resolve the Swedish economy's problems. On this there is great political unity. The disunity there is concerns how it should occur. Should we rely mainly on increased collective savings? Or should we primarily count on private interests to take care of savings, build capital and decide investments? The problem is not *whether* we have to abstain but *for whom* we shall abstain. Should we abstain for those who can afford to save, that is, shareholders and high income recipients? Or should we gather the money in commonly owned and controlled funds?

From the standpoint of justice, the answer is obvious. If we are to have a continuing equalization of income and wealth we must increase our capacity for collective savings and capital formation. Otherwise all the striving for justice in Sweden will be blocked by the fact that we need rich people to handle the saving and investment in this country. Collective capital formation is equality's only secure basis. This is a truth that equality's enemies seem to be more conscious of than its friends.

The funds can be said to contribute to more equal distribution of wealth in three different ways:

1   The build-up of collective funds shifts the growth of wealth from private persons to commonly owned funds and thereby lays the basis for a continued equalization of income and wealth.
2   Profit sharing gives employees a share in the profits that must occur in order for industry to function and invest for employment and development.
3   Increased share ownership through the funds gives employees a progressively increased share in the dividends that are paid by firms.

Solidaristic Wage Policy and Company Profits

One of the original motives for employee investment funds is the need to prevent wage restraint in high profit firms from leading to increased profits for shareholders. As is well known, the profit situation of firms varies. In firms that are doing well it is often possible to take out higher wages than in the labor market as a whole. In part, those firms have money to spare after paying wages and normal returns. In part, they are often willing to pay higher wages because they need to attract labor to carry out expansion. Three different situations can then occur:

1   Wages go up, but only in these high profit firms. This breaks down the solidaristic wage policy of equal pay for equal work, for in this situation it is not the kind of work but the company's profit position that determines wages.
2   Solidaristic wage policy restrains wages in the high profit firms. This maintains the policy but excess profits that accrue to the owners occur as a result of the policy, which obviously subjects the policy to strains.
3   Wages go up in the high profit firms but corresponding wages spread to the rest of the labor market. Solidaristic wage policy is maintained retroactively and excess profits are avoided. But this drives up the general wage level and with it inflation. Too many firms risk getting into trouble because the wage level is adapted to the most profitable firms, injuring employment and growth and leading to increased inflation.

The conclusion so far is as follows. If the industrial development problem we face requires an increase in the profitability of industrial firms we must find a method to break the vicious circle that consists of higher profits leading to higher wage drift leading to higher inflation leading to lower profits leading to lower growth.

There is really only one method to counteract excess profits' negative effects and that is to decrease them. This can be brought about by compelling firms to share their profits with employees.

To make wage restraint acceptable is one of the aims of profit sharing through employee investment funds. Profit sharing will hold back wage drift and prevent the general wage level from being always adapted to what the most profitable firms can bear. With profit sharing, wage policy no longer has to be geared to the especially profitable firms. Profit sharing through employee investment funds can therefore eliminate a problem that otherwise can be insurmountable.

The 1980s—the Beginning of Deepened Welfare?

Employees are naturally conscious of the need for increased savings and strong, robust firms in order to overcome Sweden's economic crisis and defend the Swedish welfare society. But the welfare society cannot be defended by increasing injustice. The sacrifices and common efforts that are required can only be motivated if the welfare society can be developed further toward a better society, where the right to work is general and welfare is for everyone.

The reforms that can transform 1980s Sweden into a different and better society do not primarily concern increased consumption. We must certainly defend the material welfare we have achieved, indeed even increase it, in order to equalize incomes and make the efforts needed for children and the old. But perhaps the greatest gain in welfare that must be made concerns participation in the work of economic reconstruction that will absorb at least the decade ahead.

If people are enabled to participate in this work, if the reconstruction of Swedish industry is planned with citizen involvement, if the rebuilding of industry can also mean a change in production processes in the direction of forms that promote human development—in short, if economic democracy gets established simultaneously with recon-struction, then the 1980s can well be the beginning of a deepened welfare in Swedish society. That welfare is anchored not only to people's need for material wellbeing and social security but also to people's capacity to develop, learn new things, and take responsibility for their own and others' conditions.

That firms' need for risk capital has increased since the beginning of the 1970s does not diminish the need for employee investment funds but increases it.

That the more optimistic faith in rapid reform of work life at the beginning of the 1970s has now been dampened does not diminish the need for employee ownership to support the democratization of work life but increases it.

To develop welfare in Swedish society requires the democratization of work life, and that requires employee influence built on ownership.

5   The British 'Social Contract', 1973

Extract from TUC-Labour Party Liaison Committee, *Economic Policy and the Cost of Living* (February 1973).

The following is the complete text of the agreement reached by the leadership of the British Trade Union Congress (TUC) and that of the Labour Party in February 1973. The aim of the document was to provide a basis for union–government cooperation for the next time the Labour Party won political power. Such an explicit agreement would, it was hoped, prevent the debilitating conflicts over incomes policy and industrial relations legislation that had plagued the Wilson govern-ment of 1964–70.

1   The present inflation has been induced and encouraged by deliberate Government policies. For its policies have not only led to higher rents, house prices, fares and food: they have also led to a series of confrontations with the trade union movement—against the harsh background of record levels of unemployment. In addition, large-scale undercapacity working in manufacturing industry has led to increased costs. But this is not all. The Government has also chosen to redistribute income and wealth, on a massive scale, to the most privileged sections of the community—those benefiting most from investment income and capital gains, or reductions in corporation tax and estate duty. Yet at the same time, it has proceeded to introduce new and increased social charges right across the board, including dearer school meals, and much higher charges for prescriptions and dental and ophthalmic services.

2   In the two and a half years to the end of last year [1971], food prices rose by 25 per cent, rents by 29 per cent, rates by 30 per cent, fares by 42 per cent and house prices by more than half. This is the record of this Government on prices—that is, on the precise issue which more than any other brought it to office. The Government forced up rents, for example; it abandoned the cheap food policy; it presided over a huge drop in council house building—down by some 50,000 a year since 1970; and it deliberately pared down the subsidies given for commuter fares.

3   Time and time again, the Labour Movement has urged the Government to change its course. For the Government's policies have steadily undermined the possibilities of cooperation in our economic life. The Government refused to listen. Instead, it seems to have equated what it describes as its electoral mandate with a freedom to ride roughshod over the interests of great sections of the community. Certainly, it was quite unprecedented for a Government in this country to introduce legislation intended to transform the entire legal framework of one of the greatest institutions in our society—the trade union movement—without any attempt at serious discussion of the principles. The fact is that we are still living with the legacy of these serious and damaging mistakes, and a lack of confidence, which is affecting not only the trade union side of the industry, but also the attitudes of management towards investment.

4   This lack of confidence, moreover, is reflected in the serious state of the economy today. Despite the substantial increase in consumer spending during 1972 and the large increase in profits, manufacturing investment is now known to have fallen by no less than 10 percent—in real terms—in 1971–2. By choosing to stimulate the economy through an unplanned and unbalanced consumer boom, the Government has brought about a deterioration in our balance of payments, as imports have swept in to meet the demand, while goods which should have been exported have been diverted to the home market. The balance of payments surplus left by the Labour Government has been wiped out, and the trade deficit is growing at an alarming rate. This prospect can only serve to further deflate industrial confidence in our prospects for growth. Yet unless we can increase the level of our investment, our prospects for maintaining adequate growth in the long term must look decidedly grim.

5   Trade unionists are as concerned to keep down the cost of living as anyone else. They do not need to be told that what matters is real wages, not paper ones. But the problem of inflation can be properly considered only within the context of a coherent economic and social strategy—one designed both to overcome the nation's grave economic problems, and to provide the basis for cooperation between the trade unions and the Government. It must be a strategy which takes full account of the one irrefutable fact which has been so clearly highlighted by the freeze— namely that wages and salaries are very far indeed from being the only factor affecting prices. It has not been the farm worker, for example, who has been responsible for rising food prices nor has he shared in the higher farm profits which have resulted. Likewise it has not been workpeople and their families who have been responsible for rising rents. And it is surely time it was properly understood that in the composition of consumer prices as a whole, wages and salaries account for only 40 per cent—with profits, rent and other trading income accounting for 25 per cent, and imports and taxes on expenditure each accounting for between 15 and 20 per cent. Moreover, the level of wages and salaries in Britain is no more than about average for industrial countries—and their rate of increase for the last decade has been below the average.

An Alternative Strategy

6   The key to any alternative strategy to fight inflation is direct statutory action on prices—and, above all, direct action on the prices of those items that loom largest in the budgets of workpeople, such as food, housing and rents. *Food prices* must be controlled; and the next Labour Government will create the machinery to make this possible, providing subsidies where necessary to curb increases in the price of food. Special measures will be taken to deal with increases in the prices of important basic foods, such as milk, bread, sugar, meat and potatoes, including, where required, the creation of new special purchasing agencies to intervene in the market.

7   But controls on food prices will be only one part of a wide-ranging and permanent system of *price controls*. Such a system will need, first, to cover the main items in the family budget and affect the various levels of activity, from manufacturing to retailing. But second, the system will be flexible, with the powers available to it capable of being used selectively. And inevitably, in deciding to permit or refuse particular price increases, or whether or not to order price reductions, the system will have to concern itself deeply with profits, profit margins and productivity. In this way, the next Labour Government will prevent the erosion of real wages—and thus influence the whole climate of collective bargaining.

8   There must be a new approach to *housing and rents*. The next Labour Government will repeal the 1972 Housing Finance Acts. Council tenants will be given a better deal—both on rents and on security—and be given, too, very much more say in the management of their estates. For private rented tenants the aim will be the municipalisation of privately rented property— with, in the shorter term, much greater security of tenure being given to tenants in furnished accommo- dation. In addition, the Labour Government, while continuing its previous policy of helping those who do wish to buy their own house on mortgage, will end the scandal whereby the richer the person and the more expensive the house the greater is the tax relief. Surtax payers will no longer be eligible for relief at the higher tax rate and all relief on mortgages to purchase a *second* house will be abolished.

9   Far more houses must be built each year. The Government will aim to exceed the total of 400,000 new homes completed in the last full year of the Labour Government. The emphasis will be on homes for those most in need, and for those on lower incomes—with the subsidies to the public sector at least matching the £300 million plus a year which is now given in tax relief to the owner occupier. And all of this will be underpinned by the public ownership of all the *land* required.

10 A new approach is needed, too, on *transport*. Far more of our traffic must be concentrated onto *public* transport. And in addition to the provision of adequate subsidies to help contain increases in fares, the next Labour Government will carry out experiments in free public transport within our major conurbations.

11 A Labour Government will reverse the regressive social and taxation policies of the present Govern- ment, and aim for a large-scale *redistribution of income and wealth*. At present, one-tenth of British adults own between them three-quarters of the nation's private wealth—while 1 per cent of adults own about half of all ordinary share capital. (This excludes the holdings of pension and insurance funds, and invest- ment and unit trusts, which together account for about a third of total share capital; though even these funds are owned disproportionately by the higher income groups.) This distribution must be changed. The numerous tax concessions given to the rich by this Government will be reversed; and new taxes on wealth, and also on gratuitous transfers of wealth, will be introduced. The system of direct taxation will also be made very much more progressive, with the tax threshold being regularly raised as necessary to maintain the real value of the personal allowances.

12 These tax reforms must be supported by a deliberate Government decision to channel resources into the social services. *Social charges* will be phased out as quickly as possible—and prescription charges will be the first to go. For pensions, our immediate

commitment is £10 per week for single retirement pensioners and £16 a week for married couples—and the basic pension would be updated each year in relation to average earnings, not just the cost of living. The Labour Government will help to meet the cost of these urgent social requirements not only by tax changes but also by measures to cut back the level of defence spending to that of our European allies.

Investment, Employment and Economic Growth

13   Underpinning all of these policies, however, must be agreed policies on investment, employment and economic growth. And the objective must be to get faster growth in both national output and in output per man. For as we have emphasised above, wages and salaries in Britain have *not* increased faster than the average for industrial countries. What *has* increased faster is wage costs *per unit of output*—a direct result of the small rise of output in Britain.

14   Both output and output per man depend very substantially, of course, on the quality and effective management of capital equipment, as well as on up to date working methods. Yet Britain's capital equipment in many industries is rapidly falling behind the standard of our competitors. Fundamental to the British economic problem, therefore, is the problem of *investment* and, more generally, the problem of the control and the disposition of capital. The expansion of investment and the control of capital will thus be one of the central tasks of the next Labour Government. And this will mean the development of new public enterprise and effective public supervision of the investment policy of large private corporations. For it is these big firms which now dominate the growth sectors of the economy—to the extent, indeed, that no less than half of the nation's manufacturing output is already accounted for by the leading 100 companies, with this degree of concentration growing year by year.

15   In the past year both company and personal saving have been increasing, as is indicated by the improved liquidity position of companies and the high proportion of personal income which is being saved. Despite this, however, this productive investment has declined in real terms while there has been an uncontrolled flow of funds into the property market. New measures of control will be needed to channel funds into productive investment. In addition, the next Labour Government will need to assert the right to control capital movements overseas—whether in Europe or elsewhere. Already in the first three-quarters of 1972 UK private investment overseas totalled £970 million—30 per cent higher, that is, than in the whole of 1971. But in these same nine months,

inward investment totalled only £450 million—well down on the 1971 figure, which had been inflated by the boom in North Sea oil equipment. Moreover, the poor prospects for our balance of payments are, as is well-known, being further worsened by the terms of entry into the EEC. All that the Government suggest at this point in terms of increasing Britain's inadequate receipts from the Community Budget is a development of regional policy, which would be at the expense of the highly successful approach through the Regional Employment Premium, introduced by the Labour Government, which must be retained.

16   This highlights the need for a new approach on regional policy. The next Labour Government will, therefore, work closely with the trade union movement on an agreed programme to promote regional development—a programme spearheaded by effective manpower subsidies, a massive expansion in training and retraining, and investment funds for industry linked to greater accountability. And all of this will be backed by a policy of planned growth— allowing the economy to expand fast enough to keep unemployment down to a minimum level required for job changing and retraining.

Industrial Democracy and Economic Democracy

17   A new approach is needed also towards much greater democratic control in all aspects of our national life and towards greater public accountability for decision-making in the economic field. In the control of capital and the distribution of wealth there will be more economic democracy, and the growing range of functions of the trade union movement will bring about a great extension of industrial democracy. The collective bargaining process is the essential means whereby the most important factors affecting the livelihood of workpeople can be subject to joint regulation. But these areas must be extended to include joint control over investment and closure decisions.

18   In some respects, as was pointed out by the Donovan Commission, the extension of collective bargaining to deal with questions of industrial efficiency must entail the further movement of bargaining in many industries from national to plant level. But equally there has to be a development of common lines of action at national level and, indeed, at international level in dealing with the great international corporations.

19   This is one of the most complex fields of our national life, and this is the fundamental reason why policy in this field can only be based on agreement and not on compulsion, though there is great scope for seeking to reach recommendations through tripartite machinery along the lines of NEDC. But in the field of collective

bargaining, such recommendations can only be incorporated in collective agreements voluntarily reached by the process of negotiation.

20 In an earlier agreed statement published in July 1972 the National Executive Committee of the Labour Party, the General Council of the TUC, and the parliamentary Labour Party, outlined the provisions which would be included in the next Labour Government's legislation to repeal the Industrial Relations Act. They believe that the approach set out in this statement on Economic Policy and the Cost of Living will further engender the strong feeling of mutual confidence which alone will make it possible to reach the wide-ranging agreement which is necessary to control inflation and achieve sustained growth in the standard of living. Whilst the Liaison Committee will further review this subject in the coming months, it will of course be impossible to specify what will be the precise economic circumstances in which the next Labour Government will take office. Nevertheless it will be the first task of that Labour Government on taking office, and having due regard to the circumstances at that time, to conclude with the TUC, on the basis of the understandings being reached on the Liaison Committee, a wide-ranging agreement on the policies to be pursued in all these aspects of our economic life and to discuss with them the order of priorities of their fulfilment.

4

State Intervention in Postwar Western European Health Care: The Case of Prevention in Britain and Italy

ROSEMARY C. R. TAYLOR

State intervention in health care has increased in most West European countries since World War II. This chapter considers explanations for national differences in health care policies. It examines variations in solutions chosen by West European states to address a dual obligation accepted in the last four decades: to improve a population's health and expand a system of medical care—two tasks which do not always amount to the same thing. I look in some detail at one state strategy, prevention, because it is emerging as the modern panacea for the contemporary crises of cost and efficacy: health care systems that cost too much and medical care that does not seem to be making noticeable progress toward eliminating the chronic diseases that contribute disproportionately to mortality and morbidity in advanced capitalist societies. There are, however, some interesting differences among the preventive policies of West European nations. Any attempt to explain them encounters the general question that has intrigued several writers in the last decade: why the level of welfare spending varies from country to country (Wilensky, 1975). More important, it raises the issue of why there are differences in the content of welfare state measures chosen to respond to very similar material dilemmas.

I shall analyze the preventive strategies of two European nations, Italy and Britain, and discuss the USA in so far as it provides an instructive contrast. By 'strategy' I mean not simply a 'policy outcome'—particular legislative or institutional measures—but the ideological construction of prevention as the appropriate response to a perceived health problem and the range of initiatives it has inspired. I choose Italy and Britain, because they seem, at first glance, to support the argument that Western European nations are converging toward a similar post-industrial pattern of health care delivery and financing (Van Langendonck, 1972; Abel-Smith, 1965; Field, 1976; Roemer, 1977). Both have a national health service, while the USA relies much more on the private sector for its system of medical care. In their formulation of a preventive strategy, however, the three countries form an interesting continuum with the British approach moving closer to the American policy, which is very different from the Italian.

Explanations for the diverse evolution of these three national health care systems are often derived from more general models which identify the structural roots of variation in the development of the welfare state in advanced capitalist societies. They can be grouped for simplicity into four categories. Analyses (Heilbroner, 1975; Rimlinger, 1971; Marshall, 1975) that focus on the role of ideas—'changing views regarding the reciprocal rights and duties of the individual and the state' (Rimlinger, 1971, p. 10)—would tend to support Brian Abel-Smith's conclusion that different patterns of organizing and financing medical care 'have been greatly influenced by long-established differences in *attitudes* to medical care' (Abel-Smith, 1965, p. 40; my italics). A second group of studies relies on cross-national aggregate data to test models of the relation between levels and rates of economic development and social equality. They reject the significance of ideology and rely on such factors as the age of the social security system and the number of old people in the population to explain differences (Wilensky, 1975). Both theories have a certain mechanistic cast and often preclude a discussion of purposive social action. They make the political groups involved in the construction of strategies into the objects of history. Analysis of the interaction among organization, ideology, social conditions and economic development—the stuff of politics—tends to be smothered by the blanket of ideas or reduced to insignificance in the face of neat correlations between national income and social welfare.

Pluralist accounts of the development of the welfare state and/or the emergence of specific health policies do reintroduce politics into the discussion of social policy. They often have the merit of increasing our empirical knowledge of the background to particular political bargains struck at crucial historical moments in the evolution of welfare provisions in different advanced capitalist nations. However, as numerous critics have observed, they usually narrow the focus of attention so that the reader is regaled with biographical details about key 'decision-makers' or accounts of particular strategic ploys (Bevan's negotiations with the British medical profession in the postwar period is a favorite). If the terrain is expanded, it tends to document the detailed maneuvering of myriad interest groups, lobbyists, political parties and bureaucrats (Eckstein, 1960). Such studies enrich the historical narrative, but they are generally premissed on the assumption that the net result of all this activity will be the judicious construction of policy through the mediation of a benign state among competing interests. Not only does this perspective ignore the perpetuation of inequalities of power and resources, but it cannot explain (and, indeed, often denies) the existence of *systematic* variation among countries in the evolution of their health care systems. Heidenheimer *et al.* (1975), reviewing the European experience with public health services, argue that it reveals 'by no means only a series of victories of left-wing parties over right-wing parties' and they indicate the existence of different evolutionary patterns. But they fail to elaborate or capture the nature of those patterns and, describing the reasons for differences among European health care systems, they fall back on 'national traditions' (Heidenheimer *et al.*, 1975, p. 13), 'the development of the national health financing and administrative capacities and of how these are related to health care delivery' (p. 14) and the strategies of such 'players' as the medical profession and 'bureaucratic reformers' (p. 20).

Early attempts on the part of Marxists to tackle the theoretical problem of the role of the state in advanced capitalist society downplayed politics and focused on the structural constraints that shape state intervention in certain predictable directions in the field of social welfare in general and health in particular (Piven and Cloward, 1971; O'Connor, 1973; Rodberg and Stevenson, 1977). The state is faced with conflicting imperatives: to ensure long-term capital accumulation and reproduce labor power in the most cost effective

way possible. But at the same time, it must fulfill these 'functional requirements of capital' without jeopardizing social harmony. It must secure the loyalty of citizens who will continue to view the state in practice as the pluralists envisage it in theory—as the just provider of services to all. It must, therefore, fulfill 'two basic and often contradictory functions' (O'Connor, 1973, p. 6): accumulation and legitimation.

This approach had the merit of exploding the myth that Western Europe and the USA had been engulfed in a sudden health care 'crisis' in the 1970s, born of purely technological and economic factors. It encouraged the view that, in all these countries in the decades after World War II, the state faced a series of problems as it intervened in the field of social welfare. State-subsidized health care served several vital purposes: it helped to guarantee an active workforce for capital and socialized the cost; it reinforced basic work norms and tightened social control by defining what were acceptable medical reasons for absenteeism and, indeed, the very nature of illness as opposed to malingering. But since the public increasingly viewed the state, rather than the individual employer, as responsible for health care, it was the state that came to bear the brunt of popular disaffection over inadequacies. The rising sense of entitlement, which so many authors have considered a characteristic feature of the 1950s and 1960s, produced enormous political demands on the state, often for tangible services. The cost of those services risked outrunning the state's revenues. Perceived inequalities would be laid at its door. The conflicting demands of labor and capital, the tensions inherent in the accumulation/legitimation dilemma were, according to Marxists, the source of a *series* of health care crises.

The Marxist account of the fiscal crisis of the welfare state has, therefore, helped to elucidate the nature of the state's dilemma with regard to health care. It has also contributed toward a general theory of the contradictory path of welfare state evolution. However, as Ian Gough and others have argued: 'the functions of social policies must always be distinguished from their origins' (Gough, 1979, p. 54). Aside from the unresolved theoretical problem of linking the functional needs of capital to state activity postulated by this approach, it cannot account for either the content of, or variation in, various state responses to the accumulation/legitimation dilemma in welfare policy or, indeed, in any other sphere. Recent elaborations of this general approach have stressed the need to examine the content and organization of historical class struggles over specific social policies

(Navarro, 1978; Korpi, 1980b; Gough, 1979). Simply to articulate the existence of opposing class-based interests in the field of social welfare is not enough, however, since policy is rarely a direct reflection of conflict of interests. The most promising attacks on this problem have argued that the political organization of class demands on the state—in particular the composition and structure of working-class parties and unions—must be analyzed in conjunction with the internal organization of the state to understand the emergence of specific state policies. In addition, such an approach needs to be rooted in an account of the political, economic and, I would add, cultural resources available to these actors. The problem with a comparative case study is that it cannot hope to confirm or disconfirm conclusively the utility of the view sketched here, but I hope, through an analysis of preventive policies—one state response to the continuing health care 'crisis' in most West European countries—to suggest its potential.

In broad outline the problems that the state has faced with regard to health care in the postwar period are roughly similar in advanced capitalist countries, although they may have occurred at different historical moments. In the 1960s the crisis was one of access. Few questioned the value of medicine and nearly all argued that it should be extended to everyone: the elderly, minorities, people living in rural areas or other 'underserved areas'. The system as a whole should be expanded and improved until the wonders of medical science were available to all. In some countries this led to an expansion of health insurance benefits, in others to an organizational response: the construction of small, neighborhood health care facilities in communities that complained of inadequate care.

In the late 1960s and early 1970s a twofold attack on medicine and health care emerged. The concern with access continued to some degree but people began to worry more about the features of the medical system that contributed to social control. The increasing medicalization of everyday life and the overweening power of the medical profession were attacked on the grounds that they robbed consumers and patients of their natural capacities to cope with pain and disease. Critics, most notably Ivan Illich (1976), defined and abhorred the phenomenon of iatrogenesis—that doctors and drugs and scientific medicine often ended up doing more harm than good. More significant was the charge that they were not *effective*. The duplication of expensive medical facilities, the maldistribution of medical specialists, the priorities of the health care system, international rankings in rates of infant mortality—all were challenged, but most important, the very essence of modern medical care was attacked. The curbing of infectious disease (largely, in reality, through public health measures) used to be presented as the definitive achievement of scientific medicine. But the diseases which claim the vast proportion of lives in industrialized societies now are the chronic diseases of cancer, heart disease and stroke. Modern medicine has been able to make very little headway with them.

When the very usefulness of modern medicine was questioned in this way it fueled growing concern over another crisis—that of *costs*. Overall spending on health care has increased dramatically since World War II. It consumes a large percentage of the GNP (9 percent in the USA, 6 percent in Britain and 7 percent in Italy), which has created a serious political problem in those countries facing rising inflation and a steadily deteriorating economic situation. In the USA the high cost of hospitalization—the major contributor to spiraling expenditures—has not been absorbed by insurance, and so the social cost has been increased and the maldistribution of resources exacerbated. Low-income groups have not been the only ones to protest. Industry, and the auto industry in particular, turns a jaundiced eye toward medical costs as the fringe benefits it has to pay to unionized workers assume an even greater proportion of its wage bill. Regulation of various degrees of sophistication is the favorite remedy. Italy and Britain have tried to cope with the problem recently by imposing rigid ceilings on health care and social service spending by local and regional authorities.

Given that similar crises have developed in the health care systems of the three countries under study, the interesting thing to explain is the difference in state responses to those crises. A range of reactions to the current costs/efficacy dilemma have emerged in Italy, Britain and the USA. One of the most interesting and universal solutions, however, is the discovery (or in some cases rediscovery) of prevention as a panacea.

Prevention of ill-health is usually classified as primary, secondary or tertiary. In the words of the recent British Royal Commission on the National Health Service:

Primary prevention is taking measures to prevent disease or injury occurring, immunisation, good obstetric care and discouraging smoking. Secondary prevention measures are concerned with identifying and treating ill health promptly, for example through screening patients at risk. Tertiary prevention is concerned with mitigating the effects of illness or disease which has already occurred and includes rehabilitation and continuing care such as the care and after care of diabetics and terminal care. (*Royal Commission on the NHS*, 1979, p. 41)

Using this widely accepted definition I shall be mainly concerned with primary and, to a lesser extent, secondary prevention.

Italy, Britain and the USA have embraced prevention with enthusiasm in the last decade. 'Curative and caring services and related research contribute a great deal to individual treatment and their importance must not be under-rated, but on the basis of past experience a substantial improvement in national and community health is more likely to be achieved by preventive measures', argues the Royal Commission (1979, p. 42), and these sentiments are echoed in the official pronouncements on the state of health care and health care services in the other two nations. On closer examination, however, there appear to be substantial cross-national disagreements over what prevention means and what concrete measures it entails.

Basically, there are two meanings to the term which stem from two underlying, incompatible theories about the causes of illness in modern society.[1] The first theory, which focuses on the social determinants of illness (let us call it *social*), argues that disease can be largely attributed to the stress of life and the nature of work under capitalism—or at least in advanced industrial societies (Eyer and Sterling, 1977)—and to more specific environmental and work-related threats such as air pollution, carcinogenic chemicals and food additives, and industrial accidents. A preventive strategy based on this theory would entail far-reaching social changes. A study of the health of the elderly in an Italian community makes this argument explicitly:

[T]he present research revealed that the aging population of this town expressed needs that go beyond what health service alone can provide. The economic needs, the needs to use leisure time fruitfully, and the need to maintain affective ties, all of which were found closely related to the health status of the elderly, will require profound social and economic reforms. (Figa-Talamanca, 1976, p. 47).

The competing (*individualist*) theory focuses on personal behavior. The diseases of civilization—cancer, heart disease and stroke—are diseases of affluence, according to this view. People eat unwisely and too much, take too little exercise and kill themselves by driving recklessly. Prevention, it follows, means persuading individuals, through education or sanctions, to change their self-destructive habits.

A wide range of specific measures to reduce morbidity and mortality can then follow from either theory of disease and prevention. Changing health-related individual behavior can be attempted through methods as diverse as taxes on cigarettes, health promotion campaigns in schools and higher insurance premiums for consumers who persist in harming themselves. Advocates of a social theory, in contrast, have often worked through government regulatory agencies that have a mandate to protect workers and consumers against a variety of occupational and other environmental hazards. Others advocate direct action against industries with high pollution or low safety records.

A strategy of prevention can, therefore, be based on one of two competing theories and encompass a multitude of policies, programs, laws and other initiatives. Because the latter are constantly changing with changes in economic conditions and local administrations, it is difficult to locate any one country's strategy unambiguously. Italy, for example, is particularly difficult to characterize because the responsibility for many health care activities and their implementation has been delegated to the regions in the last decade and so policies vary in different parts of the country. In some Socialist or Communist controlled municipalities workers have achieved a thorough knowledge of the production process, particularly in the chemical industry, and implemented safeguards against many occupational hazards. At the national level, however, Italy's legislation with regard to environmental and occupational threats to health is poor. The United States, on the other hand, has more comprehensive legislation in areas such as toxic substances and noise, but enforcement has been hesitant and, under some administrations, minimal. The implementing structures of the National Health Service in Britain distribute money to doctors and hospitals around the country and ensure access to the public, but they are not really set up to enunciate any philosophy of health care, so the etiological theory which underlies British health related policies is often hard to determine.[2]

In terms of an overall direction, however, it is relatively easy to describe the preventive strategies of different countries in a particular historical period. In most countries, both the social and individualist theories about the origins of disease have had and still do have their advocates, but one tends to be dominant at any given time. As the eighties begin, Britain and the United States, although their health care systems are organized and financed in very different ways, have adopted fairly similar versions of an individualist strategy. Italy on the other hand, with a health care system superficially similar to that of Britain since 1978, provides one of the strongest examples of a social approach.[3] The ideological construction of prevention in each nation is well summarized in the following policy and legislative statements. In 1977, the Department of Health and Social Security (DHSS) in Britain issued a White Paper entitled *Prevention and Health*. In it they discuss an earlier subcommittee report of the Expenditure Committee of the House of Commons on preventive medicine and endorse one of its main objectives:

> The Sub-Committee are concerned to ensure that people are encouraged to take more responsibility for their own health; and say that to enable them to do so there should be a greater flow of reliable information and advice. Many of the positive steps towards healthy living which they recommend are, in their own words, 'really warnings to the ordinary citizen about what he himself can do to avoid illness and premature death'. (DHSS, 1977, p. 1)

The Foreword by Joseph Califano, the Secretary of Health, Education and Welfare in the USA, to the first Surgeon General's Report on *Health Promotion and Disease Prevention* in 1979 makes the same argument:

> This report underscores a point I have made countless times, again and again, in my thirty months as Secretary of Health, Education and Welfare: 'You, the individual, can do more for your own health and well-being than any doctor, any hospital, any drug, any exotic device.'
> Indeed, a wealth of scientific research reveals that the key to whether a person will be healthy or sick, live a long life or die prematurely, can be found in several simple personal habits: one's habits with regard to smoking and drinking; one's habits of diet, sleep and exercise; whether one obeys the speed laws and wears seat belts, and a few other simple measures. (US Department of Health, Education and Welfare, 1979, pp. viii–ix)

Article 20 of the 1978 Italian National Health Service

Law, on 'preventive activity', includes not a single reference to personal behavior and instead concentrates on a range of factors in 'working and living environments' which must be controlled or eliminated to ensure good health (**Document 1**).

To understand how states have constructed different preventive strategies we may look first at the explanations for the emergence of the individualist approach in the USA, where it has reached its most well-developed formulation and engendered a great deal of comment and debate. I shall consider three of the most commonly cited explanations. The specific theories fashioned to account for state policy in the field of health draw on the same intellectual traditions that inform arguments about the nature and growth of the welfare state. But since they have to explain the conception and implementation of particular legislation, and the funding of particular programs, as well as the emergence of general trends, they emphasize a different level of activity. Of necessity, therefore, they are more sensitive to short-term developments within the political sphere and to the strategies of political actors in a defined historical period.

According to the first explanation, scientific research has demonstrated beyond reasonable doubt that damaging lifestyles are behind the modern epidemics of cancer, heart disease and strokes. Secretary Califano's conviction about the 'wealth of scientific research' pointing to the need for individual measures is reflected in the Surgeon General's report, *Healthy People*:

> In 1964, A Surgeon General's Report on Smoking and Health was issued. This report pointed to the critical link between cigarette smoking and several fatal or disabling diseases. In 1979, another report was issued based on the knowledge gained from over 24,000 new *scientific* studies—studies which revealed that smoking is even more dangerous than initially supposed (US Department of Health, Education and Welfare, 1979, p. 9; my italics)

Assailing popular wisdom and public misinformation, Elizabeth Whelan argues in the Heritage Foundation's *Policy Review*:

> The Delaney Clause, the EPA 'Principles', the OSHA regulations and even the new interagency proposal seem to be so intent on preventing cancer *at any cost* that they have overlooked some obvious

and sometimes disturbing scientific realities. (Whelan, 1979, p. 40)

She deplores the skepticism and antagonism which have greeted the 'few scientists who have stepped forward to report the facts about chemicals, cancer, the environment and health' (Whelan, 1979, p. 45) and concludes firmly:

Air and water pollution, modern food technology, and 'industry' are not at the root of our cancer problem. The parts of the cancer causation puzzle now assembled point directly to harmful aspects of our individual habits, particularly cigarette smoking and dietary excesses. (Whelan, 1979, p. 45)

Advocates of a second explanation (Crawford, 1979, Salmon and Berliner, 1979) argue that concern over rising health costs lies behind the narrow view of prevention. Particular actors—large corporations and state—stand to benefit (by a drop in the cost of the social wage, for example) from such measures as cost-sharing insurance plans that emphasize the necessity of changing individual habits. They stand to lose a great deal from analyses indicating the importance of social and environmental factors for health that might encourage political efforts to impose new restrictions on industry. They have, therefore, publicized and promoted, if not actually generated, the individualist approach.

Finally, Marc Renaud has argued in a provocative paper that state intervention in the field of health care will inevitably ignore larger environmental influences on health. There are 'structural constraints which preselect the issues to which the state in capitalist societies is capable of responding' (Renaud, 1975, p. 559). The first and easiest option for the state will be to blame individuals for their own bad health. But one must not look to the 'Machiavellian wills of some powerful individuals or groups under the control of some medical empire' (Renaud, 1975, p. 560) to explain the limits to state action. It is rather the result of the 'deeply embedded and camouflaged logic of the capitalist social order in health' (p. 569), 'the institutionalized relationships between capitalism, health needs, medicine and the state' (p. 560).

Examining only the American case, for the moment, none of these explanations provides a satisfactory account of the emergence of a narrowly focused state policy on prevention. The argument that the empirical findings of science accumulate and gradually yield a body of data that persuades policy-makers of the appropriateness of the individualist approach ignores what we know of their social construction. Much of the data now heralded as conclusive proof that indulgent personal habits cause ill-health has been around for a while. What we need to account for is the 'discovery' of this knowledge and the way it has been used. Moreover, British sociologists of science argue that it is not only the political manipulation of data that we need to fear: the procedures and conclusions of scientific and medical research themselves are, like all other cultural products, the contingent outcome of interpretative social acts (Bloor, 1976; Mulkay, 1979). Michel Foucault's book (1975) on the emergence of clinical medicine in France is a compelling account of how a revised 'way of seeing' structured new versions of medical experience for doctors and patients alike. Such work argues for a skeptical look at the claim that scientific research alone has dictated an individualist approach to prevention in the 1980s.

Blaming corporate pressure for the individualist approach is also unsatisfactory. Theoretically this argument is based on a view of the state as a simple instrument of capital, and of ideas as the direct reflection of capital's interests. It is also not clear that costs could be controlled or that corporations would gain substantially from preventive measures of this kind. Holtzman has argued, for example, that in times like the present when unemployment is high,

[I]t might even be argued that with labor in plentiful supply, there is little incentive to improve the health of potential workers. As the demand for skilled labor diminishes, it may not cost too much to train a replacement for a worker who dies prematurely or who becomes disabled. Companies could even save money by premature deaths; long disability and retirement payments would be reduced. (Holtzman, 1979, p. 35)

Nor does this argument explain how and why the life-style emphasis has captured the public imagination. It is implausible to attribute the recent addiction of Americans to exercise and 'healthier' diets solely to corporate avarice. Politically such an explanation is also problematic, because it essentially dismisses many of the 'preventive' alternatives in the health care field— self-help groups, holistic health advocates and practitioners—as the peddlers of reformism and the victim of co-optation. It overlooks the genuinely progressive movements of the 1960s and 1970s within health care to demystify medicine and teach patients to rely on each other and their own resources.

While Renaud is careful not to allocate blame for restrictive state intervention and preventive policies to specific individuals or groups, he does not cast much light on the politics of policy development. Politics, in fact, almost disappears from his account. His emphasis on the overall tendency of capitalism to commodify health needs leads him to omit the details of that process. While he does admit the possibility of the emergence of the class struggle and thus partial reform—'timid efforts ... to partially implement a new, more preventive and more community-oriented medicine' (Renaud, 1975, p. 569) under particular historical conditions—it remains for us to spell out those political and economic circumstances.

These explanations, while unsatisfactory or incomplete when applied to the American case,[4] become even less convincing when we turn to the comparative question. It is true that Italy, Britain and the USA were all concerned about health care costs. Their preventive policies were inspired to a greater or lesser extent by that concern. Yet this fact cannot explain why the nature and content of those policies were so different.

The DHSS acknowledges in *Prevention and Health* that an important impetus for British initiatives on prevention was, indeed, costs:

The enquiry was undertaken in response to the Expenditure Committee's concern at the growing cost of the National Health Service and the high and increasing share of total NHS expenditure which was being devoted to the hospital services, most of which are curative services, compared with the relatively small sums spent on prevention. (DHSS, 1977, p. 1)

The DHSS also argued that preventive measures should be guided by the assumption that individual lifestyles were the key to change. However, it denied that its position on the content of preventive programs was dictated by cost considerations:

The effectiveness of a preventive strategy depends to a large extent on people's attitudes and behaviour. This general thesis is well worth stating right from the start. So also is the point that it is no part of the Government's policy at any time to regard prevention as a cheap option. Prevention may be cheaper than cure, and expansion of preventive services may be able to contribute to the more effective use of limited resources. However,

prevention can sometimes be expensive. (DHSS, 1977, p. 6)

The USA, too, was concerned about costs. The etiological theories of disease that emerged in that period appear to be informed, in large part, by that concern. The secretary of HEW argued:

We are a long, long way from the kind of national commitment to good personal health habits that will be necessary to change drastically the statistics about chronic disease in America ... And meanwhile, indulgence in 'private' excesses has results that are far from private. Public expenditures for health care that consume eleven cents of every federal tax dollar are only one of those results. (US Department of Health, Education and Welfare, 1979, p. ix)

His report confirmed that:

There are three overwhelming reasons why a new, strong emphasis on prevention—at all levels of government and by all our citizens—is essential.
First, prevention saves lives.
Second, prevention improves the quality of life.
Finally, it can save dollars in the long run. In an era of runaway health costs, preventive action for health is cost-effective. (US Department of Health, Education and Welfare, 1979, p. 9)

One of the principal architects of the Italian National Health Service Law displayed a similar concern for escalating costs. In the fifteen years prior to the reform, and particularly since 1967, the mutual benefit societies' expenditure on health care had risen at a rate notably greater than that of GNP. He cites as one of the three major obstacles to the realization of a national health service 'the growing imbalance between the economic costs that confront the community and the health benefits perceived by individuals' (Berlinguer, 1979, p. 14; translation mine). It is not, however, the costs of individual 'private excesses' which he blames. Instead he points to the rate of growth of health insurance costs and compares it with the expenditure on public health services, which since 1975 has remained stationary (Brenna, 1978, p. 2; cited in Berlinguer, 1979, p. 42).

Thus all three nations did generate a preventive program partly in response to the threat of uncontrollable health care costs. But this threat did not inevitably dictate a program oriented toward changing unhealthy individual habits. Similarly, scientific and medical research on the roots of chronic illnesses do not differ markedly from country to country. Where there are differences in the kind of research funded, international scientific networks quickly disseminate the findings. Yet the accumulated body of evidence has not automatically led to similar recommendations about the prevention of illness. Rather, different governments accept different standards of evidence or draw different conclusions from the same scientific findings.

We find in the British White Paper, *Prevention and Health*, for example, that the government rejects evidence (recommendations concerning saturated fats and screening for breast cancer) about the advisability of certain personal behaviors which is accepted in the USA. It argues that other British government experts 'may have assumed certainty where none in fact exists' (**Document 2**).

Finally, Italy, Britain and the USA all faced the constraints of a capitalist society which Renaud documents. Yet they have generated preventive programs which differ markedly in their theoretical assumptions, their content and organization. I argue that the reasons for those differences must be sought not in a general theory of the patterns of welfare state evolution, but in specific historical accounts of state responses to the political articulation of class interests.

Italy

Compulsory health insurance and other forms of social protection developed relatively late in Italy as compared to other European nations. It was, in fact, the last form of assistance to be introduced into the country for the protection of workers. In 1943 a law was passed in favor of compulsory insurance for all employees which created a single authority to manage insurance—Istituto Nazionale per l'Assicurazione Contro le Malattie (INAM). The insurance scheme offered by INAM covered medical benefits for all employed persons and pensioners. Various special insurance schemes, however, were founded over the years for independent groups of workers such as seamen, the liberal professions, journalists, public employees, self-employed artisans, merchants and tenant farmers. This led to a confusing patchwork of insurance schemes, one for each section of the working population. Because of the cumbersome administrative structure of INAM and other insurance bodies, the monthly contributions from employers and employees which represented the majority of their funds, turned out to be consumed by their administrative expenses.

In 1974 the various insurance schemes had accumulated such enormous debts that a law was passed to 'wipe the slate clean' and erase all debts.

The system of administration and financing of public hospitals was drastically altered with the implementation, in January 1975, of Law no. 386. Public general hospitals were divided into three categories: zonal, provincial and regional according to the facilities and services which each hospital offered (Koff, 1975). The hospitals were then placed under the administrative supervision of regional bodies which, in turn, were directly responsible to the Ministry of Health.

In January 1979 the National Health Service Law was approved by the Parliament. The government delegated the task of organizing health services, including occupational health services, to each region. The new administrative units, which do not always correspond to local government boundaries, are the Unità Sanitarie Locali (USL). They take responsibility for 50,000–200,000 inhabitants and will provide medical care in the three types of hospital outlined above. In addition, they will assume responsibility for industrial hygiene and medicine, food control and pharmaceutical services. This organization of the health care system is to be implemented gradually over the five years following the adoption of the bill. Insurance schemes will continue to operate during the period of transition but will eventually disappear altogether. The hope expressed in the reform was that the mutual-benefit-cum-health-insurance system would be changed into a decentralized and democratically controlled public health service. Particular effort was made to reunify the separate activities of prevention, treatment and rehabilitation.

Disease Patterns

One of the most obvious explanations for the difference among countries in their policies toward the amelioration of ill-health is that they are simply dealing with different material circumstances: that Italy, with its relatively low expenditure on measures to change individual lifestyles and its social approach to the prevention of illness, is faced with a completely different disease pattern. There is some basis to this argument. For example, comparing rates of cardiovascular mortality, Italy has consistently maintained a much lower rate than the USA or Britain. A study of twenty advanced capitalist countries reveals that only Japan, Switzerland and France have lower rates, while in 1969 the USA ranked first and the UK eighth. In

1974 Italy was still seventeenth, the USA had fallen to third and the UK moved up to seventh (**Document 3**). Given that the research amassed on cardiovascular mortality concentrates overwhelmingly on lifestyle factors and that a significant positive correlation has been found between such factors as cigarette consumption, dietary cholesterol and major animal-food sources and cardiovascular mortality rates (NIH, 1979, p. 346), it can be argued that Italian policy-makers have concluded that cardiovascular mortality rates are not a significant problem. Controlling risk factors that largely involve personal behavior would not, therefore, constitute a major priority. However, in 1975 it was nevertheless true that diseases of the circulatory system constituted the major cause of death for the population, followed by neoplasms (*Eurohealth Handbook*, 1978, p. 327).

Looking at the data on occupational health, on the other hand, we find that in the 1970s Italy looked back on a rapidly increasing rate of occupational injuries over two decades culminating in a figure of 1,600,000 for 1973 (Assennato and Navarro, 1980, p. 222). Occupational accidents also increased in Britain and the USA during the same period, but in 1979 Italy had the highest rate of labor accidents and occupational disease per employed person in the Common Market (Terranova, 1979, p. 3). The significance of this figure can be read not in the size of its contribution to mortality rates, but in the fact that it constituted a major political problem for the Italian unions and government. In addition, Italy faced several other pressing problems with regard to health and health care which were not, or were not perceived as being, so severe in the USA and Britain. There is great inequality in health status and health services between the north and south of the country, which successive governments were pressured to remedy. In 1979 Italy had the highest perinatal death rate in Europe (Terranova, 1979, p. 2), and it has to cope with a range of infectious diseases and health problems which are more typical of nineteenth-century conditions in the other two countries. We may conclude therefore that Italy, like the UK and the USA, does have to contend with the chronic diseases as the major contributor to mortality rates, but that it has other, competing priorities which are political as well as medical problems.

The Medical Profession

Considerable weight has been given to the interests and the political power of the medical profession in various accounts of the health care sector's evolution and of the emergence of specific health care policies in different countries. We cannot afford to overlook its role (Willcocks, 1973; Alford, 1975). At first glance, however, it would seem that the orientation of the medical profession is irrelevant to the issue of prevention. After all, physicians in most advanced capitalist countries in the twentieth century spend vastly more of their time on curative than on preventive care of *any* kind. A recent comparative study concluded that 'periodic checkups and health teaching are very time-consuming, doctors are too busy with their normal flow of ill patients, and . . . they do very little preventive work' (Glaser, 1976). However, it is also true that the medical profession, by virtue of its state-sanctioned control over medical knowledge, has exerted a powerful influence over state policies concerning the organization, financing and distribution of medical care in the twentieth century. What, then, has been its stance toward preventive measures in Italy?

Italian physicians do not receive a medical training substantially different from their British or American counterparts in terms of content. The differences frequently remarked upon are that Italian medical schools are extremely overcrowded, as are the universities in general. In addition, Italian medical education is biased more toward theory and entails less clinical training than in Britain or the USA. Neither of these differences would indicate that Italian physicians are more oriented toward the principles and practice of prevention. In fact, similar criticisms to those in the other two countries have been leveled against Italian medicine for its overemphasis on curative skills and its social-control functions (Maccacaro, 1981).

Preventive remedies used in practice stem to some extent from the contemporary requirements of the doctor–patient relationship (Rosenberg, 1979). Patients in any country usually want something concrete from their physicians which will make them feel better, so that their demands exert further pressure on physicians to practice curative rather than preventive medicine. There is some evidence that Italian physicians rely more on pharmaceutical aids and prescribe more than do physicians in other nations, thereby strengthening an adherence by patients to the 'magic bullet' approach to medicine which tends to further obscure the role of larger social factors in illness. One reason for this practice is the method of payment under the insurance system that existed before the national health reform in 1978: doctors were paid by the patient visit and by the prescription, a practice unlikely to encourage the time required for preventive consultations related either to a patient's personal habits, or to his/her work history. A recent study of general practitioners confirms this impression. Only 11 percent of the doctors sampled were in favor of the national health service reform with its strong emphasis on broad preventive activities. When asked directly about their attitudes toward preventive medicine, 85 percent said that they supported it, but listed a series of obstacles which inhibited their commitment to it in practice. Most cited time, and others listed money, logistics and age as significant barriers to preventive activities (Piperno and Renieri, 1983, pp. 25–6).

The fraction of the profession which has advocated a broadly based view of prevention has suffered a decline relative to other specialties. The number of *medici condotti* ('board of health' or 'county' doctors), salaried physicians who largely practiced in rural areas and were responsible for a range of public health activities, increased from 10,300 to 10,500 over 1957–68, an increment of 1·9 percent. The corresponding increment for hospital-based doctors was 59·9 percent (from 24,000 to 38,300) and for all doctors 22·7 percent (Caruso, 1977, p. 206, table 2). One of the central reasons for the inability of public health to attract new recruits is that such work is paid relatively badly. Commenting on the lack of attention to 'surveillance at the population level' two critics argued, in 1973, that 'medical officer recruitment is a problem because the salaries and working conditions are hardly competitive' (Saracci and Donato, 1973, p. 135). The situation had not changed much by 1979 when it was estimated that those engaged in preventive work, be it in schools, factories or environmental services, could expect to make much less than the average physician's salary.

The Italian medical profession, then, like its counterparts in Britain and the USA, has emphasized curative medicine and is not likely to fight for a broad environmental notion of prevention. But since the 1970s there has been a critical difference in its structural situation *vis-à-vis* the state, which has weakened its ability to define totally the content of health-related measures. There is, first, a huge over-supply of physicians. Tuition fees are minimal and anyone who wishes may attend university and acquire a medical degree. In the last decade the universities have been subjected to a string of uncoordinated liberalizing reforms and enrollment has increased dramatically. Critics agree, however, that one of the results has been that the quality of education has suffered. The

economic crisis, in turn, has limited opportunities for subsequent employment. Medical education is no exception, so that the total number of students in medical school increased from about 25,000 in 1962–3 to about 120,000 in 1972–3, which represented 15 percent of all university students as against 7·8 percent in 1965–6 (Saracci and Donato, 1973, p. 133). In 1975 it was estimated that Italy had more than 115,000 physicians—a ratio of one physician for every 487 inhabitants (*Eurohealth Handbook*, 1978, p. 332).

The medical profession was obviously concerned that such an oversupply would limit its bargaining power, and much of its political energy in the 1970s was focused on securing limits to admission to a medical education. Toward the end of the decade, it also became clear that the profession could not successfully oppose the implementation of the national health service law which was supported by a very broad coalition of forces. It concentrated, therefore, on minimizing the threat it posed to the existence of private practice. The campaign was successful in that physicians now have the option of choosing either a full-time salaried position with the national health service, or a contract relationship which allows them to maintain a private practice.

Since its implementation, the medical profession has mounted a series of attacks on various provisions of the reform. In addition, the internal divisions within the profession have been exacerbated, because the family practitioners under contract won a substantial increase in their fees which almost doubled their income. The salaried hospital physicians, who see themselves as more committed to the principles of the reform, reacted in outrage and then struck in support of the demand that their salaries be increased by a corresponding amount. The President of the Republic subsequently refused to approve the increase for the family practitioners, thus pitting the profession in a serious battle against the state. Given these controversies, the medical profession did not see the issue of prevention as a priority, nor was it in a position to oppose vigorously or effectively a broad-based definition of prevention.

The Left and the Unions

The critical element in an explanation for why Italy evolved a preventive policy oriented largely toward work-related and environmental factors is the relative power of the labor movement and the left during the period that state intervention in the health care field was attempted. The existing structure of the health care system and the timing of state intervention are also crucial factors.

During the 1950s the labor movement in Italy was both weak and divided. The major Italian union had split and unemployment was high (Assennato and Navarro, 1980; Bagnara, 1981). In the same period Italian industry began an aggressive program of rationalization. The introduction of new technology, the inclusion of a new group of workers who had migrated from the south to the industrial north and the greater emphasis on increasing productivity had several consequences, the most dramatic of which was an increase in occupational injuries. By and large this cost of rapid industrialization was accepted by workers as inevitable. Technological progress was viewed as a natural process which had occupational accidents as its unfortunate byproduct. Workers, therefore, accepted a system whereby wages were set in some part with regard to the hazardous nature of the work involved.

After the political ferment of the early 1960s, some modest gains were made by the trade union movement. There was still a tendency to equate health hazards with money—wages or extra compensation—but workplace design and occupational health emerged as issues to be bargained over. The metal and chemical workers' unions were the most vocal on these questions and won the right, after a struggle over their national contracts in the early 1960s, for union locals to establish joint committees, with representatives from unions and management, to discuss conditions of safety at the workplace. Implementation and degree of activity varied enormously but the principle had been established.

Gradually, throughout the 1960s, the focus within the labor movement shifted so that working conditions emerged as a set of considerations equal in importance to wages and hours. One of the most critical developments in this change was the emergence of 'workers' investigations'. These had several sources (Bagnara, 1981, pp. 437–8) but consisted of a set of inquiries by groups of social scientists and trade union and/or party experts who carried out their studies together with groups of workers. Through interviews or group discussion, they attempted to understand the actual experiences of workers in the workplace and in the community and to reconstruct the nature of changes in work through the eyes of those who had experienced them. A significant study for occupational health was that done by the union local in Turin. It conducted an investigation at a chemical plant, Farmitalia, with two purposes in mind: to determine through the workers' experiences what work and health conditions were like

in the plant, and to inform workers about the injurious consequences of some aspects of their work and the substances they handled. It was during this study that criticisms of the union policy of paying in monetary terms for the risks incurred by workers developed and the slogan 'health is not for sale' was coined.

In the course of these workers' investigation an important observation about the nature of the labor-force emerged. Mechanization and Taylorization had led to the progressive deskilling of many workers. However, it was now possible to identify a series of clusters of workers, all performing the same operations and therefore confronting identical working conditions, which became known as 'homogeneous groups'. Later the trade union movement came to recognize this 'natural' structure of the laborforce and modeled its internal organization in the plant after it. These groups formed the basic unit for working out what has become known as the workers' model of health hazards. They began to demand that any expert or management evaluation or measurement of the level of risk attached to any piece of work or equipment existing in any plant must take account of the collective experience of the homogeneous group. This meant in effect a refusal to delegate health problems to experts and a requirement that the evaluation of occupational hazards must be controlled by those subject to them.

During 1968–9 extensive work was carried out on designing a method of evaluating work hazards, so that the homogeneous groups could effectively collect information and delegate certain tasks to experts (**Document 4**). Finally, a series of instruments were developed to measure the effects of health hazards over time, so that a collective memory could be built up. Given that both plants and homogeneous groups changed over time, it was thought necessary to construct a long-term evaluation of risks and a way of measuring the effect of any changes introduced.

Much of this work was initiated by rank-and-file or local labor organizations. The critical period in its development was the outbreak of labor militancy in 1968, leading to what is known as the 'hot autumn' of strikes in 1969. As a result of this industrial strife, initially unforeseen by the unions, health and safety organization changed radically within the factory. The safety committees which had been appointed by unions and management were now to be elected directly by the homogeneous groups. The delegates from these groups would not be removed from production and so would remain closely tied to both the rank-and-file and to conditions of work.

General political developments contributed to a

situation in which both this mode of organization and the analysis of health problems developed at the workplace were likely to receive serious support. Issues of health had become important in the internal political debate of the Italian Communist Party (PCI). The debate focused around local territorial control of a wide range of services, and great emphasis was placed on worker and community control drawing on participatory models like those evolved by workers inside the factory. In a conference organized in Genoa in 1967 the PCI debated and attempted to coordinate these initiatives at the national level.

In the late 1960s and early 1970s a broad political movement for reform generated a series of demands concerning the nature of work and health. The proposals from the student movement for grassroots democracy fueled the drive for worker and local control; the intellectual critiques of the nature of medicine and of health created a greater awareness of the links between health and relationships at work and in both family and community. Proposals for reform were no longer simply proposals to improve health care services; they extended much further to consider the controlling features of medical and many other institutions and the harmful reproduction of the medical model even within democratic organizations (Carrino, 1977). The movement within psychiatry and among mental health workers, inspired by the work of Franco Basaglia, was particularly influential in advancing the latter critique. The mobilization of feminists and of the Radical Party around the issues of abortion and health raised a series of questions about women's control over their own bodies and their relationship to their families.

During 1969–71, with the increase of direct union activity at the workplace, the confederations concentrated their energies on negotiating with the government over the introduction of social reforms which center–left governments in power since 1963 had failed to introduce. Known as the 'struggle for reforms', this strategy began with a series of demands over housing policy but extended to transport, education, the health services and the taxation system. The demands were articulated through general strikes on a regional basis, by meetings with the political parties and with the government. The results were by and large meager—producing a new housing law and some promises about health services. The strategy, however, was of great importance to the union confederations because of organizational interests: bargaining activities had become decentralized in favor of the individual industry unions and shopfloor

militants; the union movement as a whole felt the need to reaggregate the varying sectors of the working class around unifying aims in a period when union membership was increasing dramatically (50 percent during 1968–74). It was also important to see that the living conditions of workers' families did not deteriorate so as not to cancel out the benefits won in bargaining at the factory level (Regalia et al., 1978, p. 133).

Taken together, these factors indicate why the struggle for reforms was not explicitly abandoned by the confederations in 1971, when it had become clear that it could not generate adequate rank-and-file support. Regalia, Regini and Reyneri argue:

It allowed them to co-ordinate bargaining activities according to a scale of priorities, to regain a pre-eminent position in the trade union movement, and to obtain privileged status as a body which the government had to consult on important economic and social problems. Only by bearing in mind all those advantages which accrued to the confederations, independently of the amount of success achieved by the struggle for reforms, can one understand why the union movement was so slow to change its strategy, despite its obvious failures, the criticism (and self-criticism) it provoked, and the various demands for a change of direction. (Regalia et al., 1978, p. 134)

By 1972 the confederations took an official joint stand on health problems and occupational hazards in an attempt to tie plant conflicts to social ones and to translate the demands that had arisen spontaneously from the needs of different groups of workers into a long-term bargaining strategy. At a conference held in Rimini they demanded that the new forms of information gathering developed by many of the homogeneous groups and introduced through collective bargaining in various industries and geographic areas be extended; that occupational health experts be trained in a way which would make them a genuine aid to labor rather than a regulator of absenteeism for management; and that occupational health services be integrated in a national health service which would be regionalized. This was the same year that certain powers were transferred from the central government to the communal (local) and regional governments, with their own elected governing assemblies, as the left had been urging for some time. A number of these local governments gained left majorities and several of them, in central and northern Italy, instituted preventive industrial medicine services (Servizi de Medicina Preventiva dei Lavoratori—SML) to give technical assistance to workers in individual firms. The SMLs has a mixed record—none being implemented in the south—but demonstrated that the questions of work, health and community/worker control were now of central concern for the labor movement. The PCI, which had initially supported the union attempt to engage directly in the struggle for social reforms in 1971, put forward its own organic reform policy which, it argued, was the task of the political parties. It, too, then embraced the problems of work and health as central components of that policy.

Throughout the 1970s the debate around health problems intensified. This was partly due to the financial chaos and instability of the hospital system. The reform legislation passed in 1968 dealt with the structure and administration of the hospital agencies, and Law no. 386, passed in 1974, provided for a long-term reform of the hospital system and an immediate solution to the financial crisis (the public hospitals were on the verge of bankruptcy and the insurance companies could no longer pay their debts) (Koff, 1978, p. 23). The labor movement, in the face of worsening economic conditions—first stagnation and then recession—focused more on wages, on full employment and on influencing economic policy (Salvati, 1980; Regini and Esping-Andersen, 1980), yet did not abandon their commitment to a democratic national health service. The political parties kept the debate over health alive since, during the fifth legislature, each political party presented its own health care bill. With the elections of 1976 the PCI won 34·4 percent of the vote—up from 27·1 percent in the previous general elections—and by 1978 the PCI was explicitly included in the majority supporting the fourth Andreotti government, though not represented in the Cabinet itself. In December 1978 the National Health Service Law was approved with a broad consensus among the political parties.

Clearly, a coalition of forces produced this law, but the fact that it had such a strong orientation toward occupational health—the entrusting of industrial health services to the new Local Health Units, the creation of a new board, the Higher Institute for Occupational Safety and Prevention and the mandatory acceptance at the national level of the information-gathering techniques that the unions had won in some local contracts—can be attributed to the militancy and relative power of the unions. During the late 1960s and early 1970s they made health care into a central concern and defined health very broadly, making explicit links between social relationships at the workplace and health. By the time the major health reform was passed, the rate of unionization had steadily increased, reaching 59·9 percent in 1977, and the CGIL—the country's largest trade union confederation and the PCI's ally—had become a primary partner of the government. Accordingly, the unions had the political muscle to influence the shape of the legislation.

Britain

State intervention in the field of health care was initiated earlier in Britain than in Italy or the USA. In 1911 compulsory health insurance was established through the National Health Insurance Act which mandated general practitioner services for low-income workers but not their dependents. The poor were taken care of by municipal hospitals and physician services outside hospitals, both financed by local taxation (Anderson, 1977, p. 112). The Friendly Societies—mutual aid associations of the more skilled members of the working class—lost the reasonably strong bargaining powers they had achieved before the Act to contract with physicians to treat their members (Heidenheimer et al., 1975, pp. 15–16). Providers of medical services were able to persuade the government to force upon insurers changes they had previously resisted. As Abel-Smith has argued, state intervention essentially had the effect of rescuing the physicians from the control of Friendly Societies, 'while in Germany it initially enhanced the power which sick funds could exercise over the profession' (Abel-Smith, 1965, p. 35). The Act also brought government into disputes concerning levels and methods of remuneration and the control of medical services. Over the next two decades, instead of compulsory hospital insurance, there developed a number of voluntary non-profit hospital insurance schemes to which workers contributed what they could afford (which covered about a third of the revenue of voluntary hospitals). Charity and grants from public authorities made up the rest.

By the end of World War II, this system was universally regarded as being in a state of crisis. Aside from the damage to hospitals wrought by both lack of upkeep, and the destruction of war, serious concern was voiced over the maldistribution of specialists and general practitioners, the differential treatment received by the poor and the middle class and the financial state of the entire system (Anderson, 1977, p.

113). The Beveridge Report on Social Insurance and Allied Services had been published in 1942, proposing a serious attack after the war on the 'five giants' of want, disease, ignorance, squalor and idleness. A comprehensive health service and rehabilitation service, it declared, should be made available to every citizen on the basis of *need*. A coalition government accepted the principle of a national health service and the National Health Service Act was passed in July 1948 by a Labour government with Aneurin Bevan as Minister of Health. Bevan skillfully deflected the initial opposition of the medical profession by exploiting the splits within it, but the specialists still dominated the negotiations and enhanced their position to a much greater extent than the general practitioners (Watkin, 1978, p. 18; Doyal and Pennell, 1979, pp. 180–2). The labor movement had fought for a health service and viewed it as an important social reform, but it was not strong enough to impose its vision of an appropriate structure, so the latter was influenced greatly by compromises forged between the state, the voluntary hospitals, the insurance companies and the medical profession.

The most important feature of the National Health Service (NHS) was the assumption by the state of major responsibility for financing and planning medical care. Hospitals formerly owned by local authorities and charitable organizations were nationalized. Since non-hospital services were treated differently, this had the effect of institutionalizing the growing separation of hospital from primary care. The new service was to be *universal* (in the sense that it covered the whole population), *comprehensive* (in that it was intended to meet any need for medical care) and for the most part *free* (making benefits available on the basis of need). It, thus, differed from the pattern of medical services in many other countries where some payment is made by the user, or state services are limited to particular classes of citizen—like the elderly, the indigent or insured workers—or restricted in scope in some other way. This principle of free care was of fundamental importance to Bevan. 'The field in which the claims of individual commercialism come into most immediate conflict with reputable notions of social values', he wrote, 'is that of health' (cited in Marshall, 1975, p. 95). He was determined that the profit motive should not creep between doctor and patient in his service. He finally agreed grudgingly to a charge of 1 shilling for each prescription, but when the Labour government introduced further charges he resigned, saying that this was: 'the beginning of the destruction of those social services in which labour has taken a special pride

and which were giving to Britain the moral leadership of the world' (Marshall, 1975, p. 95).

This structure remained in operation for twenty-five years until, in April 1974, after five years of detailed discussion, a major reorganization of the service was instituted with the National Health Service Reorganisation Act. The reform was essentially an administrative one designed to integrate the former tripartite structure: the hospitals, primary care and broader environmental and public health services. Up to this point, the hospital and specialist services had been provided and financed by the Minister of Health through specially appointed hospital authorities. Outside the hospitals, general medical and dental practitioners, chemists (pharmacists) and opticians remained independent contractors, whose services were made available through the administrative machinery of about 120 executive councils which were *ad hoc* bodies partly appointed and wholly financed by the minister. The third arm of the service was the local authorities. These were usually a county or county borough charged with a range of responsibilities for health in the community, from health education to domestic help and home nursing. They differed from the other bodies in that they were not agents of the minister, but part of the local government system, financed partly from local rates (taxes).

Under the reorganized system a new Department of Health and Social Security (DHSS) decides on priorities with the Secretary of State and then agrees with Regional Health Authorities (RHA) on how these may broadly be achieved. They pass on guidelines to Area Health Authorities (AHA) with an indication of the financial allocations that may be expected. The AHAs, it was hoped, would enhance integration, securing collaboration between local authorities and health authorities. Health districts (205 in England) work with officers from the AHAs to provide a range of health services for their local population of 100,000–500,000 people (Levitt, 1977, pp. 27, 48) (**Document 5**).

The current system has met with mixed success. One initial priority of the reform—the joint administration of health and social services under unitary local authorities—was rejected as a fundamental threat to the status of the medical profession in the NHS. The separate administrations have not yet worked out serious collaborative planning arrangements which were supposed to be facilitated through Joint Consultative Committees. General practitioners are still relatively independent of the NHS administration and therefore elude general planning, making the integration of family practitioners' services with the rest of the NHS imperfect. Since the reorganization increased both the administrative apparatus and the administrative costs of the NHS, there has been much discussion as to whether one layer of the administration should be removed—the area being the current favorite choice. Inequalities of care persist as a commissioned but little distributed government study, the Black Report, makes abundantly clear (DHSS, 1980).

A series of further questions arise, as Levitt has argued, 'because the NHS is an instrument for involving the State in the lives of individual people' (Levitt, 1977, p. 216), and because the financial basis and extent of NHS operations make the Health Service a matter of great public concern. Over 80 percent of its income comes from general taxation. Less than 10 percent is derived from weekly National Insurance contributions from employees and employers and about 3 percent from direct charges for certain services, such as dental, ophthalmic and prescription charges (Brown, 1978). The NHS is now the third most expensive social service after social security and education and it employs the great majority of doctors, nurses and members of the paramedical professions—altogether over 1 million people (about 4 percent of the working population). Questions persist as to whether consumers have access to all the services they need, such as mental health, counseling and abortion. Iatrogenic (doctor-caused) disease appears to be on the increase (Levitt, 1977, p. 217). However, a Royal Commission on the National Health Service, set up to allay discontent among the medical profession (Ryan, 1977), produced, at a cost of £918,000 sterling, a lengthy report and 117 recommendations which did not threaten any serious change in the system, 'no blinding revelation', in its own words 'which would transform the NHS' (cited in Klein, 1979b, p. 848).

The Medical Profession

'We, as doctors, are mainly concerned with the individual man, woman, or child, with one individual problem after another', argued a noted British physician in a lecture series in 1950 (cited in Robson, 1973, p. 424). The concern with the treatment of the individual patient focuses the doctor's gaze on the individual case and obscures the epidemiological vision of populations and disease patterns—the cognitive foundation of public health. It leads inevitably to a greater concern with cure than with prevention. Realizing this, in 1969, Britain abandoned straight

capitation—the remuneration of doctors based on the number of patients for whom they were responsible—and added extra compensation to reward various acts of preventive medicine like immunizations and cervical smears (Glaser, 1976, pp. 86–7). This measure does not seem to have transformed the practice of British doctors. Their natural focus remains curative medicine, yet they have not been willing to yield the whole field of prevention to lay-workers and their ideas on the subject are an important factor in the policy equation.

As in the Italian case, it is a mistake to view the medical profession as a united entity. Among British physicians at present, there are some particularly strong divisions that have a bearing on the profession's stance on prevention. Junior hospital doctors have emerged as an independent and organized force; there are conflicts of interest among consultants (specialists)—between part-timers and full-timers, those working in London and those in the provinces, those working in specialties like surgery where private-practice income is possible and those working in specialties like geriatrics where such opportunities are rare (Klein, 1977). The most important division, however, has always been that between hospital-based doctors and general practitioners working in the community, a separation that was institutionalized with the passage of the NHS Act. David Armstrong has made the interesting argument that, for general practice, in an effort to escape its historical subservience, medical knowledge itself became an important element in the struggle. 'Hospital medicine', the dominant ideology, which abstracted pathology-based disease from the patient, was to be replaced by what Armstrong calls 'biographical medicine'. This 'new approach' to disease, advocated in a Royal College of General Practitioners' report in 1965, would protect patients from hospital specialists who recommended treatments 'in ignorance of the patient's underlying social and personal problems' (cited in Armstrong, 1979, p. 6). The patient and his social world were, therefore, reintroduced via general practice. 'Some doctors', claimed a speaker to the Royal College of Physicians in 1977, 'find people more interesting than physiology or pathology' (cited in Armstrong, 1979, p. 7).

Even though general practice in Britain advocated that doctors should view the hospital as filled not with cases, but with 'sick persons—people in trouble, husbands, wives, fathers, mothers, children, people with homes and jobs and lives of their own' (cited in Armstrong, 1979, p. 5), widespread adoption of an etiological theory stressing the social determinants of disease did not automatically follow. The patient had become the 'centre of the medical problematic'. As Armstrong puts it, 'the medical gaze was not to be directed to the silent interior of the body but to the patient's biography and environment' (1979, p. 5). In practice, however, the environment was relegated to a secondary position. In a recent memorandum to the Social Services and Employment Subcommittee on Preventive Medicine, the Royal College of General Practitioners had only this to say on 'the Effect of Health of the Wider Environment': 'As a College this is not our special area of interest and we are unable to comment' (*Memorandum*, 1977, p. 616).

Moreover, the individualist approach within the profession was strengthened when the only advocates for a broader view of prevention, the Medical Officers of Health (MOHs), were abolished with the 1974 reorganization of the NHS. Originally the MOH was the guardian of the health of the population of the local authority. His employment was protected by the 1848 Public Health Act, which stated that 'dismissal by the local authority was not to be the reward for "making trouble in order to protect health" ' (Unit for the Study of Health Policy (USHP), 1979, p. 13). The MOH was responsible for maternal and child health services, which were strongly oriented toward prevention, and for environmental services. With the 1974 reorganization he was replaced by the Community Physician. Community Medicine had emerged as a specialty in 1972, partly as the response to a Royal Commission on Medical Education. On paper it looked as though the new specialty would reinvigorate the broader conception of prevention. It was defined as

> that branch of knowledge which deals with populations or groups rather than with individual patients ... It requires special knowledge of the principles of epidemiology, of the organization and evaluation of medical care systems, of the medical aspects of administration of health services and of the techniques of health education and rehabilitation which are comprised within the field of social and preventive medicine. (Parry, cited in USHP, 1979, p. 20)

But in practice, the duties of community physicians have focused much more on medical administration, and the organization and rationalization of medical services, than on public health. As a consequence, or perhaps because the mandate of the specialty is so unclear, it has not been able to recruit younger doctors:

52 percent of community physicians are over 50. Overall the number of doctors involved in public health has fallen—'from about 1200 in the old public health and medical administration services to 740 in the new specialty of Community Medicine' (USHP, 1979, p. 27).

Thus the overwhelming bias from within the profession at present is toward the individualist approach. Since the British medical profession does exercise considerable power *vis-à-vis* the state, it can be presumed to have a strong influence on the formulation of health care policies (Levitt, 1977; Fry, 1976). It is true that increased state intervention has threatened 'medical dominance' in certain ways. For example, paramedical and other groups who wish to strengthen their professional aspirations or advance their claims in the health care field look to the state rather than to the patronage of the medical profession (Armstrong, 1976). However, even more so than in the USA, the medical profession retains almost total control over the content of their interactions with, and advice to, patients. As Rudolf Klein has argued:

> Within the NHS the medical profession paradoxically enjoys much more autonomy than doctors working in free-market systems. Precisely because the NHS has a strict system of financial control over the total amount of resources allocated, it has so far not had to devise a system of trying to control individual medical decisions ... Hence the irony that the only machinery for reviewing the decisions of doctors in Britain is that for checking the prescribing habits of general practitioners: the doctors who are least integrated into the administrative structure of the NHS and who have the most independent status. (Klein, 1977, p. 172–3)

The Left and the Unions

In Italy the struggle over workers' health and the specific gains and measures emerging from the struggle developed within the framework of a general discussion about a population's health, ways to improve it and the appropriate strategy to reorganize and rationalize health services as a whole. In contrast, the struggle over health and safety in Britain and the USA was in many ways unconnected to a more general discussion about health care and the provision of health services. The gains won in occupational health in the USA and the UK were achieved at different times from changes in the organization of services; they were promoted by different coalitions and administered by different government agencies. Hence, in a time of economic crisis those gains are much more easily undermined or rolled back. The attacks on the occupational health and safety administration by the Reagan administration, for example, are not even widely perceived as an attack on the levels of protection for workers' health. Instead, in many quarters, they are welcomed as part of a moratorium on the promulgation of unnecessary redtape by federal bureaucracies. They are presented as part of the general attack on waste, sinecures and make-work projects within the state, which are often seen as an important constraint on the productivity of industry.

The historical development of the trade unions and the structure of the labor movement in Britain also makes labor a much less effective advocate for a broad social approach to prevention. The British trade unions evolved along narrow craft and industry lines. Generally, their battles are on the behalf of the unionized workforce at any particular moment and much less frequently for universal benefits. Different unions have fought vigorously at various times for occupational health and safety issues. Recently, for example, the agricultural workers' union has fought to ban the use of 2,4,5-T, a weedkiller pesticide, and as a result some local authorities have stopped using it; other unions have fought against the use of asbestos; miners have won battles for compensation for black lung disease and for better protection against occupational accidents. Where gains have been achieved, however, they have been translated into specific industry health and safety programs. The unions by and large are cut off from influencing a national discourse on the social issue of health and health care services for the population at large. In addition, although there have been a number of local and rank-and-file struggles of note around occupational health, they have not always been picked up and generalized by the trade union movement as a whole. Unlike the Italian situation, where the union confederations found that articulating local health and safety issues and adopting the techniques of investigation generated by union locals would facilitate their efforts to gain control of the rank-and-file and of specific industry unions, the Trades Union Congress (TUC) historically has been unable to influence its member unions effectively and union officials have often been unable to discipline or control their rank-and-file.

Ironically, one of the most substantial obstacles to the emergence of a social view of prevention on the part of the unions, or indeed of any other group, was the institution and the structure of the NHS. A free service had been established in the postwar period when disease patterns were different and the etiology of the chronic illnesses was not in contention. Moreover, the structure of the NHS institutionalized the separation of public and environmental health services from general practice and hospital-based services and, therefore, insulated each from the discussion of the other. Any movement for reform subsequent to that time had to deal with an intact, inflexible social institution, centrally controlled, greatly influenced by the hospital consultants and, even in the last few years, the most popular social service.

The 'movements' of the 1960s and early 1970s in Britain did not entail the kind of mass mobilization that emerged in France or Italy. Students and workers were not involved in a broad coalition to promote health care and other social reforms. The women's movement was perhaps the most visible presence in struggles over health care issues, raising questions about the nature of social relationships within medicine. When a Labour government came to power in 1974, it was committed to a program of sweeping reforms which included legislation on occupational health. The Health and Safety at Work Act was passed but implementation has been slow and penalties for infringements, like those in the USA for similar infractions by employers, have been negligible. More important, occupational health issues were divorced from any thoroughgoing consideration of the nature of health, health care and the National Health Service. The 1974 reorganization attempted to integrate the three branches of the service but did not precipitate an ideological discussion of their content.

By the end of 1974, as the symptoms of an economic crisis became more visible, the government began to abandon its 'expansive' approach to public spending (Bornstein and Gourevitch, 1984). A series of budgets from November 1974 onward cut public spending on hospitals and imposed a system of 'cash limits' on government departments and local authorities to prevent their expenditures from rising to keep pace with inflation. The unions supported some of these cuts at first, but by 1976 that consensus had disintegrated. The union leadership was caught in the familiar squeeze between its loyalty to a Labour government and the demands of its rank-and-file. After a winter of industrial strife in 1978–9, Labour lost the general election in 1979 and the unions were cast as the villains of the piece. With the Thatcher government strategy of setting strict monetary targets to control inflation while cutting back on government spending, they face soaring unemployment and a reduced standard of living.

Such a situation has not provided the political space for either the trade unions or the Labour Party to argue for reconstituting the ideological basis of the National Health Service. Both have been engaged in a defensive battle for free public health care against the attacks of the Tories, who assert the necessity of increasing prescription charges and expanding private medicine (**Document** 6). The most visible fight launched by the unions around these issues from 1974 onward was to remove pay beds (set aside in NHS hospitals for the private paying patients of consultants). Apart from this, union activity was largely confined to the struggle to preserve jobs and increase wages within the health care sector. The militancy of health care unions was strengthened by the fact that the proportion of unionized workers in the health care industry had increased dramatically in the late 1960s and early 1970s. By 1974 the NHS was more highly unionized than the British laborforce as a whole, 50 percent of whose members belong to unions (Klein, 1979*a*, p. 477). This was also the period when all fractions of the medical profession were raising pay demands, so that the NHS was under siege from several quarters. By the late 1970s the situation had begun to ally health care workers seeking, for example, to stop the closing of small hospitals and preserve jobs, with consumers trying to prevent cutbacks in services.

The Labour Party, in the period before its ouster, had tried to pose as the party of economic efficiency; the Tories urge rollbacks in services and public spending. In such a climate issues concerning the etiology of disease are barely mentioned. The TUC report of 1978 does speak to the publication of the government's White Paper on Prevention but does not contest the kind of prevention proposed. In fact, it endorses the report's position on smoking, unlike some American unions which, in recent years, have fought government anti-smoking campaigns on the ground that they obscure the occupational sources of lung disease and of respiratory ailments and encourage the view that workers contribute disproportionately to their own self-destruction. The TUC complains only that not enough money has been allocated to implement the provisions of the government's preventive program (**Document** 7). In 1979 the Royal Commission on the National Health Service considered and rejected the proposal that responsibility for occupational health and medicine be transferred to the NHS. These matters were left with the Department of Employment, as in the USA, encouraging the continued divorce of discussions of workers' health and of occupational hazards from an appraisal of measures to improve the health of the entire population. In Italy, by contrast, a similar debate resulted in the transfer of large areas of responsibility for occupational health and safety to the new national health service at both national and local levels.

During the 1978 French legislative elections the issue of prevention became highly politicized, with the parties of the left arguing for a broad program of social reform and the parties of the right advocating individual responsibility for good health (Canone and Guyot, 1978). In both Britain and Italy the issue did not become the object of debate between the right and the left. In Italy the major political parties, supported by the unions, agreed on a broad social environmentalist definition of prevention. In Britain the parties were silent on the issue, arguing instead, in a situation of economic crisis, about the utility of preserving certain aspects of the welfare state. The unions were engaged in fighting a defensive battle over jobs, leaving no political actor with power on the national scene to articulate the social position.

Implications for a Theory of Social Policy

I have argued that the form of a particular state health care policy can be best understood as being conditioned by a struggle between class interests. In Britain, Italy and the USA capital sought during the 1970s to contain the cost of the social wage and to control medical costs which it perceived as contributing to rising inflation. Since the state had assumed direct responsibility to a greater or lesser degree for the financing of health services and was faced with a growing fiscal crisis, state managers were also anxious to lower expenditures on high technology curative medical care. In these circumstances the ideology that responsibility for health belonged to the individual was a seductive one (Doyal and Pennell, 1979, p. 208). Nevertheless, it failed to inform health care policy to the degree that working-class unions and parties perceived it as a direct attack on either workers' health at the point of production, or consumers' health, and to the degree that they were able to mobilize effectively in alliance with social movements to promote a broader etiological theory of disease and a social definition of prevention.

There are, of course, other factors which influenced

the success of those struggles. The structure of the state in all three countries conditioned the extent to which well-organized working-class demands could have an immediate and tangible effect on particular social policies. Giuseppe Di Palma has argued that the Italian state, 'formally centralized... otherwise porous and progressively "available" ' (Di Palma, 1980, p. 155) during the 1950s and 1960s, has not changed substantially during the upheavals of the 1970s. With the emergence of an expanding leftist culture, one saw only an 'acceleration of that process of penetration of the state by competing corporate-economic and corporate-ideological constituencies already set in clear motion during the decade of the Center–Left coalition' (Di Palma, 1980, p. 160). By the 1980s, according to Di Palma, the state has 'turned itself into a huge social service apparatus open to root-and-branch control' (Di Palma, 1980, p. 163). Built on ties of individualized patronage, it had been the province of Christian Democracy since the postwar period began, but became gradually 'available' to the left and the unions in the late 1970s.

In contrast, the British state is not linked to a particular political party or open to interest inter-mediation in the same way. It is not markedly decentralized or democratized. At the inception of the National Health Service Bevan strengthened this principle, insisting on the rationalization of hospitals: 'How', he asked, 'can the state enter into contract with a citizen to render service through an autonomous body [the hospitals]?' (cited in Watkin, 1978, p. 18). The British bipolar party system ensures frequent alternation of governments with strongly opposed ideological positions, but the 'stop–go' pattern of policy which can result is resisted by the Civil Service to the extent possible. The unions can make strong demands on a Labour government to which they are closely linked, but the union leadership is often caught between a rank-and-file impatient to press such demands and the fear that the unions will relinquish all influence if they endanger the government by their intransigence. The American case provides a third possibility. Labor can make inroads, if temporary ones, in what has been described as the 'organized chaos' of the American government's approach to health (Altenstetter, 1974, p. 72). But the political composition of the state bureaucracy changes as the two political parties alternate in government. Hence, the achievements in occupational health under Eula Bingham's tenure at the Occupational Safety and Health Administration (OSHA) can be quickly eroded by a conservative Republican successor.

The political role and organization of capital and labor and the internal organization of the state appa-ratus are critical elements in an explanation of national differences in particular health policies. They must, however, be situated within an analysis of the economic and political conditions that may facilitate or obstruct mobilization. Cultural resources take on an added importance in this comparative approach. The nature of the cultural discourse about health shaped the responses available to the opposing parties in the struggle over prevention. Two features of the American case are worth mentioning briefly. First, at the level of national policy, the terms of the debate on health have been almost completely captured by cost–benefit analysis. In the course of the petrochemical industry's efforts to fight recent health and environ-mental challenges to its activities, its appeal to risk-accounting methods has helped to generate a new political rhetoric: life is inescapably risky. The acknowledged risk of cancer from an industry's products should, therefore, be put 'in perspective' and balanced against product benefits (Noble, 1980). Secondly, the trade paperback emerged in the 1960s because of changes in the publishing industry.[5] The cultural content which proved to be the most appropriate to this new cultural form was self-help. Its themes multiply to fill the space available: how to become attractive, how to take care of your health, how to use power, and so on. The proliferation of women's magazines and talk shows in the same period reinforced the self-improvement message and was, I speculate, an important ideological resource for those actors who wished to publicize an individualist view of prevention (Taylor and Mattes, 1980). These phenomena have touched Britain to some extent but are almost unheard of in Italy.

The foregoing analysis has emphasized several factors as crucial for any explanation of the content and direction of state responses to health problems in Western European nations. Taking prevention as one of the most common strategies adopted by advanced capitalist states faced with a dual crisis of cost and efficacy in health care, I have described the struggle among different interests to define the content of this strategy. I have emphasized in particular the role of working-class parties and unions in opposing an individualist definition of prevention supported by the medical profession and capital; the political, cultural and economic conditions which lent force to their opposition; and the structure of the state they were trying to influence. I argue that the struggle among political actors is more significant in explaining shifts in health policy than new scientific information, the influence of capital, the cumulative effects of bureaucratic inertia or the logic of state intervention in advanced capitalism.

The details of the prevention case should make clear, first, that Western European countries do not seem to be converging inexorably toward one general pattern of health care policy as some authors have asserted. Secondly, the public or private character of health provision and the existence or absence of a national health service are not sufficient to explain differences in the nature of health care strategies chosen by different countries. By emphasizing the interests of and relations among different political actors, my argument resembles, in many ways, the neo-corporatist 'system of interest representation' (Schmitter, 1974, p. 93) in which peak associations (in this case the medical profession, trade unions and capital) negotiate policies with a strong state. Inevitably, an analysis which deals with the ideological construction of a particular strategy, the passage of legislation and the funding of specific programs is more sensitive to short-term developments within the political sphere and to the goals of political actors in a defined historical period (see, for example, Regini and Regonini, 1980). My account, however, differs in several crucial ways from a neo-corporatist model, and it suggests several additional factors which would have to be taken into account in a theory of state intervention in all areas of health care, or in a more general theory of social policy.

The resources and organizational capacities of political actors and the struggle among them are indeed crucial in my argument, but they do not add up to either the random competition of pluralism or the carefully structured negotiation of neo-corporatism. Neither the medical professions nor the trade unions that I describe can discipline their members and act as the unified peak associations which neo-corporatism envisages. Contrary to the assumptions of pluralism, it is the underlying balance of class forces which lends persuasive power to some groups over others and which makes a particular trade union strategy, for example, viable at a particular historical moment. And, I suspect, it is changing patterns of economic development and changes in the composition of the labor force which define the terrain over which those political actors negotiate. The transformation of Italy's export sector during the 1950s and 1960s, for example, reflected a move toward an industrial structure that emphasized heavy and chemical industries. Italy's increasing dependence on petroleum and petroleum-derived products created a highly polluting economy, and an aggressive program of rationalization caused occupational injuries to soar. All these factors generated new health problems which were then defined as significant political problems because irreconcilable class interests were at stake.

Finally, class forces are significant in one further respect. There are two crucial features of the context in which the political struggle which I have described is conducted. The first is the existing institutional structure of health care in a given country. The National Health Service in Britain limited the debate over reform and the nature of health care in several important ways. It is a structure which was forged as part of the postwar settlement between capital and labor in Britain which accounts in part for its orientation toward curative, hospital-based medical care and its neglect of preventive medicine. Secondly, the cultural discourse around health provides the metaphor within which innovations in policy are explained, justified and reinforced. This discourse has been shaped in no small part by the current conflict among class forces. It reflects the experience of everyday life for large sections of the population, but the particular uncertainties engendered by conditions of life under contemporary capitalism can be translated into individualist or social terms. In the United States specific industries—publishing and petrochemicals—have changed the language in which health is discussed in very specific ways in the last decade. These changes should be understood as part of an ongoing struggle over the terms of the debate about health and health care and not simply as a reflection of traditional attitudes about social welfare.

Notes: Chapter 4

Earlier thoughts on this subject were presented to the Boston Health Study Group, the Labour Study Group at the Center for European Studies, Harvard University, the East Coast Health Discussion Group, the Sociology Department, New York University and the 1981 Annual Meetings of the American Political Science Association. This paper benefited greatly from comments at those sessions and, particularly, from the criticisms of Lesley Doyal, Mary Ann Elston, Art Goldhammer, Joel Krieger, Peter Lange, Harry Marks, Massimo Paci, Michael Reich and the editors of this volume. Part of the research for the project was completed while I was the recipient of a National Endowment for the Humanities Fellowship and thanks are due for this support.

1   I do not take a position here on the normative question of which theory is 'better' in the sense that, if pursued, it will lead to a greater improvement in a nation's health. I ask only why

different countries have adopted different etiological theories and different preventive strategies.

2 I am indebted to Professor William Glaser for drawing my attention to this point in a private communication.

3 I have narrowed the scope of this paper in two important respects. First, the activities which could be included in a description of a country's policy on prevention include: health care services, health education programs, occupational health programs and legislation to safeguard the environment. In this paper, however, I consider only those activities which a particular country itself defines as part of its *health care* policies. Those programs which are considered to fall under the jurisdiction of a non-health-related ministry—for example, the

Department of Employment—and which are therefore not discussed in an overview of a country's health care policies are given only brief attention. Secondly, I restrict myself to a discussion of the *construction* of different governments' strategies with regard to prevention. I do not, therefore, consider the complicated question of subsequent policy implementation. In Italy, for example, it is well known that progressive laws can be undermined or not implemented in practice.

4 For an alternative explanation of why the USA has adopted an individualist version of prevention, see Taylor, 1980.

5 I am indebted to Professor Paul Dimaggio for first bringing this phenomenon to my attention.

Documents

1   The Italian National Health Service Law, 1978

Extracts from Articles 20 and 22 of Law 833, Istituzione del servizio sanitario nazionale, the law instituting a national health service in Italy, passed in 1978.

Articles 20 and 22 establish the basic premiss of the law: that most ill-health is caused by 'dangerous or deteriorating factors in working and living environments'. Although the article embodies the principles for which the labor movement fought, many of its provisions have not yet been implemented. Risk maps, for example, mentioned in clause (d) of Article 20, have been drawn up in several regions, notably Piedmont, but are non-existent in others. The law has remained little more than a general framework or set of principles. For many of its provisions it requires either further legislation at the national or regional level, or action by the local health units. There are, therefore, many opportunities for opponents of the law to weaken it.

Article 20

Preventive Activity

The preventive activity includes:

(a)   the localization, identification and control of harmful, dangerous, or deteriorating factors in working or living environments in application of the existing legislation in these matters in order to guarantee respect for the maximum untransgressable limits ... and for this purpose, the compilation of registers ... The above-mentioned tasks are carried out through tests and control of machinery, installations, and protection devices produced, installed or used within the territorial limits of the local health unit in fulfilment of the functions defined ... [above];

(b)   the communication of verified data, diffusing knowledge of it, even in the work or living environments, either directly or through the bodies of municipal decentralization, also for the purpose of administering properly the means of information ... and trade union representat[ion];

(c)   the indication of measures capable of eliminating the risky factors and to restore the living and working environments, applying the existing legislation in this matter and in fulfilment of the delegated activities ...;

(d)   the drawing of risk maps, obliging the firms to publicize the substances used in the productive cycle, along with their toxicological characteristics and their possible effects on humans and the environment;

(e)   the prophylaxis of eventual morbid events, adopting the measures capable of preventing the event;

(f)   the verification, according to the procedure envisaged by laws and regulations, of the compatibility of urban plannings, industrial projects, and productive activities in general, with the need to safeguard the environment in its hygienic sanitary aspects and to defend the health of the population and the workers involved.

In fulfilment of the functions entrusted to them in the field of preventive activity, the local health units—once they have given guarantee to protect industrial secrets in reference to letter (d) of the previous paragraph—shall resort to their own personnel, the multi-area specialized officials, according to Article 22, and personnel which, within its technical and functional competence, performs services of diagnosis, cure and rehabilitation.

Preventive measures taken in working environments—the search for, elaboration and realization of necessary measures capable of safeguarding workers' health and physical integrity—in reference to types of work not contemplated by specific legislation, such activity is carried out on the basis of the needs jointly verified with the trade union representative and the employer, in accordance with the procedure of the contracts or collective agreements applicable to the productive unit ...

Article 22

Multi area Preventive Health Centers and Services

The Regional legislation, depending on the location and consistency of the industrial plants, and the peculiarity of agricultural productive processes, handicrafts and work done at home, shall:

(a)   identify the local health units in which multi-area health centers and services shall be established to control and safeguard environmental hygiene, to prevent work accidents and professional hazards;

(b)   define the functional and interregulatory characteristics of the above mentioned multi-area health centers and services;

(c)   provide forms of coordination of these bodies with environmental hygienic services and with the services of work hygiene and medicine of each local health unit.

The multi-zone centers and services mentioned in the previous paragraph shall be managed by the local health unit in which they reside, in accordance with the modalities indicated [above] ...

2   Science and Ideology in Health Policy

Extracts from the Department of Health and Social Security White Paper, *Prevention and Health* (London: HMSO, Cmnd. 7047, December 1977), and from *Preventive Medicine*, Vol. 1, the First Report from the Expenditure Committee (London: HMSO, February 1977), pp. lxxxii–lxxxv.

These extracts are included to show that preventive policies are rarely based on indisputable scientific fact. Not only did government committees writing within ten months of each other disagree on what constituted incontrovertible evidence of risks to health and appropriate preventive measures to deal with them, but the British positions on breast-cancer screening and the risk of fat consumption have differed at various times from those of Italian and American experts. Given that many of the 'facts' on which preventive strategies are based are arguable, their underlying ideological assumptions are critical.

Prevention and Health

The Dilemmas of Uncertainty
Prevention and Health: Everybody's Business referred to the dilemmas of uncertainty and the importance of thorough assessment of all the evidence before decisions are undertaken. In making some recommendations the Sub-Committee may have assumed certainty where none in fact exists. Examples are recommendations 42 and 45 which propose action by the Government to inform the public of risks arising from the consumption of certain foods including fats, and recommendation 53 which suggests the introduction of a national breast cancer screening service for women. Whilst the Government accepts that decisions must sometimes be taken in the face of uncertainty about consequences, its assessment, in the light of expert advice, of the conflicting evidence presented to the Sub-Committee on these and other controversial topics, leads it to conclusions which differ from those which the Sub-Committee reached. Clearly the Government cannot wait for absolute certainty before taking action; on the other hand, it would seem wrong to use resources or interfere with individual liberty if there is real doubt whether the action proposed will in fact produce the benefits claimed for it.

Preventive Medicine

Conclusions and Recommendations
We have been convinced by our enquiry that substantial human and financial resources would be saved if greater emphasis were to be placed on prevention. This is not just a theoretical conclusion; it is, literally, a matter of life and death. Our recommendations cover organisation, training, advertising, finance, and last but not least, self-help.

Age-Average Mortality Rate, All Persons Aged 35–74 (1969–75)
Coronary Heart Disease (Hundreds of Thousands)

Country	1969	1970	1971	1972	1973	1974	1975	%age Change	Slope
Australia	579	588	570	551	536	541	500	−13·6	−13·0
Austria	278	281	284	282	276	296	290	4·3	1·3
Belgium	295	295	303	299	285	279	279	−5·5	−3·5
Canada	482	484	453	455	446	447	—	−7·3*	−8·2
Denmark	390	387	387	403	402	393	388	−0·5	0·7
Finland	543	524	547	513	518	520	—	−4·2*	−4·8*
France	126	126	132	134	132	134	—	6·3*	−1·7*
German Federal Republic	260	259	269	274	275	277	284	9·4	4·1
Republic of Ireland	468	449	434	475	489	500	487	4·1	7·6
Israel	510	494	497	509	488	489	448	−12·1	−7·3
Italy	211	201	201	198	209	202	—	−4·3*	−0·7*
Japan	93	93	87	83	86	84	79	−15·2	−2·2
Netherlands	314	333	326	336	322	309	314	−0·0	−1·9
New Zealand	522	533	529	514	526	502	491	−6·0	−5·6
Norway	379	373	374	361	363	355	350	−7·5	−4·8
Sweden	357	369	395	384	392	380	378	6·0	2·9
Switzerland	182	181	186	180	175	178	191	4·6	0·3
UK	439	434	435	460	456	459	451	2·5	3·7
USA	591	578	564	551	534	507	479	−19·0	−18·1
Venezuela	278	269	245	261	254	252	257	−7·6	−3·2

All rates are age-averages of the rates of the four ten-year age groups 35–44, 45–54, 55–64 and 65–74. Percentage change is 1969–75, except where otherwise designated.
* 1969–74.

Among others we examined the particular problems of smoking and excessive drinking, of contraception and abortion, screening, dental care, exercise and diet. The recommendations affect doctors, dentists, administrators, scientists, researchers, and many more, including, not least, the layman or 'patient' . . .

Our recommendations are as follows [in part]:

(42) Information about fats should be placed before the public in order to show up clearly the risks from a high intake of saturated fats, to encourage people to moderate their fat intake or switch to polyunsaturated fats.

(45) Where consensus exists about the dangers arising from the consumption of certain foods, the Government should have a duty to bring this to the attention of the public.

(53) A national breast cancer screening service for the women most at risk should be introduced. The Secretary of State should expedite as a matter of urgency the production of reports by the working groups . . .

3 Comparative Mortality Rates from Coronary Heart Disease

Chart Showing the Age-Averaged Mortality Rate from Coronary Heart Disease in twelve Countries over 1969–75, extract from the *Proceedings of the Conference on the Decline in Coronary Heart Disease Mortality*, NIH Publication No. 79-1619 (May 1979).

This chart is included to show both the mortality rates among countries, and the changes in the rates over a six-year period.

4 Worker Control and the Social Approach to Prevention: An Italian Example

Description of the Terni Local Health Service (July 1979).

Terni is a town in Tuscany which is a 'red' region in Italy, that is, one where parties of the left, usually Socialists and Communists, have gained control of many local administrations. The model outlined is typical of those developed by the labour movement, emphasizing worker initiative and control over information. Many of its features were then incorporated into the national health service law.

(1) Introduction

The service is concerned with 'job safety, the prevention of injury and disease deriving from the environment, from the way jobs are organized, and from factory conditions'.

The service is provided by the Province. As authorized in the recent 'Workers' statute', it intervenes at the requests of workers, usually channeled through local or national unions.

The service is based on the workers' knowledge of their own working conditions. After collating and analyzing worker complaints about work environments and production methods it tests for pollution in the workplace (air, water, soil, etc.) and does physical examinations of the workers.

For its personnel the Labor Health Service largely depends on other, already existing, provincial institutions. Only a few people work full-time in the program; others are available on demand from the hospital, the university, etc. The responsibilities of these institutions are specified in written agreements. The Service, then, works as an intermediary between the workers and the health and environmental specialists of the province.

Terni pioneered this model in 1972. In 1980 it will be applied by law nationally.

(2) Procedure

When the service receives a request for assistance it acts as follows:

(a) it surveys the workers about the extent of the problem—informally in assemblies or small groups, or by means of questionnaires;

(b) it formulates a coherent plan of intervention and verification, with appropriate protocols for tests on the environment and workers;

(c) it makes the tests;

(d) it informs the workers of the results, in the form of medical and environmental data presented as maps of potential risks;

(e) the workers then use these results in negotiations with management.

The service remains available for further consultation.

The purpose of the medical side of the service is not so much the early diagnosis of disease, but rather the establishment of relationships between working conditions and the health of the workers. That is, it is intended to change working conditions rather than to intervene directly on individuals.

Physical exams are conducted following 'risk protocols'. They help the doctor to make an etiological diagnosis—that is, to recognize the connection between the source of danger and the risk of disease.

Tests and samplings for pollutants are conducted in close collaboration with the workers; the place for the sampling, the time and phase of the work cycle are constantly indicated to the technicians by the workers who initiated the request.

(3)   Personnel and Equipment

The service team is composed of doctors, hygienists, chemists, biologists, health paraprofessionals, social workers, laboratory technicians, sociologists, and computer technicians.

The equipment at their disposal is that of the Environmental Laboratory, a chemical laboratory, industrial toxicology, cytology, audiology, and that of an E.D.P. Center.

(4)   The Findings of the Service

(a)   For the analyses of air and water the findings are data accompanied by an explanation provided by the specialist in hygiene. These are distributed to the provincial administration and public health officials.

(b)   In reference to conditions in the workplace the findings are data giving the quantity of polluting substance sampled, maps of risks, and an explanation provided by the specialist on industrial hygiene.

(c)   In regard to health the findings are both individual booklets of health risks (which include the results of clinical tests, symptoms reported by the worker, and other social-sanitary information) and the registers of biostatistics referring to 'risk groups' (workers sharing the same risks).

The information of (b) and (c) is provided to the worker, factory unions, national unions, and management.

(5)   Results

The service assumes responsibility for *efficiency* in its response to the requests of the workers. The workers are responsible for the *efficacy* of the results.

The work of the service is not evaluated in traditional ways, such as diseases discovered or early diagnoses, but by completely different criteria:

(a)   the number and gravity of environment pollutants identified in the workplace;

(b)   the number of etiological diagnoses in which the cause of disease or injury can be traced to working conditions;

(c)   demands of workers regarding changes in the environment and the organization of work formulated with the collaboration of the service;

(d)   actual changes in working conditions obtained by the workers.

These are the only criteria for measuring the cost-effectiveness of the service . . .

5   The British National Health Service before and after the 1974 Reorganization

Extract from Ruth Levitt, *The Reorganized National Health Service*, 2nd edn (London: Croom Helm, 1977).

The 1974 reorganization of the NHS was, as these charts demonstrate, largely administrative. It did not affect the financing of the service or the distribution of services. Critics charged that the reorganization did not address the question of whether the National Health Service was coping with the population's health problems. Current proposals to change the structure of the NHS also skirt this question and focus on whether the removal of a layer of the bureaucracy (at the area level) will save money. In this respect they are similar to the Reagan administration's plans to 'cut the fat' from the federal bureaucracy.

6   Returning Health Care to the Private Sector: The Tory Position

Extract from *The Right Approach: A Statement of Conservative Aims* (London: Conservative Central Office, 1976).

Cuts in the National Health Service have not been as severe under either Labour or Conservative governments as they have been in other areas of social welfare. Yet since 1978 there have been efforts to impose strict cash limits on national health expenditure. Although in many ways the present Conservative government is merely continuing the process of cutting public spending which was begun under the last Labour government, the philosophy behind the cuts is different in one crucial respect that emerges in this document: the desire to transfer responsibility for some portion of health care services to the private sector.

The National Health Service

The Health Service is the largest single employer in the country and one of the biggest spenders. But the demands on the service have risen even faster than the increase in resources devoted to it. The advance in medical techniques, the rise in the number of elderly people in need of hospital attention, and what has been called the 'infinity of demand' for medical care have together put an immense strain on the service. A great deal of devoted work is done every day by the medical professions and others working in the Health Service, but they have to work under increasingly difficult conditions and morale has been shaken by the divisive actions of a doctrinaire Labour Government.

When the service is short of funds for priority tasks, there is no case for holding down prescription and other charges. More important, we should encourage rather than deter private provision. Increasing numbers of people have shown that they are ready to provide more for themselves; private medical insurance has doubled and redoubled over the last twenty years. It will be our aim to encourage this trend, and in particular to reverse the run-down in NHS pay beds. There is a strong argument for seeing that pay bed revenue goes directly to the hospital concerned, where it can be spent on identifiable items of equipment.

We see no reason for quantitative controls over the development of the private sector outside the NHS. We are examining ways of providing greater financial incentives to employer–employee medical insurance schemes, for example by restoring income-tax relief. The Royal Commission on the Health Service should be looking at other ways of increasing the funds available to the service, including systems of health finance that exist in other countries.

When the statutory services are under strain, it is more important than ever that the voluntary services should continue and expand their excellent work. They add an important additional dimension to social provision. The last Conservative government sought to encourage voluntary effort and even more must be done in this direction.

The National Health Service, 1948–74

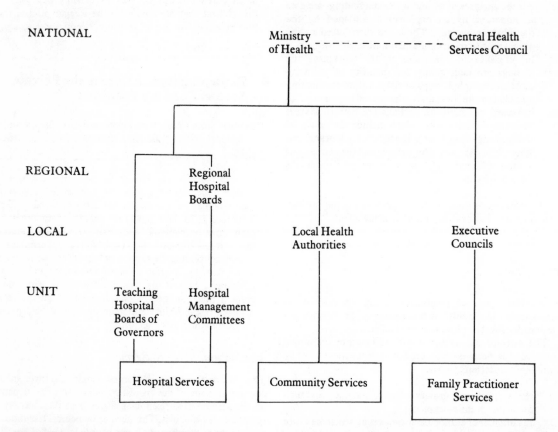

7   More Money for Preventive Medicine: The Position of British Unions

Extract from *Report of 110th Annual Trades Union Congress* (London: Trades Union Congress, 1978).

Since 1978 the Trades Union Congress has taken a more active role on questions of occupational health and safety than this document would indicate. Several unions have appointed health and safety officers at the national level and they, for example, have attempted to work through the TUC in the hopes of informing and persuading those unions that have dragged their feet over industrial health questions. The TUC has now voted to ban the pesticide 2,4,5-T and is working on a pamphlet which will analyze the occupational hazards of noise.

In January 1978, the Government published a White Paper

on Prevention and Health in response to a recent report on the subject by a House of Commons Select Committee. The White Paper endorsed the principle of wider reallocation of existing NHS services towards preventive services, with particular emphasis on giving more information to the public on the dangers of certain habits as a means of encouraging a more healthy way of life. The White Paper covered topics such as child health services, the fluoridation of water supplies to reduce dental decay in children, better dental care generally, the importance of widely available family planning and abortion facilities, the value of proper exercise and a balanced low fat diet, the wider application of screening techniques for certain diseases and congenital handicaps, and the problems of treatment of mental illness.

The White Paper also outlined the government's present position on smoking. Smoking causes seven times as many premature deaths each year as road accidents—at least 50,000. Fifty million working days are lost due to smoking and the incidence of lung cancer, which is up to 25 times more common in smokers than non-smokers, is higher in Britain than in any other industrial nation. The likelihood of contraction of an industrial disease is vastly increased by smoking. One in every three smokers is likely to die of a smoking related disease, and every cigarette shortens a smoker's life by about $5\frac{1}{2}$ minutes. Though the proportion of adult smokers has fallen sharply to less than half of all adults, there has been very little decline in smoking amongst working-class people, particularly women, among whom there are now more smokers than in 1955. The government intends to promote tobacco substitutes, control advertising further, but not ban it, restrict, but not abolish sports sponsorship by tobacco companies, levy penal taxation on the highest tar brands only, and slightly reword the health warning on each cigarette packet. The General Council welcomed the government's commitment to preventive medicine generally, which was in line with the TUC evidence to the Royal Commission on the NHS reported to Congress last year, but stressed that this section of the NHS was seriously under-financed. Preventive medicine was cost-effective in the long run and beneficial in itself, but there was no evidence of any NHS acute services being so under-used as to allow any reallocation of resources to preventive medicine. The General Council's view, that a substantial injection of new finance into NHS preventive services was essential, was expressed in a meeting with the Secretary of State for Social Services who reaffirmed the government's commitment to an expansion of preventive medicine, but stressed that additional resources were unlikely to be available in the near future.

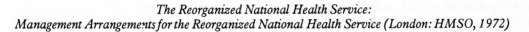

The Reorganized National Health Service:
Management Arrangements for the Reorganized National Health Service (London: HMSO, 1972)

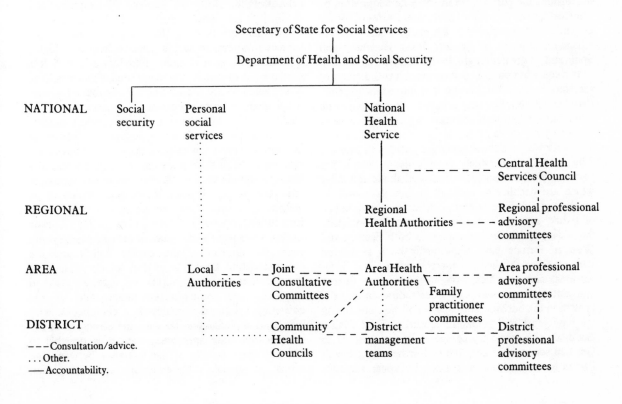

5

Education and the European State: Evolution, Rationalization and Crisis

DENNIS SMITH

Two propositions which are widely accepted, though the connection between them is still subject to considerable argument, are: first, that since the last world war Western European governments have increased the scale of their involvement in the management of finance, industry and the provision of welfare, education and research facilities; and secondly, that in the course of the last decade or so inflation and unemployment have risen to levels which are causing a serious deterioration of the rewards enjoyed by capitalists, wage-earners and the salaried middle classes, and eroding their confidence in the capacity of the political, economic and cultural systems to meet 'legitimate' expectations. The object of this chapter is to consider the part played in these developments by transformations within the institutional order of formal education. Reference will be made briefly to the education systems of France, West Germany and Spain and, at greater length, to the English system.

In a contribution to a book concerned with aspects of the state in capitalist Europe it is important to make two distinctions. The first is between those structural dilemmas and transformations which are broadly shared by all capitalist industrial societies, European and otherwise, and those which are peculiar to Europe. The second is between developments which are common to all four societies indicated above and those which are peculiar to each. A further issue will be mentioned only briefly here, concerning the question of what may be specific to *capitalist* societies. Secondary and higher education in both Eastern and Western Europe have traditionally been associated with long-established property-owning and professional classes which have been to some degree resistant to the pressures of industrialization and the growth in the bureaucratic capacity of the state during the nineteenth and twentieth centuries. Fritz Ringer has made this case very persuasively with respect to German society (Ringer, 1969). Furthermore, Frank Parkin has argued that in Eastern European societies

there is an endemic conflict between the university-based intelligentsia with its impeccable bourgeois traditions and the bureaucratic hierarchy of the ruling Communist Party, many of whose members come from 'uncultured' peasant backgrounds (Parkin, 1972).

When the focus is placed upon formal education, the distinction between 'capitalist' and 'socialist' policies may be a very imperfect predictor of differences between societies. At the level of higher education, for instance, the development of the French system has much in common with the Russian system. As Ben-David has pointed out, compared to other European and to North American cases, both academic systems are characterized by a high degree of political centralization. Both are subject to extensive and detailed bureaucratic regulation. In France and the USSR institutions of higher education have been subject to attempts by the state to impose a highly specialized division of labor (Ben-David, 1962). It is perhaps not surprising that such similarities should be found when we are considering the two major societies which share the rare experience of peasant revolution leading to the displacement of aristocratic establishments and their replacement by regimes pledged to use the state as a means of helping citizens to achieve their rights and fulfill their potential. As Lenin wrote to a French comrade in 1920: 'A Frenchman has nothing to renounce in the Russian Revolution, which in its method and procedures recommences the French Revolution' (quoted in Kumar, 1976, p. 245). In each European society the structure of the education system bears the imprint of the battles fought and the accommodation arrived at as that society underwent the transition from commercialized agrarian polity to urbanized and industrialized nation-state. If the education system is considered in conjunction with industrial organization and with the structure of the bureaucratic state apparatus, then it is possible to identify some aspects of the interplay between the forms of social differentiation and integration associated with, respectively, the transmission of culture, the use of economic power and manipulation of the capacity to exercise physical coercion.

Educational Growth, Economic Crisis and Political Frustration

Many of the contradictions and ambiguities affecting formal education in industrial societies since the last war follow from the failure of school systems to fulfill the promises which justified their rapid expansion. Education was to be a sphere of equal opportunity. The schools and colleges were to help promote economic growth. The education system was to be subject to a process of 'democratization'. Education was promoted, as it had been for over 100 years, as the principal agent of non-violent social change. It could be an active force, it was asserted. By manipulating the curriculum, for example, skills and attitudes could be developed in children which would engender fulfilling and integrated relationships in 'the present-day highly technicalised civilisation' (**Document 1**). This ideology was current among educationists in England by 1945 and had even penetrated into the upper ranks of Franco's Ministry of Education by 1969 (**Document 2**). However, by that time disillusionment was setting in.

By 1970 the annual growth rate for educational expenditure was nearly twice as large as the annual growth rate of national income in most OECD countries. This had certainly produced higher enrollments. During the twenty-five years after 1950 the number of students participating in primary education had increased by about a third, attendance at secondary schools had almost doubled and higher education had expanded its clientele by 150 percent (**Document 3**). However, the OECD Secretariat recognized that the growth was of a 'runaway' or 'unplanned' character and that it had made little contribution either to improving equality of opportunity and income between social classes, or to meeting 'the needs of the labour market'. The political consequences of these failures were becoming clear by the late 1970s. Simply put, education was becoming an extremely expensive operation and was to an increasing extent producing frustrated unemployed school-leavers. During the preceding period of postwar economic expansion passage from school to work had been relatively smooth and easy, but from the early 1970s the difficulty experienced by many in finding work exposed the lack of coordination between the two institutional spheres (**Document 4**). By 1977 the strategic planners consulted by OECD had ceased to make sanguine claims about the capacity of educational growth to promote planned social change. Instead, they were saying, in effect: 'for the past quarter-century we've been meeting the citizenry's demands for a "better life" and a "more rewarding future" by making more (and longer) educational programs available to them. Now public administrators, industrial managers, politicians and educationists have got to live with the political consequences of this, which potentially include the growth of an articulate and unemployed white-collar intelligentsia.' **Document 5** illustrates the items which were appearing on the political agenda by this time. Educationists were protesting about the effect on their projects of short-term shifts in the economic policies of governments: 'it is clear that education cannot be expected to adapt to economic cycles.' They were shying away from the uncomfortable choices being forced upon them by cuts in state spending and by reductions in 'acceptable' job opportunities for school-leavers: 'long-term development cannot be planned for a perspective other than one of full employment.'

In contrast to the previous high levels of growth in student numbers, practitioners in secondary and higher education were gloomily anticipating falling enrollments. Furthermore, the very process of expansion had tended to reduce the value of the diplomas and certificates awarded. Even the part played by teachers in the process of selection was being whittled away as various forms of 'all-in' school became widespread. By the late 1970s the crucial figure in the movement of young people from school to work was not the schoolmaster, but the potential employer. Educationists whose careers had boomed in the years of promise and plenty faced the prospect of running a mere 'parking' service for young men and women waiting to enter the job market.

To some degree these complaints were the protests of a large special interest which had allowed governments to use it as a means of satisfying voters' demands, but which had failed in the face of economic recession and decline to meet the promise, implicit or explicit, of providing students with a guarantee of security and success. In fact, the educationists' bluff had been called as early as 1970 when Michael Huberman, an official working for UNESCO, had written a brochure for International Education Year. It consisted of a wide-ranging attack upon the myths which had justified educational expansion while protecting the special interests of an elite. Huberman pointed out that while governments claimed to be 'democratizing' education they typically made primary education compulsory (hardly a 'democratic' practice) and restricted entry into higher education to those students capable of obtaining the requisite certification, thus discriminating against many working-class people who wished to obtain its benefits. Huberman called for a thorough adaptation of educational structures to make them capable of responding to the expressed wishes of individual students, perhaps through some kind of voucher scheme, rather than serving academics and administrators at the expense of students (**Document 6**). On 8 August 1970 the *Times Educational Supplement* reported that all but a few copies of Huberman's brochure had been destroyed on the orders of the Director-General of UNESCO.

Transatlantic Comparisons

Huberman's strictures were directed at European rather than American educationists and indicate an important difference between Europe and the USA with respect to the role played by universities and secondary schools. In Europe these institutions were well established long before mass primary schooling, were closely associated with the aristocracy and the church and sent their alumni into leading positions in government and the professions. As a consequence, the forms of classical knowledge transmitted within the universities and secondary schools during the nineteenth century had very high status and were considered the exclusive property and designating mark of a ruling class. In the USA neither state nor church nor an aristocracy wielded comparable influence and so none was able to bestow particular credit upon a set of exclusive educational institutions. As Ringer points out, educational institutions in the USA are not expected to confer any benefits upon their clients other than an improved capacity to perform well in the market. In other words, the skills and credentials acquired at school will enable the student to maximize his material rewards, the latter being the principal indicator, of power and position. By contrast, in Europe educational attainments and differences are *in themselves* a major indicator, perhaps *the* major indicator, of social power and position (Ringer, 1979). As a consequence, although there is a long-term tendency for educational hierarchies and occupational hierarchies in industry to be congruent in European

societies, it is possible for the two hierarchies to be in contradiction with each other (**Document 7**). For example, the current policy of the British Conservative government toward the universities is affected by the perceived 'irrelevance' of many of the latter's values and practices to the 'requirements' of industrial growth.

A further consequence of this difference between Europe and America is that the recent crisis in secondary and higher education in Europe has a dimension which is missing in the USA. In Europe the legitimizing power of traditional structures of secondary and higher education depended not only on their close associations with aristocratic, professional and governmental circles, but also upon the creation of bonds of solidarity among students who felt themselves to be members of an exclusive and specially selected minority. Expansion of secondary and higher education radically weakened this latter condition, fundamentally transforming the social milieux within which classical, liberal or 'arts' subjects had been transmitted. In effect, the elite sectors of European education systems in the postwar period have not only failed to meet the expectations of the new clients they have admitted, happily or reluctantly, but have at the same time helped to undermine the cultural supports for the traditional status hierarchy. Both processes are aspects of a broader pattern affecting all Western European societies in varying degrees. The rich cultural and material life of the nineteenth-century European bourgeoisie was made possible by its global dominance. In the twentieth century the wage-earning classes within European societies have demanded cultural and material rewards which recognize their own worth and power. In effect, they have demanded a fair share of the nineteenth-century bourgeois inheritance. The loss of global dominance by Europe makes it hard for ruling elites to resist these demands. It is also hard to satisfy them without damaging the ruling elites' own interests. The erosion of the exclusivity of the institutions responsible for reproducing traditional culture has contributed to this dilemma by weakening the effectiveness of important symbols of authority which the bourgeoisie had inherited from the aristocracy (Skidelsky, 1979).

Three Continental Examples: Spain, France and West Germany

Educational developments in France, West Germany, Spain and England cannot be considered in total isolation from each other. The cross-influences, political and ideological, are many. One might include, for example, the work of Clausewitz (inspired by Napoleon's military example) at the Military Academy in Berlin; the influence of the German idealist Krause upon the Spanish educationist Francisco Giner; and Matthew Arnold's enthusiasm for his 'French Eton' which provided state support for middle-class education. However, the part played by formal education in perpetuating, magnifying or dispersing class conflicts within recent decades has varied significantly from one society to another. These variations can be related to the different ways in which education has participated in the long-run processes of development or 'modernization'.

Within the context of this chapter it is only possible to give a brief indication of differences. In Spain the state has attempted to use education as a means of bolstering its political legitimacy but this attempt has been completely unsuccessful. This is clearest in the case of the universities. As Giner has argued, until the mid-1950s the Francoist regime permitted the domination of a thoroughly reactionary Falangist elite within a university system which had 'reached its lowest point in modern history: over-bureaucratised, corrupt, legalistic, unexpanding, rigid and, worst of all, dogmatic and poor' (Giner, 1976, p. 187). However, in the course of the next decade, the 'vertical' or 'corporatist' structures linking the universities to the state were weakened through the successful development of freer and more representative student organizations which acquired important links with industrial and political movements working to establish the classical liberal freedoms in Spanish society. During 1957–70 the student population at the Spanish state universities more than doubled. It more than doubled once more in the next half-decade (Giner, 1976, p. 196; see also Maravall, 1978). The rapid expansion of education, the demand for still more and the growth of autonomous student organizations together emphasized the difficulties faced by the government in implementing the strategy which had succeeded naked Falangism. This strategy was to placate the ubiquitous demand for reforms in a way which would broaden access to social rewards without actually extending the boundaries of political participation.

An important part of this strategy was the publication of *Education in Spain* by the Ministry of Education. It was soon nicknamed the *Libro Blanco* (*White Book*). This report surveyed the backwardness of Spanish education at all levels and proposed wide-ranging reforms (**Document 2**). It created, temporarily, a climate of intense optimism.

During the early 1970s popular expectations which had previously been low were sharply raised and then bitterly disappointed. The implementation of a new *bachillerato* (secondary school certificate) was repeatedly delayed. The Ministry of Education found itself in prolonged dispute with the Asociación Nacional de Catedráticos de Institutos, representing the most influential state secondary-school teachers. Student strikes, the closing of faculties for months on end, absenteeism by professors and other chronic disturbances continued. At the same time parents were faced with the new costs of paying the inflated fees of private colleges trying to teach the new-fangled Educación General Básica, a course intended in theory to be free and compulsory for all Spanish children aged 6–14. During a typical week in September 1973 the organization of primary-school teachers (Servicio Español de Magisterio) complained about the almost complete absence of school-building programs while private colleges were actually closing down by the score. Meanwhile, the Arts Faculty at Barcelona University was facing the elimination of some 300 academic options under a new plan being considered by the ministry.

A year later this heightening of discontent in the educational sphere, in effect produced by the government's own actions, was being matched by the appearance of labor unrest on a nationwide scale. In both the educational and the industrial spheres class groupings and other special interests brought into being by the processes of differentiation and integration associated with capitalist development were acquiring organization and representation, but the state was reluctant to recognize them. During the late 1970s, following Franco's death, the achievement of the classical liberal 'freedoms' provided conditions under which these groupings and interests could enter into the legitimate political arena and bargain directly and openly with representatives of the state. It is unlikely to be clear for some time what lasting accommodations will result from this process. A return to military repression can hardly be ruled out as a possibility.

The Spanish case offers a sharp contrast with the French in a number of ways. The French state has a much longer ancestry and, much more clearly than Madrid, Paris is the nation's capital not only in the political sense, but also in the sense of being the commercial and cultural center. Also, as Michel

Crozier suggests, participation within bureaucratic hierarchies has played a great part in shaping the French experience of authority and status (Crozier, 1964). By contrast, in Spain to a much greater extent than in France, official hierarchies are experienced as an imposition, sometimes useful and sometimes inconvenient, upon particularistic connections which generate more powerful and lasting obligations. France has always been the more stable and well-integrated society in so far as this means that a series of closely interlocking hierarchies in government, business, education and elsewhere share a common interest in the maintenance of established values, routines and patterns of distributing rewards. Of all Western European societies, France most completely epitomizes Kumar's conclusion:

> The centralisation and integration of political authority, whether or not itself originally accomplished by revolution, takes away that looseness in the structure of society which previously allowed revolutionary groups to 'take shelter' in the interstices of society, among its uncoordinated parts. (Kumar, 1976, p. 255)

Despite the experiences of May 1968, only two years later Pierre Bourdieu and his collaborator, Jean-Claude Passeron, published a book stressing the covert service which educationists performed in favor of maintaining existing structures of class domination:

> If the freedom the educational system allows the teacher is the best guarantee that he will serve the system, the freedom allowed to the education system is the best guarantee that it will serve the perpetuation of the relations prevailing between the classes. (Bourdieu and Passeron, 1977, p. 126)

The firm grasp over the development of education taken by Napoleon and the very late development of universities in France tended to inhibit the emergence of an 'academic estate' defining itself in opposition to government policy. When the pressure to introduce scientific and business instruction into the schools became very strong in the late nineteenth and early twentieth century (**Document 8**), the government was able to insist that non-classical subjects were not syphoned off into separate institutions, but taught within existing *lycées*. Once established within the schools, however, the new 'modern' curriculum was 'gradually assimilated to the traditional form of secondary education. It became less vocational and

more academic' (Ringer, 1979, pp. 118–19). As a consequence of these compromises, the division between traditional arts subjects and modern scientific subjects failed to acquire great political or social significance in French education.

To summarize, the French academic system manifests a great degree of centralization focused upon the metropolis and a high degree of congruence between the values and practices expressed in the political, educational and industrial spheres. Bourdieu has neatly identified the prevailing culture as being a subtle amalgam of the elitism of the big bourgeoisie and the Jacobinism of the petty bourgeoisie. By contrast, the Spanish system is characterized by a high degree of formal centralization in tension with strong pressures in favor of the expression of regionally based political, cultural and economic formations and of class-based interests not represented within 'official' structures. Recently, the latter have begun to obtain expression within the 'legitimate' arena but stable accommodations between the state and other interests have not yet been established. The education system remains starved of funds and a potent source of continuing disorder and discontent.

In the German case a distinctive long-term trajectory was followed. A flourishing traditional academic culture whose impact was felt in both England and Spain and which existed within a relatively decentralized educational system was confronted during the nineteenth century with a strong centralizing movement, during the course of which the state successfully developed the schools and colleges as a means of imposing order in public bureaucracy and industrial organization. A complicated system of state-run examinations linked to academic privileges took shape. Almost all the disciplines taught in the university became subject to the influence of examinations which the German bureaucracy developed to ensure that high standards were imposed upon the ranks of mining engineers, health inspectors, jurists, chemists, teachers and other occupational groups whose efficiency was important to a modernizing society:

> The level of examinations were linked first with the civil service, and after the industrial revolution industry had to accept the same standards to compete in recruiting labour. The links of the German system are possibly best seen in the case of apprenticeship, where the industry and trade unions cooperate to lay down the *Berufsbild*, the theoretical

part of which is translated into educational terms in the *Berufsschule*. (Musgrave, 1967, p. 264)

This aspect of the German education system won many admirers, especially in England. The Prince Consort and Lyon Playfair had plans during the 1850s to develop South Kensington as the metropolitan center of an English system organized along broadly similar lines.

One point above all is to be stressed with respect to the German system: the strong residual resistance mounted by supporters of the traditional curriculum, closely identified with the prestige of 'German culture' and the status of the upper class. Fritz Ringer has shown that the resisting forces retained most of their bases within the academic system. Growth in the modern sector occurred alongside established institutions which were neither transformed, nor replaced. Although the state successfully enforced the introduction of new subjects and institutions, the result was 'a dichotomy at the heart of the system, a set of status differences and value conflicts in which the high industrial present was opposed to the early industrial past' (Ringer, 1979, p. 65).

The British Case

These sketches of the Spanish, French and German patterns of development help throw into relief peculiar characteristics of the English education system which may now be considered at greater length. English society is distinguished from continental examples by the gradual pace of industrialization and the considerable extent to which it occurred outside the control of the state. The provision of mass education was not conceived of as a means of stimulating economic growth (indeed legislation for compulsory attendance did not appear until the 1870s by which time industrial development had been under way for a century), but rather as a means of coping with the political and social consequences of the growth which had already occurred. Education gradually superseded formal religion as the means for instilling in the young the moral grounds of status and authority. Above all, involvement in the provision of education gave the leadership of the old agrarian order a way to recoup some of the losses to its position sustained as the growth of the manufacturing cities and the bureaucratic state increased the power of officials, 'experts' and urban businessmen.

Although it was undergoing a long-term decline in its power, the Anglican church controlled an impressive national bureaucracy, and its clergy were deeply committed to rural values. This bureaucracy provided a useful cutting-edge which allowed the gentry to secure a deeply entrenched position in the educational sphere. Churchmen held powerful positions at Oxford and Cambridge, in the public schools and in other endowed schools, as principals of teacher-training colleges and in the National Society, whose funds were the major source of voluntary support for elementary schools. The authority of the rural order was threatened by the expansion of bureaucratic devices such as the external examination, but the educational bureaucracy was made subject to traditional influences to an extraordinary extent, especially after the ancient universities regained long-lost intellectual prestige in the late nineteenth century. As a consequence, the potential development of a powerful hierarchy of scientific educational institutions, including higher grade schools sponsored by the local school boards and provincial science colleges supported by businessmen, was prevented from coming to fruition.

The educational legislation of 1899 and 1902 had the effect of imposing in many parts of the country a clear distinction between elementary schools which would prepare most children during 'the school years available . . . for the work of life' and secondary schools for the few which would be distinguished by the prominence given within them to a literary curriculum borrowed from the public schools. In contrast to Germany, the English 'mandarins' committed to the traditional curriculum and the structures of status and authority with which it was closely associated were remarkably successful in avoiding subordination at the hands of a scientific–bureaucratic elite. The higher grade schools run by the school boards, which in some of the larger provincial cities such as Birmingham and Sheffield had reached very high standards of provision for technical education, came under very great pressure either to restrict their activities within a much less ambitious 'higher elementary' framework or to qualify as 'secondary' schools by introducing a greater element of literary instruction into the curriculum.

These changes were driven through with a confidence which derived from their compatibility with the new set of justifications for the authority of the ruling establishments in English national life, expressed through the writing and preaching of T. H. Green, Benjamin Jowett and other idealist scholars at the ancient universities. The transformations in the consciousness and aspirations of university teachers, their pupils and, eventually, members of the public schools, professions and middle-class occupations with which such men became associated were extremely significant.

The twin threats of the over-mighty state and an over-assertive populace were to be diminished by emphasizing the public duty of solid middle-class citizens to care for their neighbours. In effect, the missionary work of the Evangelical parson was to be taken over by lay professional men. This credo justified men such as the philosopher J. H. Muirhead, who obtained employment at the University of Birmingham, in maneuvering to maximize the influence of a liberal curriculum. Like his colleagues, he had a contempt for money-making as a goal and was hostile to narrow academic specialization, especially in the applied sciences: far better to be an 'all-round chap' with a due sense of public responsibility and a capacity to exercise authority.

It is important to emphasize that the 'public school spirit' provided a common frame of reference for networks of 'old boys' who belonged to establishments which were in other respects deeply opposed to each other. In has eased the transition of English society from a decentralized rural polity to a more bureaucratic urban–industrial nation-state. Through the development of the professions, central and local government and, above all, the education system itself many of the norms of status and authority of the pre-industrial society have been preserved. Furthermore, the relatively long period over which industrialization occurred, in conjunction with the resistance by both landowners and urban businessmen to a Prussian-style state apparatus, has meant that bureaucratic regulation, the market and status norms were, by the turn of the century, in an ambiguous relationship with one another. None of them was clearly established as the major principle of social coordination. In view of the incompatibility among important aspects of the cultures and practices of the major English establishments (for example, between the strong residual particularism of the county hierarchies, the orientation of the City to the market, and the bureaucratic concerns of the civil service), collaboration among them was well served by an ethos such as the 'public school spirit'. This ethos stressed the importance of close bonds established before entry into specific occupational groups, decreed that individual character was of great significance whatever one's vocation, and placed enormous value upon mutual tolerance.

The local authority (municipal) grammar schools which developed after 1902 transmitted the ethos of liberal culture and the social values of the public schools into the ranks of the middle and lower-middle classes in the provinces. The strong departmental boundaries which developed in the provincial universities encouraged a high degree of 'subject loyalty' among secondary-school teachers who were trained there and who were themselves the mentors of future elementary-school teachers. As a consequence, vertical loyalties were strengthened and horizontal bonds which might have formed the basis for a challenge to established authority were weakened. As long as the local authority grammar school was a pale copy of the public school, the pupils to whom the former gave 'sponsorship' were in a weak position to challenge the domination of the latter.

The pattern of sponsorship in secondary education, through which loyal subordinates were recruited through the grammar school to staff lesser managerial positions in commerce, local government and the education system itself, was complemented by the institutionalization of the 'collection' curriculum, that is, the maintenance of strong insulation between different subjects or disciplines (Bernstein, 1973). The collection curriculum performed an important political function. It permitted the admission of potentially threatening areas of scientific knowledge into the established framework of secondary and higher education, allowing them into association, but not too close association, with the genteel disciplines of liberal culture. The latter were recognized as being clearly superior. In this way two 'evils' were avoided: the development of completely separate high-level scientific teaching institutions; or the appearance of educational institutions in which scientific learning was completely integrated with the arts and subordinated the latter to its requirements.

These political effects had economic and social consequences, notably a failure to harness educational investment to the task of encouraging technological innovation in industry and a degradation of the social classes most directly involved in manufacturing. The huge waste of resources this entailed was, in effect, financed by England's early lead in industrial development and the profits of the London-based international network of trade and finance. The attempt to restrict working-class education within the confines of the elementary school and to stigmatize technical education as 'inferior' was congruent with the fact that, at the time of World War I, Britain had one of the narrowest electoral franchises in Europe (Matthew *et al.*, 1976, pp. 724–5).

However, the bases of this early twentieth-century

settlement were soon to be undermined. The industrial conflicts of 1910–22, combined with the experience of war, demonstrated the necessary dependence of the state bureaucracy and all establishments which looked to it to guarantee law, order and property, upon the cooperation of organized labor. Between the early 1920s and the end of World War II, a series of innovations occurred in the industrial, political and educational spheres which put into practice a strategy which had been painfully learnt by British governments in the decade leading up to the General Strike. Keith Middlemas describes this strategy as follows:

Is it unreasonable to assume that, earlier than in any other industrial country, British governments began to make the avoidance of crises their first priority? That even before the era of full suffrage they had discovered how to exercise the arts of public management, extending the state's power to assess, educate, bargain with, appease or constrain the demands of the electorate, raising to a sort of parity with the state the various competing interests and institutions to which the voters owed allegiance? That they sought to avoid, by compromise, crises in sensitive areas like wages and conditions, public order, immigration, unemployment, or the position of women, abolishing Hobbes' 'natural anarchy of competing wills' not by invoking authority (at a time of declining faith and deference) but by the alternative gratification and cancelling out of the desires of large, well-organised, collective groups to the detriment of individuals, minorities and deviants? (Middlemas, 1979, p. 18)

Formal education played its part in the new styles of social management which developed, particularly under the aegis of Stanley Baldwin and Neville Chamberlain. First, and most obviously, a slow but cumulative growth occurred in institutionalized consultation between management, unions and government at the national level, especially in the immediate prewar years. Secondly, a large program of social legislation was implemented in housing, pensions and related areas under Chamberlain's direction. Thirdly, increased attention was devoted by politicians and civil servants to means of assessing and influencing public opinion. Finally, there occurred the gradual implementation of a tripartite system of 'post-elementary' (later called 'secondary') education which allowed technical and 'modern' schools to grow up in the shadow of the grammar schools just as the latter had developed under the influence of the public schools.

Selection for post-primary education was to be regulated by a set of comprehensive examinations administered to all students beginning at the age of 11, referred to as the '11-plus' examination.

A common characteristic of all these developments was their capacity to prevent or deflect the formation of social coalitions between class fractions, whose members were strategic within the national division of labor but excluded from its benefits. The chronological coincidence of the General Strike and the Hadow Report on the 'education of the adolescent' is intriguing. The latter, through its wholesale commitment to examinations for all, promoted a new means of justifying the social inequalities which were under attack by the trade union movement. The bureaucratic device of the examination transformed conflicts of interest among social classes into problems of individual categorization which diverted attention from the underlying power structure. By 1938 about three-quarters of the school population was subject to 'Hadow' arrangements which were elaborated further by the 1944 Education Act. In a workforce whose ranks were by no means completely organized by the unions, educational experience in elementary, 'post-primary' and secondary schools may have provided a fairly effective alternative way of instilling occupational expectations.

The arrangements described above survived until the 1960s. Three aspects may be emphasized. First, the national educational, industrial and political institutions of English society were heavily oriented to performing as smoothly as possible the tasks of *distributing* material and cultural rewards among competing interests. Secondly, these patterns of distribution reflected and reinforced the veto power of influential bodies that had established themselves at the level of national decision-making during the century after 1850. These bodies may be considered to constitute an inner and an outer ring. The latter consisted of those interests which had played a central part in the political system of the nineteenth century and whose influence had helped shape the educational settlement of 1902: the churches, the ancient universities, the great public schools, the legal and medical professions and the municipalities. The former consisted of the interests whose mutual relations came to dominate national life after World War I: the City, the civil service, the trade unions and industrial management. Each of these interests had developed its own traditions, patterns of recruitment and valued objectives before becoming enmeshed in the political framework of regular consultation and mutual compromise which developed between the wars. Since English society did not experience the processes of wholesale reconstruction and 'rationalization' which were undertaken by the state in France after the Revolution and by the occupying powers in Germany after World War II, the shift toward 'corporatism' entailed the acceptance of a continuing high degree of latent conflict over ends and means in the management of English society. This leads to the third point, that historically the major function of the English education system has been to socialize generations of English children into the compromises between contradictory principles of social organization which are typical of the society. Through the schools they are taught to respect inhibitions and insulations which are devoid of intellectual justification but which have enabled powerful interests, such as the unions, the City, the civil service and the professions, controlling interdependent resources and tasks, to cooperate without pushing their differences to the level of first principles.

In the course of the last decade or so, the framework of social management built between the wars has begun to come apart. Sound management has proven more difficult, partly because Britain's declining international economic position has made the costs of placating potentially troublesome groups increasingly burdensome; partly because the political support for grammar schools, trade unions and state welfare provision has become eroded to a remarkable extent: and partly because of deliberate action on the part of governments. The number of grammar schools has been greatly reduced, especially since the support of central government was given to the implementation of 'comprehensive' schemes of secondary education in 1965. Over the same period charges to the consumer in the National Health Service have increased in number and severity while services have been reduced. Despite their relatively close relations with Labour governments, the trade unions have been subject to persistent pressure to reduce their freedom of action in industrial disputes. There have been short-term reversals of this trend, notably in the period of Harold Wilson's 'Social Contract', but the policy of the Conservative government of Margaret Thatcher has returned Britain to the previous lines of development.

The withdrawal of support for the grammar schools complements the reduction in the privileges of organized labor, since both processes mark a retreat from the compromises institutionalized in the 1920s and 1930s. These processes of bargaining eventually produced the 1944 Education Act, which in principle gave children in secondary modern schools 'parity of prestige' with grammar school children, and the welfare state legislation of the 1940s which in principle gave working-class families parity of treatment with middle-class families in matters of health provision. Both were the outcome of a 'social contract' between the state and organized labor which had made effective mobilization possible during the war.

These arrangements were underpinned in two ways: by the adherence of the provincial middle class and lower middle class to the leadership of metropolitan public school and Oxbridge elites; and by the broad acquiescence of working-class organizations in a power structure which was yielding them some rewards. Although, as Edward Shils has pointed out, intellectual and moral revulsion from the propaganda associated with the 'public school spirit' had become common between the wars in the higher levels of English society, the values of liberal culture were taken more seriously at the level of the grammar school and among the middling ranks of the bourgeoisie in the provinces (Shils, 1955). Perhaps the shock produced by the Suez adventure in 1956 helped to accelerate a process of disenchantment among these social classes which their social superiors had undergone a generation previously. The miners' strike of 1974, which had such a damaging effect on the Conservative government, finally swept away the residual atmosphere of deference which had been so assiduously cultivated in the early part of the century through the education system.

In the early 1980s a government is in power which has based its political appeal upon the supposed efficacy and explanatory power of a *single* principle, that of monetarism or control of the money supply. Practitioners within the education system are in a singularly weak position when seeking to defend their interests before such a government. This is because for the best part of a century the main task of the English education system has been to introduce its charges to the implicit values and routines of a social order dominated by a hybrid ruling class whose constituent groups had accepted a high degree of 'system inconsistency' in return for a share of the inherited rewards of Britain's early industrial lead and her advantageous position in global trade and finances. As long as they performed this basic task which underwrote the legitimacy of the entire system, educationists were permitted to pursue their own intellectual concerns and to build up their own academic empires. Formal education has, however, now lost the protection offered by its former congruence with a complex implicit status hierarchy and authority structure and is subject to sharp pressures from students, testing its products on an uncertain market, and from the state, which is anxious to decrease the tax burden. Educationists performed a vital function in the previous period and were rewarded with a high degree of freedom. For a few brief years in the late 1970s and early 1980s they had a choice either of using that freedom to 'rationalize' their internal relations in a manner which protected them from government, or of being the objects of 'rationalization' imposed from outside. That choice may now have disappeared.

Conclusion

A pessimistic reading of the current recession would suggest that Britain is experiencing at an early date a process of adjustment to relative political and economic decline which is likely to be shared by many Western European societies over subsequent decades. The way in which systems of formal education participate in the processes of intense conflict which are likely to ensue will probably differ considerably among the four societies examined in this chapter. In both France and Spain the conflicts which run through the educational sphere are very closely related to conflicts outside this sphere. In the French case this is because formal education is tightly woven into the structure of social management focused upon business and governmental elites in the metropolis. Reverberations in the industrial, political and educational orders are quickly transmitted to their neighboring spheres. In the

Spanish case formal education provides a major arena for the expression of tendencies from which the state has until recently sought to insulate itself. In other words, the education system in Spain has tended to reflect the state of civil society more quickly than political structures.

In the German case the education system during the nineteenth century (and occasionally during the twentieth) has provided a focus for traditional values and practices resisting the 'modernizing' impact of industrialization and the state. However, the combined effect of strong political controls and postwar rationalization has shifted the balance within education toward positive complicity in political and economic management. By contrast, the anguish currently being experienced within the educational sphere in Britain and the vigor with which it is being articulated are a consequence of that sphere's relative success over recent decades in keeping its distance from both government and industry. Had the education system been perceived as making a large and vital contribution to either of these spheres, it would not now be so devoid of friends. The important legitimizing function which education has performed in the recent past is now becoming something of a liability. Not least of the dangers faced by educationists is that having provided politicians, through the examination system and the ethos of 'opportunity', with a convenient means of justifying the share-out of social resources in affluent times, this very contribution may now be perceived as irrelevant or even dysfunctional. There is less need for an ethos of educational opportunity when the main political business of society is becoming recognized as not the distribution of economic rewards, but the distribution of economic penalties.

Documents

1   Proposals for Reform of School Curriculum in Britain

Extract from: *The Content of Education* ..., interim report of Council for Curriculum Reform 1945 (Bickley, Kent: University of London Press).

The Council for Curriculum Reform was set up in 1940 under the chairmanship of J. A. Lauwerys following discussions at Oxford organized by the Association for Education in Citizenship and the New Education Fellowship. The Council was dissatisfied with the rigidity of official approaches to the curriculum in England as expressed in the Norwood Report on Curriculum and Examinations in Secondary Schools. The Council for Curriculum Reform believed that the school curriculum should reflect 'both the qualities and capacities which should be fostered in all citizens and the characteristics of the new society which is in process of formation' (pp. 7–8). The report contains a full measure of wartime idealism.

Requisites for a Sound Curriculum

The main lines of a curriculum should emerge from a consideration of the needs of children at different stages of development, in relation to the conditions of the society in which they live today, and of the society of tomorrow in which they will live as adults. A very brief consideration of the existing secondary school curriculum will show how little relevance much of what is taught has to the children's needs in the present-day highly technicalised civilisation. All institutions tend to lag behind social change, and the curriculum, as one institution, is not exempt from this process. Originally a subject is included in the curriculum because there is a social demand for it. Once there, it becomes part of the established institution and any suggestion to remove it, or to vary its accepted scope, is resisted for reasons other than its social relevance. An unscientific belief in the theory of the transfer of training is the basis of much of the argument for the retention of subjects in the curriculum when they have ceased to have any real grounds for inclusion in it. This does not mean that everything taught must be of immediate practical utility. It does mean, however, that transfer must be ensured, and not merely assumed. This can only be accomplished by making clear in the minds of both the pupils and the teachers those features of the subject-matter which can be fruitfully generalised. This is particularly valuable when the social relevance of the knowledge being acquired is made plain.

This criterion of social relevance will prevent the curriculum builder from falling into the very prevalent tendency of working out the needs of the child in an artificial, abstract, and schematic manner. There is a temptation to discuss *the* needs of *the* child instead of the needs (here and now) of *this* child. Such discussions are unreal; a child's needs must be related to his or her reactions to specific situations—personal and social. The curriculum has to be so framed that it uses the psychological researches on the development of children and young people, and also the relevant sociological data.

Another prominent consideration in the mind of the curriculum planner must be the need for integration. In fact, one of the major criticisms that can be levelled at the existing curriculum is that valuable qualities are aimed at but are all too rarely achieved. Children must find the present time-table a very disjointed and piecemeal affair, mainly because of the traditional compartmentation of the subject-matter. The means whereby this evil may be remedied demand careful research. This may involve some readjustment of subject boundaries in order that the needs of the children may be more adequately met. But it is evident, from what has been written earlier in this chapter, that the re-drafting of curricula will not in itself bring about the desired integration. If it is effective, the integration will appear in the child's life and work.

At this point the search for an adequate curriculum impinges upon that of the training of teachers. There is a great need for specialist teachers who are trained to co-operate in the achievement of common ends. In many respects, increasing specialisation has made teachers as wise as owls in an ever-narrowing field but as blind as bats over an ever-widening one. Such specialists are for ever demanding more time and more facilities for their own subject, and a desire for prestige in the wider social world is reflected as a desire for prestige for their particular subject in the curriculum. In the community the lesson of co-operation for the achievement of a purpose has to be learned. In the school each specialist has to work not for an end peculiar to himself and his subject, but for the achievement of the common purpose of the educational process. This need may well lead to the development of teachers trained to integrate the activities of individual children.

2   Spain's *Libro Blanco*

Extract from: *Education in Spain* (Madrid: Ministry of Education and Science, 1969).

The so-called *White Book* (or *Libro Blanco*), published in 1969, was intended to set the course of Spanish education for the rest of the twentieth century. For a while it created a climate of optimism in Spain. However, it was beset by two contradictions. First, its ambitious plans demanded a degree of economic backing which Spain's political and class structure would not provide.

Secondly, the vision of an open and creative educational process which it offered contrasted sharply with the closed and rigid framework of Spain's political and industrial life.

The world progresses toward new forms which not even the boldest and most acute politicians have been able to predict accurately. All ideas and all facts are under revision, submitted to critical analysis, and where possible, reformulated. This universal revisionism does not spare educational systems, nor sociological, economic or political ideas, nor even the very application of ethical or religious principles, and we should not be surprised to find among men a climate of fear and desperation before this changing horizon. However, the diffusion of culture among Spaniards is a precious adventure which will reach insistently into all corners of our country. The challenge of our time is a formative and instructional education, and we are engaged in meeting it with the firm hope of obtaining the most clear cut results.

I have felt it my duty to recall this statement by the Chief of State since it synthesized well and with a clear call to our consciences the educational policy which the government attempts to develop. This policy is aimed at extending the human right to an education as far as possible. It presses for equal opportunities of access to the latter for all Spaniards, and it establishes a better correspondence between the requirements of a rapidly developing and transforming society with the orientations and performances of the national educational system. The new policy and the reform it fosters will entail in the future a thorough reform of society and of its old structures, quite like a silent and peaceful revolution, although it will be much more efficacious and profound than any other revolution in leading to greater social justice . . .

Perhaps an example will clarify what I have indicated above. Undoubtedly, the University question and the demands of its students captivate general attention, as these are 'newsworthy' items and therefore resonate in the mass media which, to a large extent, currently mold public opinion. But I am convinced that this circumstance unwittingly obscures the root of many of the problems which 'are seen' in the University, *since these are to be found, in fact, largely in the previous educational levels.* Thus, the class nature of the University, the dogmatic character of its teaching methods, the attitude of intellectual passivity which the students are forced to adopt, geared as they are only to pass exams by rote memorization.

The narrowly systematic search for a degree and the myriad other defects constitute problems which cannot be posed and resolved in isolation. Concretely, and in order to single out more clearly the above noted example, the class bound nature of the Spanish University is mostly a function of the differentiated tracks found in secondary education;

consequently, it will be impossible to correct this situation without reforming the latter thoroughly. This is, then, a problem to be found in our Universities, but one which cannot be addressed solely within them . . .

The list of what our government hopes to accomplish with the educational sector is really very long: first of all, to prepare youth for the responsible exercise of liberty, to foster social integration and national unity and civility, and to promote greater social mobility. But, in addition, it hopes to make of the educational process a continuous system, with a united and inter-related structure, and to offer the opportunity of a life long, permanent education for men and women. All this would require a substantial upgrading of the educational system's performance at every level, both in numerical as well as in qualitative terms, through an ambitious program of research which will permit, among other things, the introduction of new and modern pedagogical methods. This effort should be accompanied by an intense campaign of student recruitment and support through new and more ambitious scholarship and work-study programs, and by educational and professional orientation throughout the period of study.

Aside from these brush strokes to the general picture which the new policy proposes, it is necessary to recapitulate previously proposed and highly significant reforms such as the following: general basic education, free and compulsory until age fourteen; an overcoming of rural/urban inequalities in educational opportunities; intensive and accelerated professional training for all Spaniards before employment; unified and comprehensive education at the preparatory level, which should be free and extensive to all those with the necessary intellectual capacity; non-discriminatory access to a University with three cycles of study after a first, orientation course; University autonomy and creation of new Universities; new, inter-faculty University careers to meet the need for new middle level professionals; the creation of a truly University bound career for the faculty, with different positions and functions; etc.

3 Problems and Processes of Educational Growth

Extract from: *Educational Policies for the 1970s* (Paris: OECD, 1971).

This extract is taken from the Report of the Conference on Policies for Educational Growth which was held at Paris, 3–5 June 1970. A previous conference on a similar topic had taken place in Washington, DC a decade previously. At the Washington conference the main debates had been about the pace of educational growth (should it be rapid or slow?) and the relative importance of manpower planning as opposed to 'social demand' in setting educational targets. By the time of the Paris conference high educational growth rates were well established and education was being valued as much for its supposed contribution to the distribution of resources and opportunities as for its presumed effect on economic growth. However, there was a widespread feeling at that time that investment in education was making a significant contribution to economic progress.

A somewhat 'runaway' process of educational growth has reached levels where economic demand alone can no longer be the justification. Yet the structure of skills and qualifications resulting from the individual and social educational choices of the 1960s is increasingly out of balance with the 'needs' of society and the economy. The problem is thus no longer how to generate the growth process (which was a consequence of educational systems lagging behind the rapidly recovering economies of the Member countries in the post-World War II period), but how to harness and control educational growth more effectively to the new qualitative goals which it is to serve...

(1)   The growth of enrolments in the OECD countries during the period 1950–1965 was 32% for primary education, 87% for secondary education and 150% for higher education... In terms of absolute numbers, primary education rose from 72·6 to 95·9 million, secondary education from 24·4 to 45·6 million, and higher education from 3·9 to 9·8 million...

	Primary	Secondary	Primary and secondary	Tertiary	Total
	As a Percentage of Population:				
	5–14	10–19	5–19	20–4	5–24
Developing Member countries					
1950	49	6·7	37	2·4	29
1965	58	17	53	7·4	44
Other Member countries					
1950	80	30	74	9·6	58
1965	81	42	82	21	69
All 23 Member countries					
1950	75	26	67	8·4	53
1965	77	38	77	19	65

(2)   From the above it will be seen that the broad structure of growth had two principal features:

(a)   biggest absolute growth in terms of numbers in primary (because of demographic trends) and

secondary education (because of democratization), and

(b)   highest rate of growth in higher education.

(3)   However, the percentage of the age-group enrolled in education shows marked differences as between the developing Member countries and the rest.
(4)   These features of past growth will to a significant extent determine the patterns of future growth:

(a)   in the advanced Member countries the quantitative growth of primary and secondary education is bound to slow down because of both demographic trends and the high percentage of the age group now enrolled;
(b)   the democratization of secondary education in these countries in the 1960s will give rise to an increasing social demand for higher education in the 1970s, and one of the major problems of policy in the future will be how to respond both to this and to the expansion of adult education;
(c)   in the developing Member countries the growth of secondary education will continue to make a major claim on resources, but economic development will at the same time call for a high rate of growth in higher education.

(5)   The process of educational growth has resulted in an annual growth rate for educational expenditure which is nearly twice as large as that for national income (between 1·5 and 2 in all OECD countries) and extrapolations of educational expenditure and national income growth to 1980 lead to the conclusion that if present trends continue 10% of national income will be devoted to education in eight OECD countries, 5–10% in seven countries, and under 5% in five countries... The problems of financing education are in consequence likely to be considerable in the 1970s.
(6)   The output of qualified people from OECD educational systems as part of such rapid growth has been adequate in global economic terms, but there are growing structural problems arising from a mismatch between the labour market and educational output of school leavers and graduates.
(7)   Indeed, the main driving force behind growth has been social demand and democratization rather than adjustment to the needs of the labour market, and it is therefore important to note that education has only very partially succeeded in increasing equality of educational opportunity ... or equality of income distribution...
(8)   A consequence is that in the 1970s the accent will be on the major structural and qualitative changes needed to make education more effective in terms of economic, social and individual goals...
(9)   In planning for such changes it must be frankly recognized that the growth of the 1960s was a runaway rather than a planned process ... and that new planning approaches and methods will be needed if growth is to be made responsive to policy...

4 Education for What?

Extract from *Education and Working Life* (Paris: OECD, 1977).

By the late 1970s it was becoming evident that rates of economic growth were too low and rates of unemployment too high to fulfill the expectations being generated within educational systems. A Joint Working Party was set up under the aegis of OECD to investigate the links between education and working life. It reported at a time when the contribution of education to economic growth was being seriously questioned. The difference in tone between **Document 4** and **Documents 1** and **3** will be evident.

Trends and Prospects in the Economy, in Employment and in Education

The view that is taken of these issues and the policies that are applied will be most realistic if they are placed in the context of the realities of the current and prospective socio-economic situation of the OECD area. In this connection three main time-horizons can usefully be taken into account.

(1) The Short Term

The OECD area is recovering from a recession that has been more extensive, deeper and longer than any other during the postwar years. The nature of the problems of education and working life has been changing rapidly as the employment situation evolves. In most countries levels of manpower utilisation have fallen since 1973; recorded unemployment is at high rates, and increasing in duration; underemployment, indicated by reductions in productivity, has risen; and in several countries total employment actually fell in 1974 and 1975, which is unusual, and shows little sign of rapid recovery. In most OECD countries it is a well-established objective to encourage contra-cyclical increases in training; and trends in enrolments may have been influenced further in that direction by individual decisions to prolong general education or to seek training.

(2) The Medium Term

The economies of OECD countries, which are continuously transformed by the growth of consumption, production and technical change, are being further altered by the major changes since 1972 in the economic relationships between the OECD area and the rest of the world. In most countries medium-term prospects for expenditures on formal education are that their rapid growth since the early 1960s will not be sustained at the same rate, although education services will continue to evolve to meet new needs and objectives and demographic changes. Expenditures on training may rise: several governments have announced planned increases for the next few years. However, where training is financed by payroll taxes any

expansion is likely to be slow. Most OECD countries, which hitherto had experienced a period of overall scarcity of manpower during the rapid growth of most of the postwar period, have now entered a phase of prospectively lower levels of manpower utilisation. Since its inception the aims of the Organisation have included achieving the highest sustainable economic growth and employment. Following the meeting of the Manpower and Social Affairs Committee at Ministerial level in March 1976 the Council of the Organisation adopted a Recommendation on a General Employment and Manpower policy in which 'OECD countries re-affirm their commitment to full employment as a goal of policy'. Nevertheless, the economic situation and prospects in the OECD area are such that, in most countries, the moderate rate of recovery in output is expected to absorb unemployment more slowly than in previous upturns and to make future patterns of employment more uncertain than usual in times of recovery.

(3) The Long Term

There is even greater uncertainty about the form that socio-economic development will take in the more distant future under the influence of endogenous changes or how far its direction can be changed by public policy. Awareness of the growing economic, human and environmental costs of growth has created a need and a willingness to explore the possibilities of a more positive social policy. It must be anticipated that the penetration of the labour force by an increasing proportion of more highly educated citizens will have profound influences on the capacity of OECD economies, on expectations and on human and political relations at work.

The Transition from Education to Working Life

For the economy the movement of young people into working life is the most important single way in which the labour force and its average level of education is renewed and developed. The same is true for the personnel of most enterprises. Yet there is growing agreement that for a large proportion of young people, preparation for working life is inadequate and that the transition to working life is often unnecessarily difficult and slow, particularly for low socio-economic categories and for women. This is further compounded by the views that many young people hold about the unsatisfactory nature of work opportunities that the economy offers.

Employers are often reluctant to employ young people because many of them lack appropriate vocational skill and employment experience. In some employers' views, some young people do not possess the basic skills of literacy, numeracy and communication, or the personal qualities that many employers prefer. The initial contribution of new entrants to production is often low, and even negative. During favourable economic conditions some employers may be prepared to accept these costs as part of the total cost of renewing their personnel, but others prefer older workers or women returning to the labour force who are already trained or more likely to work regularly. When they do employ young people, employers often engage in a search, that is not always successful, for people with specific skills or the ability to adapt to the circumstances of the enterprise. Some enterprises do not provide training, including induction, if they are not convinced of the usefulness of it or if they fear that, in periods of relatively high employment, they may lose the personnel they have trained.

For the age group as a whole and for many individuals within it, the transition from education to firm establishment in working life takes several years. Boys and girls complain that they are often inadequately or wrongly prepared in school and that counselling is not satisfactory. There is a marked seasonal pattern in unemployment while school leavers are absorbed into employment. Once in employment, opportunities during working life to acquire experience, education and training, responsibility and income are often limited by traditional employment structures and practices and by the absence of facilities for further education and training.

Although relatively little is known in detail about the problems of transition, which are obviously different for each individual, it seems clear that they vary significantly among different age-groups and types and levels of education and training.

These difficulties during the transition impose opportunity costs: individuals lose income and work satisfaction, employers and the economy lose production both currently and in the future, as well as the outlays on recruitment. While part of the high rates of turnover among young people performs the useful role of allocating the labour force among employers and jobs, part of it entails waste in the form of loss of output and is one of the sources of inflationary pressure.

In the current recession the costs have fallen heavily on young people. In many countries the arrival in the labour force of a large cohort of boys and girls leaving school, especially after compulsory education, has coincided with a stagnation or even a fall in the level of employment. National rates of unemployment among young people have ranged up to 20 per cent in some Member countries, and double that figure in some regions or among certain categories of them. For many young people their first experience of life in the labour force is unemployment; and it is now increasing in duration, although not necessarily more than among older workers. In these circumstances pressures on liquidity among enterprises have not only denied many young people an initial work experience, they have also reduced training opportunities, especially long-term ones such as apprenticeship.

More particularly, there is growing concern for the categories of young people, upon whom these costs fall most heavily of all because they are especially vulnerable. The transition to an employment corresponding to their qualifications, expectations and aspirations, either in the first job or later, which is difficult and frustrating at all levels of education, may be particularly protracted and entail more broken employment and unemployment among the young school leavers with lower levels of education and no training. There are many young people, often from families whose socio-economic status is low, who experience problems at school, including difficulty in learning, who leave school early without either formal qualifications or vocational skills, who experience corresponding difficulties in obtaining an initial job or stable employment with opportunities to obtain training, more than a very low income, or the prospect of subsequent personal development during working life. Moreover once in types of employment that are low level or unstable, or both, they tend to be considered suitable only for that type of work.

5   New OECD Strategies for Education

Extract from *Education Policies and Trends in the Context of Social and Economic Development Perspectives* (Paris: OECD, 1977).

In 1977 a 'group of experts' from the education ministries of six OECD members (Germany, the USA, Norway, France, Sweden and the UK) met to assess the broad implications of declining rates of economic growth and high levels of unemployment. In contrast to the atmosphere of Paris in 1971 (see **Document 3**), it was acknowledged that 'educational reform did not fully succeed in meeting all the users' needs while, at the same time, it generated new demands as well as new forms of dissatisfaction' (Introduction, p. 6). The 'experts' recognized that unemployment had become a serious threat for young people. They hoped to prescribe 'new roles and functions as well as new strategies for education' (p. 7).

[I]t is clear that education cannot be expected to adapt to economic cycles and, more particularly, that its long-term development cannot be planned for a perspective other than one of full employment; . . . the higher levels of educational participation and attainment among all groups of the population which have resulted from the massive growth of education in the postwar period represent a major social change of a secular nature; future policies for education have to take account of the consequences and irreversibility of this development.

(1)   Summary of Trends

Changing Patterns in Educational Growth and Demand
Most of those of the Member countries which, in the past,

experienced high levels of educational growth, now witness a slowing down in their rate of expansion accompanied by greater diversification of their educational systems. Overall expansion, however, will continue, particularly in those Member countries which are still in the process of development, thereby making it possible to reduce the existing marked disparities in participation rates among social groups.

The fall in the birthrate in many countries since the middle sixties (and, in particular, since 1972) has resulted in a decrease in enrolments at the primary school level and this will continue until 1980/85, reaching lower and upper secondary levels. It is to some extent compensated by increased demand at pre-school level due to growing enrolment rates. Non-compulsory secondary education, in many countries, can be expected to continue to grow up to the mid-eighties—in some cases notably in the technical and professional branches—and to diversify in a variety of directions in response to the demand from young people between 16 and 19 years of age and also from adults. Beyond that date it will in its turn be affected by the fall in population. At all these levels improvements in the quality of education and in the use of resources in equipment and manpower (e.g. reduction in some countries of the teacher/pupil ratio and of the number of pupils per class) will remain a high priority for educational policy-makers.

In many Member countries, the demand for post-secondary education has stabilised or is growing only slightly. This is not unconnected with a decrease in the relative advantages conferred by degrees and similar credentials.

In all Member countries there is a marked increase in the demand for adult education—full-time, but particularly part-time—including courses leading to occupational and technical qualifications.

The result of these changes is to shift emphasis in educational policy-making from efforts to meet demand in terms of numbers to increased concern for qualitative considerations. This development is related to the unsteady evolution of enrolments and has consequences for the factors affecting enrolment trends.

Relations between Education and Employment
The changes outlined above, especially those touched upon under [the above] section, cannot be considered simply in terms of educational policy. In many Member countries, along with a levelling off of the demand for higher education, there is considerable youth unemployment concentrated among those young people with low educational attainment or no professional qualifications.

Although there has been some dissatisfaction and restlessness among the better qualified young people over their employment prospects—and this is particularly true of young teachers in some countries at this time—they have nevertheless often had sufficient choice and, perhaps, the social and educational background required to come to terms with their situation. Increasing numbers of young people gaining higher education qualifications may, however, well present short-term social and employment problems even at a time of full employment, which it would be unwise to ignore—though this should not be interpreted as denying the fact that for the individual the more education he has the better are his chances to secure satisfactory employment. Finally, even if economic recovery attains greater momentum, sharpened awareness of the needs in social policy or in ecology would call for increased educational policy concern over disadvantaged groups and new content in education for the preparation of people as responsible citizens.

As a result of past educational expansion, the selection which used to take place in the course of school life will in future take place increasingly at entry into the first job. This may be a healthy development, but its consequences should be noted. The problem of entry into active life, rendered all the more difficult by the shrinkage and segmentation of the labour market, has become the primary preoccupation for young people, calling for precise responses on the part of national authorities and a more socially conscious attitude on the part of the employers.

Those Member countries which have been strongly affected by a fall in the birthrate will experience an increased aging of their population. This evolution of the demographic structure will result, on the one hand, in an increase of the ratio of the old non-active to the active population (which could result in an increase of the social burden on the active population) and, on the other hand, in a decline of the rate of entry of young people into the active population in relation to the corresponding rate of exit.

The present state of the economy of many Member countries results in a high level of unemployment among young people, affecting in particular certain groups—unqualified youths, young women, youth in underprivileged regions, young migrants and the handicapped. This segmentation process is likely to increase the share of these specially vulnerable groups in total unemployment. The transition from school to active life is accompanied by risks, difficulties, disappointments and increasing frustration. This position has potentially negative long-term psychological effects upon individuals and might bring in its train undesirable social and political consequences. In response to such a situation, education systems are increasingly led to assume a retentionist function; they should do this by offering coherent and adequate opportunities for training, often within a recurrent education framework. Training having only a 'parking' role is an offence to the young people concerned and a disservice to society. Unless it can provide the student with training for a useful job, and he can see that this is so, he will be encouraged to feel disillusioned, resentful and negative in his attitude towards education and society. On the other hand, nearly any kind of education is preferable to actual unemployment, and the primary policy objective in such a situation should clearly be to provide meaningful education for all young people who want it.

The employment prospects of young people, and how they are related to education, are difficult to identify and plan for very far ahead, depending as they do upon the evolution of the means of production (related to the demand for more or less qualified manpower to operate the capital involved), the demand for goods and services, the rhythm of economic development and, essentially, upon the improvement of the employment situation. The recognition that forecasting the timing and magnitude of changes in these elements is most hazardous makes it all the more necessary to build into planning the capacity to cope with uncertainty.

Educational Developments Vis-à-Vis New Problems in the Allocation and Use of Financial and Manpower Resources
A number of Member countries have adopted policies in favour of investments, limiting public and private consumption, together with policies aimed at a balanced budget and at reductions in public spending, all tending to restrict the growth of public expenditure on education. The high proportion of expenditure on personnel in current education expenses and the distribution of funds among the different levels of the education system create rigidities which limit the possibilities for budgetary restrictions. Such restrictions are in danger of compromising the quality of services, as of policy objectives, and of furnishing inadequate responses to new educational needs—pre-primary, remedial, adult. In some countries, the share of resources set aside for the training of unemployed youth so as to improve their chances in the labour market, though relatively increasing in a few cases, remains limited because of a lack of coordination between the administrative services concerned.

In some countries it is already the case that more young people have been training as teachers than for whom employment can now be found and this situation may become more widespread, even taking into account the increases in teacher-pupil ratios which may be necessary at various levels of the educational system. This will increasingly call for a re-definition of the modes of recruitment, training, utilisation and deployment of teachers and of the bases on which staffing ratios are established in relation to pupil groupings . . .

(2)   Responses of the Education System

The objective of a return to full employment is essentially a first priority for economic and manpower policies. If educational measures cannot but marginally contribute to this return there is nonetheless a basic responsibility on the part of the education system to facilitate the entry of young people and adults into working life by providing both general and vocational education appropriate to modern needs; present unemployment has no more than revealed the existence of this permanent need . . .

In many countries there may be need for a redefinition of the objectives of *basic education*, taking into account the need for an extended common educational experience for all children, the increased educational opportunities available outside the school, and the need to reduce existing inequalities between social and ethnic groups, regions and sexes. The function of education as an apprenticeship for social life and as fulfilment of the total capabilities of the individual, including the development of a propensity for participation in subsequent educational opportunities, must take its proper place along with the need for individuals to play their part in economic life . . .

[B]y providing *all* young people with a better basic preparation for social and active life in all its forms, the school could also overcome its failure to interest and motivate many groups of pupils and reduce the rate of drop-outs and repeaters . . .

By providing occupational qualifications, the education system has an important role to play in reducing the dangers which active members of the population, and in particular young people, find themselves facing in employment. All must thus be offered a chance to prepare for active life and to acquire marketable skills and qualifications; the numbers of those who at present leave the education system with no valid qualifications need to be reduced. Priority would need to be given to qualifications of a reasonably general nature, not rigidly tied to one particular occupation, but facilitating movement between several. In some countries, the education system needs to develop effective responses to the growing need for occupational training and also for the provision of middle-level qualifications. In most countries there is a need for measures to bring the education and training systems closer together.

A growing sphere of public responsibility, in conjunction with other agencies and groups concerned, is the improvement of the conditions prevailing at the time of transfer from school to active life and a reduction of the difficulties and dangers which assail the young during the process . . .

The existence of higher and rising levels of instruction among the population as a result of educational expansion is an irreversible social fact. Arguments postulating an excess of qualifications are not convincing. Nevertheless, the consequences of this general raising of the level of education must be carefully envisaged. On the one hand, in the future, individuals may be required to reduce the professional expectations formerly linked to a certain level of education or to a particular degree or diploma, while educational institutions may have to offer more diversified and not too specialised course programmes; on the other, employers will have to propose employment structures, working conditions, modes of participation and use of acquired skills which take into account and respond to the higher level of instruction acquired by their employees.

The concern over the change in employment and career chances for higher education graduates, while justified and necessary, bears the risk of becoming overly prominent in public concern, the media, and in policy considerations, to the detriment of other priority areas for educational and social policy. From the point of view of social ethics as well as in the interest of long-term economic and social development, the first priority for educational policy, together with meeting the basic demands of industry and the public sectors for highly qualified manpower, must lie with those at the bottom of the educational qualification scale, particularly at a time when that position means a high risk not only of underemployment, but of unemployment. It is on this principle also that a new priority for adult and recurrent education is founded. From the same social policy principle, together with the argument of the long-term needs of the highly developed economies facing a decline in the age groups entering the labour force, derives the idea of society's responsibility for providing all youth with a full vocational or professional qualification utilisable on the labour market, upon which their further education and retraining may build.

The trends and orientations outlined above will need to be increasingly reflected in the methods and scope of educational planning and management. This is an area in which technical and political issues are closely inter-related, and we have referred to these matters in the main body of our report.

6   The Demand for Democratization

Extract from M. Huberman, *Reflections on the Democratization of Secondary and Higher Education* (Paris: UNESCO, 1970).

The brochure from which this extract is taken was published by UNESCO for International Education Year. According to the *Times Educational Supplement* (21 August 1970), all but a few copies were destroyed on the orders of the Director General, M. René Maheu. This extract is part of a longer excerpt from Huberman's brochure which was printed in the *Times Educational Supplement*. Huberman carries out a frontal attack on educationists' preoccupation with creating a large and bureaucratic system of schooling.

[W]e are in the midst of a world-wide educational crisis, and one which has become more openly political than in the past. Until very recently, only specialists were concerned with the structures, content and methods of public education. At present, with the accumulation of dissatisfactions and demands from all sides, student, teacher and employer alike, we have had a number of warning signals that ministry authorities responsible for educational policy must seek remedies immediately.

The demand for democratization or open access to education is politically irresistible, although it can often be educationally unsound. The majority of educational ministries in the European continent are anticipating and deliberately preparing for an increase in the percentage of 19- to 24-year-olds in the population enrolled in a university of the order of 10 to 20 per cent during the coming five-year period. Given the present conditions of overcrowding, understaffing, heavy dropout rates, lack of specialized administration, discontent with teaching methods and curriculum and limited resources in many of these countries, the move to greater democratization could be catastrophic. But to limit enrolments on economic grounds, when this is educationally practicable, usually amounts to political suicide...

The lack of a smooth articulation between the secondary school and the university is bound up with the traditional idea of a university elite, representing 5 per cent to 20 per cent of the yearly age group. We have here a continued European heritage, passed on to developing countries under colonialism, that dates from its patrimonial—if not feudal—past. The American and Eastern European concept of eventually providing higher education for all conjures up in the minds of most university authorities the vision of mass education and a decline of standards. Education for all, the argument runs, is education for none.

If we look into the consequences, the changes necessary in structures and mentalities to actualize the ideas of self-education, student-centred teaching, and the breakdown of distance between school and outside environments, one particular problem stands out. Once it is assumed that there is no longer a proper and necessary order in which things can be learnt, nor that we can define an essential body of knowledge that all should share, the direction of the teaching staff must be transformed. The function of the university, for example, was formerly fixed by the subject matters.

What happens, then, when this body of knowledge is no longer fixed: when good scholarship becomes less essential than good teaching, for which very few university professors have been trained; when what the student hears becomes more important than what the teacher says; when fixed cycles of attendance are replaced by intermittent leaving and re-entry; when facilities for education are available outside institutions of learning; when students are learning to teach themselves?

The answer depends on whether we feel that universities should be managed as a civic democracy, a 'community of scholars' or an administrative corporation. When students demand representation on governing boards, they often picture the university as made up of special interest groups, each having its own preserve and its claims to control in varying degrees according to a certain number of responsibilities. The academic staff tends to see claims of formal democracy or civic equality as out of place in the practice of education.

There is something misplaced in these discussions of whether or not university students are adult enough for 'participation' when 6-year-olds in British primary schools have devised their own curricula for several years and progressive secondary schools have used democratic councils with equal voting rights for pupil representatives as an essential part of education itself.

The optimal solution—and one to which a great deal of organizational theory is being devoted at present—is that management be designed according to the kinds of decisions that are to be made, ranging from the 'pyramidal' to the 'participative'.

If we have not dealt in detail with specific reforms or remedies, we seem to be clear at least about the evolution and the present state of our dilemma in democratized education. We have seen that the most obvious solutions turn out to be counter-productive. Wider access by itself is less a solution than an invitation to a greater crisis . . .

[S]o-called 'shadow systems' in education are springing up throughout the world. They allow for a natural compensation and balance against deficiencies in the formal education system. As unorthodox and new institutions, they are more flexible and innovative. More important, they often create a challenge for the formal establishments which can set off major reform on a nationwide scale.

The most recent phenomenon in developing and market-economy countries seems to be inspired by the Danish example. The idea is simply that of giving money directly to the student rather than to the state. The university student then takes the amount that he costs the state and goes to any accredited institution, of which there are likely to be many sorts.

A number of American and British economists and educators have looked into this solution in depth. They argue that the establishment of 'full-cost privately financed education', funded by government stipends, would be more fair than the present system. The institution would be obliged to meet the needs of the student, not the reverse, since he would be in fact 'buying' his education as he would any service, and would then be far more demanding.

The same type of solution has been proposed for developing countries on different grounds. In most parts of the world, there are few welfare programmes for poor and lower class children or students. The drop-out rate is much higher among middle and upper-strata pupils simply because they make up the majority of those enrolled beyond the primary level. To give each child or parent the equal amount for the choice and purchase of education for the family (all in controlling the spread of expensive or exclusive schools) would then ensure full democratization for a far longer period. An 'educational coupon' scheme has even been proposed for Latin America.

This is not to say that the coupon scheme is the best solution for modern education and its democratization, but rather that all these trends and demands are beginning to converge. The divorce of the school from its environment, the need for individual patterns of teaching and learning, the related demand for 'open-ended' education with an accent on adaptability and independence, the creation of interdisciplinary programmes, examination criteria set closer to the aptitude for continuing self-instruction, the achievement of mass education by a variety of patterns and sequences: there is increasing evidence throughout the world of similar requirements and a similar evolution.

7 Weber and Education

Extracts from M. Weber, *Gesammelte Politische Schriften*, as quoted in F. K. Ringer, *Education and Society in Modern Europe* (Bloomington, Ind.: Indiana University Press, 1979), p. 16, and as reproduced in M. Weber, *Economy and Society*, edited by G. Roth and C. Wittich (Berkeley, Calif.: University of California Press) appendix II, pp. 1400–1.

Document 7 is included to indicate the double legacy that the elite education systems of nineteenth-century Europe bestowed upon industrial society. First, university education and attendance at secondary schools typically signified membership of a privileged high-status group possessing 'cultivation'. Secondly, the diplomas and certificates which were important outward signs of high status were also instruments in the implementation of rationalization and bureaucratization.

Differences of 'cultivation' are nowadays undoubtedly the most important specific source of *status group* differentiation, as contrasted with property and differentiation of economic function, the sources of *class* formation . . . Differences of 'cultivation' are . . . one of the very strongest purely psychological barriers within society. Especially in Germany, where almost all privileged positions inside and outside the civil service are tied to qualifications involving not only specialized knowledge but also 'general *cultivation*' . . . All our diplomas also—and principally—certify the possession of this important *status* qualification.

[T]he Germans perfected the rational, functional and specialized bureaucratic organization of all forms of domination from factory to army and public administration. For the time being the Germans have been outdone only in the techniques of party organization, especially by the Americans. The present world war means the world-wide triumph of this form of life, which was advancing at any rate. Already before the war, the universities, polytechnical and business colleges, trade schools, military academies and specialized schools of all conceivable kinds (even for journalism) reverberated with urgent demands propelled by the schools' recruitment interests and the graduates' mania for benefices: The professional examination was to be the precondition for all well-paying and, above all, secure positions in public and private bureaucracies; the diploma was to be the basis of all claims for social prestige (of *connubium* and social *commercium* with the circles that consider themselves 'society'); the socially proper, guaranteed 'salary' [rather than the 'wage'], followed by a pension, was to be the form of compensation; finally, salary increases and promotion were to be dependent on seniority. The effects can be seen inside and outside of governmental institutions, but we are here only interested in the consequences for political life. It is this sober fact of universal bureaucratization that is behind the so-called 'German ideas of 1914', behind what the literati euphemistically call the 'socialism of the future', behind the slogans of 'organized society', 'cooperative economy', and all similar contemporary phrases. Even if they aim at the opposite, they always promote the rise of bureaucracy. It is true that bureaucracy is by far not the only modern form of organization, just as the factory is by far not the only type of commercial enterprise, but both determine the character of the present age and of the foreseeable future. The future belongs to bureaucratization, and it is evident that in this regard the literati pursue their calling—to provide a salvo of applause to the up-and-coming powers—just as they did in the age of laissez-faire, both times with the same naïveté.

8 Durkheim's Vision of Education in France

Extract from E. Durkheim, *The Evolution of Educational Thought*, trans., Peter Collins (London: Routledge & Kegan Paul, 1977).

This extract from Emile Durkheim's lectures on the development of secondary education in France (initially given in 1904–5) is included to illustrate the ideology that secondary education should be concerned with the general development of the reflective faculties. The occasional obscurity of Durkheim's argument demonstrates the profound difficulties confronted by defendants of this tradition when faced with the demand for high-level vocational training. What place was the latter to have within secondary and higher education? What relationship should it have to the classics?

A secondary education can be valuable at least to some future professionals in economic life, yet it should not and it cannot, without losing its identity, be organised with these professions specifically in mind. To avoid betraying its own nature it must not take as its aim the preparation of people for a life in industry or commerce, any more than one in the law or the army, since its essential characteristic is that it does not initiate people directly into any particular profession. This does not mean that I am disputing the value of the industrial or commercial schools in which future practitioners in industry and commerce are moulded directly on leaving primary school. On the contrary I believe that within these careers there are certain functions which need not theory, not highly-developed speculative faculties, but practical qualities; and there are grounds for arousing and exercising these qualities without delay in children who have a greater aptitude for them than they have for reflection. It is only that although these schools follow directly after primary schools as do our colleges and *lycées*, we must beware of confusing them with secondary schools as we have just defined them. For each kind of school is orientated in a quite different direction; they must employ quite different methods and draw inspiration from a quite different spirit. Each constitutes a category of educational establishment which it is of the utmost importance to distinguish. If, failing to recognise these differences, we lump them together under the same headings, we run the risk of talking about both of them at once and consequently of no longer knowing what we are talking about. It is this confusion which has resulted in the fact that people have often confused two very different questions: First, how should we organise an education especially designed for commerce and industry? Second, is it possible to develop a genuinely secondary education which would nurture the reflective faculties in a general way, but which does not include Greek or Latin? And people have thought that having solved the first question the second was also solved by the same token, or *vice versa*.

By secondary education we mean exclusively that education which prepares people for the university and which is specifically defined by the absence of any immediate vocational concern. The features of this education in the whole gallery of our academic system are thus sharply defined. How it is to be distinguished from technical education and from schools concerned with practical application, we have just explained. Like higher education it is directed towards the reflective faculties, but it develops them in a general way whereas higher education makes use of them in a specific form, and in this way we can distinguish the former from the latter. The line of demarcation with primary education is perhaps more vague. Primary education does not prepare people for vocations; it too, at least today, aims to arouse reflection to the extent that in these times no one can be without it. Thus when people think that classical languages are not necessary to secondary education, it is difficult to say where one of these kinds of education ends and the other begins. There are only differences of degree, which are virtually imperceptible at the frontiers. There is nothing less justifiable than the barriers which currently separate these two kinds of school; they are barriers constructed exclusively out of illegitimate prejudices and we must hope that they will be broken down.

6

Regional Policy and Planning: Convergence and Contradiction

JAMES R. LEWIS

This chapter examines the character of regional policy and planning measures within Western Europe since 1945, in an attempt to illuminate both the nature of the contemporary state apparatus and its relationships to different social classes and movements. Western Europe is defined here as comprising the nine coterminous members of the European Community (EC) and the two Iberian applicants for EC membership (namely, Belgium, Denmark, France, Federal Republic of Germany, Republic of Ireland, Italy, Luxembourg, the Netherlands, Portugal, Spain and the UK). The state interventions considered here are those specifically concerned with the location of economic activities at the inter- and intra-regional scales, which will be collectively described as regional policies and have usually been formulated in response to the perceived emergence of a 'regional problem' or, often closely related, the need to allocate governmental resources within a particular region.

At the outset it is useful to distinguish between such policies on the basis of their objectives and scales of operation, since their forms of implementation and the social contradictions embodied in them differ considerably. Thus *regional policy*, in the strict sense, can be defined as that which seeks to affect the distribution of employment within the national territory, generally by the use of spatially selective infrastructural investment, financial incentives and development controls but including, for nationalized industries and government departments particularly, administrative fiat. Clearly, this sort of policy depends on the selection of some regions as ones requiring intervention but it has also tended to be sectorally selective in its emphases on the creation or movement of manufacturing employment. In contrast to this set of policies, *regional planning policy* is concerned with the location of a wider range of activities within a given area. Regional plans range in content from a list of expected ministerial spending on physical infrastructure (for example, communications facilities or

housing) to a detailed land-use projection. This variety of content, coupled with national variations in the administrative level at which plans are formulated and executed, means that the mechanisms for implementation differ enormously. They can range from central government decision at one end to the autonomous application by a regional authority of land-use controls to prevent 'inappropriate' developments.

Neither regional policy, nor regional planning policy, involves a large proportion of total national state expenditure, but they can be significant components in the allocation of public funds to private capital. In the UK, for example, regional policy expenditure for 1971–81 totalled £5,000 million (Committee of Public Accounts, 1981), or an annual average of some 25 percent of all state spending on the category of trade, industry and employment. For individual capitals, the availability of regional policy incentives can be of even greater significance as the maximum grant officially offered within the EC range of 15–50 percent of a new investment and this is increasingly being supplemented for large projects. Other national policies may, of course, have differential consequences between regions—from those related to nationalized industries through agricultural measures to those on social services—which may reinforce or undermine a regional policy. It is, however, sufficient at present to indicate that the latter can be important under certain circumstances.

At the level of the EEC there is a similar apparent neglect of regional policy in that the expenditure of the European Regional Development Fund (ERDF) from its inception in 1975–mid-1979 was only 1,725 million units of account (u.a.)—some 5 percent of the Community budget (EEC, 1980). However, even if the activities of the European Coal and Steel Community are ignored here, over 2,000 million u.a. worth of grants and loans were advanced during 1978 alone for regional development purposes from other sources such as the European Social Fund (for retraining workers), the Guidance Section of the European Agricultural Fund (agricultural modernization) and the European Investment Bank (industrial and infrastructural projects). As in the case of nation states, other Community policies may offset the effects of these programmes, so that one of the aims of the ERDF 'quota-free' section is to reduce any such adverse impact (for example, agricultural assistance in South-West France resulting from the impending admission of Spain), even if this occurs outside the nationally designated areas for regional assistance.

Turning to the subnational level it is much more difficult to establish the relative importance of regional planning. While the expenditure on regional plan preparation and monitoring is relatively small, the amount of public and private investment directed by it can be considerable. A further complication is that expenditure by local government on, say, infrastructure or education is often linked to national regional policy. On top of this, some regional planning investments are also part of urban plans, so that any generalization about the role of regional planning at this level is likely to owe more to its definitional assumptions than to actual measurements of expenditure.

Taken together regional policies, with their limited scope and expenditure, might seem an unlikely terrain on which to tackle such a difficult theoretical question as that of the role of the state in late capitalism. However, there are three main reasons for regarding this terrain as an attractive one and a brief statement of them has the further advantage of allowing the themes present in the documents to be introduced. First, direct and systematic involvement of the state apparatus in the location of economic activity is, with the exception of British attempts in the 1930s, a phenomenon of the post-1945 period. Regional policy and planning are, thus, hallmarks of the current phase of capitalist development, elements in the general conditions provided for accumulation. They were not, however, introduced simultaneously, nor have they remained unchanged since, so that the timing and form of intervention reflect the perception of a problem requiring intervention and the position of the government at the time. Hence, the details of the policies have varied considerably, even in a single country, and so have the justifications presented for them. **Documents 1** and **4** illustrate this in the criteria used to judge regional policies in the UK in 1964 and 1979, respectively. Whereas the parliamentary discussion of the problems of North-East England was dominated by questions of reducing unemployment and

improving social conditions through government investment, the tone set some fifteen years later by Sir Keith Joseph, was one of the limited cost-effectiveness of such investment and thus the need to reduce it.

Secondly, although seldom stressed, the state does have the role of maintaining territorial integrity, something that can be threatened by uneven regional development. This often requires interventions over and above those associated with the containment of class struggle. Regional policy and planning interventions are good illustrations of such interventions, showing the necessity of an overtly discriminatory strategy, but also bringing the problems created by this to the fore. Such problems are increased by the formal arrangements in a parliamentary democracy in which members of the legislature represent the people of a particular area and are, thus, alert to signs of territorial prejudice. Thus, **Documents 1, 3** and **4** are littered with 'special pleading' for assistance, objections to discrimination and claims for the success of policy. Each of these reports of debates in the House of Commons has members of the opposition parties arguing that their constituency deserves special treatment, while ministers and government party members proclaim the success of present policies, while seeking to show some concern about the problem being debated.

Thirdly, regional interventions are indicative of the contradiction present in all attempts to plan capitalist society, that between the state's concern to generalize the commodity form and its use of non-commodity relationships to do so (Offe, 1975). Thus, at one level, there is the problem of evaluating interventions in terms of market-based norms, one that has become increasingly prevalent as public expenditure is re-examined in light of the general fiscal crisis of the state. **Document 2** captures the ironies of this situation as it compresses extracts from a UK parliamentary committee on regional policy that concluded that it was almost impossible to judge the effects of such policies. Some nine years later, a similar committee still reached identical conclusions (Committee of Public Accounts, 1981). However, there is another level at which this contradiction operates. Regional interventions must seek to limit the effects of a process of uneven development, fueled by individualized accumulation imperatives, not simply to give a government short-term electoral advantage, but also to sustain both popular belief in the viability of the system and in the legitimacy of state power within it. While successful intervention can promote the idea of a class-neutral state, failures—be they due to 'insurmountable' economic forces, administrative incompetence or poor political judgement—may lead to a questioning of the role of the state or the operation of the capitalist system, or both. In **Document 3** a report of the debate on the creation of a development agency for Scotland, criticism both of the workings of the 'English' state and, from Mr Canavan, of the capitalist economy, is a clear theme.

Hence, regional policies can be regarded as a useful prism through which to view the capitalist state. These opening remarks should have suggested ways in which this image of the state in capitalist Europe will be 'distorted' in comparison with that of other chapters, while the three sections below will present a summary of the features revealed. The first section examines the evolution of policy, stressing the initial variety of national experiences but the increasing convergence of strategy. This is followed by an evaluation of the overall effects of the policies—both intended and unintended—and the third section deals with future developments.

The Evolution of Regional Policies

In general, regional policies claim to address the problem of uneven regional development, usually understood in terms of an imbalance between the employment available in an area and the numbers seeking employment there. Employment conditions have usually been taken as the prime index of regional disparities, with unemployment seen as expressing too slow a rate of capital accumulation to absorb the labor power available or 'regional depression', while labor shortages are an indication of over-rapid accumulation or 'regional congestion'. Given some spatial mobility of labor, there will usually be some migration in search of employment from areas lacking opportunities to places in which employment is thought to be available. Thus, outmigration has become regarded as another useful indicator of depressed areas. However, since migration is not exclusively a response to the possibilities of employment, but also reflects general living conditions, aspects of social welfare are nowadays considered as well. The most widely used indicators are those of health, education and housing provision (all of which are directly affected by state policies), of environmental and cultural amenity and of income or GDP per capital, a summary measure much favored by the ERDF.

Clearly, intranational differences in levels of employment, types of employment, migration rates and living conditions are a long-standing feature of all countries. However, regional disparities have not been regarded as creating a problem—let alone one which the state apparatus by itself could solve—until recently. Regional policies have only been adopted either as a consequence of popular protest within the deprived area, which may be echoed in parliamentary politics, or because of the fear that the kind of inefficiency expressed in pockets of high unemployment might adversely affect the national rate of accumulation. The 'regional problem', then, concerns the state when it threatens to disrupt existing political arrangements or reduce national growth. The latter concern in particular has led 'liberal' analysts to examine regional policies in terms of the correction of market imperfections in the national interest (Richardson, 1978). In contrast, Marxist analysts have stressed the former role of the policies as part of the accommodation of anti-capitalist protest and pointed out that the 'regional problem' is usually one for the mass of the population and not for capital (Damette, 1980). Indeed, much recent work has argued that capital actually benefits from the presence of regional inequalities (Secchi, 1977; Massey, 1979; Lipietz, 1980)—a point developed below.

The specific forms of regional uneven development have had an important influence on the evaluation of policies in different European countries (for an alternative approach to classification, see Carney and Lewis, 1978). As an initial distinction we can simply separate regions of slow accumulation from those of rapid accumulation as two basic expressions of unevenness, then subdivide the former according to the type of economic activities prevalent there.

Thus, there are regions where slow accumulation is primarily due to remaining pre-capitalist forms of production or obsolete capital in agriculture. Such areas often have long histories of outmigration but the rates are now being greatly increased by the 'industrialization' of agriculture. Hence the movement of 10 million people from the agricultural regions of the original EC Six between 1955 and 1975 (Romus, 1979, p. 206). The impact of outmigration can be judged by the fact that 4 million of these migrants came from the *Mezzogiorno* (southern Italy) alone and that rates of population loss even higher than this 20 percent have occurred in parts of Iberia (for example, Extramadura in Spain—22 percent over the same period of Trás-os-Montes in Portugal—21 percent in 1960–70).

The other major type of depressed region is that

dominated by obsolete capital invested in industrial and mining activities. Here, labor shed by capitals that are collapsing or restructuring their production processes is either unemployed, or induced to migrate. Although rates of unemployment are now reaching postwar record levels in regions dominated by steel-making (for instance, Lorraine or South Wales) and most attention is currently devoted to this, it is by no means a new type of problem, having previously affected coalmining regions during the 1960s—when over 500,000 jobs were lost in Belgium, the Federal Republic of Germany (FRG) and the UK alone. There are also comparable problems in textile and ship-building areas.

Regions of rapid accumulation experience a shortage of suitable labor power, sometimes in combination with other indicators, such as inflated land prices, traffic congestion or inadequate infra-structure. Since 1945 these have been regarded as problematic only in urban-industrial areas and national political capitals. Although these two categories often overlapped, as in the case of the Paris basin which increased its population by 8 percent over 1962–8, the rates of population growth of North-West Italy (containing Milan and Turin) in the 1950s and around Barcelona in Catalonia in the 1960s were recognized as causing problems even by the national governments. More recently, the emergence of port-industrial complexes (like Dunkirk or the mouth of the Rhine) as areas of massive capital investment has created a more highly localized version of the problem in which the need for production and social infrastructure is coupled with that for coordination of the strategies of different capitals. To this tripartite division we must add a type of depressed region with a very different cause—the border region. While best exemplified along the eastern border of the FRG, a similar lack of productive investment has been noted around the border between Northern Ireland and the Republic of Ireland.

Given this variety of expressions of uneven development between regions, it has been inevitable that each country should have developed different types of regional policies and planning agencies, as a brief comparison between Italy and Denmark shows. In Italy the problems of poverty, agricultural stagnation and emigration in the Mezzogiorno were first tackled by regional policies in 1950, when a land reform program was initiated and the Cassa per il Mezzogiorno (a technical and financial agency) set up. Since one of the major reasons for this action was the wave of squatting on the *latifondi* (large estates) in

Apulia, Calabria and Sicily (see King, 1975, for further details), the initial emphasis on land reform is not surprising. However, the creation of the Cassa, with a ten-year budget of £600 million, marked a more fundamental change, even though its early activities in providing infrastructure and investment for agriculture were essentially similar to postwar reconstruction programs. From 1957 the Cassa took a more active role in the industrialization of the region, both through the preparation of industrial sites, and the provision of capital grants, low-interest loans and various tax concessions to new investors. This policy was extended to the public sector by a law requiring 60 percent of new investments undertaken by bodies like the Instituto per la Ricostruzione Industriale (IRI, a state-holding company set up in 1937) and by state-owned firms such as Italsider (iron and steel producers) to be in the Mezzogiorno. Under these circumstances it was possible to pursue a regional planning strategy based on growth centers led by major ventures such as Italsider's plant at Taranto and Fiat's assembly works in Palermo (a process of industrializa-tion subjected to trenchant criticism by Graziani, 1978). With further improvements beginning in 1968 in the incentives to private capital (including an employment-related element, the social-security concession), the region became one of the most attractive areas in Europe in terms of subsidies, and the whole operation may be seen as one extreme of state regional intervention (Di Giorgi and Moscati, 1980). Although the 'southern question' has dominated Italian regional policies over the period, there have been two other strands (Ronzani, 1980). One of these has been the attempt to attract investment to agricultural areas of the north and center of the country for which low-interest loans have been available since 1976, as has a tax concession. To further complicate the picture, extra incentives are available in the three autonomous regions of the north. The other strand emerged from the urban crisis of Milan and Turin in the 1960s, which was seen as contributing to the series of strikes there in 1968. The policy involved location controls on new investments in the area from 1971. In practice, these controls and others required by regional plans eleswhere have been difficult to operate but they do represent an attempt to resolve the problem of congestion. Thus, in Italy the scale and nature of regional disparities has led to the most elaborate system of regional policies in the EC.

In metropolitan Denmark it was also the disparities between the poorer agricultural regions and the rest of the country (and Copenhagen, in particular) that first prompted regional policies. Changing production methods in agriculture led to considerable out-migration—some 10,000–15,000 a year in the 1950s (Elbo, 1975, p. 234)—and local employment. Even after the postwar peak in unemployment, the rate was 11·7 percent for Northern Jutland in 1959, while that for Greater Copenhagen was only 3·8 percent (Guttesen *et al.*, 1976, p. 81; Jensen-Butler, 1980, p. 43), but these disparities were far less extreme than those in Italy and were seen more as a cause of national inefficiency than as a source of social conflict. The policy response thus came later and was more muted, starting with the 1958 Regional Development Act, which provided government guarantees on industrial loans for firms locating outside of the major towns. Subsequent modification during the 1960s included the formal definition of areas eligible for support (much of Jutland and the major islands), as well as the introduction of government loans to municipalities for factory construction and, in some areas only, investment grants (Strande-Sørensen, 1980, pp. 36–7). Then a comprehensive review in 1972 replaced the loan guarantee with a system of 'soft' loans and added infrastructural grants to firms, all highly discretionary.

At the same time a convergence between the processes of urban planning, hitherto confined to Copenhagen and Aarhus, and special regional planning (for example, the North Jutland plan of 1966) produced the National and Regional Planning Act 1974. Each of the eighteen county councils has to present a land-use plan for its region as the basis for the municipal and local plans (see Bogason, 1978, for the instructive example of Storstrom County). Despite the remarkable dominance of Copenhagen, which still had one-third of national manufacturing employment in 1970 and almost half the employment in the state sector in 1976 (Friis, 1980, pp. 3, 11), little has been achieved in terms of regional disincentives beyond the decentralization of a few minor government offices (including that of the Regional Development administration!).

Danish regional policies have, thus, involved far less direct intervention by the state apparatus than in Italy and an average annual expenditure of only £30 million in recent years (Jensen, 1982)—compared with the £250 million per annum by the Cassa, over its admittedly larger area, throughout 1950–70. Policies have been more highly centralized (though the local government reform of 1970 has reduced this) and less sensitive to party politics than in Italy. On the face of it, they have also been more effective as regional unemployment differentials have shrunk, and the

population flow to Copenhagen has been reversed. Furthermore, figures reveal that regional inequalities of GDP per capita in Denmark were considerably less than in Italy. In relation to an EC of Ten average of 100, the GDP per capita of the poorest Danish region —East of the Storebolt—was, at 137, far closer to that of the richest, Copenhagen—at 170—than in Italy, where the comparable figures were 35 (Calabria) and 109 (Val d'Aosta).

Despite the significance of national circumstances in the determination of regional policies, it is important to note the international convergence in policies since the start of the 1960s. Most states have come to base their policies for depressed areas, be they agricultural or industrial, on a package of fiscal and financial incentives backed up by infrastructural provision to encourage manufacturing investment (for an EC summary, see Yuill *et al.*, 1980). Of course, there are variations on the sort of arrangements summarized above, for example the FRG's allowance of up to 50 percent of capital depreciation in the border area only, a similar allowance coupled with an interest subsidy in Belgium's development zones, the grants for land purchase on selected industrial estates in France, and the preferential credit offered by regional savings banks in Spain. The conditions for elegibility also vary but the direct payment of an investment grant and/or a tax concession now form the core of regional incentives. Similarly, although the administrative level of organization varies, it is not just roads, water and sewers that are provided by the state's infrastructural investments but power, factory buildings and some highly specialized facilities—most notably deep-water harbors—as illustrated by one of the recent port-industrial complexes, Sines. In the Sines project in southern Portugal, the Portuguese state hoped to match the rapid growth achieved by Huelva in southern Spain and demonstrate a real commitment to regional policy. The plan, proposed in 1971, for a deep-water harbor, oil refinery, petrochemical plant, steel works and metal-using industries, along with the new town of Santo André, envisaged a twenty-year investment of approximately £1,330 million of which at least £350 million was to be in infrastructure. Since the 1974 revolution, the monopolies who had been pressing for this scheme have been nationalized, so that almost all the investment in the scaled-down project is now from the state. This has meant that in 1980 over 10 percent of all national investment was going into a single project with no real regional impact (Lewis and Williams, 1981; OECD, 1978). Similar, but less extreme, examples of state involvement in infrastructure as part of regional policy can be seen from Taranto to Teesside.

Before attempting to explain this policy convergence, it is useful to review which policies are *not* generally used, for they indicate the degree of selectivity by the state in policy formulation (Offe, 1974). In this category we can consider the use of employment-related subsidies, the direction of nationalized industries, the use of disincentives and policies related to the service sector. Since the abolition of the Regional Employment Premium in the UK in 1977, only Italy currently relates its regional subsidies directly to the employment in a project, despite the official concern of regional policy with the reduction of unemployment in depressed areas. Italy is also unusual in the degree of locational control exercized over nationalized industries, though Spain's Instituto Nacional de Industria and, to a lesser extent, the UK's National Enterprise Board and nationalized industries have been encouraged to direct their investments to areas of high unemployment. The implementation of physical planning restrictions, often as part of a regional plan, has dominated efforts to reduce the growth of congested regions in the hope that it will occur elsewhere instead. The first such measure was the British Industrial Development Certificate (IDC) introduced in 1947 and shortly followed by the French, who also have a special tax on new floorspace in the Paris region. Although the Italians have had the administrative and legal machinery to limit large projects in the north-west since 1971, it has been little used, while the Dutch disincentive policy dates from only 1975 and 1977 (Voogd, 1982). Even though none of these controls has been rigidly applied, they have been the most unpopular part of regional policy from the point of view of capital.

Finally, there have been few attempts to move service jobs (such as office work or education) to depressed areas, because they have been assumed to be less 'mobile' and, with fewer linkages into the local economy, less useful in creating other jobs around them than manufacturing employment. However, the French disincentives apply to the service sector, too, and Britain had both an Office Development Permit scheme during 1965–80, and introduced limited grants for mobile services in 1973 to encourage decentralization from London (see Pickvance, 1981, for an interpretation of British policy). The movement of government jobs from the political capital has, however, been much more effective in relocating service sector jobs. Denmark's policy has been mentioned and similar policies exist in Ireland, the Netherlands and the UK. Both Portugal and Spain are trying to reduce the proportion of government employees in their capital, too, though this owes more to political decentralization than to regional policy. This set of 'unusual' policies has two important features which are, by definition, unattractive to most state apparatuses. First, there are policies which would involve the restriction of private capital—be it in manufacturing or services— and these control policies have had a major impact only on the public sector. Secondly, with the exception of Italy, states do not relate the rate of incentive to the employment associated with an investment in a given location, preferring to link the financial and fiscal offers to capital investment alone.

Regional policies have, thus, tended to converge in both a 'positive' (what is used) and a 'negative' (what is not used) sense. To explain this evolution, we must refer to three closely related changes within and around the state apparatuses of Western Europe in the postwar period (and not, incidentally, to the effects of EC policies on competition or regional assistance).

The first, and most basic, is the economic relationship between capital and the state apparatus in which large capital has increasingly managed to socialize its costs of production, spreading the price of investments from the individual firm to the whole population (Habermas, 1975, pp. 50–60; Mandel, 1976, pp. 474–99). Obviously, regional policy has only been a part of this phenomenon, but its emphasis on investment grants and tax relief is typical of the new mechanisms associated with the era of monopoly capitalism (Aglietta, 1979), and required for the associated hypermobility of capital (Damette, 1980, pp. 83–91), for the provision by the state of certain forms of investment shunned by private capital because of the low rate of profit they yield. This convergence toward the socialization of investment through regional policies is closely tied to the phenomenal growth of international investment among the major capitalist countries. As multinational capitals have been able to select those national and regional locations that offered the greatest opportunities for accelerated amortization, countries wishing to attract this kind of manufacturing investment have become obliged to provide equally attractive conditions—a competitive process that has greatly intensified of late. Although standard national subsidies might seem the logical culmination, only the investment package available in Ireland—which is, in fact, regionally differentiated (Breathnach, 1982)—currently approaches this.

The trend is rather toward more selectivity with each large investment having a specific set of financial arrangements. Of course, this kind of arrangement, and much of regional policy, is irrelevant to those manufacturing capitals which are not geographically mobile and are thus unable to take advantage of such means of increasing their profitability. The only other serious objections to this system from capital have come in those few cases in which location controls have been applied to increase costs (see **Document 2**) and from some banking or insurance groups unconnected to industry who gain nothing in this allocation of state funds.

The second important change stems from this socialization of production costs and relates specifically to infrastructure provision. Here, the state apparatus has also taken on an additional coordinating role (Lapple and van Hoogstraten, 1980, pp. 124–32). By the preparation of regional plans indicating the projected availability of both physical and social infrastructure, the locational strategies of different capitals can be integrated. The need for such information and control is obviously greatest with the large-scale production complexes in which inter-industry linkages and specialized infrastructure are important—hence, the involvement of the state in port-industrial complexes like Fos-sur-Mer in France (Bleitrach and Chenu, 1982) or Tarragona in Catalonia (Carreras, 1980). Yet regional plans are also useful to capitals in other branches of production. A simple illustration of this latter point is provided in Hudson's work on North-East England (Hudson, 1981), which shows how the Hailsham Plan's identification of selected locations within the region (most notably Washington New Town) as growth points, in which both premises and labor power would be readily available, led to a concentration of investment there. However, the presence of the state is no guarantee that the accumulation process in a given location will be harmonious and that all the necessary conditions for production will be available. The expansion of Fos, for example, has been adversely affected by the current recession (Kinsey, 1978), while both Vigo and La Coruña in Galicia lacked essential infrastructure during the time that they were designated 'development poles' (Richardson and Rodrigues, 1975; O'Flanagan, 1979). There are, then, limits to the state's administrative competence in this field and also limits to its ability to gain the necessary support for its policies from local power blocs who may be adversely affected by them. Thus far, the owners of large estates and of mines have on occasion successfully resisted the injection of new industries which might raise wages but, Dulong argues, in the future whole local societies may reject this form of intervention and resist it (Dulong, 1978, pp. 101–236).

The third reason for the emergence of regional policies in their present form has been political protest over the effects of regional uneven development. This has seldom been popular protest of the illegal kind as in the Mezzogiorno (and even that was not specifically about the north–south differential), but rather protest within the social-democratic, corporatist, political model that developed in most countries—Portugal and Spain being the obvious exceptions. In this system any regionalization of party political support meant that state policies would, *ceteris paribus*, reflect the electoral calculations of the government. While this is most apparent where regional assistance is extended to an area due for a midterm election, it can also involve attempts to 'win over' an opponent's territorial base. The Christian Democrats have shown themselves aware of this in their handling of the Cassa (Nocifora, 1978), just as the 1974–9 Labour government in the UK employed a regional strategy when seeking to counter Scottish and Welsh nationalism by introducing special Development Agencies (see **Document 3**). Nor has this form of manipulation been restricted to party policies, for a common arrangement in regional planning has been the creation of an advisory council involving representatives of local labor and capital, as well as civil servants. Such groups would then dwell upon their common interest in 'beating' other regions.

Regional policies have, thus, been political but they have not been a focus for class struggle (for an alternative interpretation, see the comments on May 1968 in France in Ross and Cohen, 1975). More than most other sorts of policy, regional policies have been concerned with the management for capital of an unfortunate consequence of capitalist development—hence, the attractive form of incentives and the reluctance to use strong controls. Scase (1980*b*, p. 13) might be justified in criticizing most 'state derivation'—and 'state monopoly capitalism'—interpretations of state policies as simple expressions of the needs of capital. However, in the case of regional policies, it is difficult to identify the tensions and contradictions between capital and the state apparatus that, he claims, require a more sophisticated kind of explanation. Instead, the problems created by regional policies have been of a very different order.

The Effects of Regional Policies

Obviously, it is difficult to isolate a measurable 'policy

effect' in the changing spatial distribution of employment and unemployment of incomes and opportunities, within Western Europe. Indeed, this has posed major problems in the administration of regional policies, since it has been difficult to use norms such as 'cost-effectiveness' in evaluating them (see **Documents 2** and **4**). However, it is possible to note three general features about the effectiveness of the policies before considering the political consequences of their failure.

The first point is that the policies have certainly not removed regional disparities in any of the countries and have generally done little even to reduce them. If the policies were having an impact during their heyday in the 1960s—as suggested by Brown and Burrows (1977, pp. 196–9) in their general survey, or by Keeble (1976, pp. 89–115; 1977, pp. 3–5) referring to the UK alone—this would seem to have been cruelly undone by the current recession. At the aggregate level of the EC of Nine the ten poorest regions have slipped from having incomes per capita one-third of those of the ten richest in 1970 to incomes one-quarter of the richest by 1979. Evidence from the UK shows that recent layoffs have been particularly concentrated in the traditional depressed areas (Townsend, 1981). At the same time, since 1974, in France, the rate of unemployment has risen fastest in the very areas selected for regional assistance, so that by 1979 the familiar pattern of high unemployment rates in Languedoc-Roussillon, Provence-Côte d'Azur, Nord-Pas-de-Calais, Lorraine and the agricultural west had been re-established (Mormìche, 1980).

Secondly, there is now some doubt about the contribution of regional policies *per se* to that movement of manufacturing investment which did occur in the 1960s and early 1970s. Even though the presence of regional incentives is accepted as an encouragement to capital to invest in such areas, it is clear that for many branches of production such locations were becoming more attractive anyhow as a result of changes in their production processes (see, for example, Massey, 1979; Lipietz, 1980*b*). The progressive deskilling of labor resulting from automation and standardization, allows the use of unskilled, low-cost labor for some parts of the production process, while continuing concentration and centralization of capital has given rise to firms organized on such a scale as to make the division of production between different units feasible. Under such circumstances, some branches of production have developed a separation of production functions among management (including the design of new products and labor processes), skilled production work and unskilled assembly that has been expressed spatially by the location of each separate function in the area which is most profitable for it. Thus, the control and conception functions are increasingly concentrated in the national (and international) cores, where information is most readily available and suitably trained labor can be readily obtained, some skilled production is carried out in the old industrial cities and the simplest parts of production are allocated to areas in which unskilled labor is available most cheaply. Furthermore, there is a particular attraction in recruiting such unskilled labor from those who have little experience of wage labor and, thus, of union organization—not simply because of their low wage levels, but because the hypermobility of capital makes a 'flexible' laborforce that can be rapidly adjusted to new production methods very desirable. If this is the case in sufficient branches, then the 'natural' emergence of a new spatial division of labor within the major capitalist countries is not so surprising. The partial industrialization of the French west or rural Denmark and the 'branch-plant' reindustrialization of some of the older industrial depressed regions, such as the Limburg or the Scottish coalfields, are thus a part of the same process: one in which capital takes full advantage of existing regional inequalities to increase profitability.

Regional policy may have speeded up this adjustment to new conditions for accumulation by making some industrial mobility preferable to *in situ* expansion, but the evidence of such a change occurring without a formal policy suggests that it cannot be regarded as the sole cause. Even if the recent form of industrialization in the South of the USA is ignored, there are enough cases within Western Europe of the industrialization in the south of the USA is ignored, there are enough cases within Western Europe of the (see, for example, Arcangeli *et al.*, 1980; Bagnasco, 1977; Garofoli, 1980, on peripheral areas in Italy; or Ferrão, 1979; Lewis and Williams, 1981, on Portugal). However, the view that regional policy caused decentralization has been accepted for so long that the blame for the current rapid collapse of large parts of these 'branch-plant' regional economies has been attributed to errors in regional policies. Thus, there is a widespread belief that regional policies led to an undue concentration of economically and organizationally marginal plants in the development areas or zones and so created dependent, externally controlled, economies (Firn, 1975) that are being run down at present because the decision-makers are not locally based. There is no denying that many of the depressed areas do have high proportions of multinational capital (see the evidence in Dicken and Lloyd, 1976; Yannopoulos and Dunning, 1976; Watts, 1980, rather than the crude counterassertions of Holland, 1976) and extraregional firms in their industrial structure. Nevertheless, the high rates of layoffs now observed there owe less to the absence of headquarters due to a failure in regional policy than to a further change in the scale of the spatial division of labor. The unskilled parts of some production processes (for instance, assembly of electronics) are increasingly being located outside the metropolitan economies entirely either in European countries with low wages and 'flexible' labor, such as Ireland, Spain or Yugoslavia, or in the 'Free Production Zones' of the Third World (Fröbel *et al.*, 1980; Paine, 1979). It is ironic that regional policies, having been credited with something they did not truly achieve, are now criticized for a subsequent change that they could not control either.

Finally, regional policies have been first credited and now criticized for a series of smaller effects. As the recession deepens, so the kind of employment and the kind of industrial investment associated with regional policies, as well as the effects of regional disincentives, have all been re-evaluated. As regards employment, a common criticism is that regional policy only moved low-wage, unskilled jobs—which, for the reasons just outlined, is partly true. In the depressed industrial areas such jobs have been regarded as unsuitable by the skilled workers being laid off by the shipyards or the steelworks, especially as they are pejoratively described as 'women's work'. There is, thus, a major and unpopular challenge to traditional working-class norms as households become dependent on the wages earned by women. If these kinds of personal crises are really unintended consequences of policies, deskilling and recession, this is less obviously true of the *reduction* in job availability directly due to regional policy when investment grants have been used to restructure production. To develop the earlier example of the 'growth zone' in North-East England, in Teesside, at that time the major concentration of new capital investment in the country—almost all of it supported by regional development grants—nearly 6,000 jobs were lost in the chemical sector in 1965–76. In basic metals a further 9,450 disappeared primarily in British steel (Robinson and Storey, 1981, p. 166). Under such circumstances regional policy (which could be credited with creating 4,000 jobs at the very most in this area) scarcely looks to be assisting the working class to find employment. Regional disincentives, of the IDC or floorspace-tax type, have

come in for similar criticism, though from those in the congested regions now suffering from 'inner-city' unemployment. In both Paris and London the present levels of unemployment have been attributed to restrictions on expansion there in past years, although there is little evidence to support this view. In the case of London the refusal rate on IDCs was never very high, even during the 1960s, and Dennis (1977) has shown that only 10 percent of firms leaving London in 1966–74 actually moved to the assisted areas. Employment decline was better explained by reference to complete closures (which accounted for 70 percent of the total) than to policy-induced moves.

Regional policies, thus, appear in a very different light today than they did in the 1960s. From part of the social-democratic dream of a managed capitalism which could promote equality between places as well as between people, they have become symbols, at one extreme, of the folly of state intervention in the free market or, at the other, of the class bias of state policies (see **Document 4**). However, there has also been a very important political response to the failure which combines both of these latter views—nationalism or, as Nairn calls it, 'neo-nationalism' (Nairn, 1977).

The upsurge of nationalist and regionalist movements in Western Europe in the past two decades has many causes and the actual combination of these has varied quite substantially, even within one country—as a simple comparison of the Breton and Occitanian movements (Quere, 1978) or of those in Catalonia and Euskadi, shows. Yet they all reflect the same rejection of a central government which is—in addition to any cultural repression—mishandling the resources of the area, usually by diverting them elsewhere and providing insufficient return. There is little new in this form of criticism, but if the state apparatus is intentionally redistributing resources from relatively rich regions (for example, Catalonia, or Scotland after the discovery of offshore oil), it becomes much easier to sustain a political movement and press the argument for a separate state which could avoid this redistribution.

What is even more striking is the way in which the regionalist reaction to the recession in some traditionally depressed areas has taken on a new form because of the early claims for regional policy. The commitment to moving employment to the areas where it is needed underlies regional policy and this has helped to politicize the provision of employment (obviously the nationalization of some industries and the extension of the social services have had a similar effect). At a time of rising unemployment, 'to live and work at home' has become the call of more than just the French Communist Party (Levy and Scheibling, 1978): it is at the heart of the neo-nationalists' appeal. When the state which offered this possibility to everyone subsequently appears to deny it systematically to a regionally identifiable group of people, the nationalist alternative—a state for those people—gains credence. Carney (1980) has explored this response to the central state's mismanagement of regional policies during the 1970s in Wallonia, Scotland and Lorraine and suggests two outcomes. First, regionalist movements can concern themselves mainly with the 'mismanagement' due to indifferent, incompetent, or prejudiced decision-makers and, thus, focus their demands on both devolved government and decentralized development agencies. Alternatively, they may stress the 'mismanagement' due to the class interests reflected in state policies when proposing a reorganization of government through a socialist program. In both cases neo-nationalism appears as an extension of the bargaining for a 'fair share' of economic growth set in motion by regional policies.

It would be wrong, though, to assume that regionalist movements will thus be the automatic response to the kind of legitimation crisis created by the failure of regional policies. There have been too many cases where there has been no organized reaction to mounting job losses and blighted futures or where popular reaction has been on local or industrial, rather than regional, lines to expect any major switch in the political structure. Nor should the development of nationalist and regionalist politics within countries like France or the UK be seen as an irreversible process, as the considerable variations in support for such parties, even in the past decade, show the importance of influences other than simply employment. With those caveats, however, it has to be remembered that regionalist politics have proved very hard to suppress once they become established. The present—interrupted—devolution of power in Spain (Alonso Teixidor and Hebbart, 1982) is an especially powerful reminder of the strength of nationalism, but the violence of Corsica (Kofman, 1981) and Northern Ireland can also be traced back to this source. In general terms, then, the equitable territorial allocation of resources is both a task that the state must undertake, and one in which it is almost certain to fail without real control over capital. Yet the costs of such failure have been further increased by the very claims made to justify the subsidies to capital which have dominated regional policies.

The Future of Regional Policies

In light of the problems of conducting regional policies identified above, the growing concern over inner-city deprivation and the weakening of the social-democratic compromise by capital's aggressive stance in this crisis, there is currently a reappraisal of the value of these policies by state apparatuses. Although only that of the UK has gone so far as to reformulate its policies (**Document 4**), the real value of regional incentives has been falling in other countries, while the future of the Cassa is uncertain: it reached the end of its legal life in 1980 but no new formal policy initiatives to revive declining regional economies have been taken. Even the recent French regional plan for the south-west owed more to the problems of EC enlargement and of presidential re-election than to France's normally highly coordinated system of national and regional plans (though the decentralization policy of the newly elected Socialist Party may lead to a revival of the system). This is at a time when recession in most of Western Europe means that regional disparities are being increased and the prospects for regionalist responses correspondingly improved. But, Spain apart, the state apparatuses appear to have regained some of their control. Two strategies appear to be relevant to this management of the regional effects of the crisis and appear likely to figure even larger in the future. Both involve a displacement of the expression of crisis away from the state apparatus itself.

The first involves the manipulation of the immediate consequences of the slump, so that they are spread among as many regions as possible. Such a strategy is most obvious in the steel closure program being undertaken in the main EC countries and nowhere more clearly than in the case of British Steel. Each of the recent closures or reductions in employment has been timed so as to ensure that each of the relevant regions has one in one round and none in the next. This has undoubtedly reduced the popular reaction from that which would occur if regional closures were synchronized, not least because it has proved possible to divide the union membership between one area and the next. Once the rationality of the reduction in steelmaking capacity has been accepted, a closure in, say, South Wales is less likely to meet united union action nationally for fear that the closure will simply be effected in another region. Thus, this strategy of 'playing off' one region's workers against another's—directly analogous to the politics of protectionism at a national level—seems to be effective in drawing attention away from the operations of the central state and directing it toward conflicts of interest within the working class. The threat of unemployment is proving to be a much more effective way of doing this than the tripartite discussions of regional planning councils.

The other new strategy involves the supranational level of the EC, as the community has its own regional fund. As already mentioned, this involves a comparatively small part of the budget and is intended to supplement national regional policy and planning by the provision of extra infrastructure (though this basic principle has been somewhat undermined by the acceptance of the argument that ERDF money can be used to avert cuts that would be otherwise necessary in national expenditure). There are already pressures to boost the ERDF so as to reduce the dominance of the Agricultural Fund in intracommunity transfers. The importance of community regional policy will inevitably increase as the EC expands to twelve members, for the level of regional inequalities will become much higher (Tsoukalis, 1981). Using the simplest measures, within the EC of Nine, the ratio of GDP per capita in the poorest and richest regions was 1 : 6; with the admission of Greece this has risen to 1 : 10, but the inclusion of Portugal will push it to 1 : 12. Not only is the role of the ERDF likely to expand in response to this inequality, but it also provides an easy means of transferring resources to the poorest members (EC, 1978, p. 37). Mr Mathissen, Director General of the EC regional policy, recently expressed the official view:

> Market forces have not brought about what the EC treaty calls 'a harmonious development of economic activities throughout the Community'. Since the existing disparities in standards of living constitute an obstacle to economic integration and a threat to the Common Market, public measures to foster development are required. (Letter, *Guardian*, 11 March 1981)

These measures will increasingly be at the community level as national states displace both expenditure and responsibility there. However, the immediate attraction of reducing the apparent involvement of the national state apparatus, with the attendant advantage of having 'other countries' to blame for any lack of regional policy investment, could prove misleading. Just as the parliamentary system nationally focuses attention on territorial discrimination, so the European Parliament, with its growing powers over the Community budget, could provide an opportunity for coalitions not just between political parties, but

between representatives of similarly disadvantaged regions. Obviously, there is no immediate prospect of the European MPs for South Italy, Thrace and Northern Ireland forsaking their party allies to form a new grouping, but as regional policies become more politicized at the EC level, the coincidence of regional interests will be increasingly expressed. Thus, the strategy of displacement 'upwards' is no permanent solution to the problems posed for the state apparatus by the processes and consequences of regional uneven development.

Conclusion

Regional policies have been developed to manage a deep-rooted form of inequality within capitalist Europe. By claiming to address this problem they have provided an acceptable way of offering capital part of the financial support that it needs in this era and coordinating the requirements of competing capitals and have contributed to the redistribution of some kinds of employment in the major countries of the EC. The evolution of both regional policy, and regional planning, shows the state apparatuses to have been even more responsive to the needs of large industrial capital and increasingly less concerned with the social problems that they were supposed to address within the social-democratic framework. However, the contributions of these policies have been hard to assess with market norms and the political gains from their limited overall effect on regional inequalities are becoming outweighed by the politicization of employment provision where it is demanded. Although at present most EC states are coping with the regionalist political pressures by a combination of strategies, they nevertheless continue to threaten the stability and integrity of capitalist Europe.

Note

My thanks to Ray Hudson for his comments on the early drafts of this chapter and for a seemingly endless supply of useful facts and figures. He is, of course, absolved of any responsibility for what I have done with them.

Despite the broader coverage of the chapter as a whole, the choice of documents was limited to those from the UK Parliament. The length and breadth of British experience has meant that most issues in regional policy, if not in regional planning, had been raised at some stage. Although the texts have been heavily edited to reduce the parliamentary language, much remains and gives a valuable reminder of how the issues discussed above are actually presented in a part of the state apparatus. All emphases have been added.

Documents

1 Conservative Regional Policy in the North-East

Extract from *The Problems of the North-East*, House of Commons Debate (16 July 1964).

After several years of 'weak' regional policy during the 1950s, the Conservative government increased their concern for regional disparities as the slump of the early 1960s led to a rise in unemployment in North-East England and central Scotland not long before the election due in 1964. As a result regional policies incentives increased under the Local Employment Acts and Lord Hailsham visited North-East England in 1963, subsequently presenting a program for modernizing the region based on public investment in infrastructural improvements which were to be concentrated in a 'growth zone'. A motion critical of these and other aspects of government policy regarding the North-East was introduced by the Labour Party for whom (in this extract) Mr Willey, Mr Stones and Mr Short spoke with replies from the Conservative MPs, Viscount Lambton, Mr Williams and Mr Heath.

Mr Frederick Willey (Sunderland, North): During the 1959 General Election Mr Iain MacLeod, who was then Minister of Labour and a spokesman for the Government, came to Sunderland and assured my constituents that unemployment was a passing phase. What, then, is the position in Sunderland now? We have had this exceptional recovery during the past 12 months, and we have had this pre-election boom, yet unemployment figures are almost identical: in fact they are slightly higher than in 1959. Far from being a passing phase, since 1959 we have had prolonged periods of substantial unemployment. We are now told not that a rate of unemployment of 5 per cent is a passing phase but that a rate of 5 per cent is the best we can expect from temporary Tory prosperity.

This is not peculiar to Sunderland. It is equally true of far too many other black spots in the northern region. In fact, the unemployment position overall is almost the same as it was in 1959. Not only is this a direct political responsibility; *this harsh disparity between the North East and other parts of Britain is accentuated by the Government's indifference, and made worse still by their almost provocative prejudice.* After months and months of procrastination we eventually had the Hailsham plan. This is now exposed as an amateurish, shoddy, inadequate document which does not even claim to be a plan.

What we need is continued pressure to translate the approvals into actual development as quickly as possible. I go further, and say that the actual development on the North-East Coast in itself is not sufficient. We have to take complementary action elsewhere. *We have to supplement industrial development by the cancellation of vacant premises in the congested areas. We have to regard industrial development on the North-East Coast as part and parcel of national development.*

It is because of this lack of national effort that we get this distinction in the country, this division between the two nations—those who live in development areas—those who live in the North-East—and the rest of the country. I have already given one distinction—at the height of prosperity, Sunderland has 5 per cent unemployed—but we get that disparity in every field. For instance, we are all committed to equality of educational opportunity, but there is no equality of educational opportunity between the North-East and the rest of the country. The proportion of children in the South-East staying on at school after the compulsory school-leaving age is *twice* that in the North-East.

We find this in every aspect of education. We are fortunate in the North-East in having 19 splendid technical colleges, but we have been badly let down by the Government because we are the only region that does not have a college of advanced technology.

Again, far from having the benefit of Government assistance, we are prejudiced. We have less assistance than other areas. We have been neglected by the Government.

Viscount Lambton (Berwick-upon-Tweed): I think the hon. Member for Sunderland, North, gave a false impression of the feeling in the North-East. I think that my right hon. Friend the Secretary of State for Industry and Trade would be justified in saying in reply that if the hon. Member continues to give an impression like this he will certainly throw cold water on the plans of those who are considering going into the area at this time.

The Conservative Government have put forward long-term plans for the North-East. None of these was put forward by right hon. and hon. Members opposite during their seven years of office after the war. They were perfectly content that the whole prosperity of the North-East should rest upon and the whole source of employment should depend entirely upon local industry.

Those who visit the North-East now will find the contrast between what the hon. Member for Sunderland, North, said and the great activity in that area. Sunderland is unrecognisable compared with what it was years ago. Where there was a mass of bad housing there is now a totally different and promising town. Precisely the same can be said about Darlington, the Hartlepools and Middlesbrough. There is an air of energy and purpose about the North-East which was not there in the past.

Mr William Stones (Consett): I understand that there are still 42,000 unemployed in the region and that the number of school-leavers this year in the North-East amounts to 4,000. I believe that of those who left school at the end of the last school-leaving term 600 are still without work.

This situation exists despite the much-vaunted Hailsham plan for the North-East. That plan provided for growth zones, to the exclusion of a great part of the North-East. When the plan was introduced, we on this side of the House complained and suggested that there should be a national plan governing the national economy, and that if any region required guidance and greater opportunities it should be treated as a whole and not in part. Whatever benefits may have accrued to the North-East as a result of the Hailsham plan, I am afraid that very little material benefit has been felt outside of the growth zone. In spite of new jobs provided in the North-East in recent years, we are not keeping pace with the demand for employment.

If we are to prevent this situation becoming further aggravated in the North-East, the national economy must be so geared that it can expand constantly and continuously, rather than spasmodically. *It is wrong to expect workers in the North-East who have lost their jobs to migrate, and I am sure that most people will agree that work should be provided for them in their area. The Government, Tory or Labour, must apply their minds to providing work for redundant workers, not 200 miles away but where they live.* To do this the Government must be very firmly instrumental in issuing industrial development certificates. Every effort must be made to encourage industries to go to the North-East, even if this means a greater financial inducement than already provided.

Mr Paul Williams (Sunderland, South): I was most interested to read a report in the financial columns of the *Sunday Express* only last week:

How splendidly the North-East is recovering from its depression. The three steel works there are running at or near capacity, capital industry is picking up, and there is the promise ahead of benefits to come from oil searches going on out to sea. All that is needed now is a strong twist from heavy to light industry.

All of us here from the North-East will agree with that.

A sheet steel plant, for instance, to serve the motor and consumer trades. I predict that this will come about before long. Overall, Britain's sheet steel output is working at 90 per cent of capacity and a new mill will soon be necessary.

I am delighted by the next sentence:

It is bound to go to the North-East.

I put this question to my right hon. Friend: is it bound to come to the North-East, or are we to be plagued with a plethora of questions from Scotland about it? *I give notice that, if a development of this kind is to take place, it is our hope that the Prime Minister's weight will be thrown in favour of the North-East at this time, not Scotland.*

Mr Edward Short (Newcastle-upon-Tyne, Central): The unemployment situation in the North-East has gone up and down and up and down for 13 years. The North-East has been like a yo-yo on the finger of successive Chancellors of the Exchequer. The 80,000 figure in the winter of 1962–3 was the dire result of the savage credit squeeze of the two Budgets of the present Leader of the House. The drop this year to 38,000 has been due to two factors—the 'let it rip' Budget of the present Chancellor coupled with changes in the Local Employment Act which we advocated.

The Government are like a doctor who is too inept or is incapable of diagnosing the malady of his patient, in this case the North-East. They seize the first half-a-dozen medicine bottles they can find and ram them all down the throat of the patient, hoping that one of them will cure him. If ever the need for careful, systematic economic planning was demonstrated, it is in the North-East.

The Secretary of State for Industry, Trade and Regional Development and President of the Board of Trade (Mr Edward Heath): The hon. Member for Sunderland, North, said that he wanted massive investment in the North-East. It is worth recollecting that from April 1960 to June 1964 £20·9 million went into the North-East alone from the inducements of the Local Employment Acts. With a population of 7½ per cent of the total the North-East is getting 18 per cent of the public investment going into this form of industrial inducement. I should have thought that that was sufficient demonstration of the importance of the North-East.

I believe that we are now seeing continued and excellent progress in the North-East. What is more, I believe that the people there know it and feel it. Those of us who have visited the North-East, even in the nine months in which I have held this office, can feel the change which has taken place in the whole area and in the attitude of the population. There is now a realisation of the possibilities in the North-East and the way in which they are being seized by industrialists.

Our task now is to do everything possible to encourage that, to refrain from saying things which may deter progress, and then to see the results at which we are all aiming in the North-East as a whole.

2   Regional Development and Unemployment

Extract from *Regional Development Incentives: Second Report from the Expenditure Committee*, House of Commons (London: HMSO, 1973).

This report was prepared as part of a general review of public subsidies to the private sector with an emphasis on measuring the costs and benefits of government intervention. The committee heard evidence from twenty-six witnesses, including twelve industrial firms, the Trades Union Congress, the Confederation of British Industry and academic experts (such as Messrs Moore and Rhodes).

Introduction
The problem of redressing regional imbalance in employment is an immensely stubborn one. Governments have tried to overcome it by constantly changing the kinds and levels of incentives, the rules governing their application, the extent and status of assisted areas, and the IDC (Industrial Development Certificate) regulations.

Effects of Specific Measures
How effective are incentives? Four themes in particular emerged from our evidence:

(a) Regional financial incentives in themselves, especially in the case of larger firms, were seldom thought to have instigated a major investment decision, but had more frequently influenced a locational decision.
(b) The main advantage of regional financial incentives, at any rate as seen by larger firms, was to help offset the higher costs of locating in an assisted area, or improve profitability; they constituted a marginal bonus rather than a vital element.
(c) The proportion of smaller firms or projects influenced by financial incentives appeared to be higher than that of large firms.
(d) Although many firms obviously make serious efforts to evaluate incentives and other factors in locational decisions, we did not discern any common scientific approach to this problem.

The evidence presented to us made it clear that, while the effect of IDCs has varied from firm to firm, in the case of large car manufacturers it has been substantial. Chrysler, Ford, British Leyland (BLMC) and Vauxhall all said that they had been coerced in some degree over the location of a major manufacturing complex. *All four firms claimed that there was a net continuing cost to themselves.* For Chrysler, the future annual net cost was put at £3 million after the phasing-out of Regional Employment Premium (REP) (at present about £800,000 p.a.); for BLMC, the current net cost was about £4·7 million p.a., after receipt of REP; but for Ford, the current annual figure was £1.13 million, almost entirely offset at present by REP of £1 million; similarly for Vauxhall, the additional operating costs were just over £1 million p.a., offset by REP of £850,000.

Overall Effect and Costs
The Moore/Rhodes findings were that in the development

areas in the years 1963–70 the total number of new jobs arising as a result of regional policy was of the order of 220,000 or at any rate within the bracket 200,000–250,000, after allowing for closures. This figure should be compared with that of 750,000–1,000,000 which they reckoned to be the total number of new jobs required in the same period to solve regional problems. *Regional policy had reduced the unemployment rate in the development areas by about 1·8 percentage points.* [In calculating the cost they] first examined total non-recoverable Government expenditure on regional policy in Great Britain over the period 1963–70, which they calculated to be about £1,000 million, and then divided this by the net increase in jobs in British development areas over and above the figure that they had predicted would apply if there had been no regional assistance, i.e. about 185,000 jobs. The expenditure is net of directly recoverable items such as repayment of and interest on loans, and repayment of expenditure on Government factories, but gross of clawback through taxes and similar items. *This gives an average Exchequer cost over the period of about £6,000 per job.*

Conclusion
Since the problem of economic and social disparities within Britain was first diagnosed forty years ago there have been both a substantial measure of agreement about the nature of the remedy and a continuing debate about means. At its simplest 'taking work to the workers' has been the basis of the policies of all Governments but beyond that there has been controversy. Men without jobs, children without opportunities, social and environmental decay—these are properly matters of which the stuff of politics is made. Inevitably the Government of the day has been challenged by the Opposition and pressed by its own supporters. As a result, policies have changed as Governments have changed and even within the course of a Parliament. We recognize that the evolution of regional policy must be within a political framework and that governments will inevitably wish to intervene to push the process of change along. The question is whether the basis for political choice can be improved.

Our unhesitating answer is 'Yes'. The nature of the choice, both in the size and in the allocation of resources is qualitatively no different from others that arise in the decision-making process of government. It is the task of Ministers to inform themselves about past performances and future possibilities. In particular, it is the task of their civil servant advisers to harness expert opinion to the analysis and solution of problems. We are far from satisfied that the continuing search for a viable regional policy has been backed by a critical economic apparatus capable of analysing results and proposing alternative courses. *Much has been spent and much may well have been wasted. Regional policy has been empiricism run mad, a game of hit and miss, played with more enthusiasm than success.* We do not doubt the good intentions, the devotion even, of many of those who have struggled over the years to relieve the human consequences of regional disparities. We regret that their efforts have not been better sustained by the proper evaluation of the costs and benefits of policies pursued.

Everything in this inquiry pointed to the need for Government to create a more rational and systematic basis for the formulation and execution of regional policy. We do not wish to imply that more efficient quantification of costs and benefits is a magic formula that will infallibly solve the problem of devising the most effective measures. Ministerial wisdom and departmental experience and judgement will be as necessary as ever, but they must be based, as DTI [Department of Trade and Industry] themselves said, on good information.

The attention given by successive governments to regional policy has increased, is increasing and is unlikely to be diminished. There is no doubt that a prosperous national economy makes potentially the greatest single contribution to restoring regional balance. But national prosperity is not itself a guarantee that regional disparities will be overcome or even diminished. In our view governments should pursue regional policies with the greatest intensity precisely when the growth of the economy makes disparities less obvious. There is never an occasion to relax.

3   Industrial and Regional Policy in Scotland

Extract from *Scottish Development Agency (No. 2) Bill*, House of Commons Debate (25 June 1975).

The success of the Scottish National Party (SNP) in the general election of October 1974 prompted the Labour government to introduce a new instrument of industrial and regional policy for Scotland. In this extract from the debate the views of the Labour Party (Messrs Ross and Canavan), the Conservative Party (Mr Buchanan-Smith) and the SNP (Messrs Stewart and Crawford) were expressed.

The Secretary of State for Scotland (Mr William Ross): The Bill seeks to bring to the whole of Scotland the benefits of a new executive body—the Scottish Development Agency—charged with furthering the development of Scotland's economy and improving its environment. The Bill gives the agency substantial financial resources and wide powers for carrying out these tasks.

There is no doubt that the current economic scene in Scotland is sombre but it is not one of unrelieved gloom. Unemployment has been rising progressively over the years and now 4·7 per cent of our workers are unemployed and the figures of short-time working, redundancies and job vacancies are causing concern.

The reassuring aspect of the current Scottish situation is that Scotland is proving more resilient to today's economic difficulties than the rest of Britain or countries like France or West Germany. In the past we used to be hit first and hardest in any recession. Today unemployment has risen

here more slowly than elsewhere. In the early 1960s Scotland had an unemployment rate which was more than double that of the British average. If that situation still prevailed today we should now be experiencing unemployment figures of over 8 per cent.

In the mid-1960s we were losing as many as 45,000 people each year by net emigration. The most recent figures show a net gain of population. That is something to be noted and gives an indication that the people of Scotland have more confidence in Scotland now than they had in the past. The activity associated with North Sea oil development has been a major force underlying the improving trend. It has created directly or indirectly some 40,000 jobs in Scotland. These jobs have all come about in advance of our receiving any oil and result from the massive public and private investment which has been injected into Scotland to get the oil ashore. *But much of the credit also lies with the vigorous regional policies which have been pursued by successive United Kingdom Governments over a longer period*, extending generous investment inducements to industry throughout Scotland and creating a modern infrastructure.

We still have a long way to go, however, before Scotland is able to offer the range and quality of jobs and the living environment needed for all who want to make their homes in Scotland. There are continuing problems in the rural areas, but above all, our older towns and cities, especially of Clydeside, lack the jobs and quality of life which nowadays people are entitled to expect. This is why we need the agency with adequate powers and resources to bring to the development of Scotland.

The Scottish Development Agency marks the creation of a uniquely Scottish approach to industrial development in Scotland. Policies to create jobs must continue to be based on a strong national policy, because only this can ensure that jobs are diverted from the more prosperous regions to Scotland and other areas in need of employment. Scotland has gained considerable benefits from traditional regional policies. We do not intend to dismantle them. We strengthened them last year by doubling the regional employment premium and making the whole of Scotland a development area.

It will be given an annual financial allocation of £200 million for the exercise of its functions. The Bill provides for that allocation to be raised to £300 million subject to parliamentary approval.

The sums I have mentioned are additional to the existing spending in Scotland on selective assistance, regional developments grants and the regional employment premium. It is worth noting that all these matters add up to £150 million per annum. *Those who seem to think that Scotland is getting a raw deal should consider what is being provided.*

Mr Alick Buchanan-Smith (North Angus and Mearns): We are kidding ourselves if we think that by the establishment of an agency we shall necessarily solve some of the problems that we are facing in Scotland at the present time.

What is needed is, first, the will to solve them and, secondly, the resources to solve them. No matter how many agencies or boards may be set up, these problems will not be solved unless the Government are prepared to have the will and to make available the resources to do so. The important point is that the powers are there at the moment, but the will and the resources have been lacking.

The powers of this agency are the powers of the NEB (National Enterprise Board) extended to Scotland. What we are seeing is the extension of Socialism in Scotland for Socialism's sake. I ask people in Scotland not to be kidded by what the Government are doing.

Mr Donald Stewart (Western Isles): We agree that the Bill is an effort to do something to repair the decades, if not generations of neglect of Scotland by successive Governments at Westminster. One suspects that the discovery and exploitation of Scottish oil has a good deal to do with concentrating the mind of the Government in the direction of the Bill. No country capable of commanding the resources that Scotland now has could accept any delay in the provision of substantial benefits.

Mr Dennis Canavan (West Stirlingshire): Before putting forward any ideas for a successful regeneration of the Scottish economy, it is important to diagnose what is wrong with it and why there is a lack of industrial development in Scotland. I should like to propose two major factors. The first is the lack of Government power to disperse industry. There is a maldistribution of industrial development, not only in Scotland but throughout the whole of the UK. One reason is that when the private industrialist is making a decision on where to locate industry, his main criterion is to maximize his profits. He does not think of areas of high unemployment or of social deprivation.

Successive Governments have made attempts to try to intervene in this kind of natural *laissez-faire* growth process. For example, we have had development areas, special development areas, development certificates, development grants, regional employment premium, advance factories and so on. We have seen some of the benefits from such State intervention.

In my opinion, such governmental intervention has been inadequate and *there is only one way of effectively dispersing industry. That is by being involved in the actual decision-making on the dispersal of industry*, which is normally done by the owners of industry. That is why I see an extension of public enterprise, whereby the Government are involved in the ownership, in whole or in part, of industry, as absolutely vital if the Government are to have adequate powers to disperse industry.

The second weakness in Scottish industry, in my opinion, is lack of investment. That again is not a problem that is peculiar to Scotland.

Far too often industry is dependent on the whim of private investors, many of whom are quite capable of taking money out of industry and investing it elsewhere if they do not happen to like the particular tone of the Government in power at a particular time. To my mind, however, it is not sufficient simply to take public money to prop up a private concern and bolster it up without some reciprocal public control. That is absolutely essential if the taxpayers' money is to be put into industry. There must be at least some element of public ownership and public control.

Instead of the Scottish Development Agency simply being some kind of free gifts scheme, it must be seen to be a means of extending public enterprise so that the Government have more influence on the location and dispersal of industry.

Mr Douglas Crawford (Perth and East Perthshire): The nature of the illness has been crying out for all of us to hear yet nothing has been done. It galls me and it grieves me to hear month after month when Scottish unemployment remains at an unacceptably high level, representatives of the Scottish Labour Party and the General Secretary of the Scottish Trades Union Congress (STUC) saying that something must be done. We are sick, tired and fed up of hearing the STUC representatives saying that something must be done. *Are they unable to see that the solution is staring them in the face—namely, self-government?*

The Government tell us that certain things have been done. In a way I suppose that is true, but, to quote the Latin tag, *parturient montes nascetur exiguus mus*—namely, the mountains have laboured and brought forth a mouse. The fact is that the Scottish Development Agency will have to rely on the Westminster Treasury for whatever money it receives. *Let it be put firmly on the record that no Scottish Government would produce such a puny Bill.* Once again, Scotland is being made subservient to the political will of Westminster. It is being made a poor second. Clearly the SDA is being made to play second fiddle to the NEB not only operationally but politically. Scotland, with industrial problems that are the largest in Western Europe, is being made the cat's-paw of the NEB and the Department of Industry.

Let me reiterate the position of the SNP. We shall support anything that will help Scotland, in however small a way. We shall support any devolutionary measure, however small, festooned with however much public relations. We shall give our support to this Bill on its Second Reading.

In the same week as Scottish oil was landed at the Isle of Grain and the right hon. Member for Worcester (Mr Walker) was saying that a third of Scottish oil should be sold, the Scottish Office was telling local authorities in Scotland to cut back on their expenditure. The right hon. Member for Worcester said that Scottish oil—he called it 'North Sea Oil'—would be worth between £150,000 million and £350,000 million. *That amount of money could keep the SDA going for a very long time indeed.*

4 Thatcher's Proposed Regional Policy

Extract from *Regional Policy*, House of Commons Debate (24 July 1980).

As part of their plans to reduce public expenditure the newly elected Conservative government proposed to modify regional policy by reducing the areas in which incentives would be available, lowering the rate of some incentives while increasing the expenditure thresholds and diminishing the effect of disincentive policy by raising the threshold for IDCs. These proposals were intended to save £233 million of a projected annual expenditure on regional policy of £609 million in 1982–3. This extract from the debate includes the views of the Conservatives (Sir K. Joseph and Mr R. Hicks), Labour (Mr A. Williams) and *Plaid Cymru* (the Welsh Nationalists) (Mr D. Thomas).

The Secretary of State for Industry (Sir Keith Joseph): I beg to move: 'That this House welcomes the changes which are being introduced by the Government in regional policy in order to concentrate assistance on areas most in need, to make it more cost-effective, and to remove anomalies in assisted area gradings.'

There is no loss under the Government's proposals for existing jobs in the regions. There is some reduction in the new jobs that may go to the regions in future.

The best academic assessment that can be obtained for the total effect of regional policy up to date is that the net gain in new jobs to the assisted areas, not only in manufacturing but in services, each year during the 1970s has been almost 20,000. I do not underestimate the scale of extra jobs. It is a net gain of jobs for the assisted areas.

After my recent statement, hon. Members have insisted that the loss of jobs from the withdrawal over three years of £230 million from regional policy spending will be savage. The best assessment that can be made from the academic work that has been done on the matter is that the loss of potential jobs—not existing jobs—in the assisted areas by that withdrawal over a three-year transitional period of £230 million might be about 5,000 to 6,000 jobs in the assisted areas.

There is an obstinate gap in the economic vitality of different regions in the country. In nearly every case (the assisted areas) were the depressed areas of the 1930s. In relative terms the gap has been narrowed, though because of the rise in the aggregate of unemployment the absolute difference between the unemployed in assisted and non-assisted areas has, alas, increased.

I repeat with all the emphasis at my command that *redistributing the taxpayers' money will not suffice in itself to eliminate the gap between the assisted areas.* There has to be self-help in the assisted areas. There has to be enterprise, competitiveness, high productivity and a reputation for co-operation between management and the work force in the assisted areas if they are to reach the level of employment that we all want them to reach. We need more indigenous growth in the assisted areas. That is why the changes in climate and economic context which we have set ourselves to try to achieve are so relevant to the assisted as well as to the non-assisted areas.

Mr Alan Williams (Swansea, West): Regional policy has never been about employment alone. It is about social factors as well. We inherit a population pattern which reflects the energy availability and energy resources of the nineteenth century, but in that population pattern we have the cumulative social capital—our schools, universities and hospitals—and it is an absurdity to think in terms of allowing a drift away from traditional areas of employment, a drift down to London and the South, forced there because that will be the only place where jobs will be available but where the existing social capital is already under congestion. The roads are congested, there is excessive utilization of school facilities, hospitals, and so on.

Let us not assume that regional policy is only in the interests of Wales, the North, Lancashire and the other assisted areas. It is essentially also in the interests of the prosperous areas of this country.

As the right hon. Gentleman (Sir K. Joseph) indicates, and as we all recognize, Britain, especially the regions, depends on inward investment. At present, 20 per cent of manufacturing industry is overseas-owned. My colleagues in Lancashire and in assisted areas in Scotland know what a high proportion of industry in those areas comes from abroad. The right hon. Gentleman said that we gain from inward investment, yet the cuts in regional development grants and section 7 assistance mean that we cannot reach the ceilings for financial assistance that are permissible under the EEC regulations. *Therefore, France, Germany, Belgium and our other Common Market colleagues will be offering packages of incentives that we shall not administratively be able to match because of the changes that the Government have made.*

We shall be disadvantaged in obtaining internationally mobile industry at a time when there will be the minimum of domestic mobile industry.

Mr Robert Hicks (Bodmin): Hon. Members on both sides have said that over the past few years regional disparities in the UK have been reduced. But, sadly, in my part of the UK, the far South-West, that has not happened. Whatever criterion we choose—whether it be unemployment or the level of average incomes—we find that the disparity has increased. Whether we compare average unemployment in our region with that of the rest of the UK or average income in Cornwall with the national average, we find that the gap has widened.

Therefore, in that context, I suggest the concept of some form of South-West development agency, with an agreed budget, whereby the region could sell itself in the national or international market. That is the self-help that my right hon. Friend mentioned earlier this afternoon. Would not it be a good idea if the South-West had its own development agency so that we could go out into the market and attract suitable economic activity to our region?

In the South-West we do not have a Scottish Development Agency; we do not have a Highlands and Islands Board; we do not have a Welsh Development

Agency; we do not have a Development Board for Rural Wales. The only assistance through an agency that we have is through the Development Commission which serves all the English rural regions. When we look at the average assistance that the South-West region obtains, compared with its counterparts in Scotland or Wales, we find that the budgets in Scotland and Wales for the development agencies, plus the regional development structure, are very considerable indeed compared with our receipts.

This may be the reason, or one of the reasons, why we have an unemployment problem in the South-West at a higher percentage now, compared with the national average, than the figure of five or ten years ago. That is why average earnings in Cornwall are the lowest of any part of the UK, namely, 83·3 per cent of the national average income.

One or two speakers have mentioned during the debate the dangers of a divided Britain, with the more prosperous South-East and Midlands and the less prosperous North and West and my own South-West. *I believe that this is the greatest single economic and social problem facing the country. The distribution of seats at the last general election tended to catalyse this division politically.*

Mr D. E. Thomas (Merioneth): As someone who represents a less-developed region, I know that we have been on the receiving end of the operation of market forces for many years. Regional imbalance in the case of Wales and of the other regions, is not a geographical accident. It is not a natural tendency. It is a factor in the very economic system in the countries of Britain. It results from the domination of peripheral areas by central areas. *It is a geographical inequality, a horizontal inequality, which compares with the vertical class inequality. I think that the Secretary of State for Industry, in all his speeches, exhibits his devotion to the maintenance of both.*

We have an uneven development in the concentration of capital in the South-East and the Midlands which affects adversely the development of new jobs in the regions, not only in Wales but in the other regions of the UK. Clearly, by their withdrawal of regional aid the Government are determined not to offset the operation of market forces.

In the 16 years from 1960 to 1976 the net benefit to Wales of regional policy was the creation of 76,000 new jobs. That did not offset job losses in basic industries, and those losses will be increased by the decision of the Secretary of State for Industry to axe steel making in part of my county of Clwyd, at Shotton.

The link between regional policy and taxation has been clearly exhibited in these proposals. What is regional policy if not transfer payments to the less developed regions out of the incomes of the richer classes in the more developed regions? That is the aspect which angers me most. *The Government's decision on regional assistance is part of their whole policy of favouring their supporters and blatantly favouring the class that they represent. The working people of Wales are taking note of what the Government, for whom we did not vote, are doing to the Welsh economy.*

Notes on contributors

STEPHEN BORNSTEIN is Assistant Professor of Political Science at McGill University.

PETER A. HALL is Assistant Professor of Government at Harvard University.

DAVID HELD is Lecturer in Politics at the University of York.

JOEL KRIEGER is Assistant Professor of Political Science at Wellesley College.

JAMES R. LEWIS is Lecturer in Geography at the University of Durham.

DENNIS SMITH is Senior Lecturer in Sociology at the University of Aston in Birmingham.

ROSEMARY C. R. TAYLOR is Assistant Professor in Sociology and Director of the Community Health Program at Tufts University.

Bibliography

Aaron, B., and Wedderburn, K. W. (1972), *Industrial Conflict: A Comparative Legal Survey* (New York: Crane-Russak).

Abel-Smith, Brian (1965), 'The major pattern of financing and the organization of medical services that have emerged in other countries', *Medical Care*, vol. 3, no. 1 (January–March), pp. 33–40.

Adam, N. (1980), 'L'Etat, c'est nous', *Euromoney* (October), pp. 110–24.

Aglietta, M. (1979), *A Theory of Capitalist Regulation* (London: New Left Books).

Akkermans, T., and Grootings, P. (1978), 'From corporatism to polarisation: elements of the development of Dutch industrial relations', in C. Crouch and A. Pizzorno (eds), *The Resurgence of Class Conflict in Western Europe since 1968*, Vol. 1 (New York: Holmes & Meier), pp. 159–90.

Albrow, M. (1970), *Bureaucracy* (London: Pall Mall).

Aldcroft, Derek H., and Fearon, Peter (eds) (1969), *Economic Growth in Twentieth-Century Britain* (London: Macmillan).

Alford, R. (1975), *Health Care Politics: Ideological and Interest Group Barriers to Reform* (Chicago, Ill.: University of Chicago Press).

Allison, G. (1971), *The Essence of Decision* (Boston, Mass.: Little, Brown).

Alonso Teixidor, L. F., and Hebbart, M. (1982), 'Regional planning in Spain and the transition to democracy', in R. Hudson and J. R. Lewis (eds), *Regional Planning in Europe* (London: Pion).

Altenstetter, Christa (1974), *Health Policy-Making and Administration in West Germany and the United States*, Administrative and Policy Study Series, no. 03-013, vol. 2 (Beverly Hills, Calif.: Sage).

Altvater, E. (1973), 'Notes on some problems of state interventionism', *Kapitalistate*, vol. 1 (May), pp. 96–108, and vol. 2 (December–January), pp. 76–83.

Anderson, D. D. (1980), *Germany: The Uncertain Stride of a Reluctant Giant*, Harvard Business School Case (Boston, Mass.: Intercollegiate Case Clearing House).

Anderson, Odin W. (1977), 'Are national health services systems converging? Predictions for the United States', *Annals of the American Academy of Political and Social Science*, vol. 434 (November), pp. 24–38.

Anderson, P. (1976), 'The antinomies of Antonio Gramsci', *New Left Review*, no. 100 (November-January), pp. 5–80.

Anderson, P. (1977), 'The limits and possibilities of trade union action', in T. Clarke and L. Clements (eds), *Trade Unions under Capitalism* (Glasgow: Collins/Fontana), pp. 333–50.

Andrews, W. G., and Hoffman, S. (eds) (1980), *The Fifth Republic at Twenty* (Albany, NY: State University of New York Press).

Arcangeli, F., Borzaga, C., and Goglio, S. (1980), 'Patterns of peripheral development in the Italian regions', *Papers of the Regional Science Association*, vol. 44.

Armstrong, David (1976), 'The decline of the medical hegemony: a review of government reports during the NHS', *Social Science and Medicine*, vol. 10, nos. 3–4 (March–April), pp. 157–63.

Armstrong, David (1979) 'The emancipation of biographical medicine', *Social Science and Medicine*, vol. 13A, no. 1 (January), pp. 1–8.

Artis, M. J. (1965), *Foundations of British Monetary Policy* (Oxford: Blackwell).

Assennato, G., and Navarro, V. (1980), 'Workers' participation and control in Italy: the case of occupational medicine', *International Journal of Health Services*, vol. 10, no. 2, pp. 217–32.

Bachrach, P., and Baratz, M. S. (1962), 'The two faces of power', *American Political Science Review*, vol. 56, no. 4 (December), pp. 942–52.

Bacon, R., and Eltis, W. (1976), *Britain's Economic Problem: Too Few Producers?* (London: Macmillan).

Bagnara, S., Biocca, M., and Mazzonis, D. Gattegno (1981), 'Trends in occupational health and safety policy in Italy', *International Journal of Health Services*, vol. 11, no. 3, pp. 431–50.

Bagnasco, A. (1977), *Tre Italie* (Bologna: Il Mulino).

Bain, G. S. (1970), *The Growth of White-Collar Unionism* (Oxford: Clarendon).

Baldwin, R. E. (ed.) (1965), *Trade, Growth and the Balance of Payments* (Chicago, Ill.: Amsterdam).

Barbash, J. (1972), *Trade Unions and National Economic Policy* (Baltimore, Md.: Johns Hopkins University Press).

Barkin, S. (ed.) (1975), *Worker Militancy and Its Consequences* (New York: Praeger).

Barry, B. (ed.) (1976), *Power and Political Theory* (London: Wiley).

Batey, P. W. J. (ed.) (1978), *Theory and Method in Urban and Regional Analysis* (London: Pion).

Beer, S. H. (1982), *Britain against Itself: An Essay on the Contradictions of Collectivism* (New York: Norton).

Ben-David, J. (1962), 'Universities and academic systems in modern societies', *European Journal of Sociology*, vol. 3, no. 1, pp. 45–84.

Berger, S. (1980), 'Lame ducks and national champions: industrial policy in the Fifth Republic', in W. G. Andrews and S. Hoffman (eds), *The Fifth Republic at Twenty* (Albany, NY: State University of New York Press), pp. 292–310.

Berlinguer, G. (1979), *Una Riforma per la salute: Iter e*

obiettivi del Servizio Sanitario Nazionale (Bari: De Donato).

Bernstein, B. (1973), 'On the classification and framing of educational knowledge', in *Class, Codes and Control*, Vol. 1 (London: Paladin), pp. 227–56.

Berthelot, Y., and Tardy, G. (1978), *Le Défi économique du tiers monde* (Paris: Documentation Française).

Beyme, K. von (1980), *Challenge to Power: Trade Unions and Industrial Relations in Capitalist Countries*, trans. Eileen Martin (London: Sage).

Beyme, K. von, and Ionescu, G. (1977), 'The policies of employment: policy in Germany and Great Britain', *Government and Opposition*, vol. 12, no. 1 (Winter), pp. 88–107.

Birnbaum, P. (1978), *La Classe dirigeante française* (Paris: Presses Universitaires de France).

Blackaby, F. T. (ed.) (1979), *British Economic Policy, 1960–74* (Cambridge: Cambridge University Press).

Blackburn, R. M. (1967), *Union Character and Social Class* (London: Batsford).

Blackburn, R. M. (ed.) (1972), *Ideology in Social Science: Readings in Critical Social Theory* (London: Fontana).

Blank, S. (1978), 'Britain and the politics of foreign economic policy: the domestic economy, and the problem of pluralistic stagnation', in P. J. Katzenstein (ed.), *Between Power and Plenty* (Madison, Wis.: University of Wisconsin Press), pp. 89–138.

Bleitrach, D., and Chenu, A. (1982), 'Regional planning: regulation or deepening of social contradictions? An example: Fos-sur-Mer and the Marseilles metropolitan region', in R. Hudson and J. R. Lewis (eds), *Regional Planning in Europe* (London: Pion).

Bloch-Lainé, F. (1976), *Profession: fonctionnaire* (Paris: Editions du Seuil).

Block, F. (1977), 'The ruling class does not rule: notes on the Marxist theory of the state', *Socialist Review*, no. 33 (May–June), pp. 6–28.

Bloor, Michael (1976), 'Bishop Berkeley and the adenotonsillectomy enigma: an explanation of variation in the social construction of medical disposals', *Sociology*, vol. 10 (January), pp. 43–61.

Bogason, P. (1978), 'Regional planning in Denmark', in K. Hanf and F. W. Scharpf (eds), *Interorganizational Policy Making* (New York: Sage), pp. 215–43.

Bornstein, S. (1978), 'The economy of France: the changing posture of unions and the CFDT', *European Studies Newsletter*, vol. 7, no. 5 (April), pp. 1–12.

Bornstein, S., and Fine, K. S. (1977), 'Workers control in France: recent political developments', in G. David Garson (ed.), *Worker Self-Management in Industry: The West European Experience* (New York: Praeger).

Bornstein, S., and Gourevitch, P. (1984), 'Unions in a declining economy: the case of the British TUC', in G. Ross, A. Martin, P. Gourevitch, S. Bornstein, A. Markovits and C. Allen (eds), *Unions and Economic Crisis: Britain, West Germany and Sweden* (London: Allen & Unwin).

Bourdieu, P., and Passeron, H.-C. (1977), *Reproduction* (London: Sage).

Bradshaw, A. (1976), 'A critique of Steven Lukes's *Power: A Radical View*', *Sociology*, vol. 10, no. 1.

Braunthal, G. (1965), *The Federation of German Industry in Politics* (Ithaca, NY: Cornell University Press).

Breathnach, P. (1982), 'The demise of growth centre policy: the case of the Republic of Ireland', in R. Hudson and J. R. Lewis (eds), *Regional Planning in Europe* (London: Pion).

Brenna, A. (1978), 'Il costo della salute in Italia', *Prospective sociali e sanitarie*, no. 20 (15 November).

Brittan, S. (1971), *Steering the Economy* (Harmondsworth: Penguin).

Broadway, F. (1969), *State Intervention in British Industry, 1964–8* (London: Kaye & Ward).

Brown, A. J., and Burrows, E. M. (1977), *Regional Economic Problems* (London: Allen & Unwin).

Brown, G. (ed.) (1975), *The Red Paper on Scotland* (Edinburgh: EUSPB).

Brown, R., and Kamenka, E. (1979), *Bureaucracy* (Port Melbourne: Arnold).

Brown, R. G. S. (1978), *The Changing National Health Service* (London: Routledge & Kegan Paul).

Budd, A. (1978), *The Politics of Economic Planning* (Manchester: Manchester University Press).

Calleo, D. (1978), *The German Problem Reconsidered* (Cambridge: Cambridge University Press).

Canone, François, and Guyot, Jean-Claude (1978), 'Health policy in France: a major issue in the 1978 legislative elections', *International Journal of Health Services*, vol. 8, no. 3, pp. 509–19.

Carney, J. G. (1980), 'Regions in crisis: accumulation, regional problems and crisis formation', in J. G. Carney, R. Hudson and J. R. Lewis (eds), *Regions in Crisis* (London: Croom Helm), pp. 28–59.

Carney, J. G., Hudson, R., and Lewis, J. R. (eds) (1980), *Regions in Crisis* (London: Croom Helm).

Carney, J. G., and Lewis, J. R. (1978), 'Accumulation, the regional problem and nationalism', in P. W. J. Batey (ed.), *Theory and Method in Urban and Regional Analysis* (London: Pion), pp. 67–81.

Caron, F. (1979), *An Economic History of Modern France* (New York: Columbia University Press).

Carré, J. J., Dubois, A., and Malinvand, E. (1972), *La Croissance française* (Paris: Editions du Seuil).

Carreras, C. (1980), *Geografia humana* (Barcelona: Conèixer Catalunya, Dopesa 2).

Carrino, Luciano, *et al.* (1977), *Medicina critica in Italia* (Florence: Casa Editrice G. D'Anna).

Caruso, Saverio (1977), *Il Medico della corporazione: o la socialita privata* (Milan: Feltrinelli).

Caves, R. E., and Krause, L. B. (1980), *Britain's Economic Performance* (Washington, DC: Brookings Institution).

Caves, R. E., *et al.* (1968), *Britain's Economic Prospects* (Washington, DC/London: Brookings Institution/Allen & Unwin).

Cerny, P. G., and Schain, M. A. (eds) (1980), *French Politics and Public Policy* (New York: St Martin's Press).

Claassen, E., and Salin, P. (eds) (1972), *Stabilization Policies in Interdependent Economies* (Amsterdam: Elseiser).

Clark, J. (1979), 'Concerted action in the Federal Republic of Germany', *British Journal of Industrial Relations*, vol. 17, no. 2 (July).

Clarke, T., and Clements, L. (eds) (1977), *Trade Unions under Capitalism* (Glasgow: Collins/Fontana).

Clegg, H. A. (1976), *Trade Unionism under Collective Bargaining: A Theory Based on Comparisons of Six Countries* (Oxford: Blackwell).

Clegg, H. A. (1978), *The System of Industrial Relations in Great Britain*, 3rd edn (Oxford: Blackwell).

Clegg, H. A. (1979), *The Changing System of Industrial Relations in Great Britain* (Oxford: Blackwell).

Clout, H. (ed.) (1975), *Regional Development in Western Europe* (Chichester: Wiley).

Cohen, S. S. (1969), *Modern Capitalist Planning: The French Model* (London: Weidenfeld & Nicolson).

Cohen, S. S. (1977), *Modern Capitalist Planning: The French Model* (Berkeley, Calif.: University of California Press).

Cohen, S. S. (1980), 'Informed bewilderment: French economic strategy and the crisis', Paper 335, Institute of Urban and Regional Development, University of California, Berkeley, Calif. (December).

Commissariat Générale du Plan (1979), *Options: VIIe Plan* (Paris: Documentation Française).

Commission de l'Industrie du VIIIe Plan (1980), *La Situation financière des enterprises industrielles* (Paris: Documentation Française).

Commission of the European Community (1978), *Enlargement of the Community: Economic and Sectoral Aspects* (Luxembourg: Bulletin of the European Communities, Supplement 3/78).

Commission of the European Community (1980), *The Community and Its Regions* (Luxembourg: European Documentation).

Committee of Public Accounts (1981), *Measuring the Effectiveness of Regional Industrial Policy* (London: Her Majesty's Stationery Office).

Corina, John (1975), 'Planning and the British labour market: incomes and manpower policy, 1965–1970', in J. Hayward and M. Watson (eds), *Planning, Politics and Public Policy: The British, French and Italian Experience* (Cambridge: Cambridge University Press), pp. 177–201.

Cotta, A. (1978), *La France et l'impératif mondial* (Paris: PUF).

Cowart, A. (1978), 'The economic policies of European governments', *British Journal of Political Science*, vol. 8, pts 3 and 4, pp. 285–311 and 425–39.

Crawford, R. (1979), 'Individual responsibility and health politics in the 1970s', in S. Reverby and D. Rosner (eds), *Health Care in America* (Philadelphia, Pa: Temple University Press), pp. 247–68.

Crouch, C. (1977), *Class Conflict and the Industrial Relations Crisis* (London: Heinemann).

Crouch, C. (1978a), 'The intensification of industrial conflict in the United Kingdom', in C. Crouch and A. Pizzorno (eds), *The Resurgence of Class Conflict in Western Europe since 1968*, Vol. 1 (New York: Holmes & Meier), pp. 191–256.

Crouch, C. (1978b), 'The changing role of the state in industrial relations in Western Europe', in C. Crouch and A. Pizzorno (eds), *The Resurgence of Class Conflict in Western Europe since 1968*, Vol. 2 (New York: Holmes & Meier), pp. 197–220.

Crouch, C. (ed.) (1979a), *State and Economy in Contemporary Capitalism* (London: Croom Helm).

Crouch, C. (1979b), 'The state, capital and liberal democracy', in C. Crouch (ed.), *State and Economy in Contemporary Capitalism* (London: Croom Helm), pp. 13–54.

Crouch, C. (1980), 'Varieties of trade union weakness: organised labour and capital formation in Britain, Federal Germany and Sweden', in J. Hayward (ed.), *Trade Unions and Politics in Western Europe* (London: Frank Cass), pp. 87–106.

Crouch, C., and Pizzorno, A. (eds) (1978), *The Resurgence of Class Conflict in Western Europe since 1968*, 2 vols (New York: Holmes & Meier).

Crozier, M. (1964), *The Bureaucratic Phenomenon* (London: Tavistock).

Crozier, M. (1965), 'Pour une analyse sociologique de la planification française', *Revue française de sociologie*, vol. 6, no. 2 (April–June), pp. 147–63.

Dahl, R. A. (1956), *A Preface to Democratic Theory* (Chicago, Ill.: University of Chicago Press).

Dahl, R. A. (1957), 'The concept of power', *Behavioral Science*, vol. 2, no. 3 (July), pp. 201–15.

Dahl, R. A. (1971), *Polyarchy: Participation and Opposition* (New Haven, Conn.: Yale University Press).

Dahl, R. A. (1975), *Who Governs? Democracy and Power in an American City* (New Haven, Conn./London: Yale University Press).

Dahl, R. A. (1978), 'Pluralism revisited', *Comparative Politics*, vol. 10, no. 2 (January), pp. 191–204.

Dahrendorf, R. (1964), 'Recent changes in the class structure of European societies', *Daedalus*, vol. 93, no. 1 (Winter), pp. 225–70.

Damette, F. (1980), 'The regional framework of monopoly exploitation: new problems and trends', in J. G. Carney, R. Hudson and J. R. Lewis (eds), *Regions in Crisis* (London: Croom Helm), pp. 76–92.

Dear, M., and Scott, A. J. (eds) (1981), *Urbanization and Urban Planning in Capitalist Society* (London: Methuen).

Denison, Edward (1969), *Why Growth Rates Differ* (Washington, DC: Brookings Institution).

Dennis, R. D. (1978), 'The decline of manufacturing employment in Greater London, 1966–74', *Urban Studies*, vol. 15, no. 1.

Department of Health and Social Security (1977), *Prevention and Health* (London: Her Majesty's Stationery Office).

Department of Health and Social Security (1980), *Inequalities in Health: Report of a Research Working Group* (London: DHSS).

Di Palma, Giuseppe (1980), 'The available state: problems of reform', in P. Lange and S. Tarrow (eds), *Italy in Transition: Conflict and Consensus* (London: Frank Cass), pp. 149–65.

Dicken, P., and Lloyd, P. E. (1976), 'Geographical perspectives on United States investment in the United Kingdom', *Environment and Planning*, vol. 8, no. 6, pp. 685–705.

DiGiorgio, U., and Moscati, R. (1980), 'The role of the state in the uneven spatial development of Italy: the case of the Mezzogiorno', *Review of Radical Political Economics*, vol. 12, no. 3, pp. 50–63.

Domhoff, W. (1967), *Who Rules America?* (Englewood Cliffs, NJ: Prentice-Hall).

Dorfman, G. A. (1979), *Government versus Trade Unionism in British Politics since 1968* (London: Macmillan).

Dow, J. C. R. (1970), *The Management of the British Economy, 1945–60* (Cambridge: Cambridge University Press).

Doyal, Lesley, and Pennell, Imogen (1979), *The Political Economy of Health* (London: Pluto).

Dubois, P. (1978), 'New forms of industrial conflict, 1960–1974', in C. Crouch and A. Pizzorno (eds), *The Resurgence of Class Conflict in Western Europe since 1968*, Vol. 2 (New York: Holmes & Meier), pp. 1–34.

Dubois, P., Devand, C., and Erbès-Séquin, S. (1978), 'The contradiction of French trade unionism', in C. Crouch and A. Pizzorno (eds), *The Resurgence of Class Conflict in Western Europe since 1968*, Vol. 1 (New York: Holmes & Meier), pp. 53–100.

Dulong, R. (1978), *Les Régions, l'état et la société locale* (Paris: Presses Universitaires de France).

Eckstein, H. (1960), *Pressure Group Politics: The Case of the British Medical Association* (London: Allen & Unwin).

Elbo, C. (1975), 'Denmark', in H. Clout (ed.), *Regional Development in Western Europe* (Chichester: Wiley), pp. 233–44.

Elster, J. (1976), 'Some conceptual problems in political theory', in B. Barry (ed.), *Power and Political Theory* (London: Wiley).

Esping-Andersen, G., and Friedland, R. (1981a), 'Class coalitions in the making of West European economies', in G. Esping-Andersen and R. Friedland (eds), *Political Power and Social Theory*, Vol. 3 (Greenwich, Conn.: Jai).

Esping-Andersen, G., and Friedland, R. (eds) (1981b), *Political Power and Social Theory* (Greenwich, Conn.: Jai).

Esping-Andersen, G., Friedland, R., and Wright, E. O.

(1976), 'Modes of class struggle and the capitalist state', *Kapitalistate*, vol. 4, no. 5 (Summer), pp. 186–220.

Eurohealth Handbook 1978 (1978) (New York: Robert S. First).

Eyer, J., and Sterling, P. (1977), 'Stress-related mortality and social organization', *Review of Radical Political Economics*, vol. 9, no. 1 (Spring), pp. 1–44.

Ferrão, J. M. M. (1979), *Interacção regional e divisão territorial do trabalho* (Lisbon: Centro de Estudos Geográficos, Universidade de Lisboa, 1979).

Field, Mark G. (1976), 'The health system and the social system', in M. Sokolowoka, J. Sokolowoka, J. Holowka and A. Ostowska (eds), *Health, Medicine, Society: Proceedings of the International Conference on the Sociology of Medicine* (New York: Reidel), pp. 315–29.

Figa-Talamanca, I. (1976), 'The health status and the health care problems of the aged in an Italian community', *International Journal of Aging and Human Development*, vol. 7, no. 1, pp. 39–48.

Finegold, K., and Skocpol, T. (1980), 'Capitalists, farmers, and workers in the New Deal – the ironies of government intervention', paper presented to American Political Science Association, Washington, DC (August).

Firn, J. (1975), 'External control and regional policy', in G. Brown (ed.), *The Red Paper on Scotland* (Edinburgh: EUSPB), pp. 153–69.

Foucault, Michel (1975), *The Birth of the Clinic: An Archaeology of Medical Perception* (New York: Random House/Vintage Books).

Frankel, B. (1979), 'The state of the state after Leninism', *Theory and Society*, vol. 7, no. 1–2.

Frey, Bruno (1980), *Modern Political Economy* (New York: Wiley).

Friedmann, J., and Alonso, W. (eds) (1975), *Regional Policy* (Cambridge, Mass.: MIT).

Friis, P. (1980), *Regional Problems in Denmark: Myth or Reality?* Dunelm Translations No. 4 (Durham: University of Durham Department of Geography).

Fröbel, F., Heinrichs, J., and Kreye, O. (1980), *The New International Division of Labour* (Cambridge: Cambridge University Press).

Fry, John (1976), 'Regulation and control of the medical profession in Great Britain', *International Journal of Health Services*, vol. 6, no. 1, pp. 5–7.

Gamble, A. (1979), 'The free economy and the strong state', in Ralph Miliband and J. Saville (eds), *The Socialist Register, 1979* (London: Merlin), pp. 1–25.

Garofoli, G. (1980), 'Lo sviluppo delle "aree perferiche" nella economia Italiana degli anni settarta', paper presented at Conference on Peripheral Development, Trento (October).

Garson, G. David (ed.) (1977), *Worker Self-Management in Industry: The West European Experience* (New York: Praeger).

Giddens, A. (1979), *Central Problems in Social Theory: Action, Structure and Contradiction in Social Analysis*

(Berkeley and Los Angeles, Calif.: University of California Press).

Giddens, A. (1981), *A Contemporary Critique of Historical Materialism* (London: Macmillan).

Giner, Salvador (1976), 'Power, freedom and social change in the Spanish University, 1939–1975', in P. Preston (ed.), *Spain in Crisis* (Hassocks: Harvester).

Glaser, William A. (1976), *Paying the Doctor under National Health Insurance: Foreign Lessons for the USA*, 2nd edn (New York: Bureau for Applied Social Research, Columbia University).

Gold, D. A., Lo, C. Y. H., and Wright, E. O. (1975), 'Recent developments in Marxist theories of the capitalist state', *Monthly Review*, vol. 27, no. 5 (October), pp. 29–43, and no. 6 (November), pp. 36–51.

Gough, Ian (1975), 'State expenditure in advanced capitalism', *New Left Review*, no. 92 (July–August), pp. 53–92.

Gough, Ian (1979), *The Political Economy of the Welfare State* (London: Macmillan).

Gourevitch, P. A. (1977), 'International trade, domestic coalitions, and liberty: comparative responses to the Great Depression of 1873–1896', *Journal of Interdisciplinary History*, vol. 8, no. 1 (August).

Gourevitch, P. A. (1980), 'The politics of economic policy in the Great Depression of 1929: some comparative observations', paper presented to the American Political Science Association, Washington, DC (August).

Gowland, D. (1978), *Monetary Policy and Credit Control* (London: Croom Helm).

Grant, W., and Marsh, D. (1977), *The Confederation of British Industry* (London: Hodder & Stoughton).

Graziani, A. (1978), 'The Mezzogiorno in the Italian economy', *Cambridge Journal of Economics*, vol. 2, no. 4 (December), pp. 355–72.

Green, D. M. (1978), 'The Seventh Plan – the demise of French planning?' *West European Politics*, vol. 1, no. 1 (Fall), pp. 60–76.

Grove, J. W. (1962), *Government and Industry in Britain* (London: Longman).

Grove, J. W. (1967), *Government and Industry in Britain* (London: Longman).

Gruson, C. (1968), *Origine et esprits de la planification française* (Paris: Dunod).

Guttesen, R., Hansen, F., and Nielsen, B. (1976), 'Regional development in Denmark', *Geografisk Tidjskrift*, vol. 75, pp. 74–86.

Habermas, J. (1975), *Legitimation Crisis*, trans. T. McCarthy (Boston, Mass.: Beacon).

Habermas, J. (1976), *Legitimation Crisis*, trans. T. McCarthy (London: Heinemann).

Hagen, E. E., and White, S. F. T. (1966), *Great Britain: Quiet Revolution in Planning* (Syracuse, NY: Syracuse University Press).

Hall, P. A. (1981a), 'Economic planning and the state: the evolution of economic challenge and political response in France', in G. Esping-Andersen and R. Friedland (eds),

Political Power and Social Theory, Vol. 3 (Greenwich, Con.: Jai Press).

Hall, P. A. (1981b), 'Miti culturali e realtà economiche: la programmazione francese nel confronto con l'esperienza Brittannica', *Stato e Mercato*, vol. 1, no. 1 (April).

Hamilton, A., Madison, J., and Jay, J. (1945), *The Federalist or the New Constitution* (New York: Heritage).

Hamilton, F. E. I., and Linge, G. R. (eds) (1981), *Spatial Analysis, Industry and the Industrial Environment*, 2 vols. (Chichester: Wiley).

Hanf, K., and Scharpf, F. W. (eds) (1978), *Inter-organizational Policy Making* (New York: Sage).

Hansen, B. (1969), *Fiscal Policy in Seven Countries, 1955–65* (Paris: Organisation for Economic Co-operation and Development).

Hardach, K. (1980), *The Political Economy of Germany in the Twentieth Century* (Berkeley, Calif.: University of California Press).

Harris, N. (1972), *Competition and the Corporate Society* (London: Methuen).

Harrison, M. (1960), *Trade Unions and the Labour Party since 1945* (Detroit, Mich.: Wayne State University Press).

Hayward, J. (1967), 'Le fonctionnement des commissions et la préparation du Ve Plan', *Revue française de sociologie*, vol. 8, no. 4 (October–December), pp. 447–67.

Hayward, J. (1975), 'Planning and the French labour market: incomes and industrial training', in J. Hayward and M. Watson (eds), *Planning, Politics and Public Policy: The British, French and Italian Experience* (Cambridge: Cambridge University Press), pp. 159–76.

Hayward, J. (1976), 'Institutional inertia and political impetus in France and Britain', *European Journal of Political Research*, vol. 4, no. 4 (December), pp. 341–59.

Hayward, J. (1980a), 'Trade union movements and their politico-economic environments: a preliminary framework', in J. Hayward (ed.), *Trade Unions and Politics in Western Europe* (London: Frank Cass), pp. 1–9.

Hayward, J. (ed.) (1980b), *Trade Unions and Politics in Western Europe* (London: Frank Cass).

Hayward, J., and Watson, M. (eds) (1975), *Planning, Politics and Public Policy: The British, French and Italian Experience* (Cambridge: Cambridge University Press).

Hayward, J. E. S. (1972), 'State intervention in France: the changing style of government–industry relations', *Political Studies*, vol. 40, no. 3, pp. 287–98.

Headey, B. (1970), 'Trade unions and national wage policies', *Journal of Politics*, vol. 32, no. 2 (May), pp. 407–39.

Heclo, H. (1974), *Modern Social Politics in Britain and Sweden* (New Haven, Conn.: Yale University Press).

Hegel, G. W. F. (1967), *Philosophy of Right*, trans. with notes by T. M. Knox (London: Oxford University Press).

Heidenheimer, A. J., Heclo, H., and Adams, C. T. (1975),

Comparative Public Policy: The Politics of Social Choice in Europe and America (New York: St Martin's Press).

Heilbroner, Robert L. (1975), 'Benign neglect in the United States', in H. Safa and G. Levitas (eds), *Social Problems in Corporate America* (New York: Harper & Row), pp. 63–70.

Her Majesty's Stationery Office (1975), *Report of the Royal Commission on Trade Unions and Employers' Associations* (London: HMSO).

Hibbs, D. A. (1977), 'Political parties and macroeconomic policy', *American Political Science Review*, vol. 71, no. 4 (December), pp. 467–87.

Hibbs, D. A. (1978), 'On the political economy of long-run trends in strike activity', *British Journal of Political Science*, vol. 8, no. 2 (April), pp. 153–75.

Hibbs, D. A. (1980), 'On the demand for economic outcomes: macroeconomic performance and mass political support in the United States, Great Britain and Germany', paper presented to American Political Science Association, Washington, DC (August).

Hirsch, F., and Goldthorpe, J. H. (eds) (1978), *The Political Economy of Inflation* (London: Martin Robertson).

Hirsch, H. (1978), 'The state apparatus and social reproduction: elements of a theory of the bourgeois state', in J. Holloway and S. Picciotto (eds), *State and Capital: A Marxist Debate* (London: Arnold), pp. 57–107.

Holland, S. (1976), *Capital versus the Regions* (London: Macmillan).

Holland, S. (ed.) (1978), *Beyond Capitalist Planning* (Oxford: Blackwell).

Holloway, J., and Picciotto, S. (eds) (1978), *State and Capital: A Marxist Debate* (London: Arnold).

Holtzman, Neil A. (1979), 'Prevention: rhetoric and reality', *International Journal of Health Services*, vol. 9, no. 1, pp. 25–39.

Horowitz, Daniel L. (1963), *The Italian Labor Movement* (Cambridge, Mass.: Harvard University Press).

Hudson, R. (1981), 'Capital accumulation and regional problems: a study of North-East England, 1945–80', in F. E. I. Hamilton and G. R. Linge (eds), *Spatial Analysis, Industry and the Industrial Environment*, Vol. 3 (Chichester: Wiley).

Hudson, R., and Lewis, J. R. (eds) (1982), *Regional Planning in Europe* (London: Pion).

Hunt, R. N. (1974), *The Political Ideas of Marx and Engels* (Pittsburgh, Pa.: University of Pittsburgh Press).

Hurd, D. (1979), *An End to Promises* (London: Collins).

Hyman, Richard (1977), 'Marxism and the sociology of trade unionism', in T. Clarke and L. Clements (eds), *Trade Unions under Capitalism* (Glasgow: Collins/Fontana), pp. 383–403.

Hyman, Richard (1978), *Strikes*, 2nd rev. edn (Glasgow: Collins/Fontana).

Illich, Ivan (1976), *Medical Nemesis: The Expropriation of Health* (New York: Random House/Pantheon Books).

International Monetary Fund (1977), *International Monetary Statistics* (Washington, DC: IMF).

Jenkins, P. (1970), *The Battle of Downing Street* (London: Charles Knight).

Jensen-Butler, C. (1980), 'Capital accumulation, regional development and the rôle of the state', *Arbejdsrapport*, no. 9 (Aarhus: Geografisk Institut, Aarhus Universitat).

Jenson, H. T. (1982), 'The rôle of the state in regional development, planning and management', in R. Hudson and J. R. Lewis (eds), *Regional Planning in Europe* (London: Pion).

Jessop, B. (1977), Recent theories of the capitalist state', *Cambridge Journal of Economics*, vol. 1, no. 4 (December), pp. 343–73.

Jessop, B. (1979), 'Corporatism, parliamentarism and social democracy', in P. C. Schmitter and G. Lehmbruch (eds), *Trends toward Corporatist Intermediation* (New York: Sage).

Jones, H. G. (1976), *Planning and Productivity in Sweden* (London: Croom Helm).

Joseph, K. (1974), *Reversing the Trend* (London: Centre for Policy Studies).

Kasper, W. (1972), 'Stabilization policies in a dependent economy: some lessons from the West German experience of the 1960s', in E. Claassen and P. Salin (eds), *Stabilization Policies in Interdependent Economies* (Amsterdam: Elseiser), pp. 270–86.

Kassalow, E. M. (1969), *Trade Unions and Industrial Relations: An International Comparison* (New York: Random House).

Katzenstein, P. J. (1978a), 'Domestic structures and strategies of foreign economic policy', in P. J. Katzenstein (ed.), *Between Power and Plenty* (Madison, Wis.: University of Wisconsin Press), pp. 295–336.

Katzenstein, P. J. (ed.) (1978b), *Between Power and Plenty* (Madison, Wis.: University of Wisconsin Press).

Kaufmann, H. (1969), 'A debate over Germany's revaluation, 1961: a chapter in political economy', *Weltwirtschaftliches Archiv*, vol. 103, no. 2, pp. 181–212.

Keane, J. (1978), 'The legacy of political economy: thinking with and against Claus Offe', *Canadian Journal of Political and Social Theory*, vol. 2, no. 3, pp. 49–92.

Keeble, D. E. (1976), *Industrial Location and Planning in the United Kingdom* (London: Methuen).

Keeble, D. E. (1977), 'Spatial policy in Britain: regional or urban? *Area*, vol. 9, no. 1, pp. 3–8.

Keegan, W., and Pennant-Rae, R. (1979), *Who Runs the Economy?: Control and Influence in British Economic Policy* (London: Temple Smith).

Keohane, R. O. (1978), 'Economics, Inflation and the role of the state', *World Politics*, vol. 3, no. 1 (October), pp. 108–28.

Kindleberger, C. D. (1965), 'Germany's persistent balance-of-payments disequiiibrium', in R. E. Baldwin (ed.), *Trade, Growth and the Balance of Payments* (Chicago, Ill.), pp. 230–48.

King, R., (1975), 'Italy', in H. Clout (ed.), *Regional*

Development in Western Europe (Chichester: Wiley), pp. 81–112.

Kinsey, J. (1978), 'The application of growth pole theory in the Aire Métropolitaine Marseillaise', *Geoforum*, vol. 9, pp. 245–67.

Kipping, N. (1972), *Summing Up* (London: Hutchinson).

Kirschen, E. S. (ed.) (1964), *Economic Policy in Our Time*, 2 vols (Amsterdam: North Welland).

Kirschen, E. S. (ed.) (1975), *Economic Policies Composed*, 2 vols (Amsterdam: Elseiser).

Klein, R. (1977), 'The corporate state, the health service and the professions', *New University Quarterly*, vol. 31, no. 2 (Spring), pp. 161–80.

Klein, R. (1979a), 'Ideology, class and the National Health Service', *Journal of Health Politics, Policy and Law*, vol. 4, no. 3 (Fall), pp. 464–90.

Klein, R. (1979b), 'Living with its disabilities', *British Medical Journal*, vol. 2, no. 6194 (6 October), pp. 848–50.

Klöten, N., Kellerer, H.-H., and Vollmer, R. (1978), 'The political and social factors of Germany's stabilization performance', paper presented to a Brookings Conference on the Politics and Sociology of Global Inflation, Washington, DC (December).

Koff, S. Z. (1975), 'Emergency medical services in crisis – Italian case study', *Milbank Memorial Fund Quarterly, Health and Society*, vol. 53, no. 3 (Summer), pp. 377–401.

Koff, S. Z. (1978), 'Regionalization and hospital reform in Italy', paper delivered at Annual Meeting of Northeastern Political Science Association, Tarrytown, NY (10–11 November).

Kofman, E. (1981), 'Functional regionalism and alternative regional development programmes in Corsica', *Regional Studies*, vol. 15, no. 3, pp. 173–82.

Korpi, W. (1978), *The Working Class in Welfare Capitalism: Work, Unions and Politics in Sweden* (London: Routledge & Kegan Paul).

Korpi, W. (1980a), 'Industrial relations and industrial conflict: the case of Sweden', in B. Martin and E. M. Kassalow (eds), *Labor Relations in Advanced Industrial Societies: Issues and Problems* (New York: Carnegie Endowment for International Peace), pp. 89–108.

Korpi, W. (1980b), 'Social policy strategies and distributional conflict in capitalist democracies', *West European Politics*, vol. 3, no. 3 (October), pp. 296–316.

Krasner, S. (1979), *Defending the National Interest* (Princeton, NJ: Princeton University Press).

Krause, L. B., and Salant, W. S. (eds) (1977), *Worldwide Inflation* (Washington, DC: Brookings Institution).

Kreile, M. (1978), 'West Germany: the dynamics of expansion', in P. J. Katzenstein (ed.), *Between Power and Plenty* (Madison, Wis.: University of Wisconsin Press), pp. 191–224.

Krieger, J., and Amott, T. (1982), 'Thatcher and Reagan: state theory and the "hyper-capitalist" regime', *New Political Science*, Spring 1982, no. 8, pp. 9–38.

Kuklinski, A. R. (ed.) (1975), *Regional Development and Planning: International Perspectives* (Rockville, Md.: Sijthhoff & Noordhoff).

Kumar, K. (1976), 'Revolution and industrial society: an historical perspective', *Sociology*, vol. 10, no. 2, pp. 245–69.

Küster, G. H. (1974), 'Germany', in R. Vernon (ed.), *Big Business and the State* (Cambridge, Mass.: Harvard University Press), pp. 64–89.

Lange, P. (1980), 'Neo-corporatism in Italy?: a case in European perspective', discussion paper prepared for Workshop on Neo-Corporatism and Public Policy, sponsored and organised by Western Societies Program and Center for International Studies, Cornell University, Ithaca, NY (3–5 April).

Lange, P., and Ross, G. (1982), 'Conclusions: French and Italian union development in comparative perspective', in P. Lange, G. Ross and M. Vannicelli, *Unions, Change and Crisis: French and Italian Union Strategy and the Political Economy, 1945–1980* (London: George Allen & Unwin), pp. 207–91.

Lange, P., Ross, G., and Vannicelli, M. (1982), *Unions, Change and Crisis: French and Italian Union Strategy and the Political Economy, 1945–1980* (London: George Allen & Unwin).

Lange, P., and Tarrow, S. (eds) (1980), *Italy in Transition: Conflict and Consensus* (London: Frank Cass).

Lange, P., and Vannicelli, M. (1982), 'Strategy under stress: the Italian union movement and the Italian crisis in developmental perspective', in P. Lange, G. Ross and M. Vannicelli, *Unions, Change and Crisis: French and Italian Union Strategy and the Political Economy, 1945–1980* (London: Allen & Unwin), pp. 93–206.

Langendonck, J. van (1972), 'Social health insurance in the six countries of the European Economic Community', *International Journal of Health Services*, vol. 2, no. 4 (November), pp. 491–502.

Lapple, D., and Hoogstraten, P. van (1980), 'Remarks on the spatial structure of capitalist development: the case of the Netherlands', in J. G. Carney, R. Hudson and J. R. Lewis (eds), *Regions in Crisis* (London: Croom Helm), pp. 117–66.

Lehmbruch, G. (1979a), 'Consociational democracy, class conflict, and the new corporatism', in P. C. Schmitter and G. Lehmbruch (eds), *Trends toward Corporatist Intermediation* (New York: Sage), pp. 53–61.

Lehmbruch, G. (1979b), 'Liberal corporatism and party government', in P. C. Schmitter and G. Lehmbruch (eds), *Trends toward Corporatist Intermediation* (New York: Sage), pp. 147–83.

Lenin, V. I. (1971), *State and Revolution* (New York: International).

Leruez, J. (1975), *Economic Planning and Politics in Britain* (London: Martin Robertson).

Lever, H., and Edwards, G. (1980), 'Why Germany beats Britain', *Sunday Times* (2 November), pp. 16–17.

Levitt, Ruth (1977), *The Reorganized National Health Service*, 2nd edn (London: Croom Helm).

Levy, J., and Scheibling, H. (1978), 'Régions: ici l'on casse', *Economie et politique*, vol. 9, no. 282, pp. 67–72.

Lewin, M. (1975), *Lenin's Last Struggle* (London: Pluto).

Lewis, J. R., and Williams, A. M. (1981), 'Regional uneven development on the European periphery: the case of Portugal, 1950–79', *Tijdschrift voor Economische en Sociale Geografie*, vol. 72, no. 2, pp. 81–98.

Lieberman, S. (1977), *The Growth of European Mixed Economies, 1945–70* (New York: Wiley).

Lijphart, Arend (1969), 'Consociational democracy', *World Politics*, vol. 31, no. 2 (January), pp. 207–25.

Lindberg, L., Alford, R. R., Crouch, C., and Offe, C. (eds) (1975), *Stress and Contradiction in Modern Capitalism* (Lexington, Mass.: Lexington).

Lindblom, C. E. (1977), *Politics and Markets* (New York: Basic Books).

Lipietz, A. (1980a), 'The structuration of space, the problem of land, and spatial policy', in J. G. Carney, R. Hudson and J. R. Lewis (eds), *Regions in Crisis* (London: Croom Helm), pp. 60–75.

Lipietz, A. (1980b), 'Inter-regional polarisation and the tertiarisation of society', *Papers of the Regional Science Association*, vol. 44.

Lipset, S. M. (1964), 'The changing class structure and contemporary European politics', *Daedalus*, vol. 93, no. 1 (Winter), pp. 271–303.

Logue, John A. (1980), 'Democracy inside the factory gate: the drive for industrial and economic democracy in Denmark and Sweden', paper presented to Society for the Advancement of Scandinavian Studies, Ann Arbor, Mich. (2–3 May).

Longstreth, F. (1979), 'The city, industry and the state', in C. Crouch (ed.), *State and Economy in Contemporary Capitalism* (London: Croom Helm), pp. 157–90.

Lorwin, V. R. (1954), *The French Labor Movement* (Cambridge, Mass.: Harvard University Press).

Lukes, S. (1974), *Power: A Radical View* (London: Macmillan).

Lukes, S. (1977), *Essays on Social Theory* (London: Macmillan).

McArthur, J. H., and Scott, B. R. (1969), *Industrial Planning in France* (Cambridge, Mass.: Harvard University Press).

Maccacaro, G. A. (1981), *Per una Medicina de Rinnovare*, 2nd edn (Milan: Feltrinelli).

McCracken, Paul, *et al.* (1977), *Towards Full Employment and Price Stability* (Paris: Organisation for Economic Co-operation and Development).

McCrone, G. (1969), *Regional Policy in Britain* (London: Allen & Unwin).

Mack, E. C. (1938), *Public Schools and British Opinion, 1780–1860* (London: Methuen).

Mack, E. C. (1971), *Public Schools and British Opinion since 1860* (Westport, Conn.: Greenwood Press).

MacLennan, M., Forsyth, M., and Denton, G. (1968), *Economic Planning and Policies in Britain, France and Germany* (New York: Praeger).

Macpherson, C. B. (1966), *The Real World of Democracy* (New York: Oxford University Press).

McRae, Kenneth D. (1974), *Consociational Democracy: Political Accommodation in Segmented Societies* (Toronto: McClelland & Stewart).

Maguire, J. (1978), *Marx's Theory of Politics* (Cambridge: Cambridge University Press).

Maier, Charles (1975), *Recasting Bourgeois Europe* (Princeton, NJ: Princeton University Press).

Maier, Charles (1978), 'The politics of inflation in the twentieth century', in F. Hirsch and J. H. Goldthorpe (eds), *The Political Economy of Inflation* (London: Martin Robertson), pp. 37–72.

Maller, P. (1973), *The Institutions of Industrial Relations in Continental Europe* (Ottawa: Information Canada).

Mandel, E. (1976), *Late Capitalism* (London: New Left Books).

Maravall, J. (1978), *Dictatorship and Political Dissent: Workers and Students in Franco's Spain* (London: Tavistock).

Markovits, A., and Allen, C. (1979), 'Strike divides German labor', *Democratic Left*, vol. 7, no. 5 (May), pp. 9–11.

Markovits, A., and Allen, C. (1980), 'Power and dissent: the trade unions in the Federal Republic of Germany re-examined', in J. Hayward (ed.), *Trade Unions and Politics in Western Europe* (London: Frank Cass), pp. 68–86.

Markovits, A., and Allen, C. (1984), 'The West German case', in G. Ross, A. Martin, P. Gourevitch, S. Bornstein, A. Markovits and C. Allen (eds), *Unions and Economic Crisis: Britain, West Germany and Sweden* (London: George Allen & Unwin).

Markovits, A., and Ertman, T. (1982), *The West German Trade Unions since World War II: Structural Challenges and Strategic Responses* (Cambridge, Mass.: OG & H).

Marsh, D., and Grant, W. (1977), 'Tripartism: reality or myth?' *Government and Opposition*, vol. 12, no. 2 (Spring), pp. 194–211.

Marshall, T. H. (1975), *Social Policy in the Twentieth Century*, 4th rev. edn (London: Hutchinson).

Martin, A. (1975), 'Is democratic control of capitalist economies possible?' in L. Lindberg, R. R. Alford, C. Crouch and C. Offe (eds), *Stress and Contradiction in Modern Capitalism* (Lexington, Mass.: Lexington Books).

Martin, A. (1979), 'The dynamics of change in a Keynesian political economy: the Swedish case and its implications', in C. Crouch (ed.), *State and Economy in Contemporary Capitalism* (London: Croom Helm), pp. 86–121.

Martin, A. (1984), 'The Swedish case', in G. Ross, A. Martin, P. Gourevitch, S. Bornstein, A. Markovits and C. Allen (eds), *Unions and Economic Crisis: Britain, West Germany and Sweden* (London: George Allen & Unwin).

Martin, A., and Ross, G. (1980), 'European trade unions

and the economic crisis: perceptions and strategies', in J. Hayward (ed.), *Trade Unions and Politics in Western Europe* (London: Frank Cass), pp. 33–67.

Martin, B., and Kassalow, E. M. (eds) (1980), *Labour Relations in Advanced Industrial Society: Issues and Problems* (New York: Carnegie Endowment for Industrial Peace).

Martin, R. (1978), 'The effects of recent changes in industrial conflict on the internal politics of trade unions: Britain and Germany', in C. Crouch and A. Pizzorno (eds), *The Resurgence of Class Conflict in Western Europe since 1968* (New York: Holmes & Meier), pp. 101–26.

Marx, K. (1963), *The Eighteenth Brumaire of Louis Bonaparte* (New York: International).

Marx, K. (1970a), *The Critique of the Gotha Program* (New York: International).

Marx, K. (1970b), *The Critique of Hegel's Philosophy of Right* (Cambridge: Cambridge University Press).

Marx, K., and Engels, F. (1948), *The Communist Manifesto* (New York: International).

Massey, D. B. (1979) 'In what sense a regional problem? *Regional Studies*, vol. 13, no. 2, pp. 234–43.

Massey, D. B., and Batey, P. W. J. (eds) (1977), *Alternative Frameworks for Analysis* (London: Pion).

Matthews, H. C. G., McKibbin, R. I., and Ray, J. A. (1976), 'The franchise factor in the rise of the Labour Party', *English Historical Review*, vol. 91, no. 361 (October), pp. 723–52.

May, Timothy C. (1975), *Trade Unions and Pressure Group Politics* (Lexington, Mass.: Lexington Books).

Mayntz, R., and Scharpf, F. W. (1975), *Policy-Making in the German Federal Bureaucracy* (Amsterdam: Elseiser).

Medley, R. (1981), 'Monetary stability and industrial adaptation in Germany', paper prepared for the United States Congress, Joint Economic Committee (June).

Meidner, R. (1978), *Employee Investment Funds: An Approach to Collective Capital Formation* (London: Allen & Unwin).

Memorandum by the Royal College of General Practitioners (1977). Appendix 9 of First Report from the Expenditure Committee. *Preventive Medicine, Vol. III.* House of Commons (London: Her Majesty's Stationery Office).

Michalet, C. A. (1974), 'France', in R. Vernon (ed.), *Big Business and the State* (Cambridge, Mass.: Harvard University Press), pp. 105–27.

Michalski, W. (1972), *Export Trade and Economic Growth* (Hamburg: Verlag Weltarchiv Gmblt).

Middlemas, K. (1979), *Politics in Industrial Society* (London: Deutsch).

Miliband, Ralph (1965), 'Marx and the state', in Ralph Miliband and J. Saville (eds), *The Socialist Register 1965* (London: Merlin).

Miliband, Ralph (1969a), *The State in Capitalist Society* (London: Weidenfeld & Nicolson).

Miliband, Ralph (1969b), *The State in Capitalist Society* (New York: Basic Books).

Miliband, Ralph (1972a), *Parliamentary Socialism*, 2nd edn (London: Merlin).

Miliband, Ralph (1972b), 'The capitalist state – reply to Nicos Poulantzas', in R. M. Blackburn (ed.), *Ideology in Social Science: Readings in Critical Social Theory* (London: Fontana).

Miliband, Ralph (1977), *Marxism and Politics* (Oxford: Oxford University Press).

Miliband, Ralph, and Saville, J. (eds) (1965), *The Socialist Register 1965* (London: Merlin).

Miliband, Ralph, and Saville, J. (eds) (1979), *The Socialist Register 1979* (London: Merlin).

Ministère de l'Industrie (1979), *Les Moyens de politique industrielle* (Paris: Ministère de l'Industrie); mimeo.

Minkin, Lewis (1978), 'The party connection: divergence and convergence in the British Labour movement', *Government and Opposition*, vol. 4, no. 1 (Autumn), pp. 458–84.

Minnerup, G. (1976), 'West Germany since the war', *New Left Review*, vol. 99 (September–October), pp. 3–46.

Mommsen, W. J. (1974), *The Age of Bureaucracy* (Oxford: Blackwell).

Monnet, J. (1976), *Mémoires* (Paris: Fayard).

Moran, Michael (1977), *The Politics of Industrial Relations* (London: Macmillan).

Morin, F. (1974), *La Structure financière du capitalisme français* (Paris: Calmann-Lévy).

Mormiche, P. (1979), 'Chômage et qualification dans les régions', *Economie et statistique*, no. 110 (April), pp. 23–4.

Mulkay, Michael J. (1979), *Science and the Sociology of Knowledge* (London: Allen & Unwin).

Müller-Jentsch, W., and Sperling, H.-J. (1978), 'Economic development, labor conflicts and the industrial relations system in West Germany', in C. Crouch and A. Pizzorno (eds), *The Resurgence of Class Conflict in Western Europe since 1968*, Vol. 1 (New York: Holmes & Meier), pp. 257–306.

Musgrave, P. W. (1967), *Technical Change, the Labour Force and Education: A Study of the British and German Iron and Steel Industries* (Oxford: Pergamon).

Nagel, J. H. (1975), *The Descriptive Analysis of Power* (New Haven, Conn.: Yale University Press).

Nairn, T. (1977), *The Break-Up of Britain* (London: New Left Books).

National Institute of Health (1979), *Proceedings of the Conference on the Decline in Coronary Heart Disease Mortality*, NIH Publication No. 79-1619 (May).

Navarro, V. (1978), *Class Struggle, the State and Medicine: An Historical and Contemporary Analysis of the Medical Sector in Great Britain* (London: Martin Robertson).

Nizard, L. (1975), 'Planning as the regulatory reproduction of the status quo', in J. Hayward and M. Watson (eds), *Planning, Politics and Public Policy: The British, French and Italian Experience* (Cambridge: Cambridge University Press), pp. 433–44.

Noble, David (1980), 'Cost–benefit analysis', *Health/Pac Bulletin*, vol. 11, no. 6 (July–August), pp. 1–2, 7–12, 27–40.

Nocifora, E. (1978), 'Poles of development and the southern question', *International Journal of Urban and Regional Research*, vol. 2, no. 2 (June), pp. 361–87.

O'Connor, J. (1973), *The Fiscal Crisis of the State* (New York: St Martin's Press).

OECD, *see* Organisation for Economic Co-operation and Development.

Offe, C. (1972), 'Political authority and class structure', *International Journal of Sociology*, vol. 2, no. 1.

Offe, C. (1974), 'Structural problems of the capitalist state', *German Political Studies*, no. 1, pp. 31–58.

Offe, C. (1975a), 'The theory of the capitalist state and the problem of policy formation', in L. Lindberg, R. R. Alford, C. Crouch and C. Offe (eds), *Stress and Contradiction in Modern Capitalism* (Lexington, Mass.: Lexington Books).

Offe, C. (1975b), 'Introduction to Part II', in L. Lindberg, R. R. Alford, C. Crouch and C. Offe (eds), *Stress and Contradiction in Modern Capitalism* (Lexington, Mass.: Lexington Books), pp. 245–59.

Offe, C. (1976), *Industry and Inequality* (London: Arnold).

Offe, C. (1979), 'The state, ungovernability and the search for the "non-political" ', paper presented to Conference on the Individual and the State, Center for International Studies, University of Toronto (3 February).

Offe, C., and Ronge, V. (1975), 'Theses on the theory of the state', *New German Critique*, vol. 2, no. 3 (Fall).

O'Flanagan, S. (1979), 'Growth poles, regional growth areas and regional planning in Galicia, Spain', *Tidjschrift voor Economische en Sociale Geografie*, vol. 70, no. 4, pp. 217–25.

Olsen, M. (1971), *The Logic of Collective Action* (Cambridge, Mass.: Harvard University Press).

Organisation for Economic Co-operation and Development (1973), *Monetary Policy in Germany* (Paris: OECD).

Organisation for Economic Co-operation and Development (1974), *Monetary Policy in France* (Paris: OECD).

Organisation for Economic Co-operation and Development (1977), *Towards Full Employment and Price Stability* (Paris: OECD).

Organisation for Economic Co-operation and Development (1978), *Regional Problems and Policies in Portugal* (Paris: OECD).

Organisation for Economic Co-operation and Development (1979a), *Collective Bargaining and Government Policies in 10 OECD Countries* (Paris: OECD).

Organisation for Economic Co-operation and Development (1979b), *Collective Bargaining and Government Policies* (Paris: OECD).

Organisation for Economic Co-operation and Development (1979c), *Incomes Policy in Theory and Practice* (Paris: OECD).

Otter, Caster van (1975), 'Sweden: labour reformism shapes the system', in S. Barkin (ed.), *Worker Militancy and Its Consequences* (New York: Praeger), pp. 194–234.

Pahl, R. E., and Winkier, J. T. (1974), 'The coming corporatism', *New Society*, vol. 30, no. 627 (10 October).

Paine, S. H. (1979), 'Replacement of the West European migrant labour system by investment in the European periphery', in D. Seers, B. Schaffer and M.-L. Kiljunen (eds), *Under-Developed Europe* (Hassocks: Harvester), pp. 65–96.

Panitch, L. (1976), *Social Democracy and Industrial Militancy: The Labour Party, the Trade Unions and Incomes Policy, 1945–1974* (Cambridge: Cambridge University Press).

Panitch, L. (1977), 'The development of corporatism in liberal democracies', *Comparative Political Studies*, vol. 10, no. 1 (April), pp. 61–90.

Panitch, L. (1981), 'Trade unions and the capitalist state: corporatism and its contradictions', *New Left Review*, no. 125 (January–February), pp. 21–43.

Parkin, F. (1972), 'System contradiction and political transformation', *European Journal of Sociology*, vol. 12, no. 1.

Pateman, C. (1970), *Participation and Democratic Theory* (Cambridge: Cambridge University Press).

Peacock, A., et al. (1980), *Structural Economic Policies in West Germany and the United Kingdom* (London: Anglo-German Foundation).

Peaker, A. (1974), *Economic Growth in Modern Britain* (London: Macmillan).

Perez-Diaz, M. (1978), *State, Bureaucracy and Civil Society* (London: Macmillan).

Pickvance, C. G. (1981), 'Policies as chameleons: an interpretation of regional policy and office policy in Britain', in M. Dear and A. J. Scott (eds), *Urbanization and Urban Planning in Capitalist Society* (London: Methuen), pp. 231–66.

Piperno, A., and Renieri, A. (1983), 'Profile of general practice in a period of transformation: the case of Italy', *Health and Society* (in press).

Piven, Frances Fox, and Cloward, Richard A. (1971), *Regulating the Poor: The Functions of Public Welfare* (New York: Random House/Vintage Books).

Pizzorno, A. (1971), 'Les syndicats et l'action politique', *Sociologie du travail*, no. 2 (April–June), pp. 115–40.

Pizzorno, A. (1978), 'Political exchange and collective identity in industrial conflict', in C. Crouch and A. Pizzorno (eds), *The Resurgence of Class Conflict in Western Europe since 1968*, Vol. 2 (New York: Holmes & Meier), pp. 277–97.

Pollard, S. (1969), *The Development of the British Economy, 1914–67*, 2nd edn (New York: St Martin's Press).

Poulantzas, Nicos (1969), 'The problem of the capitalist state', *New Left Review*, no. 58 (November–December), pp. 67–78.

Poulantzas, Nicos (1972), 'The problem of the capitalist state', in R. M. Blackburn (ed.), *Ideology in Social Science: Readings in Critical Social Theory* (London: Fontana).

Poulantzas, Nicos (1973), *Political Power and Social Classes* (London: New Left Books).

Poulantzas, Nicos (1975), *Classes in Contemporary Capitalism* (London: New Left Books).

Poulantzas, Nicos (1978a), *State, Power, Socialism* (London: New Left Books).

Poulantzas, Nicos (1978b), *Political Power and Social Classes* (London: Verso).

Poulantzas, Nicos (1980), *State, Power, Socialism* (London: Verso/New Left Books).

Preston, P. (ed.) (1976), *Spain in Crisis* (Hassocks: Harvester).

Przeworski, A., and Wallerstein, M. (1980), 'The structure of class conflict in advanced capitalist societies', paper presented to American Political Science Association, Washington, DC (August).

Quere, L. (1978), *Jeux interdits à la frontière* (Paris: Edition Anthropos).

Rapport sur les principales options du VIIIe Plan (1979) (Paris: Documentation Française).

Regalia, I., Regini, M., and Reyneri, E. (1978), 'Labour conflicts and industrial relations in Italy', in C. Crouch and A. Pizzorno (eds), *The Resurgence of Class Conflict in Western Europe since 1968*, Vol. 1 (New York: Holmes & Meier), pp. 101–58.

Regini, M. (1980), 'Labor unions, industrial action and politics', in P. Lange and S. Tarrow (eds), *Italy in Transition: Conflict and Consensus* (London: Frank Cass), pp. 49–66.

Regini, M., and Esping-Andersen, G. (1980), 'Trade union strategies and social policy in Italy and Sweden', in J. Hayward (ed.), *Trade Unions and Politics in Western Europe* (London: Frank Cass), pp. 107–23.

Regini, M., and Regonini, G. (1980), 'The politics of pensions in Italy: the role of labor', paper for 2nd Conference of Europeanists, sponsored by Council for European Studies, Washington, DC (23–5 October).

Renaud, Marc (1975), 'On the structural constraints to state intervention in health', *International Journal of Health Services*, vol. 5, no. 4 (Fall), pp. 559–70.

Reverby, S., and Rosner, D. (eds) (1979), *Health Care in America* (Philadelphia, Pa.: Temple University Press).

Reynaud, J.-D. (1980), 'Industrial relations and political systems: some reflections on the crisis of industrial relations in Western Europe', *British Journal of Industrial Relations*, vol. 18, no. 1 (March).

Richardson, H. W. (1978), *Regional and Urban Economics* (Harmondsworth: Penguin).

Richardson, H. W., and Rodrigues, F. F. (1975), 'Regional development in Spain: trends, policies and planning', in A. R. Kuklinski (ed.), *Regional Development and Planning: International Perspectives* (Rockville, Md.: Sijthhoff & Noordhoff), pp. 69–89.

Richter, M. (1964), *The Politics of Conscience: T. H. Green and His Age* (London: Weidenfeld & Nicolson).

Rimlinger, Gaston V. (1971), *Welfare Policy and Industrialization in Europe, America, and Russia* (New York: Wiley).

Ringer, F. K. (1969), *The Decline of the German Mandarins: The German Academic Community, 1890–1933* (Cambridge, Mass.: Harvard University Press).

Ringer, F. K. (1979), *Education and Society in Modern Europe* (Bloomington, Ind.: Indiana University Press).

Roberts, C. C. (1979), 'Economic theory and policy-making in West Germany', *Cambridge Journal of Economics*, vol. 3, no. 1 (March), pp. 83–9.

Robinson, J. F. F., and Storey, D. J. (1981), 'Employment change in manufacturing industry, Cleveland, 1965–76', *Regional Studies*, vol. 15, no. 3, pp. 161–72.

Robson, John (1973), 'The NHS Company, Inc.? The social consequences of the professional dominance in the National Health Service', *International Journal of Health Services*, vol. 3, no. 3 (Summer), pp. 413–26.

Rodberg, Leonard, and Stevenson, Galvin (1977), 'The health care industry in advanced capitalism', *Review of Radical Political Economics*, vol. 9, no. 1 (Spring), pp. 104–15.

Roemer, Milton I. (1977), *Comparative National Policies on Health Care* (New York/Basel: Marcel Dekker).

Rogow, A. A. (1955), *The Labour Government and British Industry, 1945–51* (Oxford: Blackwell).

Romus, P. (1979), *L'Europe et les régions* (Brussels: Ed. Labor).

Ronzani, S. (1980), 'Regional incentives in Italy', in D. Yuill, K. Allen and C. Hull (eds), *Regional Policy in the European Community* (London: Croom Helm), pp. 134–56.

Rosenberg, C. F. (1979), 'The therapeutic revolution: medicine, meaning and social change in nineteenth-century America', in C. F. Rosenberg and M. H. Vogel (eds), *The Therapeutic Revolution: Essays in the Social History of American Medicine* (Philadelphia, Pa.: University of Pennsylvania Press), pp. 3–25.

Rosenberg, C. F., and Vogel, M. H. (eds) (1979), *The Therapeutic Revolution: Essays in the Social History of American Medicine* (Philadelphia, Pa.: University of Pennsylvania Press).

Ross, G. (1980), 'Gaullism and organized labor: two decades of failure', in W. G. Andrews and S. Hoffman (eds), *The Fifth Republic at Twenty* (Albany, NY: State University of New York Press), pp. 330–47.

Ross, G. (1982), 'The perils of politics: French unions and the crisis of the 1970s', in P. Lange, G. Ross and M. Vannicelli, *Unions, Change and Crisis: French and Italian Union Strategy and the Political Economy, 1945–1980* (London: George Allen & Unwin), pp. 14–93.

Ross, G., and Cohen, S. S. (1975), 'The politics of French regional planning', in J. Friedmann and W. Alonso (eds), *Regional Policy* (Cambridge, Mass.: MIT), pp. 726–50.

Ross, G., Martin, A., Gourevitch, P., Bornstein, S., Markovits, A., and Allen, C. (eds) (1984), *Unions and Economic Crisis: Britain, West Germany and Sweden* (London: George Allen & Unwin).

Rothblatt, S. (1968), *The Revolution of the Dons* (London: Faber).

Royal Commission on the National Health Service (1979), report presented to Parliament, July 1979 (London: Her Majesty's Stationery Office).

Rubenstein, W. D. (1977), 'Wealth, elites and the class structure of modern Britain', *Past and Present*, no. 76 (August), pp. 99–126.

Ryan, M. (1977), 'The Royal Commission on the National Health Service – origins and prospect', *Social and Economic Administration*, vol. 11, no. 3 (Autumn), pp. 194–205.

Sachs, J. D. (1979), 'Wages, profits and macroeconomic adjustment: a comparative study', *Brookings Papers on Economic Activity*, no. 2, pp. 269–319.

Sacks, P. M. (1980), 'State structure and the asymmetrical society', *Comparative Politics*, vol. 12, no. 3 (April), pp. 349–76.

Safa, H., and Levitas, G. (eds) (1975), *Social Problems in Corporate America* (New York: Harper & Row).

Salin, P., and Lane, G. (1977), 'Inflation in France, in L. B. Krause and W. S. Salant (eds), *Worldwide Inflation* (Washington, DC: Brookings Institution), pp. 545–88.

Salmon, J. W., and Berliner, H. S. (1979), 'Can the holistic health movement turn left?' paper presented to Annual Meeting of American Public Health Association, New York (7 November).

Salvati, M. (1980), 'Muddling through: economics and politics in Italy, 1969–79', in P. Lange and S. Tarrow (eds), *Italy in Transition: Conflict and Consensus* (London: Frank Cass), pp. 31–48.

Salvati, M., and Brosio, G. (1979), 'The rise of market politics: industrial relations in the seventies', *Daedalus*, vol. 108, no. 2 (Winter), pp. 43–71.

Saracci, R., and Donato, L. (1973), 'Medical education, care and research in Italy', in *Medical Research Systems in Europe*, a joint Wellcome Trust-Ciba Foundation symposium (New York: Associated Scientific Publishers), pp. 131–42.

Sawyer, Michael (1976), *Income Distribution in OECD Countries* (Paris: Organisation for Economic Co-operation and Development).

Scase, Richard (ed.) (1977), *Industrial Society: Class, Cleavage and Control* (New York: St Martin's Press).

Scase, Richard (ed.) (1980a), *The State in Western Europe* (London: Croom Helm).

Scase, Richard (1980b), 'Introduction', in his *The State in Western Europe* (London: Croom Helm).

Schain, M. A. (1980), 'Corporatism and industrial relations in France', in P. G. Cerny and M. A. Schain (eds), *French Politics and Public Policy* (New York: St Martin's Press), pp. 191–217.

Schattschneider, E. F. (1960), *The Semi-Sovereign People: A Realist's View of Democracy in America* (New York: Rinehart & Winston).

Schmitter, P. C. (1974), 'Still the century of corporatism?' *Review of Politics*, vol. 36, no. 1 (January), pp. 85–131.

Schmitter, P. C. (1979), 'Modes of interest intermediation and models of societal change in Western Europe', *Comparative Political Studies*, vol. 10, no. 1 (April), pp. 61–90.

Schmitter, P. C., and Lehmbruch, G. (eds) (1979), *Trends toward Corporatist Intermediation* (New York: Sage).

Schnitzler, M. (1972), *East and West Germany: A Comparative Economic Analysis* (New York: Praeger).

Scott, J. (1979), *Corporations, Classes and Capitalism* (London: Hutchinson).

Scoville, J. G. (1973), 'Some determinants of the structure of labor movements', in A. Sturmthal and J. G. Scoville (eds), *The International Labor Movement in Transition* (Urbana, Ill.: University of Illinois Press), pp. 38–77.

Secchi, B. (1977), 'Central and peripheral regions in a process of economic development: the Italian case', in D. B. Massey and P. W. J. Batey (eds), *Alternative Frameworks for Analysis* (London: Pion), pp. 36–51.

Seers, D., Schaffer, B., and Kiljunen, M.-L. (eds) (1979), *Under-Developed Europe* (Hassocks: Harvester).

Select Committee on Nationalized Industries (1969–70), *First Report*, Vol. 4, House of Commons.

Sellier, François (1973), 'The French workers' movement and political unionism', in A. Sturmthal and J. G. Scoville (eds), *The International Labor Movement in Transition* (Urbana, Ill.: University of Illinois Press), pp. 79–100.

Shalev, Michael (1980), 'Industrial relations theory and the comparative study of industrial relations and industrial conflict', *British Journal of Industrial Relations*, vol. 18, no. 1 (March), pp. 26–43.

Shanks, M. (1977), *Planning and Politics* (London: Allen & Unwin).

Shils, E. (1955), 'British intellectuals in the mid-twentieth century', *Encounter* (April), pp. 1–12.

Shonfield, A. (1965), *Modern Capitalism: The Changing Balance of Public and Private Power* (London: Oxford University Press).

Shonfield, A. (1969), *Modern Capitalism* (Cambridge: Cambridge University Press).

Skidelsky, Robert (1979), 'The decline of Keynesian politics', in C. Crouch (ed.), *State and Economy in Contemporary Capitalism* (London: Croom Helm), pp. 55–87.

Smith, T. (1975), 'Britain', in J. Hayward and M. Watson (eds), *Planning, Politics and Public Policy: The British, French and Italian Experience* (Cambridge: Cambridge University Press), pp. 52–69.

Smith, W. R. (1981), 'Paradoxes of plural unionism: CGT–CFDT relations in France', *West European Politics*, vol. 4, no. 1 (January), pp. 38–53.

Sokolowoka, M., Sokolowoka, J., and Ostrowska, A. (eds), *Health, Medicine, Society: Proceedings of the International Conference on the Sociology of Medicine* (New York: Reidel).

Soskice, D. (1978), 'Strike waves and wage explosions, 1968–1970: an economic interpretation', in C. Crouch and A. Pizzorno (eds), *The Resurgence of Class Conflict in*

Western Europe since 1968, Vol. 2 (New York: Holmes & Meier), pp. 221–46.

Spencer, M. E. (1979), 'Marx on the state', *Theory and Society*, vol. 7, nos 1–2 (January–March), pp. 167–98.

Stephens, John D. (1979), *The Transition from Capitalism to Socialism* (London: Macmillan).

Stevens, A. (1980), 'The higher civil service and economic policy-making', in P. G. Cerny and M. A. Schain (eds), *French Politics and Public Policy* (New York: St Martin's Press), pp. 79–100.

Stewart, M. (1978), *Politics and Economic Policy in the UK since 1964: The Jekyll and Hyde Years* (Oxford: Pergamon).

Stoffaes, C. (1979), *La Grande Menace industrielle* (Paris: Calmann-Lévy).

Stoléru, L. (1969), *L'Impératif industrielle* (Paris: Seuil).

Srande-Sørensen, G. (1980), 'Regional incentives in Denmark', in D. Yuill, K. Allen and C. Hull (eds), *Regional Policy in the European Community* (London: Croom Helm), pp. 35–51.

Strinati, D. (1979), 'Capitalism, the state and industrial relations', in C. Crouch (ed.), *State and Economy in Contemporary Capitalism* (London: Croom Helm), pp. 191–236.

Sturmthal, A., and Scoville, J. G. (1973), *The International Labor Movement in Transition* (Urbana, Ill.: University of Illinois Press).

Suleiman, E. N. (1978), *Elites in French Society* (Princeton, NJ: Princeton University Press).

Suleiman, E. N. (1980), 'Administrative reform and the problem of decentralization in the Fifth Republic', in W. G. Andrews and S. Hoffman (eds), *The Fifth Republic at Twenty* (Albany, NY: State University of New York Press).

Tarling, Roger, and Wilkinson, Frank (1977), 'The Social Contract: post-war incomes policies and their inflationary impact', *Cambridge Journal of Economics*, no. 1 (March), pp. 395–414.

Taylor, R. (1978), *Labour and the Social Contract*, Fabian Tract 458 (London: Fabian Society).

Taylor, R. (1980), *The Fifth Estate* (London: Pan).

Taylor, Rosemary C. R. (1980), 'The politics of prevention: science, ideology and reform in contemporary American health care', paper presented to Annual Meeting of Society for the Study of Social Problems, New York (August).

Taylor, Rosemary C. R., and Mattes, Sara (1980), 'Women's health and women's magazines', paper presented at 108th Meeting of American Public Health Association, Detroit, Mich. (19–23 October).

Terranova, F. (1979), 'Health services and the state: a few thoughts about the situation in Italy today', paper presented at 2nd Conference of International Group for the Advanced Study of the Political Economy of Health, Arricia (July).

Thompson, G. (1977), 'The relationship between the financial and industrial sectors in the United Kingdom economy', *Economy and Society*, vol. 6, no. 3 (August), pp. 235–83.

Townsend, A. R. (1981), 'Geographical perspectives on major job losses in the UK, 1977–80', *Area*, vol. 13, no. 1, pp. 31–8.

Truman, D. B. (1951), *The Governmental Process* (New York: Knopf).

Tsoukalis, L. (1981), *The European Community and Its Mediterranean Enlargement* (London: Allen & Unwin).

Tufte, E. (1979), *Political Control of the Economy* (Princeton, NJ: Princeton University Press).

Turner, H. A., and Wilkinson, F. (1972), *Do Trade Unions Cause Inflation?* (Cambridge: Cambridge University Press).

Ullmo, Y. (1975), 'France', in J. Hayward and M. Watson (eds), *Planning, Politics and Public Policy: The British, French and Italian Experience* (Cambridge: Cambridge University Press), pp. 22–51.

Unit for the Study of Health Policy (1979), *Rethinking Community Medicine: A Report from a Study Group towards a Renaissance in Public Health?* (London: USHP).

United States Department of Health, Education and Welfare, Public Health Service (1979), *Healthy People: The Surgeon General's Report on Health Promotion and Disease Prevention* (Washington, DC: United States Government Printing Office).

Valance, C. (1978), 'Le retour au libéralisme', *L'Express* (24 April), p. 50.

Vernon, R. (ed.) (1974), *Big Business and the State* (Cambridge, Mass.: Harvard University Press).

Vogel, F. (1973), *German Business after the Economic Miracle* (London: Macmillan).

Von der Muhll, G. (1977), 'Robert A. Dahl and the study of contemporary democracy: a review essay', *American Political Science Review*, vol. 71, no. 3 (September), pp. 1070–96.

Voogd, H. (1982), 'Issues and tendencies in Dutch regional planning', in R. Hudson and J. R. Lewis (eds), *Regional Planning in Europe* (London: Pion).

Wadbrook, W. P. (1972), *West German Balance of Payments Policy* (New York: Praeger).

Warnecke, S. J., and Suleiman, E. N. (eds) (1975), *Industrial Policies in Western Europe* (New York: Praeger).

Watkin, B. (1978), *The National Health Service: The First Phase, 1948–74 and After* (London: Allen & Unwin).

Watts, H. D. (1980), 'The location of European direct investment in the United Kingdom', *Tidjschrift voor Economische en Sociale Geografie*, vol. 71, no. 1, pp. 3–14.

Weber, M. (1923), *General Economic History* (London: Allen & Unwin).

Weber, M. (1972), *From Max Weber*, ed. H. H. Garth and C. W. Mills (London: Oxford University Press).

Weber, M. (1978), *Economy and Society*, 2 vols (Berkeley, Calif.: University of California Press).

Whelan, E. (1979), 'The politics of cancer', *Policy Review*, no. 10 (Fall), pp. 33–46.

Wilensky, H. L. (1975), *The Welfare State and Equality: Structural and Ideological Roots of Public Expenditures* (Berkeley, Calif.: University of California Press).

Wilensky, H. L. (1976), *The 'New Corporatism', Centralization, and the Welfare State* (Beverly Hills, Calif.: Sage).

Willcocks, A. J. (1973), *The Creation of the National Health Service: A Study of Pressure Groups and a Major Social Policy Decision* (London: Routledge & Kegan Paul).

Winkler, J. T. (1976), 'Corporatism', *Archives européennes de sociologie*, vol. 17, no. 1, pp. 100–36.

Winkler, J. T. (1977), 'The corporatist economy: theory and administration', in R. Scase (ed.), *Industrial Society: Class, Cleavage and Control* (New York: St Martin's Press), pp. 43–58.

Wright, E. O. (1978), *Class, Crisis and the State* (London: New Left Books).

Yaffe, D. (1973), 'The Marxian theory of crisis, capital, and the state', *Economy and Society*, vol. 21, no. 2 (May), pp. 186–232.

Yannopoulos, G. M., and Dunning, J. H. (1976), 'Multinational enterprises and regional development: an exploratory paper', *Regional Studies*, vol. 10, pp. 389–99.

Young, S., and Lowe, A. V. (1974), *Intervention in the Mixed Economy* (London: Croom Helm).

Yuill, D., Allen, K., and Hull C. (eds) (1980), *Regional Policy in the European Community* (London: Croom Helm).

Zinn, K. G. (1978), 'The social market in crisis', in S. Holland (ed.), *Beyond Capitalist Planning* (Oxford: Blackwell), pp. 85–105.

Zoll, R. (1978), 'Centralisation and decentralisation as tendencies of union organisational and bargaining policy', in C. Crouch and A. Pizzorno (eds), *The Resurgence of Class Conflict in Western Europe since 1968*, Vol. 2 (New York: Holmes & Meier), pp. 127–60.

Zysman, J. (1977), *Political Strategies for Industrial order* (Berkeley, Calif.: University of California Press).

Zysman, J. (1981), 'The interventionist temptation: financial structure and political purpose', in W. G. Andrews and S. Hoffman (eds), *The Fifth Republic at Twenty* (Albany, NY: State University of New York Press), pp. 252–69.

Index